T0125028

On
Executive Power
in Great States

Jacques Necker

On
Executive Power
in Great States

JACQUES NECKER

Newly Revised Translation of the 1792 English Edition

Edited & with an Introduction
by Aurelian Craiutu

LIBERTY FUND

This book is published by Liberty Fund, Inc.,
a foundation established to encourage study of the ideal
of a society of free and responsible individuals.

𒂼𒄄

The cuneiform inscription that serves as our logo and as a design element
in Liberty Fund books is the earliest-known written appearance of the
word "freedom" (*amagi*), or "liberty." It is taken from a clay document
written about 2300 B.C. in the Sumerian city-state of Lagash.

Introduction, revised translation, editorial additions, and index
© 2020 by Liberty Fund, Inc.

Portrait of Jacques Necker by Joseph-Siffred Duplessis (1725–1802),
photographed by Christophel Fine Art / Getty Images.

All rights reserved

Printed in the United States of America

20 21 22 23 24 C 5 4 3 2 1
20 21 22 23 24 P 5 4 3 2 1

Library of Congress Cataloging-in-Publication Data
Names: Necker, Jacques, 1732–1804, author. | Craiutu, Aurelian, editor.
Title: On executive power in great states / Newly Revised Translation of the 1792
English Edition ; Edited with an Introduction and Notes by Aurelian Craiutu.
Other titles: Du Pouvoir exécutif dans les grands états. English
Description: Carmel, Indiana : Liberty Fund, [2020] | Includes index. |
Summary: "Necker's On Executive Power in Great States, written as the events
of the French Revolution were still unfolding, sheds fresh light on timely topics of
executive power, constitutionalism and the rule of law, federalism, balance of power,
and the dependence of liberty on morality and religion"—Provided by publisher.
Identifiers: LCCN 2020008519 (print) | LCCN 2020008520 (ebook) |
ISBN 9780865979130 (hardback) | ISBN 9780865979147 (paperback) |
ISBN 9781614872870 (epub) | ISBN 9781614876632 (kindle edition) |
ISBN 9781614879336 (pdf)
Subjects: LCSH: Executive power—France. | France—Politics and
government—1789–1799. | France—Politics and government—
1789–1799. | Constitutional law—France.
Classification: LCC JF251 .N43 2020 (print) | LCC JF251 (ebook) |
DDC 352.23/50944—dc23
LC record available at https://lccn.loc.gov/2020008519
LC ebook record available at https://lccn.loc.gov/2020008520

Liberty Fund, Inc.
11301 North Meridian Street
Carmel, Indiana 46032

Contents

Jacques Necker's Reflections on Executive Power in Modern Society

There is no real liberty,
or at least there is no secure freedom,
if there is an authority
without balance in the state.
—JACQUES NECKER

An Unduly Neglected Political Thinker

Referring to her beloved father, Germaine de Staël once wrote that Jacques Necker (1732–1804) was "the only individual who had shown himself profoundly skilled in the art of governing a great country without ever deviating from the most scrupulous morality.... Eloquence had not hurried him away beyond the limits of reason, nor had reason ever deprived him of a single emotion of true eloquence."[1] It would not be inaccurate to say that posterity has not been fair to Madame de Staël's father. As Boissy d'Anglas once claimed, "Of all statesmen, Necker has been treated with the greatest injustice. Many have spoken about him; few have known him, and even fewer have

---

1. Germaine de Staël, *Considerations on the Principal Events of the French Revolution*, ed. Aurelian Craiutu (Indianapolis: Liberty Fund, 2008), 475. Two other sympathetic portraits of Necker can be found in Germaine de Staël's "Du caractère de M. Necker et de sa vie privée" (*Oeuvres Complètes de Madame la Baronne de Staël publiées par son fils* [Paris: Treuttel and Würtz, 1821], vol. 2, 261–90) and Auguste de Staël's "Notice sur M. Necker" published in the second volume of *Oeuvres diverses de M. le Baron Auguste de Staël* (Paris: Treuttel and Würtz, 1829). Madame de Staël's portrait of Necker in *Considerations* was criticized for its excessive praise which, according to Talleyrand, bordered on idolatry. See the latter's caustic remark as quoted in Ghislain de Diesbach, *Necker ou la faillite de la vertu* (Paris: Perrin, 1978), 464–65.

wanted to know him."[2] He has remained to this day poorly known among political theorists and historians of political thought.

A former resident minister of the Republic of Geneva in Paris, Necker was often envied by his contemporaries for his fabulous wealth. Many scorned him for being a petty bourgeois, mostly concerned with promoting his own reputation and increasing his considerable fortune. As a Swiss Protestant, he may have found it difficult at times to live in a predominantly Catholic country. The fact that he proved to be an able steward of the French royal finances in difficult times—he served three times in the royal government without accepting any remuneration—did not help much either to endear the wealthy Genevan banker to his contemporaries. His critics dismissed him as a proud bureaucrat who lacked the necessary skills for weathering political storms and whose judgment allegedly was of the second order. For example, in Talleyrand's opinion, Necker had few ideas and no firm principles of administration; others viewed him as a poor orator and listener, plagued by constant fear. Furthermore, Necker's writing style was seen as pompous or trivial, which explains why many underestimated him as a political writer and religious thinker.

Nevertheless, nobody can deny that Necker played a key role in the history of France. Appointed director of the Royal Treasury in 1776, he became famous as the author of the *Account to the King* whose publication in January 1781 caused strong controversy and sensation. It was the first time in the history of the kingdom of France that its finances were made public. Necker's plans for reforming the Old Regime focused on revamping the administration of provincial assemblies and paying more attention to the rising power and demands of public opinion.[3] As a practical man who had a good sense

2. Boissy d'Anglas as quoted in Robert D. Harris, *Necker: Reform Statesman of the Ancien Régime* (Berkeley: University of California Press, 1979), 241.

3. Both Necker's *Compte rendu au roi* (1781) and his *De l'Administration des finances de la France* (1784) commented on the power of public opinion. For more details, see Jacob Soll, *The Reckoning: Financial Accountability and the Rise and Fall of Nations* (New York: Basic Books, 2014), 136–46. On Necker's views on public opinion, see Léonard Burnand, *Necker et l'opinion publique* (Paris: Honoré Champion, 2004).

of what was feasible and desirable, Necker understood that the country needed an entirely new political structure to grant legal sanction to the participation of the Third Estate in the most important political deliberations of the kingdom. In May 1789, as minister of Louis XVI, he presided over the convocation of the Estates-General[4] but his hopes for reform were dashed in the following months. Necker was dismissed by Louis XVI on July 11, after the advisors of the king convinced him to cut his ties with his loyal minister. Necker's removal from office was one of the main causes of the popular revolt that eventually led to the fall of the Bastille on July 14. Recalled by the king, Necker enjoyed a triumphal return to Paris a few weeks later, when he was received like a hero and acclaimed like a savior in the streets of the French capital.[5]

Plagued by doubt and anxiety and suffering from poor health, Necker decided to abandon the political scene in early September 1790. In an obvious attempt to cast doubt on his integrity and credibility, the National Assembly had asked him to present a complete account of the government's expenditures and revenues from May 1789 to April 1790. Confronted with a hostile audience, Necker decided to retire to his home at Coppet on the shores of Lake Geneva (also known as Lake Léman) in Switzerland, but not before lending the French government a considerable amount of money—two million livres—which was never repaid during his lifetime.[6] From Coppet, he anxiously followed the political affairs in the French capital but never returned to France. Necker's conception of moderate (constitutional) monarchy, based on the joint exercise of sovereignty by the king and Parliament, bicameralism, royal veto, and a strong executive power, found few supporters among the deputies of the Constituent Assembly in 1789–91. A few years later, he criticized the main principles of

---

4. This was the first time in more than a century and a half that the Estates-General convened; the previous meeting had taken place in 1614.

5. Necker's triumphant return to Paris is described in Staël, *Considerations on the Principal Events of the French Revolution*, 165–72.

6. The story of Necker's loan is recounted in Othénin d'Haussonville, "La liquidation du 'dépôt' de Necker: entre concept et idée-force," *Cahiers staëliens*, 55 (2004): 153–206.

the Constitutions of 1795 and 1799 which, in his view, did not provide a solid foundation for a stable and free regime in France. Necker died at Coppet on April 9, 1804, at the very moment when Napoleon's ambition of exercising absolute power was about to be fulfilled.

When Auguste de Staël edited Necker's complete works in fifteen volumes in 1821, the public was surprised to discover how prolific the former minister of Louis XVI had been. The wealthy financier was not only the author of a monumental two-volume history of the French Revolution (*De la Révolution française*, 1796), but also, in 1792, of the present volume, *Du Pouvoir exécutif dans les grands états*, one of the most important books ever written on the role of the executive power in modern society, as well as two important books on religion and politics, *De l'importance des opinions religieuses* (1788) and *Cours de morale religieuse* (1800). His final book, *Dernières vues de politique et de finance* (1802), was the swan's song of a friend of liberty worried about the prospects for freedom in France and Europe.

While some historians have paid attention to Necker's writings on political economy, none of his *political* works has been re-edited in English for over two centuries, and we still lack a general biography of the former minister of Louis XVI in the English-speaking world.[7] The situation is slightly different in France, but even there Necker's political works have been neglected by editors.[8] One reason for this oversight might have to do with Necker's political moderation and his role as a "trimmer"[9] who sought to keep the ship of the state on an

---

7. One notable exception among English-speaking historians is Robert D. Harris, author of an academic trilogy on Necker. In addition to *Necker: Reform Statesman of the Ancien Régime*, Harris also published *Necker and the Revolution of 1789* (Lanham: University Press of America, 1986) and finished a third unpublished volume, *Necker and the Revolutionary Decade* (Special Collections and Archives, Moscow: Idaho: University of Idaho Library, Collection: manuscript 2007-031).

8. One exception is worth noting here: Necker's *Réflexions philosophiques sur l'égalité* were republished in 2005 by Les Belles Lettres in the collection "Bibliothèque classique de la liberté."

9. For the definition of the trimmer, see Halifax's classic essay "The Character of a Trimmer." Halifax wrote: "This innocent word *Trimmer*, signifieth no more than this, That if Men are together in a boat, and one part of the company would weigh it down on one side, another would make it lean as much to the contrary; it happeneth

even keel in turbulent times. Marcel Gauchet was right to claim that "Necker has against him the unconditional proscription that attaches to the memory of the vanquished. His handicap suffers, moreover, from the fatal handicap of moderation."[10] Necker fully embraced the label of moderate and the concept of the golden mean. As he once acknowledged, his political career perfectly illustrated "the persecutions to which a spirit of moderation exposes public characters in times of trouble and agitation.... They are struck by all the crossing hands, and as they are passed by the accelerated march of the passions, as they are left behind by new ideas and modern systems, they fall into disrespect, and their character is accused of feebleness."[11] This is exactly what happened posthumously to Necker himself.

The Ambivalence of the Executive Power

In light of the challenges we face today, we would be well advised to take a new look at Necker's ideas on executive power in modern society. We must begin by noting that the very concept of executive power played a rather limited role in the writings of classical thinkers. The leadership provided by Pericles or Plato's philosopher-kings had little to do with the complexity of the executive power as we know it today. Aristotle mentions it occasionally in his *Politics*, but he did not use the exact term ("executive"), preferring instead to write about one-man rule or monarchy. The concept of executive power emerged much later and became a theme of sustained reflection only in Marsilius of Padua's *Defensor pacis* (*Defender of the Peace*). Marsi-

---

there is a third Opinion of those, who conceive it would do as well, if the Boat went even, without endangering the passengers" (Marquis of Halifax, *Complete Works*, ed. J. P. Kenyon. London: Penguin, 1969), 50.

10. Marcel Gauchet, "Necker," in François Furet and Mona Ozouf, eds., *A Critical Dictionary of the French Revolution* (Cambridge, Mass.: Harvard University Press, 1989), 287; on Necker's paradoxical "excess of moderation and audacity" and his limitations, also see François Furet and Ran Halévi, *La Monarchie républicaine* (Paris: Fayard, 1996), 77–79.

11. Jacques Necker, *On the French Revolution* (London: T. Gadell, Jun. and W. Davies, 1797), vol. 1, 308. On Necker's political moderation, see chapter four in Aurelian Craiutu, *A Virtue for Courageous Minds: Moderation in French Political Thought, 1748–1830* (Princeton University Press, 2012), 113–57.

lius argued that the source of all political power and law is the people and made a distinction between the sovereign (that makes the laws) and the government (that must execute the laws). According to Harvey Mansfield,[12] the real doctrine of executive power was developed in Machiavelli's *The Prince* (1532), a book often considered the origin of modern political thought due to its sophisticated advocacy of an extensive power. The nature, functions, and limits of executive power were subsequently discussed in Hobbes's *Leviathan* (1651), Locke's *Two Treatises on Government* (1690), Montesquieu's *The Spirit of the Laws* (1748), and the *Federalist Papers* (1788).

Two things combine to make the executive power different from other powers in the state and confer on it a special place in the architecture of constitutional government: it is simultaneously indispensable and ambivalent. First, the executive power is a necessity since there can be no political commonwealth without some form of executive as the main locus of decision-making. Second, the executive power can, in fact, be a very strong power, similar in some respects to the power of an absolute monarch. This resemblance might account for the traditional skepticism of republican thinkers toward the executive power, motivated by their fear that it could easily degenerate into tyranny. The extent of the power of the executive is demonstrated by the fact that it has the authority and ability to adjust quickly and effectively to emergencies and evolving circumstances. In particular, the executive has the right to wage war and, in some cases, it is allowed to go beyond the law, or even ignore it altogether in the interest of preventing anarchy or civil war.[13] As such, unlike its legislative and judicial counterpart, the executive, through its use of discretionary power (the "prerogative"), is expected to compensate for the absence or shortcomings of the laws in order to avert chaos and preserve the common good. At the same time, it must always remain subject to the rule of law so that power does not become absolute.

Can this twofold complex task ever be successfully achieved in

---

12. Harvey C. Mansfield, *Taming the Prince: The Ambivalence of Modern Executive Power* (New York: The Free Press, 1989). Necker is absent from Mansfield's book.

13. See, for example, Locke's extensive discussion of the executive prerogative in chapter 14 of his *Second Treatise on Government*.

practice? This is a difficult question to answer. Rousseau himself struggled with it in *On the Social Contract* (1762), in which he drew a sharp distinction between the sovereign and the government. His solution shed light on the fundamental ambivalence of a power which is constructed in such a way that it must be simultaneously "subordinate and not subordinate, both weak and strong."[14] It is worth pausing for a moment to reflect on the dual nature of the executive power. On the one hand, as Rousseau insisted, the executive is merely an agent that acts to advance the will and interests of the sovereign, being entrusted merely with the execution of its laws or decrees. On the other hand, it is also an independent actor on the political scene, pursuing its own agenda, but always in competition with the other two powers in the state (the legislative and the judiciary). As an agent, the authority of the executive is formally limited and, on paper, it is relatively weak. Yet, as a political actor, the power the executive commands is considerable, since the laws are powerless by themselves and must be applied, executed, or enforced by the agents of the executive power. As Hamilton remarked in the *Federalist Papers*, a wise legislator would seek to give the executive all the means and "energy" it needs to properly fulfill its key functions. At the same time, a prudent legislator must also be careful to tie the hands of the executive through carefully designed constitutional and legal rules—the most prominent being the separation and balance of powers—that could prevent the executive power from becoming arbitrary or tyrannical. How can one create a viable executive power that is neither weak nor passive and make sure that it may never become tyrannical or arbitrary in the hands of one individual or several persons?

It is no mere coincidence that two original answers to this important question were proposed from a couple of different perspec-

14. Mansfield, *Taming the Prince*, xvi. On the difficulty of defining the exact nature and attributes of the executive power in the American context, see Charles C. Thach Jr., *The Creation of the Presidency, 1775–1789: A Study in Constitutional History* (Indianapolis: Liberty Fund, 2007). For the modern French context, see the comprehensive work of Nicholas Roussellier, *La Force de gouverner: le pouvoir exécutif en France XIXe–XXIe siècles* (Paris: Gallimard, 2015) and Pierre Rosanvallon, *Le bon gouvernement* (Paris: Seuil, 2015), 37–108.

tives at about the same time—late 1780s and early 1790s—on both
sides of the Atlantic. In America, the state delegates to the Constitutional Convention who met in Philadelphia in the summer of 1787
struggled to define the scope and the limits of the executive power,
along with the attributions of the office of the president. The Articles of Confederation had not provided for a clearly defined executive
power and opposition to a unitary executive remained strong in light
of the general skepticism toward the power of the British monarch.
The idea that a strong unitary executive power, "instead of being the
fetus of monarchy" as James Wilson put it, could be "the best safeguard against tyranny"[15] seemed implausible in the eyes of many at
that time. In the end, in order to avoid stalemate or prolonged controversies, the delegates chose to leave the authority of the president
and the executive somewhat undefined with regard to a number of
important issues, among them foreign policy questions.

Subsequently, Alexander Hamilton (writing under the pseud-
onym Publius) made a persuasive case for an energetic executive in a
republican government in several essays (Nos. 67–77) included in the
Federalist Papers. Publius acknowledged that it was important to give
the executive a vital role in the constitutional architecture of the new
republican system so that it could produce good administration, the
true test of any government. A believer in the need for a strong executive capable of undertaking "extensive and arduous enterprises" (*Federalist* No. 72), Hamilton had to overcome the classical association
between monarchy and executive power and had to respond to those
who remained skeptical about placing power in the hands of a single
individual at the federal level. He also had to show how it would be
possible to deal with necessities and emergencies in a constitutional
manner, while also allaying the concerns of those who feared that
undertaking extensive enterprises would open the door to arbitrary
power. The doctrine of the separation of powers, along with the provision of unity and duration to the executive, was supposed to be part
of the answer to this conundrum. Yet, the powers not only had to be

15. James Wilson's intervention in the debate on executive power from June 1, in
The Anti-Federalist and the Constitutional Debates, ed. Ralph Ketcham (New York:
Penguin/Mentor, 1986), 43.

properly separated from each other, but also judiciously blended and balanced, so that they could cooperate and effectively defend themselves against mutual encroachment.

It is well-known that Hamilton's views on executive power differed in tone and substance from those of Madison; the latter gave the pride of place to the legislative in which he saw, in Locke's footsteps, the soul of a political commonwealth. A few years later, in 1793–94, after George Washington issued an official proclamation declaring America's neutrality in the war between France and Britain, the two founding fathers, writing under the pseudonyms of Pacificus (Hamilton) and Helvidius (Madison), engaged in a public controversy on the role of executive power in foreign policy questions and the limits on its power to interpret the laws.[16] Their exchange shows that our founding fathers were keenly aware of—and concerned with—the impact of contingency and political emergencies. Focusing on the prerogatives of the executive power, which must be strictly limited to executing laws rather than making them, Madison argued that this branch does not have the legal power to declare neutrality and make treaties (he granted the right to declare war to the legislative body). The executive power, Madison argued in 1794, "has no constitutional right to interfere in any question whether there be or be not a cause of war,"[17] a position denied by Hamilton, whom Madison accused of trying to introduce new principles into the text of the Constitution. The disagreements between Hamilton and Madison on the functions and limits of executive power reflected, in fact, the spirit of the constitutional text which was silent on several key issues pertaining to the executive and thus avoided a narrow definition of the office of the president. In the end, the framers of the Constitution opted for a certain degree of flexibility with regard to the prerogatives of the executive power, while also acknowledging the importance and diffi-

16. The entire debate can be found in *The Pacificus-Helvidius Debates of 1793–1794*, ed. Morton J. Frisch (Indianapolis: Liberty Fund, 2007). It is worth adding that Jefferson sided with Madison (against Hamilton and Washington) in his attempt to deny what they both took be a dangerous overreach of executive power into foreign affairs.

17. Ibid., 90.

culty of properly determining the functions of the executive in a large state. This approach made possible an open-ended debate on the nature, purpose, and bounds of the executive power as well as its relation with the legislative and judicial powers.

The French Exception

The French took a different route, explained by Necker in *Du Pouvoir exécutif dans les grands états*, written at about the same time as Hamilton and Madison were debating the role of the executive in foreign policy affairs in America. Necker's work, completed by April 1792, almost half a year after France received its first written constitution, did not pass unnoticed in the French press.[18] Several reviews appeared in widely read journals of different political persuasions, from *Journal de Paris* (July 17) and *Ami des Patriotes* (July 21) to *Journal de la Cour et de la Ville* (July 23) and *Mercure de France* (August 31). With a few exceptions, the reception of the book was reserved or critical, given Necker's open endorsement of the English model and its unwritten constitution that did not have many partisans in France at that time. Necker found vocal critics not only among the Jacobins, who had little or no appreciation for the moderation of the former minister of Louis XVI, but also among the ultraconservatives, who continued to view him with skepticism due to the role he had played before and during the initial stages of the Revolution. Outside of France, *Du Pouvoir exécutif dans les grands états* was more positively received, especially in Germany, being immediately translated into English and German.

In *Considerations on the Principal Events of the French Revolution*, Madame de Staël referred to her father's work on executive power as "the best guide that can be followed by men called on to make or to modify a constitution of any kind" and "the political chart in which all the dangers that are found in the track of liberty are pointed out."[19] In making this claim, Staël was certainly influenced by her

---

18. For a fuller account of the reception of Necker's book, see Grange, *Les Idées de Necker*, 63–66. The context in which the book was written is discussed in chapter 4 of Harris, *Necker and the Revolutionary Decade*, 84–114.

19. Staël, *Considerations*, 298.

love for her father, but her assessment was not far from the truth. Although Necker's *On Executive Power in Great States* should be on the reading list of anyone interested in executive power and constitutionalism, it may not be easy for us today to fully appreciate the breadth, depth, and originality of Necker's book. Consisting of seventeen long chapters in two parts amounting to six hundred pages in the original French, it is certainly much more than a simple book on the concept of executive power. In many ways, it is a very French book that emerged from the peculiar context of the French Revolution, written as events were still unfolding, with no endpoint in sight. When he sat down to write the book, Necker had left the political scene not long before. In September 1791, the legislators ratified the country's first written constitution; soon after that, the members of the Constituent Assembly were replaced by an inexperienced group of deputies in the newly elected Legislative Assembly. The Terror of 1793–94 had not yet occurred, but Necker's analysis foresees it. The days of the monarchy were numbered and its demise was both imminent and unstoppable, after the Constituent Assembly had made the king the first public functionary and stripped him of key prerogatives. In early 1792, as Necker was completing his book, the power of the Jacobin clubs was rising, but they did not entirely dominate the political scene yet.

There are several reasons why Necker's *On Executive Power in Great States* is worth reading today. First, the originality of Necker's book derives in part from the fact that in its pages, the political thinker meets the politician who had been at the helm of the affairs of the country in turbulent times. Far from being mere theoretical speculations, Necker's ideas on the role of executive power had a firm foundation in political reality. The politician had a sense of what had gone wrong and when, while the theorist drew on the works of his predecessors who taught him a few important lessons about what a good regime entails. In these pages, Necker restates the fundamental principles of his *moderate* political philosophy, proving that he was a moderate both by temperament and principle, a spirit who distrusted extravagant positions and sided with prudence against fanaticism. As an admirer of the unwritten English constitution, Necker never ran after novelties and was respectful of the accumulated knowledge of all ages and nations. In his view, the experience of the past counted more than the abstract speculations of those who, in his own words, "have taken up their residence in the middling regions of philosophy" (see below, p. 135). Distrusting all forms of enthusiasm, political and religious, Necker was skeptical about intransigent and extremist positions on all sides of the political spectrum. He denounced "the threatening influence of a blind fanaticism" and devoted particular attention to those who pursued the impossible dream of absolute equality.[20] Invoking the example of England, Necker pointed out that in a great kingdom like France, there could be neither public order nor general liberty once all ranks have been leveled and all differences of wealth and status abolished. At the same time, Necker opposed those who used fear and planted the seeds of distrust among citizens in order to better advance their own agendas.

During his entire political career, and especially in 1788–90, Necker assumed the role of a mediator between parties, fully committed to the common good and keenly aware of the difficult challenges he faced in a climate dominated by chronic distrust. He acted as a trimmer seeking to keep the ship of the state on an even keel.[21] Moderates, Necker argued, "find themselves surrounded by party rage without being in favor with any side, and have for them only the uncertain chance of the justice of posterity, or the low, and trembling voice of the honest men of their age." Exposed to the crossfire of the extremes and the ridicule of public opinion, "they are struck by all the crossing hands, and as they are passed by the accelerated march of the passions, as they are left behind by new ideas and modern systems, they fall into disrespect, and their character is accused of feebleness."[22] That is why, Necker believed, moderation is a difficult virtue only for courageous minds: "Ideas of wisdom and moderation commonly escape the wavering mass of people who regard absent-

20. Necker, *Oeuvres Complètes* (Paris: Treuttel and Würtz, 1821), vol. 9, 331. See, for example, chapter 18 below, entitled "Whether Absolute Equality Is a Necessary Condition of Liberty."

21. See Staël, *Considerations*, 113–14.

22. Necker, *On the French Revolution*, vol. 1, 308.

mindedly the conduct of statesmen, people whose attention can be caught and whose suffrages can be gained only by colorful novelties and striking exaggerations" (see below, p. 133).

One must also add that Necker's moderation was linked to a conservative type of liberalism that, in his view, was particularly needed in a country prone to succumb to various forms of political radicalism. On the one hand, Necker recognized that justice ought to be the main object of all government and unambiguously acknowledged the power of public opinion. On the other hand, he expressed reservations about any constitution that vests too much power in the hands of the people. For the many, Necker believed, are susceptible to be carried away by their passions or be ensnared by demagogues who pander to them in order to gain their favor. "In the courts of princes," he wrote, "men whisper their flattery; in the midst of a democracy, they flatter the people to the sound of a trumpet" (see below, p. 269). Eventually, the demagogues turn into intolerant chiefs of sects who measure virtue and vice, merit and demerit, according to the opinion that people have of the doctrines they profess. Thus, the political scene becomes divided between the forces of the good and evil, and a ruthless campaign is launched to purge the world of the alleged elements of darkness.

An Original Form of Constitutionalism

The second reason that makes Necker's *On Executive Power in Great States* a must-read is that it offers a sophisticated case for an energetic and limited executive power. It invites us to explore the complexity of the latter and its key role within a constitutional framework of what Necker dubbed "intertwined powers." The originality of Necker's approach must be duly underscored here, and a comparison with Locke's *Second Treatise on Government* is in order as well. One of Locke's main claims was that the soul of a commonwealth is the legislative rather than the executive power, a view also held by Rousseau. Necker challenged the idea that the supreme power in a state is the legislative power as an expression of the general will of the people. In his book, he also took the deputies of the Constituent Assembly to task for failing to create a sound balance of powers and for describing the weakening of the executive power as "a victory gained by liberty."[23] At a time when all the existing authorities, together with all the passions, appeared to have joined their forces against the authority of the king, Necker stood by the embattled monarch. He provided a sophisticated argument in favor of a constitutional monarchy based upon the model of the English constitution, in which the monarch reigns but does not govern, and in which the nobility as an intermediate body provides an indispensable rampart to the throne.

In Necker's opinion, finding a proper role for the executive power is arguably the most difficult political problem that requires "a precise rule, an exact conformity, from which it would be dangerous to depart" (see below, p. 10). He believed that all the different branches of politics are intimately connected with the prudent constitution of the executive power, "the moving force of a government" (see below, p. 10). Even the slightest inattention to establishing its particular role and proper functions in the structure of a political constitution might have significant large-scale consequences. The executive power must always be vigilant and effective and "its influence depends on an infinity of means entirely distinct from its institution" (see below, p. 12). While it ought to enjoy all the prerogatives meant to give it the proper energy, authority, respect, and duration that it needs, the executive power should also be limited so that it may never become arbitrary.

In stressing this point, Necker took up and redefined the complex issues of the separation and balance of powers. It is important to distinguish between the two concepts, for the latter is only one of the forms in which the separation of powers can appear (the other one is the specialization of functions). The doctrine of the balance of powers has historically been grounded in the recognition of the supremacy of the *legislative* power.[24] Far from implying a strict separa-

---

23. See below, 158. Compare and contrast Necker's analysis with the account given by Guillaume Glénard in *L'Exécutif et la Constitution de 1791* (Paris: PUF, 2010), 11–13. Glénard argues that the Constitution did, in fact, establish such a balance of powers.

24. Michel Troper, *La Séparation des pouvoirs et l'histoire constitutionnelle française* (Paris: Librairie générale de droit et de jurisprudence, 1980), 121.

tion between the legislative and the executive powers, it refers instead to the balance between the executive and legislative powers sharing in the exercise of the legislative functions. The different authorities sharing in the legislative functions can be the lower and upper chambers of Parliament, the ministers as agents of the executive power, the (constitutional) monarch, or the head of the state in a republican regime. This point can also be applied to understanding the executive power and the sharing of executive functions. Necker sometimes seems to treat the executive power as singular, in the sense that it can only be held by one actor (in this case, the monarch). Yet, it is possible to extend his theory to imply that the executive functions can be exercised by other powers as well, which in turn would require a discussion of the executive power from the standpoint of the optimal distribution of the executive functions shared by all the powers in the state.

As Henri Grange argued,[25] the first step Necker undertook was to redefine the meanings of both the executive and legislative powers. In a well-ordered government, these powers ought to share, in various degrees, in the exercise of *both* the legislative and the executive *functions*. On this view, the executive power means, in Necker's words, *organe de gouvernement* (providing the necessary leadership), while legislative power should serve as an *organe de contrôle* (providing the equally needed supervision). Next, Necker complemented the theory of the functional separation of powers with that of *l'entrelacement des pouvoirs*, loosely translated as "intertwining of powers," dependent upon the existence of effective links between the executive and the legislative. In the absence of such links and sharing of (legislative and executive) functions, Necker maintained that total confusion and ruthless competition for power would dominate the political scene. The powers of which a government is composed are intermixed by means of various ties that make possible their dialogue and cooperation while holding each other in check. "Were we to discard these principles of *union*, and substitute laws of equilibrium in their stead," Necker wrote, "it would be necessary, if I may so express

25. Henri Grange, "De l'originalité des idées politiques de Necker," in *Cahiers staëliens*, 36 (1985): 54–55.

myself, to place a sentinel on the confines of every vanity, every sort of self-love, every individual ambition" (see below, pp. 40–41). In his view, the existence of such links and sharing of functions between powers is essential to creating a sound and balanced constitution: "They are *ties* then, not counterpoises, *proportions* not distances, fitnesses not vigilance, which most contribute to the *harmony* of government" (see below, p. 41; emphases added).

According to Necker, the Constitution of 1791 was based on an extreme version of the doctrine of the separation of powers that lacked such ties and proportions. This doctrine was fiercely held "as an explicit ideological position"[26] that excluded the idea of the necessary division of sovereignty or the sharing of the legislative functions. Such an extreme version of the separation of powers amounted, in fact, to a rejection of the doctrine of balance of powers. According to Necker, the attention of legislators ought to have been focused on the necessity of balancing and blending the two main powers in the state by judicious means. He advocated the presence of ministers in Parliament as a means of creating the necessary "harmony" between the legislative body and the administration, a harmony which he saw as indispensable to the regular functioning of the government. "If that harmony were to disappear one day," Necker wrote, "if it were replaced by a system based on mistrust and suspicion, everything would become contest, everything would be shaken; and we would quickly discover that anarchy and confusion are the greatest dangers against which a free constitution must protect itself" (see below, p. 95).

It must be noted that Necker justified the need for intertwined powers by specifically referring to the effective sharing of the legislative functions between the executive and the legislative body in En-

---

26. M. J. C. Vile, *Constitutionalism and the Separation of Powers*, 2nd ed. (Indianapolis: Liberty Fund, 1998), 194. For a recent comparative analysis on this topic, see Christoph Moellers, *The Three Branches: A Comparative Model of Separation of Powers* (Oxford: Oxford University Press, 2015). Necker was certainly aware that doctrine of the balance of powers in America was grounded in the recognition of the supremacy of the *legislative* power. He referred to the American system of checks and balances while making his case for the supremacy of the *executive* power.

gland and the United States. Across the Channel, in Necker's view, the king's ministers are almost always de facto members of Parliament and play an important role in parliamentary deliberations by contributing their knowledge of affairs and judgment of circumstances. "Far from being considered in either house as inferiors to be silenced or made to speak with the mere waving of a wand," the king's ministers "are ordinarily expected to open the discussions on new measures useful to the state, or to offer the first observations on the proposals made by other members of the legislative body" (see below, p. 96). Either by being able to propose new draft laws or by familiarizing themselves with the laws proposed by other representatives of the nation, the ministers are able to assist with their knowledge and experience in the drafting of parliamentary bills and in the discussion of their details. As such, their presence in the lower chamber does not infringe upon the separation which ought to be maintained between those who exercise legislative and executive powers.

A similar situation can be found in the United States, where the executive power has close ties with the legislative and possesses effective (if limited) means of proposing and participating in the drafting of the laws. It will be recalled that in America, the Federalists proposed a form of separation of powers within a scheme of shared functions according to which all three departments of the federal government share in the exercise of the legislative functions. In their view, Congress ought to propose laws, the president may veto proposals, and the Supreme Court should be allowed to overturn laws agreed upon by the Congress and the president. Similarly, the Federalists paid particular attention to creating a system in which all three departments may share in the exercise of the executive functions. In their opinion, Congress (with presidential approval) ought to be able to create executive agencies and delegate regulatory authority to them (it can also retract that authority, and even abolish executive agencies it has established). The Senate must appoint federal officers nominated by the president. The Supreme Court also has executive powers insofar as it oversees the administration of the federal judiciary in legal matters. Finally, Congress is entrusted with the exercise of judicial functions such as the impeachment and removal from federal office, and, more important, control over the appellate jurisdiction of the Supreme Court. In turn, the president can nominate judges and issue pardons. In other words, the separation of powers within the context of shared functions or responsibilities requires collaboration for action to occur. The Federalists wanted a sharing of functions, such that no federal department could ever have a monopoly of power in any of three arenas: law-making, execution, and adjudication. For this reason, it would be inappropriate to refer to executive power as if it were only an attribute of the executive. That creates a false opposition between the executive, legislature, and judiciary that does not exist in reality.[27]

If Necker defended the intertwining of powers (*l'entrelacement des pouvoirs*) as an essential condition of liberty in a representative government, it was because he strongly believed that there can be no real freedom if there exists an authority without balance in the state. The mere existence of such a power—be that of the monarch, the nobles, or the people—without an effective counterpoise would be a serious threat to liberty and constitutionalism. At the same time, all powers not only must have the necessary resources for being able to compete for supremacy in the state but also the possibility of acting in concert to pursue common goals. Four years later, in his book on the French Revolution, Necker reiterated this point when making a renewed case for creating a constitutional framework in which all powers exercise mutual and effective vigilance over each other. His advice and choice of words were revealing. Necker recommended to all the friends of liberty "to establish a constitutional alliance between the executive and legislative powers" and insisted that "their *prudent association*, their *artful intertwining*, will always be the best security for mutual circumspection and efficacious vigilance."[28] Worth noting

27. I would like to thank Russell L. Hanson for his comments and for encouraging me to clarify this issue.

28. *On the French Revolution*, vol. 2, 127; all emphases added. Here is the original French text: "On doit chercher à établir une liaison constitutionnelle entre le pouvoir exécutif et le pouvoir législatif; on doit songer que leur prudente association, leur ingénieux entrelacement seront toujours la meilleure caution d'une circonspection mutuelle et d'une surveillance efficace" (*Oeuvres Complètes de M. Necker*, vol. 10 [Paris: Treuttel and Würtz, 1821], 133).

here is the difference between Necker's emphasis on the need for a judicious intertwining of powers and the more radical interpretation espoused by vocal critics of the monarch such as Bertrand Barère, who believed that the executive power will always be "the enemy of the legislative power"[29] and will always seek its destruction.

Necker's Critique of Revolutionary Radicalism

The third reason for which we should read Necker's book today is that it offers a comprehensive analysis and critique of the French Constitution of 1791, which he viewed as fundamentally flawed and destined to vanish soon after its ratification.[30] Necker's analysis of the constitutional text occupies more than half of his entire work on executive power. Unlike his daughter who believed that the Constituent Assembly ought to be praised for the abuses which it destroyed,[31] Necker concentrated on its internal contradictions and poor design. In his opinion, the greatest error of the 1791 Constitution stemmed from its ignorance of the true nature and role of the executive power and its failure to establish a sound balance between public order and liberty. The Constituent Assembly, he argued, "constantly regarded the king as a rival, instead of having the courage, as a legislator, to consider him as the principal actor in a monarchical government, and to prudently grant him, on time, his share in government" (see below, p. 118). Obsessed with the doctrine of extreme equality which became the watchword in France, the deputies quickly abandoned the etiquette to be observed toward the monarch and his ministers, treating them with vulgar familiarity and cynicism. Thus, the king was granted the title of the "first public functionary" instead of being respected as the hereditary representative of the entire French nation. At the same time, the Constituent Assembly created a flawed legislative body, consisting of a single chamber, elected for a short period of time (only two years compared to six or seven years in England), and

29. Barère as quoted in Rosanvallon, *Le bon gouvernement*, 46.

30. On Necker's views on the Constituent Assembly see Harris, *Necker and the Revolution of 1789*, 707–41.

31. See Staël, *Considerations*, part II, chapters 22–23 (273–84), part 3, chapter 2 (291–98).

virtually unable to make the necessary revisions of the constitutional text. The short duration and frequent elections in France raised significant challenges. The effect of any transient authority was to increase the eagerness to act, the willingness to take bribes, and the impatience to distinguish oneself among one's peers through radical proposals and extravagant actions aimed at achieving short-term populist goals.

In several chapters of the book reminiscent of Burke's critique in *Reflections on the Revolution in France*, Necker denounced the errors and excesses of the new legislators of France, who were engaged in a risky political adventure. Searching for an illusory uniformity in "the vast plains of equality" (see below, p. 174) and in love with their new abstract metaphysics, they began by tearing down ancient customs and mores and ignored the lessons of prudence and tradition. Overconfident in their theories, they attempted to begin everything anew, while relying mostly on abstract principles rather than the lessons of experience. Thus, they regarded France like a mere chessboard where they could move all individuals as they thought fit. In the end, inebriated by their passion for novelty and equality, the authors of the first written French constitution created a system in which liberty was only "a simple device, morality a mere maxim, and happiness a vain boast" (see below, p. 186). In practice, dissent was condemned as treason, and virtue was identified with blind submission to the new order.

Necker attributed the faults and the imperfections of the Constituent Assembly not only to the deputies' excessive attachment to uniformity and equality at the expense of reason, morality, and liberty but also to their penchant for intrigue, their unbound ambitions, and their "mad passion for new systems" (see below, p. 24). The new political instructors of France believed in their hearts that they were able to govern the whole world by two words: liberty and equality. They ostentatiously displayed their patriotism as a banner which justified their actions and allowed them, in fact, to persecute all those who differed from them in their opinions. Necker's merit was to have highlighted the analogy between the new eloquence, bereft of measure, harmony, taste or decorum, and the new type of politics, devoid of moderation and prudence, and carried away by excessive enthusiasm for abstractions. The legislators of France, Necker argued, invented a novel language that reflected the decay of civility and the decline of mores and standards of taste. They coined new verbs that expressed their exaggerated sentiments and boundless pride.[32] And they disregarded the lessons of religion, ignoring that those who are not influenced by religious morality may often have no other motive than selfish interest and no other law than their personal gratification. Necker believed that religion alone can restrain human beings in the exercise of their passions and teach them their duties. It is religious morality alone that can render them at the same time severe toward themselves and indulgent toward others, moderate in the exercise of their rights, and determined to fight for justice for all.

Even when the new legislators sought to imitate other models, Necker believed that they "sometimes exaggerated known truths, sometimes arranged words in a new order, and sometimes called things by different names, thus giving an appearance of originality to the most literal imitations" (see below, p. 219). They focused their entire attention on the *Declaration of the Rights of Man* without properly considering how its articles were to be connected to the constitutional articles. To be sure, the Constituent Assembly began the work of legislation without having formed any coherent plan regarding the means necessary for the proper functioning of the executive power. The French deputies declared the government monarchical, but did not properly examine the degree of consideration, influence, and authority which the monarch needed to discharge effectively the functions of the executive power. Necker also criticized the ways in which the legislators approached the twin issues of the participation of the king in the legislative power and the prerogatives of the monarch, from granting mercy and the distribution of favors to nomination to various employments. They viewed the king's ministers with skepticism and treated them with arrogance, reserving for them only a de-

---

32. This is how Necker describes the consequences of these changes with regard to taste and language: "Taste is no longer necessary, and must become every day more and more perverted, when everyone wants to write and speak, and in the midst of this universal rivalry, each endeavors to surpass the other by using the most savage expressions and the most repulsive images" (see below, 279).

graded status, incompatible with their quality as first agents of the supreme power in the state. Fearing the influence of aristocracy, the deputies of the people chose monocameralism over bicameralism and paved the way for the domination of a single chamber that absorbed all power in its own hands. Thus, the Constitution of 1791 placed on one side a single permanent and strong Assembly and on the other side "an executive power, without prerogatives, without the means of effecting either good or ill" (see below, p. 159), stripped of all exterior splendor and deprived of majesty and respect.

Such an unbalanced constitution had nefarious consequences that made possible the rise of an authority without counterpoise in the state, an omnipotent legislature unwilling to compromise and listen to its critics and rivals. This absolute authority acted in the name of the sovereignty of the people, ignoring the fact that the people, as Necker put it, could only be a pure abstraction in a large kingdom of twenty-six million souls. As a critic of popular sovereignty, Necker had to confront the Jacobin theories of popular sovereignty inspired by Rousseau. In his political and historical writings, and especially in his reflections on equality that concluded his work on the French Revolution, Necker endorsed the concept of complex sovereignty. In his view, "the sovereignty in a free country, in a wisely organized political society, can never exist in a simple manner,"[33] and the existence of a mere majority may never serve as a title and justification for the unlimited exercise of sovereignty. In order for sovereignty to be limited, Necker pointed out, it must never be simple: "The sovereignty, not in its abstraction but in its reality, must be considered as a mixed idea, as a compound institution, and its primary elements are eternal reason and eternal justice."[34]

France, England, and America

Finally, *On Executive Power in Great States* offers an innovative comparative analysis of three political and constitutional traditions: French, American, and English. Necker appreciated both the wisdom

---

33. Necker, *Philosophical Reflections on Equality* in *On the French Revolution*, vol. 2, 404.

34. Ibid, 402.

of the English unwritten constitution and the judicious combination of powers in the U.S. Constitution.[35] "England, in its unity, America in its system of federation," he wrote, "present to our view two admirable models of government" (see below, p. 213). In the footsteps of Montesquieu's *The Spirit of the Laws*, Necker held England as a mirror which his readers could use in order to find the true principles of liberty. America was also present in Necker's book as a model of a democratic republic whose principles were going to be analyzed in detail four decades later in Tocqueville's *Democracy in America*.

To understand Necker's appreciation for America's system of checks and balances it is important to remember that the French took a strong interest in the American federal and state constitutions from the mid-1770s until 1792. America was seen as mankind's best hope, an asylum open to the oppressed of all nations. In a letter to Richard Price dated March 22, 1778, Turgot, whom Necker knew quite well, made precisely this point. "It is impossible not to wish ardently that this people may attain to all the prosperity to which they are capable," he wrote. "They are the hope of the world. They may become a model to it."[36] Translations of eleven American state constitutions made by the liberal-minded Duke de la Rochefoucauld d'Enville in 1783 circulated widely in France. A few years later, during the parliamentary debates on controversial topics such as the royal veto and bicameralism in the Constituent Assembly, numerous references were made to both the English and the American examples. If the lightning originated in France in 1789, when the Old Regime collapsed, the true light came, in fact, from America and its novel constitutional experiment that had been completed in Philadelphia in 1787.[37] The Amer-

35. On Necker's views of America, see Grange, *Les Idées de Necker*, 350–58.

36. Quoted in Richard Price, *Observations on the Importance of the American Revolution and the Means of Making It a Benefit to the World* (Dublin: White, Whitestone, Bryne, and Co., 1785), 1–2. Also see Philippe Raynaud's entry, "American Revolution," in *A Critical Dictionary of the French Revolution*, 593–603, and Marc Lahmer, *La Constitution américaine dans le débat français: 1795–1848* (Paris: L'Harmattan, 2001).

37. See Susan Dunn, *Sister Revolutions: French Lightning, American Light* (New York: Farrar, Straus, and Giroux, 2000).

ican experiment was highly important for the French because it was the first successful example of combining popular sovereignty with self-government and representative institutions.

There were, no doubt, other important reasons for the French interest in America during the last decades of the Old Regime. Some referred to the American example in order to combat the influence of English ideas in France. For them, England represented the past of mankind, while America stood for its future. This idea came to the fore, for example, in Condorcet's *L'Influence de la révolution de l'Amérique sur l'Europe* (1786), a book in which he argued that America was a step ahead of Europe in the fight against superstition, ignorance, despotism, and intolerance.[38] As such, it was believed that America had the honor of teaching mankind an important lesson: that human beings are actually capable of governing and perfecting themselves. Nevertheless, in the end, the French deputies entrusted with the task of giving France a new constitution did not follow the American example. Trusting their own reason, they believed they were called to do better than America. In the words of one of the deputies, Rabaut Saint-Étienne, "*Il fallait surpasser l'Amérique*" ("we had to outperform America")[39] when it came to establishing a new declaration of rights.

Necker disagreed with this view. He dismissed the idea that the French could do better than the Americans with regard to establishing the foundations of a new constitutional structure. Such a pretention, he believed, was nothing but an expression of arrogance and ignorance on the part of the French deputies. Necker took issue with those "political metaphysicians" who (wrongly) pretended that they agreed in principle with the sage legislators of America but were, in fact, reluctant to imitate the Americans' morality, religious spirit, and domestic virtues. A case in point was the elaboration of the famous *Declaration of the Rights of Man* in the summer of 1789. The French

38. On Condorcet's interest in America, see Echeverria, *Mirage in the West*, 153–54; also Condorcet, *Writings on the United States*, ed. and trans. Guillaume Ansart (State Park: Pennsylvania State University Press, 2012).

39. See Marcel Gauchet, *La Révolution des droits de l'homme* (Paris: Gallimard, 1989), 48–59.

legislators viewed it as a philosophical distillation of moral and political imperatives conceived in the same spirit that produced many abstract books on government. Key rights such as the right against self-incrimination, illegal seizures, and the right not to be deprived of property arbitrarily ended up missing from the French document. Unlike the French, the Americans did not conceive of their Bill of Rights as a set of abstract first principles serving as a preamble to their constitution. The first ten amendments to the U.S. Constitution were adopted only after a long and intense debate, in which the defenders of the constitutional text approved at Philadelphia in September 1787 had to respond to the critiques of the anti-Federalists who lamented the absence of such a bill of rights in the original text.

Necker did not believe that the French should have imported wholesale all of its principles or institutions, nor did he claim that the American Constitution could ever work in France in the same way it operated across the ocean. He argued that there is a striking difference between a constitution grafted upon ancient laws and mores, such as the American one, and a constitution antecedent to the existence of a government, such as the one drafted by the members of the Constituent Assembly in France from 1789 to 1791. The Americans, Necker went on, enjoyed peculiar geographical conditions and had unique mores adapted to their particular institutions. In the New World, he opined, vanity and self-love had not yet established an absolute empire, being restrained by morality, nor were people condemned there to ignorance and poverty. The labor market and the distribution of property allowed them to be independent and prosperous. Furthermore, unlike the national debt and finances of France which had spiraled out of control during the last years of the Old Regime, America's national debt was moderate. The Americans did not have to keep a large and expensive army to wage war or protect themselves against foreign invasion. Necker did not preclude the possibility that one day America might evolve in the direction of France, and its social and political order might become more susceptible to revolutionary turmoil and disorder. But that day, he suggested, was still far away, and the French ought to pay close attention to what America had to teach them in political affairs.

Necker highlighted two lessons that might be learned from across

the ocean: the organization of the executive power and the functioning of the federal system. Regarding the office of the president, he
pointed out that "the prerogatives attributed to the President are sufficient to show that the United States have secured the activity of
government in a more firm and respectable manner than we have
done in France" (see below, p. 210). Those prerogatives, he insisted,
were sufficient to ensure the maintenance of public order, the timely
nomination to various employments and offices of administration, as
well as the exercise of the right of pardon and the executive veto. On
all of these issues, the Americans proved to be more judicious than
the French. The Americans also chose bicameralism, recognizing the
necessity of—and the benefits deriving from—having two chambers
instead of one. The federative system offered additional benefits by
combining force and order, providing security and good administration, and circumscribing civil government within the limits "which
the weakness of human beings renders so necessary and proper" (see
below, p. 254). It is also worth pointing out that for all of his appreciation for the American system, Necker never envisaged the possibility of an executive power chosen by the people, a radical idea that
had been contemplated, however, by Condorcet and Brissot in 1791.

The Power of Moderation

In publishing his great work on executive power, Necker sounded
an alarm to all the friends of liberty across Europe. He claimed to
have written his book not as a party man, but from that pure and
untainted affection that he professed for France, his adopted country. Necker hoped that the ideas of his book might be able to deter
the friends of freedom elsewhere from adopting a government and
a constitution similar to that of France. The stakes were very high
and the margin for error quite small. "We might, perhaps, allow ourselves to consider this government as an amusement of the mind," he
warned, "as a work of the imagination, had it not led to the most fatal consequences, had it not produced the saddest effects" (see below,
p. 331). In particular, Necker warned that it would be impossible to
create a stable and effective political constitution in which the executive power was ignored and in which all legitimate authorities were
forced to compete against each other in the absence of an adequate

balance between them. Necker also worried that the people might be seduced by new promises and bribes and predicted that their leaders would invoke the treacherous conduct and conspiracies of the alleged enemies of the revolution in order to justify stronger measures inimical to liberty.

If Necker wrote his book as a moderate, his moderation was not always a recipe for success. His political career was a mixed success during his first ministry and a failure toward the end, especially after February 1790, when the finances of the kingdom spiraled out of control during his third ministry. As François Furet once remarked, similar to Guizot's case, "Necker the philosopher was a victim of the failure of Necker the political leader."[40] It is important to remember, however, that Necker did not oppose necessary reforms. Although he remained a staunch supporter of constitutional monarchy and the English model, he was prepared to accept a republican system, similar to that established in the United States. Nevertheless, it would be hard to deny that Necker's capacity to understand the psychology of other political actors was limited. His critics claimed that he was incapable of providing effective leadership, preferring instead to delay or to allow things to drift. Because he feared the rise of Jacobinism, he may have been too insensitive to claims for—and aspirations to—equality and political democracy. Finally, he lacked the ability to build coalitions and did not have the capacity to "confront the destructive and violent side of politics"[41] in an effective manner.

Nevertheless, the course of events in France confirmed Necker's general political instincts and darkest intuitions and vindicated his political acumen posthumously. France needed several decades to make an arduous apprenticeship of liberty, but not before going through the dark period of the Terror of 1793–94 and the absolute regime of Napoleon Bonaparte (the latter was extremely hostile to Necker and his family). The Charter of 1814 and the Bourbon Restoration finally brought about the type of political regime that Nec-

---

40. François Furet, "La monarchie et le règlement électoral de 1789," in *The Political Culture of the Old Regime*, ed. Keith M. Baker (New York: Pergamon Press, 1987), 386.

41. Gauchet, "Necker," 289.

ker had envisaged in 1792, a tempered constitutional monarchy and a parliamentary government, based on competitive elections, separation of powers, and freedom of the press.

Necker wrote *On Executive Power in Great States* more than two centuries ago, worried that the French legislators had misinterpreted the nature and misjudged the significance of the executive power. The debate on how to empower the executive to respond effectively to emergency situations without endangering the constitutional order has continued to this day. This issue—how to create a simultaneously strong and limited executive power unable to overstep its bounds—is certain to remain of interest as we continue to discuss controversial and complex topics such as the administrative state, emergency powers, and the growing presidential power at the expense of legislative authority of the Congress in the United States.[42] Finally, through its critique of political fanaticism, Necker's book reminds us of the importance of moderation, that rare and exquisite virtue without which, as John Adams once put it, "every man in power becomes a ravenous beast of prey."[43]

AURELIAN CRAIUTU
Indiana University
Bloomington

42. The importance of the modern presidency is discussed in Steven Skrowonek, *The Politics Presidents Make: Leadership from John Adams to Bill Clinton* (Cambridge, Mass.: Belknap, 1997). The discretionary powers of the president are examined in Clement Fatovic, *Outside the Law: Emergency and Executive Power* (Baltimore: Johns Hopkins University Press, 2009) and Benjamin Kleinerman, *Discretionary President: The Promise and Peril of Executive Power* (Lawrence, Kans.: University Press of Kansas, 2009). On the rise of the administrative state, see Philip Hamburger, *Is Administrative Law Unlawful?* (Chicago: University of Chicago Press, 2015).

43. *The Political Writings of John Adams*, ed. George A. Peek (Indianapolis: Bobbs-Merrill, 1954), 89.

Note on the Present Edition

Du Pouvoir exécutif dans les grands états was originally published in French, in two volumes, in 1792; an English translation came out that same year in London under the slightly modified title *An Essay on the True Principles of Executive Power in Great States.* The publisher of the English text was listed as G. G. J. and J. Robinson, but the name of the translator was not disclosed, a practice common at that time. Upon its publication, Necker's book was reviewed in France and abroad; a full list of the reviews can be found in Grange, *Les Idées de Necker,* 629–30. *Du Pouvoir exécutif dans les grands états* was reedited in French in 1821 as volume 8 of Necker's fifteen-volume *Oeuvres Complètes de M. Necker,* under the editorship of Auguste de Staël.

In preparing the present edition, we have started from the text of the 1792 English translation (also published in two volumes) and followed the French text from volume 8 of Necker's *Oeuvres Complètes.* The original translation contains many inaccuracies and archaisms and occasionally leaves out entire sentences. As a result, significant changes had to be made almost on every page in order to offer an accurate translation; missing passages were also added where appropriate. We have changed the translation of the title to reflect the original French text. This new edition also includes an introductory study as well as a critical apparatus meant to provide a historical background for the general reader. The explanatory notes appear at the bottom of the page, preceded by an arabic number to distinguish them from Necker's notes (marked with symbols). Typos and archaic punctuation in the original translation have been corrected silently, and English spellings have been Americanized throughout. A bibliography was added at the end, containing information about primary and secondary sources relevant for understanding Necker's political thought as well as his context.

It is a pleasure to acknowledge the support received from Liberty Fund in bringing this difficult and long project to fruition. Special thanks are due to the Board of Liberty Fund and its president for endorsing this project, and to Laura Goetz, whose expert advice on the translation and editorial assistance has been much appreciated.

A. C.

AN

ESSAY

ON THE

TRUE PRINCIPLES

OF

EXECUTIVE POWER

IN

GREAT STATES

TRANSLATED FROM THE FRENCH OF

M. NECKER

And if each system in gradation roll,
Alike essential to the amazing whole;
The least confusion but in one, not all
That system only, but the whole must fall.
                    POPE's *Moral Epistles*

VOL. I

LONDON
PRINTED FOR G. G. J. AND J. ROBINSON,
PATERNOSTER-ROW
MDCCXCII

Introduction

The time is not far distant, when the inhabitants of every country were interested in the projects and hopes of the French nation; the time is not far distant, when it was imagined that the first kingdom of Europe would add new lustre to its exalted destiny, and furnish the example of a happy regeneration in political principles. It was impossible to observe without emotion the first dawn of freedom amidst a people possessing so many claims to celebrity; and everywhere the eyes of mankind were fixed with admiration upon the memorable epoch, when a monarch, heir to a power, the limits of which were unknown, formed himself the generous resolution of circumscribing them; and when, disdaining the ambition of an unbounded authority, he surrendered himself to the emotions of a virtuous soul and was seeking guarantees for all the good things he wanted to achieve.

Every soul of generous feeling, foreigner or native, was intellectually present on that great and important day,[1] when the august bene-

---

1. It was on the occasion of the opening session of the Estates-General on May 5, 1789, that the three orders were brought together for the first time since 1614. On that occasion, Necker gave an important and long speech. For more details, see Robert D. Harris, *Necker and the Revolution of 1789* (Lanham: University Press of America, 1986), 403–45; Aurelian Craiutu, *A Virtue for Courageous Minds: Moderation in French Political Thought, 1748–1830* (Princeton: Princeton University Press, 2012), 119–26. On the Estates-General and the French political context before the convocation of the Estates-General, see Roland Mousnier, *Les institutions de la France sous la monarchie absolue, 1598–1789* (Paris: Presses Universitaires de France, 2005);

factor of France, surrounded by the deputies he had called together, deliberated with them upon the means of establishing forever the public felicity. If we cast our eyes at this period over the different countries of Europe, we shall say, that the first representatives of the French nation had to acquit the debt of gratitude which was felt to the king by the whole human species; we shall say, that these representatives held in their hands the cause of the universe; so much did all hearts associate themselves to the success of their important mission. It was a source of general satisfaction to see this great mass of citizens, whom unjust customs had vexed in so many ways, rise from their abasement and obscurity; and, however ungrateful they may have been, the splendid act of the monarch, which gave substance to their rights and their dignity, will hold its rank in the memory of mankind; for a great moral idea, existing in itself and independent of events, triumphs over misrepresentations and survives all passions. I well remember how Europe, whose diverse reactions I am recounting now, witnessed with discomfort our first controversies and those well-known rivalries which prevented the French legislators from advancing upon the new path opened before their eyes. Even after this epoch of the revolution, which the National Assembly had consecrated in its annals, foreigners did not yet permit themselves to despair of our cause. The singular coincidencies of the times, the majesty in which distance envelopes great events, and which hides their insignificant causes, still supported our character abroad; and not even those deplorable excesses with which the first moments of the insurrection of Paris were stained could destroy the general partiality for a great people, marching forward to a great object, with the wild disorder of great passions. It was believed that generosity would follow in the train of victory; it was hoped that discretion would accompany and modify the triumphs of force. With how much patience and forbearance did the inhabitants of other countries excuse the errors of the French and the faults of our first legislators! They still trusted that,

François Furet and Ran Halévi, *La Monarchie républicaine: La Constitution de 1791* (Paris: Fayard, 1996), 41–73; and Ran Halévi, "Estates General," in François Furet and Mona Ozouf, eds., *A Critical Dictionary of the French Revolution* (Cambridge, Mass.: Harvard University Press, 1989), 45–53.

in the last moment of revision, in the result of the final dispositions of the Constituent Assembly, order would give her hand to the support of liberty. Mistrust had long taken possession of the sober and thinking inhabitants of France, before foreigners would allow themselves to harbour it. The great mass of mankind remains attached to its long-held impressions; it is an immense body that moves all together and that cannot be guided or changed by complex ideas. It was not therefore till after long resistance that foreigners abandoned our cause; it was by a sort of constraint that they withdrew from us their attachment; and they felt a deep and lively sorrow when they saw their wishes frustrated and their hopes vanish. Their interest diminished and their hearts were alienated from us when they beheld the progressive increase of disorders in the kingdom; when they beheld the continual abasement of all regular authority and the sacred maxims of liberty converted into a pretext for every species of tyranny. Their interest diminished and their hearts were alienated from us, when they saw the people blinded by the hypocritical adulation of those who aspired to dominate in their name; when they saw in the legislative body, the timid weaknesses of virtue and the daring insolence of vice; when they saw the base complaisance of a National Assembly towards men whose reputation was so greatly tarnished by their past that they would not have been permitted, according to the laws of the ancient republics, to make any proposals however useful to the public adoption. But above all did foreigners shrink from us with terror, when they heard the story of successive deeds of injustice, barbarity, cruelty; and when they alone sometimes lent an ear to the distressful cries of the victims. The generous and the virtuous of every country abandoned also the cause of the French nation, when they witnessed its ingratitude towards a monarch, whom that very nation had described with great pomp by the glorious appellation of *the Restorer of Freedom*; when they saw the shameful pleasure that was taken in idly wounding the heart of the best of princes, and that he was abandoned, in the hour of adversity and in his retirement, to the vile and dastardly insults of the most contemptible of beings, who, a little before, and while the shadow of power remained, had servilely cringed and licked the dust beneath his feet. Finally, all nations despaired of us, when they saw morality and religion rendered the laughing stock of our politicians, when they observed the presumptuous hopes of that criminal philosophy which, having thrown aside the mask, pretended to substitute its dry lessons for the balm of piety and the heavenly teachings prepared for our weak nature. Unfortunately, today people everywhere have lost hope in the fortune of France and her best friends abandon themselves to the darkest predictions. They perceive the arrival of the last term of illusion; they see the moment approach when the bitterest tears will be shed over the rich harvest which has been left to perish, when the least prudential effort might have saved it. You who have accomplished all this, with what remorse ought you not to be stung! It is not your country only, it is all Europe that demands an account of that liberty of which fortune had rendered you the guardians; of that liberty which, sagaciously directed, would have captivated the affections of the whole universe, but which, in your unskilful hands, has become an instrument of fear and a signal of terror. Blind and wretched guides of a nation deserving of a better lot, you have sacrificed even her renown! Could you for a moment but quit the narrow cell in which your vanity has enclosed you; could you but hear what is now said of a people whom you have misled, your remorse would be eternal. It is said that their spirit of imitation, acceptable with regard to what is fashionable, changes into hyperbole in political affairs and renders them incapable upon all occasions of moderation and prudence. It is said that their mildness of manners was the effect of their submission, and that their true character at length displays itself. It is further said that they have absolute need of a master, and that liberty is a happiness of which they are neither worthy nor capable of enjoying. Such is the language which is now held throughout Europe; nor is it at all to be wondered at. Nonetheless, it would be unjust to impute to the natural inclinations of the French people wrongs that belong to a system of government which was unknown to them; wrongs that introduce anarchy and the relaxation of every social tie. Among the different motives then, which may induce us to expose the vices of this constitution, it may be one to remove the obloquy which rests upon a great nation, by showing the true cause of the various disorders to which France is subjected. In this subject I have a particular interest, I who have united my name in so many different ways to the glory of being French; and if, while I fulfil a task which I have so much at heart, I annex no other title to my work than reflections on *Executive Power*, it is because all the different branches of politics are in my opinion closely connected with the prudent constitution of this social power. Every thing would have gone on well among us, if we had taken care to place ourselves under the protection of a benignant guardian; time would have done the rest, time would have brought the seeds that we planted to maturity and perfection.

I have never ceased to remind the National Assembly of these fundamental truths. I have done it at all times during my administration; and I have done it again during my retirement, when I hastened the publication of my last work[2] so that it could appear prior to the revision of the constitution. It will, however, be seen that our legislators, sometimes through ignorance, and at others through weakness, have constantly diverted their attention from the idea which ought to have been ever present to their minds; it will be seen how they have neglected real precautions from a blind attachment to certain maxims; how they have preferred the office of high priests of a new sect, to the honourable functions of philosophical lawgivers; how vanity led them early astray from duty, and how they have more anxiously sought the applauses of the people, than the inestimable satisfaction of one day meriting its benedictions. It is by rendering justice to these men, by exhibiting them in a true point of view, and assigning them their proper place, that I shall save the honour of the nation; for there is not a people upon the face of the earth whose manners would not be totally changed, if they were suddenly carried back to the state of natural liberty, or if they were merely brought near to it by weakening the authorities destined to guaranty the public order. Envy, jealousy, the mere aversion excited by the unequal distribution of property, sentiments that are contained within bounds by the power of the laws, would then present the most terrible spectacle,

---

2. Necker refers here to *De l'administration de M. Necker par lui-même*. The book was written in less than six months after Necker's departure from France in September 1790 and was published in Lausanne in April 1791. For more details, see Grange, *Les Idées de Necker* (Paris: Klincksieck, 1974), 61–63.

since liberty would become the ally of all the passions that instigate us to the abuse of liberty. The barriers that divide the savage from the civilized man, are much stronger in appearance than they are in reality; they were erected many ages ago, and their very antiquity offers itself to our imagination as an index of their indestructibility. But it is no less true that a few simple moral principles constitute these barriers, and one or two of these principles, pushed to an extremity, would suffice to unite the spirit of independence and the spirit of tyranny, the equality of the early age with the corruption of the later one. A slight inattention to the executive power, in the structure of a political constitution, may bring on this confusion and a mistake of this kind reminds us of that black cloud which, appearing in the midst of a blue and brilliant atmosphere, terrifies the experienced navigators, and which, at first almost an imperceptible point, blackens by degrees the prospect, and forecasts the bursting of a most terrible storm.

I do not know whether this work will be the means of conveying useful instruction to the French nation; I fear that they will be capable of listening to the truth only when they will begin to shake off those slavish chains in which they are held by their polemical writers. But foreign nations, who have not yet parted with that best and most honourable species of independence, freedom of opinion, will perhaps hear me, and it is to them that I pay today the tribute of my thoughts with greatest confidence. Let them reverse, for their own happiness, the exaggerations that have caused our ruin; and let us one day derive wisdom from them! We have wanted to instruct them, but it has been with the trumpet of discord and from the towers of Babel; and the opposition of our hearts and the confusion of our tongues have equally discredited our lessons. Our morality and our virtues would have been the best proof of the soundness of our philosophy, as our happiness would have made more converts than the most rhetorical language. I recollect the time when, in publishing the result of my long reflections on the finances of France, I employed these words: "Yes, generous nation, it is to you I dedicate this work." Who, alas! would have supposed that, in the revolution of so small a number of years, the period would arrive when I could no longer make use of the same expressions, and when I should be obliged to direct my attention to other nations, in order to derive fresh courage to speak of justice and morality! Oh! why is it not now permitted me to say: "To you I address this work; to you, a nation more generous than at any former period, since liberty has developed your character, and freed it from its shackles; since you are free from the yoke of slavery; since you have made a fair trial of your strength, and obey no laws of which you were not first the authors!" Oh! what transport would it have given me to be able to adopt a language like this! The feeling still exists in my bosom, but it is now an exile and a vagabond upon the face of the earth. I am incapable of forming any new political alliances, and I am not less incapable of indulging, even in fancy, the favourite idea and the single passion with which my soul was so long filled.

CHAPTER I

General Reflections on Executive Power

The executive power is the moving force of a government. It represents, in the political system, that mysterious principle which, in moral man, unites action to the will. So various are its relations, so extensive is its influence, and so great the space, so to speak, which it occupies in the social order, that the adjustment of its limits and the accurate adaptation of its means to its end offer to the human mind one of the most comprehensive subjects of reflection.

The eminence of the legislative power and the rank it holds in the general scale of authorities strike the imagination in a more forcible manner, yet in the first conception of this power, all is simple, and its existence depends on no exterior circumstance. The functions which it must fulfill may be executed by an assembly of men possessing the confidence of their fellow citizens, though this assembly should not have been constituted according to the best principles, and in the most perfect manner. The formation therefore of the legislative body cannot be placed in the number of problems difficult to solve; and it certainly does not require, like the institution of the executive power, a precise rule, an exact conformity, from which it would be dangerous to depart.

It is of little importance either to happiness or to liberty that the legislative body be formed, as at present, of seven hundred and forty-five deputies; rather than of six, seven, eight, or nine hundred. Scarcely is it of greater importance for happiness or liberty that the assembly be composed of deputies nominated by each department, in the combined ratio of number of inhabitants, degree of contribution, and extent of soil, and not in the simple proportion of population and public burdens. The duration of each legislature may also be fixed at three, rather than two years, without any important consequence for the advantage of the kingdom. And the age and degree of property necessary to be eligible are equally issues whose precise determination is of little interest to the safety of the state. Lastly, even the grand question respecting the formation of the legislative body into one or two houses, though the most interesting of all, acquires no real importance till the moment that its connection with the executive power be seen; for if it be considered only as it relates to the framing of laws, it is obvious that a part of the inconveniences resulting from a single house may be remedied, by modifying with different statutes the dangerous rapidity of its deliberations and decrees.

It may without exaggeration then be affirmed that the constitution of the executive power forms the essential and perhaps sole difficulty of every system of government.

This power, though second in appearance in the political scale, acts there the principal part; and if by a fiction we were for a moment to personify the legislative and the executive powers, the latter in speaking of the former might borrow the well-known words of the Athenian slave, and say: *All that this man has said, I will perform.*

The laws would in effect be nothing more than counsels, than so many maxims more or less sage, without this active and vigilant authority, which assures their empire and transmits to the administration the motion which it needs. When it passes certain limits, this power is alarming to liberty and may endanger the constitution itself; and when stripped of the prerogatives that compose its strength, it is incapable of fulfilling its important destination, and its place remains as it were vacant amidst the social edifice.

It is therefore by the efficacy of this power and its prudent adjustment that the primitive intention of political society is accomplished; and it derives its perfection from the most exact combinations, where all is proportion and everything in equipoise.

Very different, however, from the legislative power, which may begin its career the moment it is installed and the persons appointed to exercise it are legally assembled, we may almost say of the executive power that when created, it does not yet existence, as its influence depends on an infinity of means entirely distinct from its institution.

In reality, the constitutional laws would in vain define the functions of the executive power, would in vain ordain that a general respect should be paid to it, would in vain determine that this power should be exercised, whether by a monarch elective or hereditary, or by a senate composed of a certain number of persons, eligible in a certain way. All these conditions would give to this power neither energy nor life; and while the legislative body, with its thinking or its eloquent members, might multiply at its pleasure laws and decrees, the executive power, if not invested with all the prerogatives necessary to its authority and its credit, would uselessly attempt to enforce its rights and accomplish the ends of its institution.

This power has no existence but by the union of all the properties which form its essence; it derives its energy both from the real assistance given to it, and from the continual support of habit and of imagination; it must have its rational authority and its magic influence; it must act, like nature, by visible means and by an unknown influence.

We should not be astonished by the necessity of such a union. For nothing is so extraordinary in the moral order than the obedience of a nation to a single law, regardless of whether this law is the expression of the will of one man, or the outcome of a representative assembly.

Such a subordination must strike with astonishment the people capable of reflection, if only because of its opposition to the general laws of the physical world, where the motion of bodies is proportioned to their masses and their power of attraction.

The obedience of a very great to a very small number appears then to be a singular circumstance, an almost mysterious idea; yet we believe to be simple what has long existed in the moral order, and we observe with all the familiarity of habit the greatest phenomena of the universe.

At present however, when we have stopped all the wheels of the old political machine; when we have changed or displaced them; when we see also order everywhere subverted, obedience everywhere opposed, it is time we should acknowledge that the motion, which is most simple in its effects, frequently depends on the organization whose springs are the most complicated and whose proportions the most astonishing.

The executive power has the same end, the same destination in all governments; its functions therefore may be easily defined and separated from those which exclusively belong to the legislative body. But when we want to organize this power; when we wish to make choice of the elements proper to constitute its strength; when we wish to assure an action free from abuse, a motion without destruction; and would apply all these proportions to an immense rotation to an immense space, we perceive the difficulties of such a theory. And the National Assembly might perhaps be pardoned for having ignored or overlooked them, if all our misfortunes, those which we have already experienced, those which we feel at present, and those which we have still to apprehend, were not to be referred to this first fault. This fault we shall long have cause to regret, and in order one day to find a remedy, it is first necessary to be conscious of it in its full extent and in all its consequences.

CHAPTER II

The Formation of Executive Power, with Reflections on the Conduct Observed towards It by the National Assembly of France

We have just shown that the formation of the executive power is the most important and perhaps the only difficulty attending a political constitution; and we have observed at the same time, that the welfare of the state and the most important interests of a nation depend on the wise and prudent solution of this difficulty.

If the members of the National Assembly of France therefore, examining with a persevering and serious attention a question of such magnitude, had erred in their conclusions; if seeking to establish a perfect equipoise between the security of public order and the maintenance of liberty, the balance, from inadvertency, had declined in their hands, the weakness might have been placed in the number of errors from which the title of legislator does not exempt men. But how can they defend themselves against a heavier charge, a charge which, if founded, would give us reason to call in question their political science, and tarnish the glory after which they most anxiously aspire, that of talents and genius? Yes, it is on the very eminence where they have placed themselves, it is amidst the homage that attends them like their shadow, that I dare call them to account for a fault, the source of all the evils and troubles of France, and of which no example is to be found in the history of political legislations.

This fault, the consequences of which have been so great, is having absolutely forgotten the executive power, when they ought to have been mindful of it; it is having mistaken its nature and imagined that the law was sufficient to create it; it is having presumed that, in order to have a king, it was only necessary to declare his crown hereditary, and his person inviolable and sacred.

We shall throw some degree of light upon these propositions by following for a moment the path of our legislators and ascending to the origin of their labours. This arrangement of our reflections will be the more proper, as the National Assembly itself, either seduced by the attractions of method, or confiding in the absolute authority of its will, has followed a sort of hierarchy, well calculated without doubt to diminish its effort of reflection, but which could not correspond at all to the parallel hierarchy of moral ideas.

The Assembly then, giving the priority to the examination and recognition of the rights of man, next proceeded to the choice and adoption of the constitutional articles of its new political system; and having assigned the third place in the order of its labours to the task of constructing laws for the regeneration of all the branches of government, postponed to the last the organization of the executive power.

The Assembly doubtless supposed this to be its rank. But though it be true that, in the order of action, the executive power comes next after the legislative, whose decrees it ought to execute, it is otherwise in the order of thoughts generating the social system; it is otherwise when we consider the moment in which the different powers should be constituted and receive the properties necessary to their existence and duration. Then no supremacy can be admitted; and since in a political system, the movement proceeds not from without, but is inherent in all the parts, by separating the formation of the executive power from that of the other constitutional combinations, there would be a danger of our becoming the authors of an imperfect work, a work lame and sickly from its birth.

The winds and the waves do not act upon a vessel till the moment that it is completed, till the anchors are raised, and the sails spread; but if the constructor, in planning the different parts of his learned edifice, had not taken into his estimate the degree of pressure of all the powers that were to impel or to resist it, the vessel would remain in port and would be unable to make its way in the ocean.

Thus the National Assembly, from the moment its attention was occupied by the declaration of rights, from the moment it thought of fixing the constitutive articles of its political system, ought to have made the necessary enquiry, not only as to what were the general conditions on which the solid existence of an executive power depended, but also what were the particular conditions which this institution required in a kingdom like France.

In that case, the Assembly would first have seen that the utility of such a power was in proportion to the importance of public order; next it would have seen that the maintenance of this order, the guarantee of property, and the common desire of mankind to enjoy in tranquillity the habitual feeling of personal safety, were the spirit and object of all political associations; and seeking to secure to us these advantages, seeking at the same time to protect liberty from the dangerous influence of useless authorities, the Assembly would have discovered early the true means of reconciling interests apparently opposite; and fixing its opinions, at least respecting the different elements of which the executive power ought to be composed, and the laws of equilibrium absolutely indispensible to the activity of government, the Assembly would have had the result of these considerations present to its mind in the course of its labours and studies, and would have perceived its application from the first step.

Then, and if it had judged that in a kingdom consisting of twenty-six millions of souls, and with an impetuous and fickle nation, it was impossible by elevating beyond measure the imagination of the people to escape the dangers of anarchy, the Assembly would have avoided saying to them without any real utility that, *men are born and continue equal in rights;*[1] it would particularly have avoided addressing them in legislative and proverbial maxims, maxims which are easily

---

1. Reference to Article 1 of the famous *Declaration of the Rights of Man and of the Citizen,* adopted in August 1789: "Men are born and remain free and equal in rights. Social distinctions may be founded only upon the general good" http://www .constitution.org/fr/fr_drm.htm. For more details, see Marcel Gauchet, "Rights of Man," in Furet and Ozouf, eds., *A Critical Dictionary of the French Revolution,* 818–28.

retained and transmitted; and it would further have avoided misleading its mind by including among those rights, and under the title of *imprescriptible*, all resistance to oppression, a vague, uncertain, and always dangerous idea, when the application of it is abandoned to the eternal ignorance of the multitude.

Finally, when the National Assembly passed from the Declaration of Rights to the examination of the constitutional articles,[2] it proceeded blindfold in the discussion, since it had acquired no knowledge relative to the conditions necessary for the establishment of the executive power, and since it was absolutely ignorant both how these conditions could be combined with such and such parts of the constitutional articles, and how they could be made to assort with the limited degree of authority which the Assembly was disposed to accord to the head of the state. Thus, the most simple and most reasonable constitutional articles would have been found to have been connected to the previous questions that I have pointed out, and which never entered into the deliberations of the Assembly. Let us apply these observations to a few examples.

The Assembly rightly placed in the first rank among the constitutional articles, *that the French government is monarchical.* I am far from thinking the National Assembly to have possessed either the right or the power of changing a fundamental disposition, consecrated by all the instructions and stamped with the seal of public opinion. But

---

2. Three weeks separated the passing of the *Declaration of the Rights of Man* on August 26, 1789, from the rejection of bicameralism and the adoption of the suspensive veto by the members of the Constituent Assembly in September. Of particular significance are the speeches given during this important period in the Constituent Assembly, collected in François Furet & Ran Halévi, *Orateurs de la Révolution française*, vol. 1. *Les Constituants* (Paris: Gallimard, Bibliothèque de la Pléiade, 1989). A few speeches in particular stand out. Lally-Tollendal's discourse in favor of bicameralism (August 31) restated the classical case for prudence, while Mounier's speech from September 5, 1789, one of the most important discourses in the Constituent Assembly, defended bicameralism and absolute royal veto. Mirabeau also advocated the latter in an important speech from September 1, 1789, while Necker defended the suspensive veto.

considering this question here in a speculative view, and supposing the Assembly invested, as it has pretended to be, with an unlimited power of pulling down every thing and building anew, would it not have acted prudently, if, previously to declaring the French government *monarchical*, it had inquired what degree of consideration, influence, and authority it was necessary to secure to the monarch to enable him to discharge the functions of the executive power in a kingdom such as France? For even admitting that this inquiry and this knowledge might have made the Assembly worry about the extent of means that must be lodged in a single individual, an individual however bound to secure public order, the protection of the state, and the activity of the administration, it would have led to the further consideration whether those alarms, well or ill-founded, ought not to make the Assembly prefer a republican government to a monarchical one. And thus it would not have itself led a part of the nation to deal with a question which is still debated today, and which should have been placed first in the order of political discussions.

Similarly, the hereditary succession was also connected with the institution of the executive power and the degree of force proper to assign to it. For though this succession might seem at first view, a subject of umbrage, and a reason for reducing the authority of the monarch, yet as it is a circumstance that leaves to chance the qualities of the prince and the influence attached to his personal worth, it enforces the necessity of sounding the royal authority upon real prerogatives, upon prerogatives adequate to supply the deficiency inevitable from the failure of sentiments of respect, whenever, in the course of the numberless casualties of nature, time brings to the throne a sovereign lacking the various gifts which command the respect of the people.

I shall bestow a cursory attention upon other constitutional articles. The National Assembly in determining, at first tacitly, and afterwards in a formal manner, the indivisibility of the kingdom, could not act in this respect from a perfectly enlightened judgment, before it had thoroughly explored, or at least taken some view of the question of the executive power; for, as the indivisibility of the kingdom implies a proscription of a federative government, the Assembly thus bound itself to invest the monarch with the required authority to govern, from a single center, an immense kingdom; and the dangers or the inconveniences of this authority ought to have been taken equally into the final deliberation of the National Assembly.

It was also not a matter of indifference that the National Assembly should have bestowed some attention upon the difficulties attending the organization of the executive power, prior to decreeing constitutionally that the legislative body should consist only of a single house. For had the Assembly been aware that, among the different means that might be selected for organizing such a power, one of the mildest and most judicious was the maintenance of that instinctive and habitual respect, independent of all reflections, which the people in all nations of the world pay to the head of state, it would without doubt have inquired how this respect could be kept alive without distinction among ranks; and this moral and philosophical inquiry would have influenced in some degree the deliberations on the formation of the legislative body as a single chamber.

Further, when the National Assembly decreed constitutionally the permanence of the legislatures, without imposing them the obligation to interrupt their meetings, it could not be sure of the propriety of the measure, since it had neglected to examine at the same time whether the proper means existed of counterbalancing the inevitable diminution of reverence that would inevitably result as to the monarch, placed continually in the presence of a numerous and powerful body, towards whom all the hopes, all the fears, and all the regards of the nation would be incessantly directed.

It would be still easy for me to show in what manner the grand question of the executive power bore a direct relation to the rest of the constitutional articles decreed in the month of September 1789,[3] but it would be superfluous to extend further these reflections.

The conduct of the National Assembly during the period when the fundamental articles of the constitutions were approved will astonish us even more. It was natural to presume that, after having absolutely forgotten the formation of the executive power in the discussions which preceded the adoption of those various articles, the Assembly would at least have given it a general attention, before

---

3. Necker refers here to bicameralism and executive veto.

starting the work of legislation; but so far from doing this, so far
from seeking to focus on the prerogatives necessary to the supreme
chief of the government, it pursued a plan directly calculated to divert its attention from the subject. The Assembly divided the examination and elaboration of all the laws of the administration among
its various committees, each of which, in its department, determined
the part of the monarch as it pleased. This the committees did, frequently without at all considering whether they acted in union with
the committee of constitution, and without inquiring whether there
was any general plan for the formation of the executive power, and
how each part of the administration was supposed to contribute to
it. The various committees also, prior to their making their report to
the Assembly, did not inquire whether the members of the Constitutional Committee were to assist at the meeting, and the Assembly
never thought of demanding the opinion of this principal committee on the reforms which the other committees proposed, according
to their particular fancies, but always seeking to reduce the ancient
prerogatives of the monarch. The consequence was that the executive power found itself composed only of those prerogatives which
had escaped the destruction by the various committees of the National Assembly, all deliberating and acting separately, and without
any kind of concert.

Thus the ecclesiastical committee, influenced by the opinion that
the people were competent to the choice of bishops and inferior
clergy, reserved to the king no share in these elections, not even the
right of assent or approbation. The committee of judicature adopted
the same idea respecting the nomination of judges civil and criminal, and formed its plans according to this principle. The committee
of contributions conceived that the choice of tax officials would be
better if an invariable rule of promotion were fixed and excluded as
useless every degree of influence and appointment on the part of the
government. The military committee also, in establishing rules regarding the advancement of army officers, rules to which the monarch had to strictly obey, did grant him, however, a small role in their
nominations, and even that, not with a view of giving to the executive
power its necessary consideration, but in order that there might exist

for distinguished talents a hope independent of the law of seniority. The marine committee followed nearly the same principles; and as to the National Gendarmerie, which it was thought unnecessary to make an exception, the royal prerogative was still further restricted. The pension committee, persuaded that every sort of favour would be more regularly distributed by the National Assembly than by the government, carried this principle so far as to deny the king the privilege of bestowing a gratuity of a hundred franks without the consent of the legislative body. Lastly, the constitutional committee itself, when occupied with the particular organization of the departments, districts, and municipalities, forgot, like the rest, the necessity of securing to the executive power some means of consideration and influence, and reserved to it no share in the nomination of persons called to exercise in the interior of the kingdom the functions of police and administration, to direct, proportion, and recover contributions, and to watch over every part of public order. The organization of the national guards was regulated in a similar manner, and I could extend these examples still further; but I have cited enough to show that each committee, thinking only of the object of the administration which it was to plan, neglected entirely the part necessary to be assigned to the executive power, in order to invest it with the consideration indispensible to its existence. The committees had received from the Assembly no instruction to do this, so that the blame of their conduct falls not upon them. Besides how were they of themselves to ascertain the degree of royal influence that ought to be preserved? Each of them pursued its labours separately, and none of them could have determined to what degree it was supposed to contribute to the construction of the executive power. They treated this power as if it had been a supernatural and pre-existent faculty against which each of them indiscriminately was called to direct its attacks; while in reality the executive power, amidst the complete annihilation of the government, could only derive its activity and existence from the means of influence and ascendancy which should be reserved to it; and these means depended on the mode in which the royal authority was to be displayed in each department of the public administration.

It was neither to the different committees of the National Assembly, nor to any of its deputies in particular, that the appreciation of the means proper for instituting the executive power ought to have been confided. Such an important legislation belonged to the Assembly itself; and it ought not only to have preceded the work of legislation, but it also merited to have been considered jointly with the determination of the principal articles of the constitution.

The Assembly having destroyed all the obligations, all the principles, all the usages, all the habits, and all the kinds of respect that, under the preceding government, had given lustre and support to the executive power, it was no longer sufficient to declare that this power should reside in the hands of the monarch. It was necessary, after mature deliberation, and with every possible assistance of human intellect, to form a picture of the prerogatives requisite to enable the king to exercise the august function confided to him. It was necessary, in the presence, as I may say, of public order and of liberty, carefully to investigate the point of conciliation between two interests equally dear, and to obtain by dint of reflection that precise measure, that just proportion, which might escape the vague enquires of systematic minds, and the discernment of which is reserved for the calm researches of reason and the penetration of genius.

This rational and judicious organization of a power destined to maintain public order and the observance of the laws, an organization important both on account of its object and its necessity, might have raised our thoughts to the moment when the sovereign Author of nature, after having created man, determined in the depth of His wisdom, what degree of force and activity He should add to the most valuable of His gifts, the gift of liberty.

When the National Assembly had once fixed its opinion regarding the necessary means to secure to the executive power its proper ascendancy and consideration, each of the committees, instead of supposing that the sole will of the law gave to this power its full completion, instead of supposing that it was already too great, when as yet it had no existence, could have endeavoured to construct the department of the general administration that came within its province in such a way that it might harmonize with the principles established by the Assembly; and thus the executive power would have been modelled, not at hazard and without any system, but according to a well-arranged plan, the result of the first deliberations of the legislator.

It appears then, that whatever difference of opinion we may suppose to exist regarding the inefficiency of the executive power, as it has been constructed by the accidental combination of the particular ideas of each committee, or by the laws they made, each on its own, with regard to the essential parts of the public administration, it is not less certain that the National Assembly departed from the line which its functions imposed as a law upon itself. It will be no less incontestable that the Assembly began the work of legislation without having formed any plan regarding the means necessary to the construction of the executive power; and that thus, deprived of the capacity of judging the necessary prerogatives of the executive power, it listened in vain to the reports of its committees, without being able to know whether it was right or not to banish, as much as possible, the influence of the monarch from the nomination to all appointments in the church, the army, the navy, the police, the magistracy, the finances, and the administration.

The Assembly and its committees have thus seen themselves constrained to adopt as a guide a maxim of Montesquieu, developed by Rousseau in the *Social Contract*, which is, that *the people ought to do of itself whatever it is competent to do well, and what it cannot do well it should do it through its ministers.* But both philosophers are speaking expressly of democracies; and even in such governments a principle of this nature cannot be admitted in an absolute manner. Nor is a democracy able to dispense with an executive power; and in order to form this power such prerogatives must be given to it as shall secure the necessary degree of consideration to cause it to be respected. As democracies however exist only, and can only exist, in small states, public opinion is there so considerable an aid to the executive power, that this power can accomplish its object and maintain public order with very feeble means. But to apply the maxim of Montesquieu to a kingdom like France, is one of the greatest faults that a legislator can commit.

If indeed, in a political constitution, the executive power were invented for the convenience and amusement of the person who was to exercise it, it would be right to bestow on it such prerogatives only as the people should think proper to reject; for every degree of preference would belong to the nation, either because of its sovereignty, or on account of the immensity represented by its collective existence. But a distribution directly the reverse would become fitting, if the executive power were considered as the cornerstone of political society, if it were regarded, in the light it ought to be regarded, as the protector, the guarantee of public order, and the power that gives motion to the general administration. Then it would be incumbent, for the sake of the welfare of the state and the interest of the nation, first to examine and ascertain what prerogatives were necessary to render this power effectual; and after having fixed them, with all the precaution that a love of liberty inspires, the overplus that remained, if I may be permitted so to express myself, would fall to the people to be exercised in elections and other associations indirectly connected with the general administration. It is against a useless authority that the people should feel resentment, never against that which is instituted for their own advantage. This is what they would have been told and what they would have felt, had there not been a greater eagerness to please than to serve the people, and had there not been a desire to make the spoils of the executive power the instrument by which to seduce them.

In the meantime, individual interests, personal projects, the secret and dark career of intrigue, the daring attempts of undisguised ambition, the mad passion for new systems, and the errant knighthood of metaphysics, all those forces forming a league against the sane reason, sometimes united, sometimes not, would have had, over the mass of virtuous and upright minds, but a feeble influence, if the National Assembly, by a preliminary discussion, had taken measures to ascertain and determine, before it entered on the work of legislation, what degree of force it was necessary to accord to the executive power to constitute its essence. The Assembly would then have had an instruction that would have served it as a guide and a model to which it might constantly have referred; and the Assembly would certainly never have consented that this power should be composed of the scattered remnants of prerogative, the entire work of chance.

Then also the directors of this Assembly, those haughty and imperious guides, would not have had the temerity to suppose that the
executive power could be created by their sole fiat, by a single word
from their lips; but in a moment of modesty would perhaps have
thought that the mortals do not have the right to say to the paralytic,
surge et ambula, rise up and walk.[4]

4. On Necker's views on the Constituent Assembly, also see Harris, *Necker and the Revolution of 1789*, 707–41. A trenchant critique of the errors of the Constituent Assembly can also be found in the first volume of Necker's *De la Révolution française*; the original text can be found in *Oeuvres Complètes de M. Necker*, vols. 9–10 (the relevant pages on this topic are vol. 9, 254–300). From the very beginning, Necker noted, the Assembly was under a grave delusion with regard to its power and possible accomplishments. The deputies, he wrote, "have fancied that they were enlightened more than others, by science and meditation, and yet they have conducted themselves like the chief of a horde of barbarians, by destroying all the solemnities of the moral world, and making uniformity by an universal debasement" (*On the French Revolution* [London: T. Gadell, Jun. and W. Davies, 1797] vol. 2, 336).

CHAPTER III

In What Manner the Question of Executive Power Ought to Have Been Treated by the National Assembly

In great affairs, and in the various exercises of thought, the questions most difficult to determine are those in which the mind has to fix limits and to draw with accuracy a line of demarcation between contending principles. There are political problems of the highest importance in which this difficulty does not exist. Thus, the distribution of powers, their line of separation, the formation of the legislative body, all these political dispositions, along with many others, doubtless require just views and considerable comprehension; but for the solution of questions to which I allude another and higher type of intellect is required, and among these questions there is not one that presents so many nuances to take into account, so many uncertainties to be cleared, as the prudent and deliberate choice of the means necessary to give to the executive power the activity which it needs, without violating political liberty or endangering it. The task is arduous, and neither the force of reasoning, which from proposition to proposition leads at last to truth, nor that metaphysical spirit whose rapid flight frequently attains it sooner, are adequate to its accomplishment. In this business, the mind is called to a fugitive point, it must direct itself towards a goal which presents itself in different ways. It has uncertain forces to calculate, apparent oppositions to reconcile, vague limits to fix, and the general system of proportion that it must observe depends upon countless combinations and relations. It requires therefore the union of various species of talents to properly organize the executive power in a great empire; particularly when the old foundations have been demolished, and when the soil on which they stood, dug up in every direction, doesn't indicate any trace of the old edifice.

Every thing thus seemed to point out to the National Assembly the necessity of searching for a model, not in order to slavishly conform to it, but to assist it in fixing its ideas amid the immense void which its destructive genius had spread around it. This model was near at hand, a circumstance that was our misfortune; for had it not existed on the banks of the Thames, but been transmitted down to us in old traditions, extracted from a Chinese or Arabic manuscript, and found by chance in some library, or mysteriously confided to the chiefs of our legislators, their ambition to pass for inventors would perhaps have led them to doubt, whether deriving their ideas from the extremity of the globe, or from remote antiquity, was not tantamount to being the authors of them; and we should have enjoyed the English government in an improved state, a government more free than that which we have at present, and assuredly happier.[1] We should have had at least an executive power capable of preserving public order, without exciting fears for the maintenance of the

---

1. As an Anglophile, Necker belonged to and continued a distinguished tradition. The fascination for the English model can be found in many works of that period, from Montesquieu's *The Spirit of the Laws* (1748) to Jean-Louis de Lolme's *The Constitution of England* (1771) and beyond. The monarchiens (Mounier, Clermont-Tonnerre, Malouet, etc.) were also convinced Anglophiles who, for all their differences from Necker, shared with him a strong admiration for English political institutions. Part 6 of Madame de Staël's *Considerations* also offers a panegyric of England as a political model. On the political image of England in France, see Grange, *Les idées de Necker*, 307–49. The fascination exercised by English culture, institutions, and mores in France is explored in Josephine Grieder, *Anglomania in France 1740–1789: Fact, Fiction and Political Discourse* (Geneva: Droz, 1985). A recent synthesis on this topic can be found in Tanguy Pasquiet-Briand, *La Réception de la Constitution anglaise au XIXe siècle. Une étude du droit politique français* (Paris: Institut Universitaire Varenne, 2017).

constitution; and as the opinion of the nation might have been directed with greater facility towards prudent ideas which had stood the test of experience, than towards wild and unprecedented systems, the most perfect satisfaction would have prevailed for the present, with the additional certainty of its continuation, and general tranquillity would have been its first sign. Oh! on what trivial causes do great events depend! This common maxim could never be applied with greater truth and force than to the political situation in which we have been placed, and in which we still find ourselves.

I draw the attention to the executive power, to that branch of the constitution which is inseparable from every other. It is thus, that in my opinion, the example of England might have served to direct the meditations of the legislators of France. They had to combine and organize a power, the guardian of public order, the principle of the entire activity of government; and since, in so serious a business, prudence would not permit them to be guided solely by conjecture and surmises, they ought to have sought in the most temperate monarchy of Europe for a knowledge of the elements that enter into the formation of that power. And being aware, as they could have been at the same time, that the English government, with all its prerogatives, had, so to speak, only barely enough authority to maintain order and prevent abuses of liberty, they would naturally have been led at least to fashion their ideas in conformity to such instructive observations.

Forewarned in reality by the experience of a century in a neighbouring people, what sort of combination of means and prerogatives was required in a free nation to give efficacy to the executive power, had any particular parts in this combination not met with their approbation, or struck them as presenting various disadvantages, they might have modified these in another manner; but sure of an object of comparison, and having it always present to their thoughts, even in deviating from it, they might not have wandered into error.

Such, as it appears to me, was the most simple mode of proceeding, and what would certainly have been recommended to the legislators of France, not by vanity, not by an ambition to pass for inventors, not by presumptuous confidence, but by that plain good sense, before which I am every day disposed to bend the knee with greater respect, in consequence of seeing how dearly in all transactions we pay for the contempt in which it is held. Oh! You who conceive it so base and low, you, our grand metaphysicians, you could have found it if, in taking the Assembly with you in your ethereal circle, you would have ascended a little higher in your winged chariots.

In treating such an important question, it was surely right to seek for information by examining what were the elements of which the executive power of England was composed; it was reasonable to consider whether the degree of prerogative with which that power was invested proved in any respect injurious to public liberty; and supposing for a moment we had been led to this belief, it was our business to have sought how to guard against such a danger; but on no account ought the security of public order and interior tranquillity to have been abandoned, blessings so dear so inestimable, and the enjoyment of which is the chief object of people's desire when they renounce their individual independence to form a society.

In studying the history of England from the revolution of 1688, it would have been seen that the national constitution, respectfully maintained, had experienced no important change, and that political liberty, under the different guardian powers, had remained unchanged; these are essential truths, which I shall examine in further detail later.

What a wealth of information, what a useful assistance could experience have afforded us, had we been disposed to consult it! Nonetheless, it cannot be repeated too much, it is experience that furnishes us with the extract of the knowledge of all ages and of all people, and incessantly turning its spindle around the most subtle ideas and most imperceptible in their origin, gives them the consistency adapted to our use; but unfortunately they then assume the name of common maxims, and we begin to despise them. But the moment approaches when, after having imprudently discarded the tie that unites them, we shall find in their composition every degree of intellect and of thought.

I propose, in the following chapters, to draw a parallel between the organization of the executive power in England, and the elements of which this power is constituted today with us. This comparison will serve not only to show the extreme weakness of the authority which, in France, is to watch over the maintenance of public order; but will also naturally lead me to justify what I have advanced, in the beginning of this work, regarding the intimate union that exists between the formation of the executive power, considered in all its relations, and the various constitutional laws of a nation. It is, I conceive, by applying general ideas to real objects that they become additionally instructive, or at least are the more easily understood.

CHAPTER IV

The Formation of the Legislative Power

It is impossible at the present moment to turn our eyes to the political state of France and of England, without being struck with a great truth; that in one of these countries, enjoying the most perfect civil and political liberty, there exists the happy art of preserving the social harmony, of maintaining public order, and of securing the activity of government; and that in the other, all these advantages are indiscreetly exposed to danger and surrendered into the hands of chance.

This proposition deserves to be considered in different ways, and in the course of its investigation I shall examine various parts of the civil and political systems of the two kingdoms; I shall show their connection with the constitution of the executive power, and shall point out at the same time the relations of this power with order and liberty, with order and equality. I shall confine myself to the main ideas of the subject, and without engaging with the speculations of witty minds, I shall particularly attach myself to that method which can offer a link between uncertain opinions.

I shall first direct my attention to the composition of the legislative power, this commencing point in the social scale.

Everyone knows that in England, the legislative body, under the name of Parliament, is formed of two houses; that their joint will constitutes the law, and that this law is fully sanctioned by the monarch.

Everyone also knows that one of these two divisions of the legislative body, denominated the House of Commons, is composed of representatives elected by the nation, and that the other, called the upper house, consists of peers of the realm, an hereditary dignity of royal investiture.

We perceive at first sight the majesty of a legislative body constituted in this manner, and the influence it must have on public opinion; on public opinion, not as some would mould it, by the aid of factious ideas and constrained sentiments, but as it exists, and ought to exist, in European countries and in the midst of the immutable circumstances that govern us.

The House of Commons, like all elective assemblies, represents, or is at least the substitute of the general will,[1] a will changeable because of its generality, and because of the impassioned elements of which that generality is composed. Such a division of the legislative body, the most powerful as to number, credit, and energy, is wisely situated near another division, which, less numerous, but unchangeable in its condition and functions, represents more particularly the constant interest of the kingdom.

There is thus, in the union of these two houses, a character of harmony, as well as a sort of compact and firmness; and we see how they mutually assist each other in order to obtain the consideration with which a legislative body cannot dispense, and how, united, they acquire the degree of force necessary to defend reason against the enterprises of restless spirits and the incursions of malevolent geniuses.

It is different with a legislative body composed, as in France, of a single house. In that case it soon becomes the object and levelling point of all the passions. Every one being aware that a majority of opinions is all that is necessary to decide the most important interests of an empire, exterior combinations are formed; individual societies and political clubs put things in train to effect that majority, and

---

1. Necker's original term, *voeu général*, differed from Rousseau's famous *volonté générale*. On the distinction between the two concepts, see Grange, *Les Idées de Necker*, 267–71 and Craiutu, *A Virtue for Courageous Minds*, 148–49. Necker's strongest refutation of Rousseau's ideas on equality and social contract can be found in his *Réflexions philosophiques sur l'égalité*, written in 1793 and included as an appendix to the second volume of *De la Révolution française*. The full text can be found in *Oeuvres Complètes de M. Necker*, vol. 10, 341–500.

assiduously study the art of directing a deliberating assembly; the art of moving it as they please by intrigue, by false reports, by alarming publications, and every other species of influence. All these manoeuvres would be defeated, if the suffrage of two houses was necessary to the formation of laws; the spirit of faction would then cease to be encouraged, and the sources of an infinite number of disorders would no longer exist. Morality would also gain in another way by this change; for its authority is wholly lost when a great part of the nation is enticed from a domestic and laborious life in order to engage in a licentious career of political passions and the variety of plots which those passions generate.

The National Assembly imagines that it reigns alone, since it is the sole legislator: but does it know the extent to which it is obliged sometimes to share power with its partners? This part is beyond calculation; for it is not seldom that those who speak from fear or act from imitation are disposed to exceed the opinions of those who dominate over them, in order to acquire by this exaggeration the character of free agents. The English House of Commons would much rather have to harmonize with the upper house, than to exist under the yoke which is placed on the assembly of France; a yoke so terrible that it allows no independence of opinion and freedom of thought; and on such conditions I know of no authority that is desirable, at such a price I know of no civil dignity that can be honourable.

It is true that there are in France two legislative sections, but the organization of both is monstrous; one is the National Assembly, the other that combination of political societies to which it is obliged to accommodate itself. And we shall deceive ourselves if we imagine that by destroying these societies, the evil would be entirely remedied; for they contribute to the force of the legislative body and supply the want of consideration that must inevitably result from its composition. Respect can now no longer be imposed but by the power of numbers; this is a consequence necessarily arising out of the system of perfect equality when established in a great empire; an important reflection, which I shall more particularly investigate in another part of this work.

We have directed the reader's attention to the advantages of a regular division of the legislative body into two houses; but we have considered the question only as it relates to popular commotion and a spirit of turbulence and faction; we shall now observe that such a constitution would have the happiest influence on the deliberations of the legislative body itself.

It is not possible to subject the opinions of a legislative body to any regular mode of censure because, in that case, the idea, which it is so necessary to preserve, of its superiority, would no longer exist; by becoming however a legislative body, it does not cease to be an assembly liable to all the errors, all the indiscretions and weaknesses which are the lot of humanity. The establishing therefore of this censure in the very bosom of the legislative body itself, by dividing it into two houses, was a beautiful and truly ingenious idea. Each chamber is thus obliged to form to itself a model of wisdom, and to have it continually in view, since this wisdom is in ordinary circumstances the most certain means of unity of opinion. It is different with a single house, which must seek to distinguish itself by extreme ideas, such ideas alone being formed to catch the crowded and capricious theatre whose suffrage and applause are the objects of its ambition. The rejection of the plan of two houses when constructing the legislative body, and the formation of this body into a single deliberating assembly, is nearly like giving to the empire of the passions the preference over the authority of wisdom. No one is ignorant of the facility with which the assent of numerous auditors may be obtained, either by the subtlety of argument, or by the insinuating power of eloquence, particularly when certain circumstances are laid hold of by which to act upon the mind. It has wisely been ordained in the French constitution that the projected laws shall be read three different times, at intervals of eight days; but permission being at the same given to depart from this rule in *urgent* cases, this urgency, decreed every instant, has become a mere form, which may be employed whenever one pleases. In a word, as altercations and quarrels are more frequent at the table of high gamesters than at any other, so when an assembly decides of itself the fate of the empire, hatreds, divisions, and jealousies must reign there with greater force, than if that assembly had represented only a portion of the legislative power.

Not one of these observations is applicable to the English Constitution; and its firmness, its consistency, the calm it diffuses, the judicious conformation and strict observance of the laws, and the regular action of the executive power, all these happy circumstances are in a great degree to be ascribed to the division of the legislative body into two houses, whose agreement in opinion fixes the sentiments of the rest of the nation, attracts respect, and is followed by obedience.

The institution of the first of these two houses concurs in the same end, though in a different way. By the existence and intermediation of the peers of the kingdom, the majesty of the throne, so necessary to the support of public order and to the peaceful course of the administration, this imposing majesty is essentially preserved to the king of England. The peers serve as a pillar and an escort to the royal dignity, as a necessary class instrumental in forming ideas and sentiments of respect for the head of the state. Public opinion needs these gradations and arrangements in order to form the notion of a superior office without an equal. Where the distance between the prince and the people is too great, the imagination loses itself; where the distance is too small, that would bring about all the dangers of habit and familiarity. The idea of a king has something extraordinary about it; as long as it is seen favorably, it must be supported by public opinion, by this opinion which reinforces it, and which itself needs to be carefully maintained and nurtured.

It was in order to adhere faithfully to the system of perfect equality or to maintain the quackery of it, that the National Assembly rejected the institution of two houses of legislature, of which England and America afforded examples; but as they deviated from the system in two very considerable instances, appointing a monarch at one end of the social scale, and at the other excluding from every political office those who did not contribute a certain amount of taxes, it is difficult to conceive in what consisted the necessity of observing the most rigorous levelling principles between these extremes.

The system of jealous vanity to which many abandoned themselves, after having been gilded with a specious varnish of philosophy, has been the source of many mistakes. They wanted only a single chamber and a single rank, and thus by stripping the legislative Assembly of all the aids afforded by our ancient manners, and trusting too quickly to their metamorphosis, they eventually brought the Assembly into contempt before a complete change of opinions occurred. No doubt, a much safer approach would have been adopted if, in a monarchical government, the Chamber of Deputies would have been given more prestige and authority by being united to another one composed of the most considerable men of the nation either for rank or landed property, and at the same time reserving to the Chamber of Deputies a greater power, and the right of originating all acts of taxation and finance.

The Constituent Assembly has demonstrated no knowledge of the effects of imagination on a numerous people. It presumed that it had the power to create the majesty both of the throne and of the legislative body without the assistance of any idea conducive to the rule of law. Time has already proved its mistake, and will prove it still more completely when the first enthusiasm which supports new opinions shall subside, and shall leave them to the sole protection of reason.

The English, who have reflected for a longer period than ourselves on political constitutions, would stop believing that their monarchical government could exist for a long time, should the House of Commons, by an unexpected revolution, ever compose of itself the legislative body. All human beings are constantly moving forward; this is the inevitable effect of the agitation of their faculties, and the particular tendency of their imagination. Thus, the commons would tend to put excessive pressure on the monarch, if the peers were not there to serve as a buffer; they would soon tear apart the veil of opinion that surrounds the throne, and that forms its constitutionalist greatness, and after having thus shaken the respect for the monarch, they would make him, without intending it, useless to the state, and the balance of government would be wholly destroyed.

In the meantime, if we may thus reason, in a country where the house of national representatives is composed of men distinguished by their education, and attached to the interest of the state by their having considerable landed property,* with how much greater force will these reflections apply to a legislative assembly, the members of

---

* The representatives of counties are required to possess estates of six hundred pounds sterling a year, and the representative of towns estates of three hundred a year.

which are elected and take their seats without proof being required of their possessing any fortune?

This remarkable difference between the two countries has numerous consequences and direct implications for the executive power, because its task becomes easier in proportion as respect for the laws is augmented. Now, till the most ancient and most natural opinions are entirely changed, such citizens, as are attached to the well-being of the state by ties of property, and whom fortune has blessed with the means of acquiring the various kinds of influence resulting from education, these people will always give to the laws of which they may be the authors a character of superior reverence. Let us never forget that the obedience of a very great number of men to the deliberations of a few individuals is a surprising phenomenon in the moral order of things; and that we therefore hazard considerably by neglecting any of the means calculated to influence the opinions of men. We may sometimes by the aid of multiplied punishments, emanating from force, be able to dispense with this respect, but it is a sentiment indispensibly necessary to the mild, regular, and durable operation of a political system.

The idea, no doubt, that first presents itself, when we proceed wholly upon general principles, is that in his personal affairs every man has a natural right to choose for himself; but these philosophical reflections do not always accord with practical truth. The mistake lies here in the word *choice*, a term which signifies a reflexive impulse towards what is most agreeable to our habits and interests. The application of the word, as thus defined, admits of no difficulty, in the case of an individual placed within a narrow circle of personal interests, possessing sufficient light to direct him towards what is most for his advantage, and expressing his sentiments in a direct manner; but none of these circumstances take place in the act of nominating the delegates of the people to the National Assembly. If the individual nominates them himself, it is most commonly from the opinion of another that he forms his decision; if they are nominated by the mediation of a body of electors in the choice of whom he has participated, he runs the risk resulting sometimes from the passions and sometimes from the partialities of that body; lastly, the majority of suffrages being understood to bind the minority, it is frequently a very small number of voices that determines the preferences. To give the people therefore their true interest for their guide is no violation of their rights, when that interest is to be interpreted by legislators in whose wisdom they have placed their confidence; for that interest is a much surer warrant of the opinion of the people than their opinion is a pledge of their interest.

Had the National Assembly then, like the English, the Americans, and all other nations, considered property, and a property of an important kind, as securing the attachment of the citizens to public order and the interests of the state, they would have essentially served the people and the nation by making the possession of such property a condition of advancement to the dignity of legislator.*

A man without property is not a complete citizen, since he has no interest in the majority of public affairs; and I cannot conceive how the deputies of the National Assembly, whose sole possession is a rich fund of words, can take upon themselves to influence, by all sorts of means, the decision of questions, the result of which is perfectly indifferent to them, or at least affects them only by philosophical affinity. These men, though certain that they shall take no part in the chances of war other than by exclamations and *bravos*, certain also that they shall not have to lament their fields ravaged and their houses on fire, are nonetheless the ardent promoters of political conflicts. How many thousands of men daily pass from life to death amidst the cries of grief and despairs, it matters not to them; they undertake for nothing but the crowning of their exit with an apotheosis. How many others have their fortunes wrecked by the disorder of the finances, the usual consequence of political troubles, yet, they aren't concerned by that; they know that their own fortune is safe in the impenetrable asylum of nothingness. Indeed, one must conceive a very high idea about the right granted by the place of birth or one's

---

*I have frequently regretted that the Notables, assembled in 1788, did not make property a necessary qualification to the being admitted into the states general. The king, influenced by their opinion, would, I believe, have assented to the measure; but they were more accommodating than the Notables in former instances, at least as to the admission of the nobles.

baptism in order to imagine that with a mere certificate from the parish register signed by the local priest, one has a right to come forward and preach the ruin of a nation, and to prescribe to others sacrifices in which they have no share. Nothing appears more bizarre than such a pretension, especially if we compare its humble origin with the momentous consequences to which it may lead.

One might ask whether the constitution has not in reality served the executive power by freeing the deputies to the legislative body from the obligation to present any proof of property, since the chance is hereby greater of being able to act upon them by secret means.

This assertion obliges me to consider what political rank it is necessary to assign to corruption. It may supply in certain governments the want of proportion between the different established powers; but in organizing these powers or when reflecting on how to build a constitution, the legislator will never think of favouring corruption by making it one of the elements that are to compose the authority of government. For, leaving aside for the moment the immorality of such a system, it is obvious that he can admit among his arrangements no force whose degree of pressure and influence is uncertain. He ought, by the prudent accord of all the parts of the social constitution, to prevent abuses of power, and should not try to secure political harmony by means of such abuses.

The members of the National Assembly have often shown their distrust of sources of corruption; but whenever the question had been raised whether they should content themselves with a smaller salary, or whether they might not make a temporary sacrifice of a part of it to purposes of benevolence, orators have always been found whose eloquence could dissuade them from measures of this kind, by insisting on the necessity of representatives in the capacity of legislators to enjoy an income that should be a sufficient security against the suggestions of personal interest. The certainty, however, of twenty-eight francs a day for a period of two years is no very powerful safeguard; and the moment they employed, for the purpose of retaining their earnings entire, the principles of morality, it is strange that they did not consider as a more natural and effective means of independence, the necessity of property as a condition for being admitted among those called to govern over the destiny of France.

An even more important idea suggests itself to me upon this important subject. One of the most praised features of the English Constitution is the equilibrium of the different powers, and the stability of such a renowned constitution is attributed to this sage combination. Some praise it from reason and reflection, while others repeat the same words even stronger merely from imitation. I will not contest this opinion; but I will allow myself to present one idea in particular. I believe the stability of the English government is not due solely to the balance of authorities, but that it must be attributed to the accurate, wise, and delicate harmony, as it were, that subsists between the condition and the respect for persons who must exercise these different powers. I see in England a House of Commons composed of representatives of the nation, a House of Peers and a monarch entrusted with the executive power. I maintain that the union of these branches depends in a considerable degree upon the gentle and gradual transition that exists in the eyes of public opinion between the majesty of the king, the high dignity of the peers of the kingdom, and the personal importance which the deputies of the commons derive from their landed property and their liberal education; and I will add that the harmony of the constitution would probably expire, if either the peers ceased to be mediators between the crown and the representatives of the commons, or if the personal estimation in the majority of these representatives did not bring them nearly to an equality with the social eminence of the peers. I leave my ideas to the consideration of sensible and reasonable people; but I would be seriously mistaken if they were not true and do not contain in fact a very important truth.

It is impossible to establish harmony between different powers by the sole effect of a jealous watchfulness and a mutual distrust. Neighbouring nations, indeed, may thus keep each other in awe, with the aid of their citadels, their fortresses, and their standing armies; but the powers of which a government is composed, powers intermixed in various ways, and the exercise of which devolves on men subject to frailties and passions, how could they agree with each other, how would they remain in their place without nicely calibrated reciprocal relations? Were we to discard these principles of union, and substitute laws of equilibrium in their stead, it would be necessary, if I may so express myself, to place a centinel on the confines of every vanity, every sort of self-love, every individual ambition. They are ties then not counterpoises, proportions not distances, fitnesses not vigilance, which most contribute to the harmony of government; and the reason that we are continually calling the attention of legislators to the necessity of balancing one power by another, and not to the advantage of blending them by judicious and natural means is, that in moral ideas, as in physical objects, the nuances escape us, while contrasts attract instant observation and never fail to impress us.[2]

The National Assembly imagines that, by pulling down every eminence and forcibly establishing a perfect level, they have superseded the necessity of proportions in the political system. But a monarch remains, and there must be steps of descent from his throne to the vast plains of equality; a great and numerous people remains, and it is necessary that, without the aid of habitual coercion and punishments, it should respect its legislative colleagues and yield obedience to their decrees. These are problems not easily solved, but they ought at least to be examined.

It should not be forgotten that the first National Assembly[3] possessed means of elevation which succeeding ones will not enjoy; for not only was it in a certain degree composed of distinguished individuals from the late existing orders of the nobility and clergy, but the arduousness of it task, its enterprising spirit, its combats and its success, by creating it numerous enemies, have given it considerable brilliancy. I am as yet unable to ascertain what degree of lustre the

2. The emphasis on the importance of the "intertwining" of powers (*l'entrelacement des pouvoirs*) is a key and original theme in Necker's political works and serves as a complement to the classical theory of the separation of powers. For more information, see chapter 5, below; also see Grange, *Les Idées de Necker*, 272–305; Craiutu, *A Virtue for Courageous Minds*, 150–54.

3. For more information regarding the composition of the Constituent Assembly (1789–1791), see Edna H. Lemay, Alison Patrick, Joël Félix, *Revolutionaries at Work: The Constituent Assembly, 1789–1791* (Oxford: Voltaire Foundation, 1991); Timothy Tackett, *Becoming a Revolutionary: The Deputies of the French National Assembly and the Emergence of a Revolutionary Culture (1789–1790)* (University Park, Pa.: Pennsylvania State University Press, 1996).

second Assembly will derive from its relation with so many memorable events and the gravity of the circumstances in which it is placed; but in the future it will be from themselves, from their individual persons, that the legislators will have to derive their principal consideration; and I end with another very bold idea, but that is not without reference to one of the characteristic features of the French nation. Never was a vaster edifice undertaken than that of the new political constitution. The art and labour of between seven and eight hundred architects were devoted to it, and twice had the earth revolved around the sun, when this immense task was still unfinished. Stones have been accumulated upon stones, materials heaped upon materials, machines raised upon machines, and we are terrified at this prodigious mass which seems to brave the hand of time. But I question whether the solidity of this important work, this work of so many days, can withstand the impression that the ignoble or absurd formation of a National Assembly may one day make on the minds of men. It is more important to be upon our guard against this sort of accident than against the attacks of a foreign enemy; in spite of the metamorphoses we are witnessing today, I believe that no other people will ever be affected more than the French by the incongruity of tones and manners. This trait of our character, the most subtle of all, will, I believe, survive the former amenity of our manners, and be at least the last to yield to the terrible hand of the reformers. Frenchmen may, in testimony of the devotion of their patriotism, cut their hair short behind, or let it grow before, but the genius and temper of a country are not so pliable, and it is much easier to make ourselves ridiculous than to shut our eyes upon the ridiculousness of others.

In the meantime let care be taken as to that contempt of forms introduced by our young and unexperienced philosophers, that contempt for all sorts of ideas which do not immediately flow from the small number of abstract principles which their brains are able to contain. Experience will teach that the proportions of power, the grand object of attention to a legislator, are not to be supported without the assistance of opinion; and this opinion, continually fluctuating on account of the numerous elements of which it is composed, will always attach itself to persons as to a center of repose.

These latter reflections will admit of no striking application as long as the present enthusiasm shall subsist, an enthusiasm that, together with the motives in which it originates, exalt in our imagination both the persons and the characters of men; but with time all this will subside, and it is for days of tranquillity and moderation, for those long periods of political existence, that permanent laws should be made.

CHAPTER V

The Participation of the Monarch in the Legislative Power

We have seen in what manner the formation of the legislative body, by influencing the general sentiments of respect and deference for the laws, seconds or counteracts the government in the exercise of its functions. We shall perceive still more easily how the intervention of the chief of the state in legislative acts is intimately connected with the dignity of the throne and the efficacy of the power of which the monarch is the depositary.[1]

In the English Parliament, a bill does not have the force of a law till it has received the royal sanction; and decrees of accusation, known by the name of bills of impeachment, are the only exception to this general rule.

It is not thus in France. The new constitution has imposed various restrictions on the sanction of the monarch, some limiting the duration of it, others its application.

The right of opposition, called the *suspensive veto*, that is accorded to the sovereign by the constitution can no longer prevent a law from taking place, after three successive legislatures have persisted in wishing it. In England, on the contrary, a law is never effectual without the

---

1. On constitutionalism, separation of powers, and balance of powers, see M. J. C. Vile, *Constitutionalism and the Separation of Powers*, 2nd edition (Indianapolis: Liberty Fund, 1998).

assent of the king; and this admirable prerogative establishes a striking difference between the splendour of the two Crowns.

What I have now said by no means destroys the observations I have heretofore made on the suspensive veto, both in my latest work and in a Memoir that has just been published.[2] Those observations had a particular object. I wanted to demonstrate that depending on the form of government, a veto, subject to certain restrictions, would have in it more reality than an unlimited right of opposition. In a government where the legislative body consists of a single house, the royal veto cannot be a prerogative of mere parade, cannot be a prerogative, as in England, never to be called into use. The power given to the king of resisting hasty or inconsiderate decisions becomes here a valuable deposit and security; and if it be rendered inert, only one authority would exist and every kind of equipoise would be entirely destroyed. The interest of the nation therefore requires that the king should be emboldened to use this prerogative; and he would never be disposed to do it in the midst of a constitution whose political powers are so unequally distributed, if the monarch had an unlimited power to reject the wishes expressed by the representatives of the nation. These conditions are almost fulfilled by a right of opposition overridden by the vote of three legislatures. I grant that the exercise of such a right is but a kind of appeal to public opinion; but the term of that appeal is sufficiently long to give the victory to reason, and this victory is the only one of which a good king needs. Besides, though the nature of this veto is simply suspensive when applied to laws of general and durable administration, it becomes an absolute veto as to temporary laws meant only for the exigencies of the moment. This suspensive veto would never have been granted to the king by the constituent assembly in its later sessions; for limited as it is, it little accords with the authority that the constitution ascribes to the people, and with the weak condition to which the executive power has been ultimately reduced. Moderation on the part of

2. Reference to *De l'Administration de M. Necker par lui-même* (1791). Necker had also previously published *Mémoire sur les administrations provinciales* (1781) and *Mémoire d'avril 1787* in response to a discourse given by M. de Calonne in the Assembly of Notables.

government would still be necessary in the use of this right of opposition. What would be the consequence if it were absolute in all cases
and circumstances, and thus it became the object of every clamour
and the pretext of every discontent?

It is not therefore the limitation of the right of the veto granted
to the king, but the necessity of this limit, according to the principles
of the constitution, that ought to be considered as the factor affecting
the majesty of the throne.

None of the reflections I have made on the suspensive veto would
be sufficient if the modification of constitutional articles were submitted to the approval of the monarch, as was the case in England;
for as these changes may influence the prerogatives of the Crown
and maintenance of the social equilibrium, a veto of limited duration would not be applicable to such an order of things. But it is well
known that the prerogative of the French monarch has been reduced
to the sanction of laws of administration; and so many provisions
have been included under the articles of the constitution, these immutable articles independent from the will of the prince, that, by this
means, the royal authority finds itself infinitely circumscribed.

Many of the laws of simple administration, and those of the most
important kind, have not been made subject to the royal sanction.
Such in particular are the different legislative provisions *regarding the
exercise of the constitutional police, the administrators, and the municipal officers,* vague expressions easily susceptible of being arbitrarily
extended. But the most extraordinary exception is that of the *decrees
which relate to the fixing, the extension, and the collection of public contributions,* which according to the constitution ought not to be submitted to the approval of the monarch.

A disposition more degrading to the royal majesty cannot be
imagined; and it is difficult to conceive how legislators could resolve
to represent the king as unconnected with the dearest interests of the
people. Of what worth is the title of hereditary representative of the
nation, which the constitution has bestowed on him, if he be no longer to represent that nation at the very moment that the sacrifices it
is required to make are under discussion? Has it been remembered
that, in a kingdom called upon to pay five or six hundred millions, so

vast a contribution extends to all places, persons, and things; is connected with them all by an infinity of relations, known and unknown; and that to be excluded from this grand whole is to be less than a simple citizen?

The weak arguments alleged to induce the Assembly to pass such a constitutional provision cannot be put in competition with the dangers attached to a failure of the respect due to the chief of the nation, and to the weakening of the executive power, which is the consequence. But this interest, great as it is by its intimate union with public order, was never reverted to in the course of debates. It cannot be too often repeated that the Assembly continually acted as if it supposed the power destined to guarantee the execution of the laws existed by itself; or as if it hoped to give that power life and action by the sole efficacy of its own words.

It has been said that the Estates-General possessed in all ages the right of consenting to taxation. No doubt; but *to consent,* in the French language, does not mean to act without the concurrence of others.

It has been said that on the 17th of June 1789,[3] the National Assembly had, of its own authority, reinstituted or imposed anew the existing taxes without any interference on the part of the king. This is more artful than true; for the taxes were already established and properly collected, and the Assembly did nothing more than unite its own will with the will of the monarch, made manifest before.

It has been said that contributions proportioned to the wants of the state being absolutely necessary, should the king refuse or defer his sanction to decrees for continuing the taxes till the next meeting of the legislature, the result would be general disorder, which might overturn the constitution. But were a king to act thus, either he must be in the state of lunacy foreseen by the National Assembly, or he must have become a magician to forbear with impunity to pay the soldiers, sailors, stock-holders, and the emoluments of the caps for

3. On June 17, 1789, the deputies of the Third Estate declared themselves the National Assembly and later took an oath to stay in session until they would give the country a new constitution.

the National Assembly itself; and the most singular circumstance of all would be that, while indulging in all these mad acts, he would likewise rob himself of his civil list.[4]

It has been further said, that the king might refuse to abolish taxes burdensome to the people, or might admit only of such as should be favourable to the rich. Can a supposition like this be seriously entertained, while the constitution has subjected the king to the necessity above all things of gaining popular favour?

This truth will undoubtedly be perceived when considering the exact opposite of the previous claim which was maintained in another quarter of the house, where it was asserted that the king, to render himself popular, might refuse his consent to those taxes which should be most disagreeable to the multitude, and thus contend for public favour with the National Assembly. Every thing in this supposition is chimerical, except the rival jealousy of the Assembly; and the orator, to excuse himself, thought it right to remind his audience of the principle, too often repeated from the tribune, that the executive power and the legislative power must eternally be enemies. Enemies! if such be the result of the constitution, what greater criticism can be pronounced upon it? All the labours of legislators should be to reconcile these two powers; and the success of their efforts would have been the proof of their wisdom.

But it is not only as it interferes with the majesty of the throne that I see cause to blame the constitutional article depriving the king of his sanction to decrees for fixing, extending, and collecting the taxes. If ever the union of two opinions and two wills is necessary for consecrating national laws, if ever the welfare of the state and the interest of the people require that union, it is to the institution and choice of taxes that this truth deserves to be applied. A system of this kind might exist, the branches of which would extend to the fundamental principles of political order. Of this I will give you an example. Let there be substituted, as has more than once been proposed, instead of the present taxes, which operate equally upon property measured by its absolute extent, another sort of tax, the operation of

4. The annual sum paid by the government to the king to cover official expenses related to his office.

which should be regulated by a scale progressively drawn from the extent of each property; such a distributive mode of taxation which would subject the rich to exceptional sacrifices would exhibit a striking resemblance to the Agrarian laws which were so frequently the topic of tumult and debate in the Roman republic. Yet the king, the hereditary representative of the nation, must remain a simple spectator of such an upheaval; nay, he would be required, according to the constitution, to proclaim and enforce the execution of such a law, for which his ministers would become responsible.

I ought further to observe that, in the regulation of all taxes, the consent of the chief of the administration, and the sober investigation which ought to precede his consent, cannot be indifferent to the welfare of the state. It has been said that, if it were necessary to know the opinion of ministers, that opinion need only be asked in the presence of the Assembly. But in what character must they give their opinion on such a subject? They could not give it in the name of the nation, since they are not the representatives of the nation; they could not give it in the name of the king, since the consent of the king relative to taxation has been rejected and, as it were, exinguished by law. In treating this question, and giving their opinion in a legislative deliberation, ministers would then suddenly exercise a function foreign to the trust reposed in them by the king, and having no legal connection with either of the two constituted powers. The monarch would imperceptibly find himself reduced to the quality of an elector of ministers, and transformed, if I may say so, into a sort of active polling mechanism for the greater ease of national assemblies. All this might be very indifferent under a certain system; but it must be allowed that this and many other circumstances can neither be reconciled with the respect due to the monarch, the dignity of the throne, the quality of chief of the administration, the activity of the executive power, the title of hereditary representative of the nation, nor with any of the great advantages attached to monarchical government.

It has been said that the Assembly would shield the love of the people for the king from their inconstancy by not making him a party in the establishment of taxes; but let it also be considered that neither will he have any share in their abolition or in their reduction; besides, from the taxes not originating with him, the simple prerogative of the sanction, which ought to have been preserved to the chief of the nation, would never have subjected him to reproach.

I am also at a loss to conceive what agreement can exist between two legislative ideas which seem so evidently at warfare; the one is the imposing of taxes without the approval of the king; and the other is the granting to his authority every necessary power to secure their exact payment. Is not this affording to the negligence of administration, or to its want of will, a very natural excuse? Does this not amount to giving it the right to claim that the obstacles originate in the ill choice of taxes, or in the injudicious manner in which they have been laid?

Is there not, lastly, a kind of contradiction and inconsistency in absolutely excluding the king from the system of taxation, while his sanction is required for all expences and loans? For he is thus made a party in engagements, without being a party in the means taken to fulfil such engagements.

The most simple and common observations often give birth to sublime ideas, when such ideas have any relation to the subject in question; and I cannot help saying to myself at this moment, it is a misfortune to France that roads which have long been open should serve as avenues to the temple of reason; for had it been necessary now first to open them, our ardent labourers in legislation would have been satisfied with that honour, and would then have led us by the shortest and best paths.

CHAPTER VI

The Limitation of the Powers
of the Legislative Body—
Revision of the Constitutional Articles

The three united wills of the commons, the lords, and the king form in England the legislative power; and this power, thus constituted, has properly no limitation.

The code of the ancient laws of England has been fully entrusted to the guardianship of the three wills that compose the legislative power, and whatever they unanimously decide is considered legal.

Public opinion protects with its shield the principles that essentially interest national liberty, but it leaves to the three powers which govern England, powers so admirably constructed, the faculty of correcting or modifying the small imperfections of the social edifice.

The English do not understand how an assembly of deputies, convened from time to time, should surpass in understanding the united science of the three political guides to whom the nation has given its confidence.

The English, long emancipated from the schools of legislative philosophy, no longer fall on their knees before those words, repeated amongst ourselves with so much pomp, before those imposing words *general will* and *national sovereignty*, those vague ideas whose regular application is impossible, and which become a source of error and delusion when forced from the circle of abstractions, to be converted into active maxims and practical truths.

The general will, the sovereignty of the nation, can never exercise a real authority without being made known, without quitting their moral essence, in order to assume in some manner a corporeal form. You, the legislators of France, have acknowledged, as interpreters of the general will, a certain number of deputies, chosen by electors whose nomination is vested in a portion of the people; yet, while submitting all these deputies to the same mode of election, you have told us that some of them represented the nation to enact laws of administration, and others to enact constitutional laws; thus all is supposition, all is arbitrary in this arrangement. How can the English be said to forsake principle, as you affirm, because, without any distinction of circumstances, they acknowledge, as interpreters of the general will, the united sentiments and the ideas of the king, lords and commons? The principle consists, according to you, in the sovereignty of the nation, in the supremacy of the general will; but the English constitution has not violated this principle; it has only, like the French constitution, given an interpreter to authorities purely abstract; and the question is which of the two nations has been least mistaken in its choice.

The English nation was not willing that the essential foundations of the social fabric should be shaken at every interval, by deputies legally invested with such a power.

The English nation was not willing that minor alterations, but such as experience strongly recommended, should be rendered impracticable. Corrections which depend on a general system of redress will always be uncertain, on account of the difficulty of combining a plan of general revision with the circumspection that great innovations demand, and of adapting it, at the same time, to less important amendments.

The English therefore, without going as we have done, to the flame of metaphysics to kindle their lamps, but guided by the light of good sense or of experience, a light less dazzling but more steady, the English have supposed that the same powers worthy of regulating their civil and criminal, their commercial and financial legislation, and all the active departments of their government, were equally capable of superintending the movement of the political machine, and of rectifying such wheels as time might impair or experience prove to have been originally defective.

The English, persuaded that men skilled in the knowledge of the well-being of a state, if they have at the same time a real interest that should lead them to desire the continuation of that well-being, are the best interpreters of the *perpetual* will of a nation, a will still more vast than the general will,[1] have placed the public welfare under the entire guardianship of the three powers established by their constitution.

Public opinion which surrounds these powers and the necessity there is that they should harmonize with it, gives the nation the most perfect tranquillity regarding the use that will be made of the authority with which they are entrusted. It is impossible to conceive in politics of a system of precaution that ought not to end in confidence; for the controllers and the controlled, the superiors and those who act under them, are in all cases men; if therefore a sufficient provision be made for the existence of this confidence in the scheme of the authors of a constitution, they have discharged their function as far as the imperfection of human affairs allows it to be discharged.

We shall here present a contrast that will show to what strange ideas men are obliged to resort, when in forming a political constitution, they want to reform it, as they have constituted it, by the aid of suspicions and distrust.

The seventh section of the French constitution gives a minute account of the mode of proceeding to be adopted in the revision of that work. I shall first cite it entire to enable the reader to follow easily the remarks I have to make upon it.

Title VII
Revision of the Constitutional Decrees

I. The national Constituent Assembly declares that the nation has the imprescriptible right to change its constitution; nevertheless, considering that it is more conformable to the national interest to make use only, in a way prescribed by the constitution

---

1. Here Necker uses the term *voeu perpétuel*, that is, the permanent will of the nation, always focused on its long-term well-being, which he distinguishes from the *voeu général*, the general will or temporary desires of the nation, focused on its momentary desires and interests. On this important distinction, see Grange, *Les Idées de Necker*, 267–71.

itself, of the right of reforming such articles as experience might prove to be inconvenient, they decree that the mode of proceeding shall be, by an Assembly of Revision, in the following form.

II. When three successive legislatures shall have manifested an unanimous desire for the alteration of any constitutional article, the revision demanded shall take place.

III. The ensuing legislature and that next following shall not be at liberty to propose the reform of any constitutional article.

IV. Of the three legislatures who shall hereafter have power to propose alterations, the two first shall not attend to this business till the two last months of their final session, nor the third till the end of their first annual session or the beginning of their second.

Their deliberations, on such subjects, shall be accompanied with the same forms as legislative acts; but the decrees by which they shall have manifested their desire shall not be subject to royal sanction.

V. The fourth legislature, augmented by 249 members to be elected in the different departments, by doubling the ordinary number furnished by each department according to its population, shall form the Assembly of Revision.

These 249 members shall be elected after the nomination of representatives forming the legislative body shall have been terminated, and a separate *procès-verbal* shall be made thereof.

The Assembly of Revision shall only be composed of one house.

VI. The members of the third legislature which shall have demanded a change, cannot be elected in the Assembly of Revision.

VII. The members of the Assembly of Revision, after having taken together the oath "to live free or to die," shall swear individually that they will confine their decrees to the objects presented to them by the unanimous wish of the three preceding legislatures; that they will maintain, in other respects, with all their power, the constitution of the kingdom decreed by the national Constituent Assembly in the years 1789, 1790 and 1791, and that in every thing, they will be faithful to the nation, the law, and the king.

VIII. The Assembly of Revision shall then proceed without delay in the business to be submitted to its investigation, and as soon as its work shall be terminated, the additional 249 members shall withdraw, having in no case the power of participating in legislative acts.[2]

Let us take a cursory view of this scaffolding invented by our legislators in order to improve certain parts of the present, or erect a new structure, so urgent and so highly necessary.

We perceive at first sight that they have rendered immutable for ten years not a small number of principles worthy of immortality, but three hundred and twenty-nine articles,[*] of which several have been already disproved by the imposing voice of experience. Our first legislators have commanded the government to march, without giving it any principle of motion, and have at the same time laid an injunction on their successors neither to aid it, nor release it from its setters. They have sown all the seeds of disorder by instituting a political system in which no proportion has been observed, and have prohibited the equipoise to be restored till the period which they have thought proper themselves to fix. There have never been more despotic testators than them and never legatees more obedient and docile.

Though an improvement of the constitution was rendered morally possible after a ten-year waiting period, yet upon a nearer inspection of the conditions imposed on every sort of change, it is obvious that no modification even of the smallest part of the new French system can be possible without a concurrence of circumstances beyond all the rules of probability.

For example, what is required merely to render legal the convocation of an assembly authorised to pronounce upon the passing or rejection of a certain proposed amendment? It is required that three

---

[*] There are not 329 constitutional articles distinctly numbered; but several of the articles, reckoning by the figures, contain different injunctions under one head, which injunctions are distinguished from each other only by being broken into paragraphs.

2. The entire text of the Constitution of 1791 can be found in *A Documentary Survey of the French Revolution*, 230–62.

successive legislatures, the two immediately succeeding the Constituent Assembly counting for nothing, shall perfectly agree, not as to a principle, not as to a general idea, but as to a new constitutional article expressed by one of the legislatures with all the precision of a decree. Let us suppose that by chance, three succeeding legislatures were to agree upon the propriety either of making property necessary to be eligible to the National Assembly, or of forming in future the legislative body of two houses, or of increasing the royal prerogatives; the unanimity of their opinion regarding the general principle would not authorise a convention of the Assembly of Revision, unless their desire regarding the nature of the change itself, and that desire expressed by a decree, be also *uniform*. How can a concurrence and similarity of this kind be expected? I know no instance upon record of such complete agreement, except the grammatical agreement of adjectives and substantives; and to require that the self-love of different men, all of them Frenchmen, all of them authors smit with the ambition of distinguishing themselves, should thus harmonize, is subjecting every amendment of the constitution to conditions which we may well despair of ever seeing fulfilled.

It seems as if the drafters of the project of revision, adopted by the Constituent Assembly, had been sensible of the embarrassment in which this project involved them; for they endeavoured to evade it by a construction that has by no means the clarity which a question of such magnitude required. The expression, *when three successive legislatures shall have manifested an unanimous desire for the alteration of a constitutional article*, does not clearly tell us whether it shall be sufficient, for the convocation of the Assembly of Revision, that three successive legislatures desire any kind of change in this or that article of the constitution; or whether it shall be further necessary that they should agree as to the nature of the change. These ideas, so extremely different, are distinguished only by a grammatical subtlety in the choice of the article that precedes the word *alteration*. Let us explain this singularity, truly extraordinary in a business in which the fate of an empire is interested. *To manifest an unanimous desire for* the *alteration* signifies in the French language that the unanimous desire shall determine the particular kind of alteration; but *to manifest an unanimous desire for* an *alteration* would denote that the unanimous desire respected any alteration whatever. Is it possible that grave legislators should have wished to separate two ideas of so opposite a nature by so imperceptible a line? Is it possible they should no otherwise have distinguished them than by the difference between the definite and indefinite article, had they not themselves been perplexed? But they have not by this artifice saved their reputation; for the latter interpretation would be of no more avail than the former, or would at least be attended with equal though different inconveniences, since it would give to the Assembly of Revision so extraordinary a power that neither the preceding nor subsequent legislatures would be willing to acknowledge it. Supposing three succeeding legislatures would actually agree on placing property among the conditions necessary in future to be eligible as a representative of the nation; it would remain with the fourth legislature alone to fix the quota of that property. Supposing them also to be of the same opinion as to the establishment of two houses; to the fourth it would again belong to determine upon the nature and attributes of this new branch of the legislative body. We thus see that the power devolving on the fourth legislature would be immense, and far superior to the influence of the united wish of the three preceding assemblies.

Let us then abide by the literal sense which the article of the code of revision presents; a sense which seems also confirmed by the obligation imposed on the legislatures of passing their desire of a change in the constitution into a decree, since this form is more applicable to precise than to general ideas.

It is no less true that the Constituent Assembly failed to express itself with the clarity which a measure of such great importance required; and I shall have the occasion to show that, in another difficult situation, it expressed itself with a similar obscurity.

But to continue my remarks. A miraculous coincidence between the precise wishes of the three legislatures will not be sufficient to legitimize a new article of the constitution; it will only give the power of convoking a more numerous legislature than the preceding ones, and to that fourth legislature will the right belong of declaring, whether the desire of the three former ought to be received or rejected.

In short, as if all these shackles were not sufficient, little difficulties of execution are interposed, which will equally obstruct the revision of the constitutional code.

Two months only are allotted to the legislatures for their deliberations on the constitution; a very short period, particularly when we consider that every projected decree must be read three times, and at intervals none of which is to be less than eight days.

It has further been ordained, and that also constitutionally, that if the third legislature, in accord with the two preceding ones, should demand a change in the constitution, none of its members can be eligible to the Assembly of Revision. Now this assembly will possess in addition to its own, the legislative functions; and the members of the third legislature therefore, by having voted for a change in the constitution, will forfeit their right of being eligible to the next legislature. Such a condition, which is truly penal, will be a restraint on their suffrages, by making their private interest militate against the convocation of an Assembly of Revision.

The motive in which this measure originated is obvious. The constitutional committee wanted to prevent the deputies, who should decide the alteration of a constitutional article, from becoming judges of their own decision by having a seat in the Assembly of Revision. But on the same principle, they ought to have excluded the deputies of the first legislature that voted for the alteration from being eligible to the second, and the deputies of the second from being eligible to the third; for, by the constitutional code, the third legislature has no more influence than either of the two preceding ones in the convocation of an Assembly of Revision, since it is the unanimous desire of the three which can alone authorise that convocation.

But it is impossible not to see that all that part of the French code, which relates to the revision of constitutional decrees, has been drawn up in a haste in stark contrast to the importance of the object.

I have already said enough on this issue; but I cannot help still pointing out the oddity that may be the result in particular of one of the regulations adopted by our first legislators. According to their system, an entire uniformity of opinion between three *succeeding* assemblies is required to any amendment whatever in the constitution. It is the word *succeeding* that I highlight here for the moment, and I say that, by this regulation, the majority of the French nation, the majority of its representatives, the majority of legislatures, might earnestly wish for a change in the constitution, without ever having the power to effect it; and even that national sovereignty so ostentatiously cited, would thus be fettered and kept at bay by a mere form. Let us develop this point in a few words.

The legislatures A and B shall be of the same opinion regarding some particular change in the constitution.

The legislature C shall think differently; thus, the opinions of the two former will be of no more avail than if they had never been expressed, since there must be a similarity of desire in *three succeeding* legislatures to authorise a convocation of an Assembly of Revision.

Afterwards shall come the legislatures D and E agreeing perfectly in sentiment with the legislatures A and B.

But if the legislature F, which is to follow D and E, shall not think as they do, their opinion will be of no effect.

We have already, upon the supposition we are making, four legislatures out of six, whose unanimous desires are superseded and annulled by the contrary sentiments of the other two. The hypothesis may be extended infinitely further, and through the whole the smaller number will be found to prevail over the greater.

Such, however, is the possible result of the constitutional article of which I have been treating.

How many other reflections of still greater importance might suggest themselves, when examining the method devised by our legislators for proceeding to the revision of constitutional articles? Has it been considered what a multitude of intrigues and cabals would arise from the circumstance of any one of the principal articles becoming a subject of contention, and the amendment of it adjourned from legislature to legislature, in the midst of a thousand contending passions, and after having been discussed in all kinds of political clubs? Have we sufficiently reflected on the impossibility of a proposal, separated by the course of deliberations from those articles which should serve it for modification or for balance, being understood precisely in the same manner by successive legislatures? The Constituent Assembly, after a discussion of two years and a half, appears not to have fully comprehended the entire complexity of our new political system, a system which was, however, its own child; and yet, it is expected that in the space of two months, a new legislature can select a few defective parts, replace them quickly, and transmit this shapeless whole both to succeeding legislatures and to the public opinion placed above them. A proceeding like this would scarcely be applicable to a constitution generated by the wisdom of ages, that had undergone the trial of every sort of event, and which, as a result, displayed only a few defects; for in that case, it was of little importance whether the best method for correcting these small imperfections was adopted or not. Thus in England, since the period of the revolution, and since government and liberty have been both secure, the inequality that subsists in the representation of the different parts of the kingdom in Parliament is borne without dissatisfaction. It is well known that this inequality has never been the spring of a single law contrary to the common interest of the state; it is further well known that a nation, united in its principles and its conscious felicity, has as its best representative the spirit of morality and reason when this spirit is still honored in its midst; and we also know that, as soon as public opinion will give more importance to the inequalities which people complain about, these inequalities will be definitively changed. But they are unwilling to redeem such an imperfection, or imperfections greater than this, by the slightest innovation upon the authority of and respect for the king and the Parliament, of those two powers whose agreement constitutes the true security for all the blessings that the English enjoy.

Nonetheless, these reflections are a reproach to the genius of the French legislators; since, by a contrary proceeding, they have rendered incorrigible, both as to its principles and its moral effects, a constitution new in all its parts and already at open war with experience; a constitution destitute of the necessary means for the maintenance of order and true liberty; a constitution in which men of discernment in all countries have discovered imperfections of every kind.

In my last publication[3] I invited the Assembly to limit itself to a small number of constitutional articles; and ten or twelve, I believe, might have been sufficient to give to the fundamental principles of the French government and to civil and political liberty, all the stability that can be derived from national conventions. I am well aware

3. *De l'Administration de M. Necker par lui-même* (1791).

then that the resemblance of those articles with the positions of the king, on December 27, 1788,[4] prior to the convocation of the Estates-General, would have been apparent, and this is precisely what the Assembly wanted to avoid making it obvious. Be this as it may, by reducing the constitutional articles to their proper size, a degree of solemnity might have been given to them which would have impressed them on every mind. It might have been considered, whether it would not be expedient to insert them at length in the oath of allegiance and fidelity required of the citizens. By acting thus, our legislators would have paid due homage to this religious bond; whereas, by obliging the inhabitants of France to swear *that they will maintain with all their power the constitution decreed by the Constituent Assembly, in the years 1789, 1790, and 1791,* and by composing that constitution of 329 articles, they exact a rash oath, which the best informed men are liable every instant to violate without knowing it. A form like this is truly an original idea, in which we can perceive nothing of the genuine character of a legislator.

After reducing the constitutional decrees to a small number of principal sections, on which an enlightened nation can never vary its opinion, it would have been at the same time wise if the Assembly had ranged in a second class such dispositions as required to be sanctioned by the authority of experience. Then, in order to give time for obtaining that sanction, had they restrained a legislature or two from making alterations, such a restriction, rational in itself, would also have had the greatest advantages. On the one hand, the foundations

---

4. On December 27, 1788, Louis XVI announced that the representation of the Third Estate will be doubled in the meeting of the Estates-General scheduled for the spring of 1789, but indicated at the same time that no other changes would be made. Necker authored a forty-two-page report addressed to the king (*Rapport fait au Roi dans son conseil*). He also commented on this decision in the first volume of *On the French Revolution;* his account can be found in *Oeuvres Complètes de M. Necker,* vol. 9, 64–69. For an overview of the projects for reform in the last years of the Old Regime, see ibid., 3–175; François Furet, *Revolutionary France: 1770–1880* (Oxford: Blackwell, 1995), 17–40; Jean Egret, *Necker, ministre de Louis XVI* (Paris: Honoré Champion, 1975), and Egret, *The French Pre-Revolution* (Chicago: University of Chicago Press, 1977).

of social order and public liberty would thereby have been secured from every kind of commotion; and on the other, modifications of a different nature, the expediency or necessity of which should be acknowledged, would have been rendered easier and more expeditious. Many of the American states have conducted themselves in this manner; their legislative body may make alterations in the constitution, but certain essential articles have been excepted from that. As for us, we have thought nothing too sacred to become the subject of controversy. Supposing therefore the first legislature, that is regularly authorized to revise the constitution, should propose new measures for weakening the royal authority, or even plainly and without disguise a republican government; I ask whether this proposition, the discussion of which is reserved to the second legislature and will take place only at the distance of twenty-two months, will not, during that interval, end up annihilating the authority of the monarch and the activity of the executive power reposed in his hands? Thus public credit will be entirely destroyed, at the moment when one legislature should propose the expediency of bankruptcy to the consideration of the legislatures that follow.

Has anyone ever imagined that, according to the law of revision adopted by our legislators, it would be neither more nor less difficult to change the monarchy into a republic than to modify the most trivial article, inserted, no one knows why, in the constitutional code? I will give a single example which offers a contrast with the previous reflections. In the second article of the 14th Chapter of the constitutional code, it is provided that the king shall nominate *the surveyors general of works, the sub-surveyors of civil edifices,* and *only one half of the surveyors of administration* and *the sub-surveyors of works.* Now I would like to ask whether these exact proportions are so closely related to eternal truths that their details were worth inscribing in the immutable constitution of the French empire?

I should never end were I to point out everything that is whimsical and dangerous in the plan invented by our legislators for correcting the defects of the constitution. It is to the vicious formation of the legislative body that some of these singularities are to be attributed. It was made to consist of a single chamber, and the legislators were afraid of trusting to that chamber the power of modifying the most trifling articles of the constitution. They would not even dare to grant it the right of summoning a national convention, at the very moment it deemed the revision of certain constitutional decrees necessary; and it was this which led them to require, for every kind of change, the unanimous wish of three succeeding legislatures, as well as to subject the expression and efficiency of that wish to puerile formalities, unworthy of the dignity of the subject to which these formalities are applied.

No doubt, if anything could increase the attachment of the English to the essential principles of their constitution, it would be to observe our legislators, with the advantage of all preceding experience, and hoisted, if I may be allowed the expression, to the pinnacle of their theoretical and metaphysical system, troubled and confounded in their operations, and mistaking subtlety for perfection, and singularity for genius.

CHAPTER VII

The Convocation and Duration
of the Legislative Body

Here also we shall have an opportunity of remarking in what manner the dignity of the throne and the supremacy of the monarch have been constantly cherished by a free people. The English have conceived that the action of the executive power depended on that, and they have never forgotten that this authority was supposed to secure public order and regularity of the social movement. Whatever consideration therefore could be given to it without endangering the principles of the constitution, they have not hesitated to bestow. These are the sound political views; whereas our aim has been to compose trophies of liberty out of the entire spoil of government, by leaving the care of the general harmony to chance.

In France, the legislative body must assemble by itself, at an appointed period; and the primary assemblies, in which begins the election of the new deputies, are to be convoked every two years by the departments, without any previous notification or any authority for that purpose on the part of the monarch. Finally, the legislative body being once assembled, the prorogation and resumption of its sessions depend entirely on its own will.

In England, a parliament cannot subsist longer than seven years; but the constitution empowers the monarch to shorten its duration. The new elections are ordered by royal proclamation, and to the authority of the monarch it equally belongs to determine the opening of Parliament, and to suspend its sessions.

These august prerogatives give no umbrage to the English people and excite in them no apprehensions. A wise nation does not construct its system of government altogether upon the basis of suspicion; suspicion has no place, when the best form of prudence has accomplished its task. How can it be supposed that the king of England should fail to convoke the Parliament at the proper season, when it is already settled that no taxes can be levied but by the authority of Parliament, and none of the expences of the government be paid; and when the laws relative to these subjects, as well as laws which secure the discipline of the army, have force only for the term of one year? The right of appointing the period at which Parliament shall assemble is no longer anything than an honorary prerogative of the king, and only entrusts to the monarch the power of choosing between different days within a very short period; a power which, thus circumscribed, may frequently be essential to the public interest. If the king of England were to acquire the power and feel the inclination to levy taxes of his own authority, of what use would be the faculty attributed to the Parliament of assembling without his sanction even if they had this faculty? The kingdom would then be in a state of revolution; no question of mere form could either ruin or save it; its destiny would depend upon the joint effort of all citizens, lovers of liberty and of the laws of their country. On the contrary, by wanting to accumulate precautions after precautions, and by sacrificing upon every occasion the majesty of the throne, a system of mistrust has been introduced from which there is no return; and which, by perpetually multiplying occasions of offence and irritation, renders mistrust every day more unavoidable. It is thus that, in France, an attempt has been made to introduce a social order without any mutual civility and deference; but the chains of iron, which have been employed to this effect, will not equal in duration the silken cords which bind together all the parts of the English constitution.

The important prerogative, enjoyed by the English monarch, of dissolving the Parliament and ordering new elections, was not essentially applicable to the French constitution; since that constitution has limited the duration of legislatures to two years, a period too short for any considerable change in the sentiments of the electoral assemblies to be expected. It would therefore be useless to have recourse to a new election if, during the short life of a legislature, the reprehensible conduct of its members should suggest such a measure. But we cannot consider in the same light the liberty given to each legislature to continue its sessions without interruption; for as this interruption will depend solely on its own will, we may be assured that it will never take place. How indeed can we be so absurd as to imagine that they will be disposed to quit a theatre on which they have only two years to exhibit? The period will be thought too important, too brilliant, for a moment of it to be renounced. A political existence of twenty-four months is scarcely sufficient to give each deputy time to record his eloquence in the Logographe, and to send down to his district or municipality a few of his words that seem outstanding to him. Out of the 745 members, there will probably in all cases be 740 perfect novices in the career of glory. It will be necessary they should make a trial of their strength in this contest; it will be necessary that they should enjoy, some their success, others their hopes, and others their share in the common triumph. What will be two years for so many gratifications! Let's add that the twenty-eight francs a day, punctually paid, may be likewise an imperceptible tie; this is only a supposition, but surely the thing is possible. How delightful also will it be to these gentlemen, to issue daily their orders to their first servant, the king of France! How delightful for some of them, to go in solemn procession four by four and cause the folding doors of the palace of the representative of the Capetian race to be opened to receive them! How delightful to summon at their bar, with a word, all the ministers! Nobody will ever be able to voluntarily give up functions so captivating as these ones!

Nonetheless, if the sessions of Assembly are at no time interrupted, and if according to the constitutional law, one legislature must succeed immediately to another, their permanence will be established both by fact and by right; and in these conditions, the executive power will remain without influence and consideration, since the habitual presence of a more efficacious authority must keep it constantly in obscurity. And as business naturally searches for the real power, provided the center of that power be always accessible, all proposals, communications, and requests will be made to the National Assembly. The Assembly, easily consenting to increase its authority, will become every day more than the preceding day the center of all wishes and of all types of power. It will only reserve to the government certain tasks of an unmanageable or an unpopular sort, reserving to itself the privilege of censuring its measures while prudently hiding behind the events.

The king of England, notwithstanding his eminent prerogatives, would, I am certain of that, be unable to preserve the consideration essentially necessary to his political functions, if the constitution had not granted him the right of suspending the sessions of Parliament. He hereby judges of the moment when, the regular business being at an end, there would be reason to apprehend that the activity of a numerous assembly might degenerate into a dangerous commotion, and insensibly give birth to a spirit of faction and intrigue. A social order is a work of wisdom and of proportion. This our legislators were unable to perceive because they drew all their lines from an abstract principle and extended them as far as it was possible to do it. This is their principal fault and the source of all our misfortunes. This truth meets us at every step. They said: The nation is the sovereign power, the legislative body is composed of its representatives; they have therefore the liberty to deliberate, debate, and decree as long as they please. But the nation is the sovereign only in a certain manner, the legislative body is its representative only in a certain manner, and as a consequence, its power must exist only in a certain manner. This is what the English, those philosophers in practice, feeling a due respect for experience, were able to see and acknowledge. Their meditations and experiments had prepared the way for us; but vanity and presumption would not permit us to take advantage of this assistance. Our legislators had the pretention to start anew; and in such a long and wearisome journey, their strength failed them, and that at a considerable distance from its end.

I have yet to present a few observations on the period fixed for the duration of legislative assemblies. This period in France is limited to two years; in England it may extend to seven; but, if viewed in its connection with public order, the term of two years will be found to be productive of great inconveniences. Uniformity of principles in legislation and their stability have always been the most effective way of securing obedience in the people and their respect for the laws. But how can we entertain the slightest hope of this permanence and harmony if there be a continual change of legislators? The first effect of a too transient authority is an eagerness to act and an impatience to distinguish itself; and as time is necessary for enjoying the honours of wisdom and prudence, when men invested with considerable power are deprived of this time, it is natural that they should pursue a glory whose harvest may be more speedily reaped. That glory normally consists in proposing exaggerated and absurd principles, in strong measures and a specious heroism; and such proceedings, dangerous at all times, are even more so at the moment when the revolution is already complete, and when all that is necessary is the spirit which preserves and perfects.

We must also be careful about this continuous repetition of learning and of apprentices resulting from the too frequent renewal of legislators. How much time must be lost! What portion of apprenticeship must be endured by the nation from each successive assembly! How often must the mere ceremony of learning to spell in political science be repeated! For legislation is not only the business of national assemblies; their power and their taste for authority lead them to take part in administration; their committees divide the government of the kingdom, and by the time they have learned their business, they are obliged to give place to their successors, who, in turn, begin all over again, and are indeed compelled to do so in order not to lose their way in an unknown land.

Finally, it is a fault against social order to assemble the people too frequently for the purpose of elections, and thus continually to revive in them the consciousness of their strength. "What! Are not the people our sovereign, our master; and can we have too many opportunities of knowing their will?" Such is the objection which men who hope to govern this master will repeat without thinking, those who imagine to gain its sympathy with their servile flattery in order to establish their own tyrannical authority. I leave them to their consciences; it would be disgraceful to contend with the hypocrisy of such characters.

It is in good faith that another mode of reasoning is adopted. By a renewal of the members of the legislature every two years, they are placed, it is said, more out of the reach of seduction. On the contrary, will not a transient legislator, seeing his return to the rank of private citizen at so short a distance, be more easily corruptible than if his political existence had been of longer duration? Will he not be more easily corruptible with a very narrow space of time in which to conceal his shame, than if he were obliged to endure or to dissemble it for a series of years? I am not expert in calculations of corruptibility, but I will venture to make one on the present occasion. Suppose a government, attentive above all things to purchase through its favors the good will of the legislature, is it not obvious that it would in this respect have more means of seduction, if the authority of the legislature were confined to two years than if it were of much longer duration? In such a short period, those who are corruptible cannot reject vague promises, since there is not enough time to fulfill them; and from the moment when it is possible to use the currency of illusions, people have inexhaustible treasures at their disposal. Whereas, on the contrary, when the deputies hold their appointments for six or seven years, as in England, the moment of performance must arrive, and promises therefore cannot be employed but with moderation and precaution.

But whether these calculations be just, or whether there be others of greater or less force, let us equally disdain them all. Let us fix our attention on nobler and more dignified objects, and say that the virtuous man is always secure from the influence of corruption, and the man prepared by his character for such sort of seduction yields in a moment as much as in a day. Let us assiduously then cultivate principles of honour and of virtue, and never imagine that any thing can make up for their absence. They alone act in every sense and serve us in all cases. They alone fight for us and protect our weakness. They alone also, when they are held in veneration, assure to nations tranquillity and happiness, and suffice to mark out to the true legislators the path they ought to pursue.

CHAPTER VIII

The Judiciary Power

The National Assembly has diffused the same spirit through all its institutions, and wanting to assimilate everything to its favourite principle, has constantly sacrificed everything to one single idea. Liberty, guaranteed by the power of the people, has formed the sole object of its speculations; while public order, guaranteed by the authority of government, has never occupied but by accident any share of its attention. The truth of this remark will be found in the manner in which the judiciary order has been constructed.

The judges, according to the new constitution, are to be nominated by electors, the choice of whom lies with the people; the particular appointment of the public accuser depends also on their choice, and new elections are to take place every six years.

In England, the judges are nominated by the king and can be removed from their offices only in case of misdemeanor.

The difference is considerable, both as connected with public order and with the majesty of the throne.

Independence, that first trait of character in a judge whose function it is to suppress vice and avenge innocence; that sacred quality and the virtues of impartiality and firmness that are its handmaids, all these qualities can never exist in their plenitude, if the continuation of the magistrate in his office or his removal to a more desirable post be made to depend on the suffrage of those very men over whom it is most necessary that a severe authority should be exercised.

There are doubtless judges whose characters will always entitle them to the rule of exception; but I am considering the question as connected with human nature in general, and I see that by placing the arbiters of our dearest interests between fear and hope, we subject to the influence of personal motives persons, of whom it has always been said that they ought to be as impassible and impartial as the law itself.

Meanwhile was there ever a constitution in which the virtuous firmness of a magistrate would seem more necessary? Justice is publicly to be administered, in the midst of a people informed of their strength and inebriated with their power; in the midst of a people kept in irritation by the habitual spectacle of the disparities of lot, inevitable in an old nation in which wealth increases day by day; in the midst of a people, naturally passionate, and over whom the curb of morality is held more loosely every day; in the midst of a people, in short, who now approach their rulers with the sword of vengeance in one hand, and in the other the party-coloured list of every honorary and lucrative office, to which they alone have the privilege of nominating. In this state of things it will be with their eyes fixed on their masters and renumerators that magistrates, elected by the people, will in civil causes, where they are the sole umpires, decide between the parties, and in criminal ones will direct their charge to the jury and record the verdict. Reduced, however, to the number of three, four, or five at most, should all the judges of the tribunal be present, their responsibility almost becomes personal; but who does not know with what facility magistrates can dissemble their partiality, by cloathing it in the form of that justice of which they are the sole interpreters? I have said that in England the judges are appointed by the king, and are not removable but in case of misdemeanor. It is proper to add that they cannot be members of the House of Commons. Thus have the English taken as much care to preserve the independence of their judges, as we have neglected this important consideration in the whole arrangement of our judiciary code.

Let us also observe that the judges in France, subject every six years to new elections, can never acquire the prestige and influence resulting from a long exercise of and steady respect for their functions. Reputation is slowly acquired in the judiciary profession; purity of heart and rectitude of judgment do not discover themselves with the same promptitude as talent; thus only time can reveal these precious qualities and attract towards them the homage of the people. At the same time, as often as we deprive these magistrates of the necessary means for gaining personal consideration, we expose them more to the temptations of interest; and we ought never to drive to despair the love of reputation, a sentiment that has so many dangerous passions for its rivals.

Finally, it is a duty we owe to the inhabitants of a country to give them, as arbiters of their fortune and their honour, not only men worthy of such a function, not only men whom a small number of electors, influenced by different motives, have approved, but men whose long display of judiciary virtues have added dignity and lustre to the reputation of a tribunal; that precious lustre which diffuses a calm through civil life and tells us, long before we stand in need of justice, that, whenever the day arrives, we shall find it administered to us by magistrates, who know what justice is, and are surrounded with the necessary consideration to enforce and maintain it.

The present state of the judiciary order in France offers us no picture like this, nor is it possible it should. Which of us, for instance, though residing in the very centre of Paris, could discover, by the public voice, the opinion he ought to entertain of the judges of the first, the second, the third, and so on as far as the sixth *arrondissement* of the capital? And supposing that we began to acquire some insight into the business, it is probable then that new magistrates would by that time be appointed to the same tribunals. The method of distinguishing them by numbers also serves to render our attention more vague and more painful. Precisely the same mode has been adopted to designate the regiments of regular troops. I believe that, by discoloring everything, our legislators wanted to establish equality in the realm of imagination.

The judges in England are chosen from among men enjoying the highest distinction both for their knowledge and their moral character, and it is seldom that the public voice does not anticipate the nomination of the monarch. This choice is doubtless made easier where, as in England, all the superior functions of the judiciary order are executed by twelve magistrates only. The fact that the laws require them to go the circuits makes a higher number of judges unnecessary. But in France, where no such form is introduced, and where local tribunals have been multiplied in proportion to the different sections of the kingdom, it would not have been reasonable that the nomination of all the members of these tribunals should have vested in government; and the monarch would himself have been willing that some sort of restriction should be put upon his choice. But, instead of adopting, in this respect, a system of wisdom and of deference, the royal dignity has been degraded in the very forms of the law, for the following are the words of the constitutional article: "Justice shall be gratuitously rendered by judges, chosen for a time by the people, and installed by letters patent of the king, *who shall have no power to refuse them.*"

Who shall have no power to refuse them! Thus the monarch is introduced into this important article of political orders merely as an assistant and a straw-man; and the king of the French is obliged to give letters of instalment to any judge that shall be pointed out to him, whatever proofs government might possess of the immoral conduct of this new arbiter of our honour and our property. There is something tyrannical in this restraint, and the very expressions of such a law are incompatible with the majesty of the throne, and the respect that is essentially necessary to the supreme head of administration. The contradiction indeed strikes us at every turn in the systematic innovations of the Constituent Assembly, the strange contradiction of wishing to attach to the royal authority the obedience of the people and the activity of government, and at the same detaching from the chief of the state all the most important interests of the nation. Our legislators have supposed that opinion would always follow their instructions. But accustomed to obey only where it felt confidence and respect, opinion was confounded by our subtle philosophical reflections, and confusion has spread everywhere.

There is another sort of magistrates, as well in France as in England, whose mode of appointment is different in the two countries: I mean those public officers whose daily business it is to attend to the preservation of good order. By our new constitution these functions are divided among justices of the peace, commissaries of police, and municipal officers; in England they devolve on the justices only. The towns and boroughs indeed have municipal officers, but they limit themselves to inspecting the general parts of the police such as the regulating, cleaning and lighting the streets, the inspecting of provisions that are of indispensible necessity, etc. Sometimes however, the chief municipal officer is at the same a justice of the peace, either by a commission from the monarch, or by virtue of an ancient prerogative annexed to his office.

Thus it appears that, with only a few exceptions, the magistrates of the police are, in England, nominated by the king; and they cannot be removed unless for misdeameanor, or their removal be requested by either house of Parliament. The commission of the justices of the peace is commonly bestowed on such persons as enjoy the fairest reputation in the counties where they reside, and those who, from their rank or other circumstances, are most likely to command natural respect.

The monarch in France has no more influence in the choice of justices of the peace and commissaries of the police than in the election of the other magistrates; the nomination is made by the people, without the smallest interference of the king, and the elections are to be renewed every two years.

The observations I have made on the different practice of the two countries regarding the appointment of judges in civil and criminal cases are equally applicable here. The executive power will always be feebly assisted by magistrates of police in the hands of the people, and subject to frequent changes; a great timidity must necessarily be the result of such a system, and experience proves the truth of this remark. It is extremely difficult to draw the exact line between the use and abuse of the functions of police; it is necessary to place upon the officers exercising these functions a variety of salutary restraints, and this circumstance, combined with the short tenure of their authority, will render the maintenance of order in large cities impossible. And from time to time, circumstances will oblige them to resort to strict measures and means of inquisition incompatible with the principles of liberty.

Let us now direct our attention to the nomination of juries.

The English convinced, both from experience and from reflection, of the importance of the executive power and the difficulties that attend its formation, have neglected no means of consolidating it consistent with safety. Guided by this thought, or by a sort of political instinct which frequently supplies the place of reason, they have introduced the authority of the monarch wherever its appearance was not likely to prove injurious to civil and political liberty.

The application of this principle can be seen in every part of their constitution, and is found even in the circumstances attending the formation of juries.

The citizens who are called upon to serve on what are called *grand juries* or *juries of indictment (jurés d'accusation)* are, in England, appointed by the sheriff of the county, a civil officer charged with various functions and nominated by the king.

The same civil officer makes out the list of citizens who are to serve on *small juries (jurés de jugement)*, and of these the accused has a right to challenge a certain number fixed by law.

In France, the *grand juries*, which consist of eight persons only, are drawn by lot from a list of thirty, which is made out by the Procureur-Syndic of *the district*, subject to the approbation of the governing board of the department.

And the *small juries*, to the number of twenty, from a list of two hundred, are drawn up by the Procureur-Syndic of *the department*, subject in like manner to the approbation of the governing board; regarding this list, the accused, as in England, has the right of challenging a certain number according to the terms prescribed by the law.

It is a matter of public notoriety in England that the juries are invariably constituted of persons most worthy of this sort of confidence; and no discontent ever manifests itself on this subject. Thus no inconvenience results from the jury-lists being composed by a representative of the monarch, and the dignity of the throne derives additional lustre from the circumstance. May the loss of that dignity in France, by the preference given to the Procureurs-Syndics of department and district, be the only disadvantage that will be felt; may no sort of partiality be the consequence; may these administrators, chosen for a time by the people, have always the same prestige and influence as the royal officer in England, to determine the citizens to accept the functions of jurors! At the present moment however, everything seems to indicate that the majority wish to be excused from this important mission, and we have reason to be terrified at the danger of its devolving upon men totally unworthy of the trust.

The formation of the jury lists by an officer of royal appointment has afforded an opportunity for the application of a principle that appears to be regarded by the English as of no trivial importance. The grand juries, whose business is to determine whether a supposed delinquent, arrested by the order of a justice of peace, ought to be brought to a criminal trial, are uniformly chosen from a class of citizens distinguished for their education; but the observance of the same rule is not thought necessary in the appointment of the other sort of juries, who are definitively to pronounce whether the person, declared a suspect by the decision of a grand jury, be actually guilty of the crime that has been laid to his charge.

This distinction, originating from an ancient usage in England, has not been introduced without reason. The evidence from which one has to determine the actual guilt of the accused is derived from positive facts, or a concurrence of certain circumstances which appear as evident; and here nothing is required to the discovery of the truth but probity and attention. On the contrary, in judging of the propriety of submitting the accused to a criminal trial, one is commonly obliged to decide from loose documents and presumptions more or less vague. It is therefore necessary that the citizens to whom so delicate a function is confided should possess more penetration and a more cultivated understanding than are required in the former instance; it is moreover necessary that by their rank in society, they should be in possession of those general principles, which serve as a scale to measure the degrees of innocence and guilt; and all these conditions are all the more indispensable, because grand juries are obliged to proceed with a certain rapidity, that the administration of justice may not be prolonged beyond certain limits. Finally, in England as well as in France, the small juries are directed by the judge; which the grand juries neither are nor ought to be, since such a proceeding would render the power of the judge too great. Add to this a remark still more important than all the rest, that, in neither country, has the person accused the right to challenge the members of the grand jury, which is one more reason to be very scrupulous in their nomination and use every guarantee provided by their education and rank.

There is no such thing in France; it is likely that the grand juries will be less select than the small juries, because the latter will be selected from the whole extent of a department, and by the Procureur-Syndic of this superior administration, while the members of grand juries will be chosen from the inhabitants of a district, and nominated by the Procureur-Syndic of this subaltern administration.

I know that it may be said, in answer to all this, that men having been declared equal by the constitution, the reasons for distinction no longer exist. But the act of declaring men equal does not make them so; and the indestructible hierarchy of disparities of education will always contradict these legislative axioms.

I am led by this reflection to a last observation on the subject of the judiciary code. In England, the House of Lords alone is the judge of the delinquency of its members on criminal matters. And I do not know how I could justify this prerogative to our outrageous levellers, to our philosophical upstarts who, in the enthusiasm of their new rank and on the heights of their pedantry, do not want to admit a single exception in the midst of a monarchy.

I appeal then to wise people and I ask whether it is not an inhuman abuse of the metaphysical doctrine of equality to apply its principles to the serious business of a criminal trial and to enjoin, for example, a prince of the blood royal to think himself judged by his peers, when he shall be judged by men whose rank is at an immeasureable distance from his own?

One cannot help remarking to what an extreme general principles are capable of misleading men in politics. *Men are born and remain equal in rights.*[1] This axiom which has become so familiar would seem, at first sight, to give assurance to the accused, that all, universally, should be judged by their peers. No such thing! A second inference is drawn from the same axiom, which is that all men are peers; and notwithstanding the contradiction in point of fact, they are held as such, are ordered mutually to judge one another; and thus is the spirit of the trial by jury changed in one of its most essential points.

The National Assembly which has constantly made political authority to reside in the hands of many, would have done well to have applied the same republican spirit to its philosophical speculations,

---

1. See Article 1 of the *Declaration of the Rights of Man and of the Citizen* (1789).

and not have subjected such a multitude of things to the empire of a single maxim.

The unlimited application of a general principle never appears more offensive than when legislative dispositions are deduced from it contrary to the views of universal justice. The word *peers*, thus employed in matters of criminal jurisdiction, seems intended to announce some kind of sympathy among the individuals who judge each other; and this sympathy does not consist only in their mere descent from a common parent of the human race, or in the similarity of their organs and structure; it depends essentially upon a concord of habits and ideas arising from education, fortune, and rank, an inevitable outcome of the social movement. It is this sympathy which gives to the accused a manly confidence in the recollection that they are tried by their peers, and this confidence is the good which the introduction of the institution of juries in the kingdom was intended to give. Therefore, the very spirit of the institution is subverted when it is subjected to a mode from which the original spirit has been removed, when men are appointed to decide upon a prince of the blood royal, who are in no possible sense his peers; neither his peers in reality, nor in the general opinion of mankind, nor in their own mind. Nonetheless, this is precisely what we have done in France; for according to the new laws, not merely a prince of the blood, but a brother of the king, the queen herself, and the heir apparent to the Crown, if they be suspected of any crime, are to have for their grand jury eight persons, selected by lot from a list of thirty, which list has been drawn up at the commencement of the new year by the Procureur-Syndic of a district. All this may appear very sublime, enchanting, and heroical; but if examined in cold blood, is the last refinement of absurdity; an attempt to bring us back to an uncivilized state, when we are in reality in society; an attempt to make us view everything as the reverse of what it is; an attempt, from the realm of clouds, to try upon a real world, laws fitted for an ideal world, or for a world in theory.

CHAPTER IX

The High National Court

The Parliament of England derives considerable importance, and as a result an additional degree of authority in opinion, from a privilege peculiar to the House of Lords; I refer to the right of judging all state crimes, all misdemeanors, of which charges are initiated by the House of Commons.

This institution which gives new lustre on the legislative body; this institution, which pacifies the feelings of a generous nation by consigning to men of perfect independence the inquiry into deeds of which she undertakes the prosecution; this institution, so admirable in every point of view, has been substituted in France by a high national court, a whimsical and complicated idea, and of which I shall endeavour to point out the principal defects.

Electors, chosen by the people, are to nominate, in each department, two jurors, whose business is to examine the reality of any crime, denounced by the National Assembly as a crime against the state.

These jurors will form for the whole kingdom a panel of one hundred and sixty-six.

From this number, at the time of forming the high national court, twenty-four are to be taken by lot, who, unless challenged by the accused, are to constitute the jury of trial.

The right of challenging extends as far as forty, drawn successively by lot from the whole panel; but it cannot be carried further without the prisoner submitting his reasons to the examination and decision of the high judges of the court.

These judges consist of four, chosen in like manner by lot from the magistrates of the tribunal of annulment.

The National Assembly nominates two of its members who, by the appellation of great prosecutors of the nation, are to manage the prosecution.

Let us now take a general view of these diverse circumstances.

And in the first place, what is it that we see in the room of that stable and majestic tribunal, which in England judges the crimes of state, shelters under the wing of its reputation the weak and the powerful, and secures impartial justice to the nation? We see a number of jurors, everywhere unknown but within the limits of their respective districts, and who, the instant any charge has been voted by a legislature, must put themselves in motion from every extremity of the kingdom, and descend preceded by terror, two by two, from the mountains of Auvergne, the Alps and the Pyrenees, to arrive at Orléans in order to render their sentences; this being done, they are to return again to their homes, after having seen, perhaps, the blood of the victim poured out.

No institution which produces a continuous agitation would deserve the smallest estimation, though in every other respect it should be perfect; but the one we are considering is sullied with a flagrant principle of injustice. It submits the most important of decisions, that of the life or death of a human being, to a jury, collected from every quarter of a kingdom twenty-five thousand squares leagues in extent, and whose names and reputation, it is probable, will be totally unknown to the unfortunate subject of their judgment. Besides, transported all of a sudden from their distant abodes to the town in which the prisoner is confined, and where he may himself never before have resided for a day, they will have no ready mode of obtaining information as to his manners, character, and former habits of life. Yet so congenial, so essential are these conditions to the spirit of the trial by jury that, in England, injunctions are laid on the sheriff to make choice, as far as lies in his power, of such persons for jurymen, whose residence is only at a small distance from the place where the crime has been committed; and, consistently with the same principle, when it is a foreigner who is arraigned, generous care is taken to add to the usual jury a certain number of his countrymen. This moral nation, whose indulgence consists in actions, not in words, has gone even further. Conceiving that the right of challenging ought to be afforded every assistance, and reflecting that nature stamps sometimes on the physiognomy of men the levity or harshness of their character, the jurors, in an English tribunal, are made to appear personally before the prisoner, who, taking a view of each as they are named, is allowed a sufficient interval to exercise that right within the limits fixed by the law. We, on the contrary, present to the unhappy being, arraigned for a capital crime, an uninteresting and inanimate list of jurymen, composed of persons collected from all parts of the kingdom, and whose reputation can be known to himself or to his friends only by chance or by correspondence with every district in France. In this state of things, the privilege of challenging is almost imaginary. Meanwhile, if this right has always been regarded as an essential condition, as a right inseperable from this form of trial by jury, with how much greater force will not the principle apply to times when political divisions engender all sorts of prejudice and distrust?

I go further and inquire why the English, so much attached to the trial by jury, have not admitted this form of trial in instances of crimes against the state; and I would like to refer this decision to a great and just sentiment. I believe that, being moved by emotion at the idea of making a charge against a single individual in the name of the whole nation, and being generously anxious about using greatest force against the greatest weakness, they have resolved to stand acquitted to their honour and their conscience by means of a peculiar solemnity given to the trial. Feeling in this manner, they were willing that so serious an authority should devolve, not upon jurors, those transient beings emerging one moment from obscurity to return to it the next, assembled for a short space of time and then scattered over the face of the kingdom; but upon a permanent body of men, of long established reputation, and presenting in every respect a durable responsibility. I may be mistaken; but if the English have not been influenced explicitly by these motives, it is to a secret sentiment, equal and frequently superior to reasoning, that they must have yielded; for there is an instinct of great ideas and great things which never fails to act upon human beings, taken as a whole, when they are not misled by the spirit of singularity or the vague excursions of metaphysics.

The four grand judges who are to direct the proceedings in the high national court and apply to the decision of the jury the punishment decreed by the law are to be chosen by lot from the magistrates forming the tribunal of annulment. These men, too, will be very little known, since the members of the tribunal of annulment are elected by the different departments of the kingdom, are renewable every four years, and the lot may happen to fall on the most obscure among them. Besides, the private reputation of a judge is not in this case sufficient; it ought to be a public, it ought to be a universal reputation, so to speak, to satisfy a nation, when that nation is made the prosecutor of a single individual.

Let us next direct our regard to the two deputies of the legislature, who, under the title of great prosecutors of the nation, are to manage the prosecution. They will participate in all the proceedings of the trial; will represent, before twenty-four jurors and four judges, the most powerful body of the state; and will at least suggest by their presence that the seven hundred and forty-five deputies, in the name of whom they act, have their characters at stake in not having voted lightly a capital indictment. What a want of equilibrium, what an alarming disproportion presents itself in an institution like this! And yet the life of a human being, of many human beings depends on it.

The English House of Commons delegates in like manner certain of its members to substantiate and manage its charges before the House of Lords; and it is from there we have derived our idea of great prosecutors; we have only changed the name, a rule we observe invariably whenever we copy. But how could we avoid being struck by the difference between the circumstances, a difference sufficient to transform a wise regulation into a form of oppression? In the mission given to the deputies of the House of Commons, we find nothing overbearing or severe, because the accusation is brought before the court of peers, before a tribunal consisting of 250 members, or almost that, as is well known, will not be awed by the circumstance of the commons being the prosecutors, and which will easily preserve the most perfect independence of opinion. But the House of Commons of England would be ashamed to proceed by a committee of solicitors, in a court of twenty-four jurors, whose reputations are in a state of embryo, whose characters are yet to be born, and who, leaving out of the question all considerations of respect, and taking only the circumstance of numbers into account, would be in a state of manifest inferiority when compared with the principal section of the legislative body. What would Englishmen say, were it only to be proposed that the grand juries, appointed to determine indictments in common criminal matters, should nominate deputies to act in their name and sit in court by the side of the small juries? Such an idea would excite a general outcry and reprobation; and yet, between these two types of citizens, there is no other difference than a slight superiority of condition on the part of those who form the grand juries. But we have given to an assembly, forming the whole legislative body, the right of appointing procurators before twenty-four persons chosen by lot to be part of a small jury. This is all we have done, this is the result of our sublime science! We have borrowed from our neighbors only a form, and have left its moral spirit behind; a spirit that has constantly been neglected by us, because in its various applications it admitted of no distinct name, because it presented no palpable figure, and because, armed as we have been only with geometrical instruments, we were unable to find them. We have systematically rejected and suppressed those impulses of the soul, which attain to all ideas, and never wanted in a single instance to give way to that sensibility that modifies the reasonings of the mind, applies them to our common nature, renders us good, indulgent and generous, and teaches us far better than speculations the secret of our social union.

Oh! should the reflections presented in this chapter be read by you, utter strangers to me, who from all corners of the kingdom will be called to the high national court; you, who will determine the fate of the unfortunate beings shut up in the prisons of Orléans, reflect that you are going to sit in judgment on your fellow citizens without their consent, since they will be ignorant whether they ought or ought not to reject you in the exercise of their right of challenging. Reflect also that you will have before your eyes the prosecutors of the legislative body, of that body at present the only existing power in the state, and whose reputation is intimately related to the severity of your decisions. Let the consciousness of your important duties suffice to move you, and make yourselves the protectors and support of the imprudent and the unfortunate ones! Let your soul rise to the level of your functions, and your wisdom take a rapid survey of their difficulties! Have the eyes of an Argus[1] for the discovery of innocence, and the kindness of a God to direct their employment! Above all, lend no ear to the spirit of party; give no quarter to the whispers of blind passions! They and the colors in which they are attired will pass, and you will be left alone with your conscience. Anticipate that moment, and consider nothing as lasting, but only those opinions dictated by a candid and tempered reason, those opinions founded upon the basis of that universal morality which the present generation, in spite of all its efforts, will not be able to uproot.

But it is not only to these general principles that I would like to direct the attention of the judges and juries of Orléans. I dare invite them also to reflect that, in the first moments of a revolution, severity would border upon injustice. It is necessary that men should have time to acknowledge the new power that is set up; it is necessary that they should have time to enlighten their conscience and divest themselves of their former sentiments. And, when the revolution has oppressed, in every possible manner, a certain class of citizens; when it has stripped them of their names, their rank and their fortune; when it has afterwards given them up to the discretion of a disorderly multitude whom no laws could restrain, a multitude that has refused to pay them the little that remained of their ancient rights, that has burnt their homes, ravaged their fields, and committed the most horrible outrages towards their persons and their families, the attempt to throw only upon them the yoke of the law, the wish to render them the victims at once of oppressions which have driven them to despair, and of the consequences of a natural sentiment of vengeance, all this is the consummation of tyranny. Finally, and this procedure is absolutely inexplicable, the types of crime reserved for the investigation of the tribunal of Orléans was left without any explanation. Having

1. In ancient Greek mythology, Argus (or Argos) was a giant with a hundred eyes.

copied the Americans in so many things, we ought to have imitated them in the generous care they have taken to define accurately what are to be regarded as treasonable offences; and the following are the words of their constitutional article upon this subject.

"Treason against the United States shall consist only in making war against them, or in adhering to their enemies, giving them aid and comfort."[2]

Such are the limits which a mild and virtuous people, at the moment of their emergence from the horrors of civil war, have thought proper to assign to the most dreadful types of accusation, and the most capable of vague interpretations. Oh! They no doubt, still under the influence of the first principles of morality, regarded as a public calamity the spilling of a citizen's blood. Undoubtedly, they are still strangers to the sentiment that makes others disposed to look for and find crimes everywhere. Above all, they have not learned yet the ferocious idea of maintaining a government by the axe of the executioner; they rely upon the appeal of happiness and general interest, and after making their country the asylum of peace and of the virtues most endearing to human beings, they probably feel compassion rather than hatred for those who still remain their enemies. If we compare these ideas and sentiments with the discourses and conduct of many of our legislators, it would be impossible not to be horrified by the contrast. It is in severity, in punishment, and vengeance that they have placed their confidence. They have even contrived that the spirit of the party should arise from the tenor of the constitution, and at the same time, they punished the effects of that spirit with insatiable rigour. Alas! If amidst the unique harmony of the universe, if amidst the solemn scheme of this order, we place goodness as a ref-

2. Article 3, Section 3 of the US Constitution defines treason as follows: "Treason against the United States, shall consist only in levying War against them, or in adhering to their Enemies, giving them Aid and Comfort. No Person shall be convicted of Treason unless on the Testimony of two Witnesses to the same overt Act, or on Confession in open Court.

"The Congress shall have Power to declare the Punishment of Treason, but no Attainder of Treason shall work Corruption of Blood, or Forfeiture except during the Life of the Person attainted."

uge for the frailties of mankind, what indulgence do we not owe to
the political transactions of men in a society, where everything is in
tumult, and universal chaos and confusion still subsist! I do not know
whether in such a disorder, the crimes of state belong only to those
who commit them, and whether the blood of those victims, whom
the law has condemned, will not fix an indelible stigma on that system of government, from which so many errors have flowed and so
many calamities originated.

CHAPTER X

The Right of Pardon

The spirit of philosophy, that spirit which, by asserting the rights of humanity, has attracted such a great attention, is so disfigured by its usurpers, that they have thought to be able to propose the abolition of the right of pardon as a reasonable and wise measure. This abolition has not been formally pronounced; they have contented themselves, as yet, with suspending the right by definitely delaying to address the core of the question; an expedient invented with a view of burying by oblivion the ideas that a sense of shame prevents them from openly rejecting. Meanwhile, since the reign of the National Assembly, the monarch has found himself divested of the most august of his prerogatives. All condemnations, all capital sentences, whether more or less severe, have been immediately carried into execution, and the word clemency has been blotted from our language. Its place was doubtless needed for the many barbarous names introduced by our new manners. Noble exchange, admirably calculated to honor the present epoch of our history! It will certainly give us the merit of originality, since there is not another people on the globe where the right of pardon is not established.

It has been said that, since criminal justice must constantly be administered by juries, this form of trial would exclude all kinds of errors, all forms of partialities; and that, as a result, there would be no reason for wishing that any authority in the state have the power of changing the sentence of a tribunal.

At the moment when I write these reflections, juries are as yet not established; and I cannot but express my astonishment that, during the existence of a jurisprudence, acknowledged by the Assembly itself to be defective, the suspension of the right of pardon has been so rigorously observed. Are we certain that no instance has occurred during the interval in which its application would have been just? And has the Christian morality never reminded us that, in the calculations of mercy, a human being, a single human being, is a great and invaluable number?

Next, I would like to examine whether the trial by jury really supersedes in all circumstances the right of pardon. The English and the Americans have thought otherwise, for with them, this right exists in its plenitude, and yet they had adopted, long before our legislators, the institution of juries. But I know well that examples, even the best ones, have little influence upon men who have placed themselves in the very center of theory. I shall therefore approach them only with the weapons of argument; and I venture to affirm that, on various accounts, the right of pardon is particularly necessary in countries where the trial by jury is introduced.

Such a form of trial admits of no modification. On the one side, are the jurors who have simply to inquire and decide whether the crime found in the indictment has been committed voluntarily by the person accused of it; and on the other side, is the judge, who opens the book of the law and pronounces the penalty decreed therein. Between these judiciary acts there is no place for the spirit of moderation, which other tribunals, judges at once of the fact and the degree of the punishment, are frequently led to exercise.

We may add that from the partition, as it were, of the business between the jury and the judge, the edge of that repugnance, so natural in human beings to all acts of severity, is blunted. The jurors judge merely of the fact, have not before their eyes the punishment due to the crime; and the magistrates, who come after them, consider themselves simply as the organs of the law bound to deliver its commands.

And what is the country where the abolition of the right of pardon ought to excite the least regret? It would be a republic, pervaded by a sort of kindred spirit and sentiment of morality, two factors which throw a shade of mildness and forbearance over all acts of authority. It would be a republic where the tribunals, judges at once both of the fact and the penalty, would have the power of combining with the nature of the offence, the degree of uncertainty that often remains, however strong be the evidence; where the tribunals have the power of combining the factors that may be alleged as extenuating circumstances with those that cannot and ought not to be omitted; the power of taking into account the previous behavior of the defendant along with the great services rendered by his family and sometimes by the defendant himself. These are the diverse considerations which enter into the opinion and sentiments of the judges in the exercise of their authority and which lead them to mix with the principles of severity a spirit of indulgence, and to soften, by natural equity, the rigid justice of the law.

Nonetheless, republics, in which, as I have indicated, a government of confidence is established—and many such republics exist— have been uniformly of opinion that the deviations from the law would be safer in the hands of a body superior to the judiciary tribunals; and to such a body has the right of pardon been entrusted by them. It is then in France, and in France alone, that this right no longer subsists; and yet how many circumstances are there, of which I have made no mention, that would render it more necessary there than in any other part of the globe? It is in the midst of a people whose language is that of menace, of a people aware of its force, agitated by the violence of passion, and given up implicitly to every type of guide, of a people who have so frequently shown themselves cruel and terrible, that the juries and judges will exercise their functions and pronounce their decisions. It is further in the midst of a people which have assumed to themselves the right to dispose of all favours that can seduce everyone that the judges and jurors are required to maintain their independence; and it is subject to all these limitations inherent to such a situation that the sentences of the law are to be immediately followed by their execution. Such an idea is frightening.

Let the reader recollect also in this place what I have said upon the judiciary institutions and the High National Court. The first princes of the blood may be accused and thrown into prison upon the decision of eight jurors, by a fiction of law declared to be their peers, and selected by lot from a list of thirty drawn up by the Procureur-Syndic of a district. In the High National Court, all persons, denounced as criminals against the state, are to be tried by individuals whom they do not know and by whom they are unknown, and have to plead against the prosecutors who shall be appointed to prosecute the accusation in the name of the most powerful body in the state. Finally, it is at a moment when the spirit of party carries everything before it, when the attention of the multitude is directed to one idea only, and when, through an illusion that has been widely cultivated, one single imputation can unite in itself every type of reproach and blame; it is at such a moment when, in a few words, the general effervescence can easily contaminate all spirits, that they have dared to confide in a justice so sure, impartial and intrepid, as to authorise the abolition of the right of pardon. I cannot tell what other men think, but for myself, at a juncture like this, the idea of an absolute and final judgment, with no room for appeal or hope, suggests itself to my mind under the most frightening colours.

I go further and ask whether we can gently take upon ourselves the functions of a judge or a juror in a country where the right of pardon is abolished? Shall I declare that such and such person ought to be brought to criminal judgment, ought to be accused of a capital crime, when my voice can send him to death, and when at the same time I might feel in my breast a sentiment of commiseration and of equity that would lead me to desire his pardon? Why should I consent to be the instrument of a law that has no appeal to pardon? Why should I degrade myself to this miserable condition? The juries and judges of France ought with one voice to demand the reestablishment of the right of pardon; morality dictates it, honour requires it of them. They conceive that they acquire new importance if their judgments cannot be changed, and they are deceived. Vanity leads them to regard a will executed without appeal as a circumstance peculiarly honourable. But it is not so; neither jurors nor judges have a will of their own, because the former speak in the name of the truth, the latter in the name of the law. And since these functions, thus divided, carry with them no stamp of sovereignty, and it is of the utmost importance to the consideration of jurors and judges that the right of pardon, by being revived, should draw a line and fix a distance between the conviction and the execution of the sentences.

The king of England not only enjoys the right of pardon in its fullest extent, but his signature is also necessary to carry criminal sentences into execution. Let it be observed however, on the other hand, that the judges of England, returned to London after their circuits in the provinces, are at hand to instruct the monarch as to the circumstances of each particular offence. The French constitution having established a criminal system of a very different sort, and the tribunals residing in all parts of the kingdom, the information to be conveyed to the government, regarding the due application of the royal clemency, must be precarious and uncertain. This circumstance, combined with the great territory of France, would naturally have subjected the exercise of the right of pardon to certain modifications; nor would these wise modifications have diminished in any degree the power of the monarch, since the ancient system had limited his prerogatives, not by express law, but by the nature of things. It had been customary for the courts to cause their sentences to be executed without delay. Thus only Parliament had the power—and, indeed, a very extensive one— to ask in time for the pardon of the king. The monarch wanted to reduce in general the celerity of executions in order to gain the necessary time for always knowing the motives; and his intension on this subject had been solemnly declared. But in the end, there is a distance between modification and limitation on the one hand, and on the other hand, the rash decision to abolish the right of pardon, or to exclude the king from exercising his most august prerogative, the sacred patrimony of his ancestors. Alas! We surely have not yet acquired a right of taking away from our countrymen in general their right to appeal to the clemency of the monarch! Were our security better than now with regard to the administration of justice, we would still not have this right; in moments of great danger, one needs a hope, a vague protection beyond the usual known guarantees. This is how people feel, and our eternal nature is not one of the habits that a legislator may command us to sacrifice. But such has been the result, such is the masterpiece boast of that cold and logical spirit, which has banished from our midst the authority of sentiment, and of all those grand and simple ideas which follow in its train. Thus we have broken the chain of virtue which unites us with the Supreme Being and have obliterated our most precious resemblence to His divine perfections. Never had we so much need as now to believe in a merciful and benevolent God, and it is now that we have resolved neither to be benevolent nor merciful. Guides without compassion! You make us see the frightening traces of our ferocity, you show us the bloodstained fragments which begin to cover our unfortunate land; and after having struck despair into our bosom through this frightening display, you will tell us that there is no protective power, no possible recourse; you will tell us that we have nothing more to expect or look for in heaven or on earth. You will reassure us that everything is the work of chance and that, in this blind lottery, your dry heart, your unbending spirit is one of our best chances; and you will tell us that we would do well to follow your advice and become insensitive like you. Please leave me alone! I fear you much more than all the tigers of the desert; my soul wishes to nourish itself from other thoughts and longs for another perspective without needing your help. The slightest hope and the smallest uncertainty, at least those born out of our weakness and limited understanding, will give her more courage than all your arrogant maxims. I do not want to abandon you, mild and timid spirits, I do not want to leave you with these sad thoughts. I will present you a more comforting picture by bringing to your attention one of the most ancient usages of that moral and wise nation which I am so often obliged to present as an example. I remember a fact deeply engraved in my memory and which I now find extremely comforting. Upon his accession to the throne, the king of England is reminded of the rights of clemency and mercy of which he is the august depository and which he is bound to exercise. The following is one of the questions addressed to him at his coronation by the archbishop who officiates on that solemn occasion; and to each of which the king answers: *This I promise to do.*

"Will you to your power cause law and justice, in mercy, to be executed in all your judgments?"

How beautiful, how touching is this question! Thus after having called upon the monarch to promise that he will cause law and justice to be executed, then follow these words, these beautiful words, *in mercy*. Words like these give us, as it were, at one stroke the character of a nation. Yes, this right of pardon and mercy must be placed somewhere as a sacred deposit; we need it for the honor of our legislation and the reputation of our manners. For clemency is a debt we owe to human nature, much like justice is a debt we owe to our political societies.

CHAPTER XI

The Formation of Ministry

In the parallel I have drawn, the mode of constituting the ministry in the two kingdoms, whether we consider the circumstance in itself or as connected with the executive power appears, as one of the most important matters.

In England, the ministers are almost always members of Parliament. Some have a seat in the upper house by right of birth, others in the lower house by the suffrages of the people. The assistance of several of them in parliamentary deliberations is deemed so essential, that were the person at the head of the finance, for example, not elected to the House of Commons, the king would be under the necessity of making another choice. No one in England thinks it possible to conceive how the proceedings of the legislative body could be founded on sufficient information, or be judiciously adapted to the situation of affairs, without the constant intervention of the principal members of the government. Accordingly, in the House of Commons, the prerogative of making proposals on matters of finance is ordinarily left to the minister for that department, not in his quality of minister of the king, but as being the member of Parliament best qualified by his functions to know what the circumstances and the interest of the kingdom require.

It is idle to suppose that the separation which must be maintained between the legislative and the executive powers is not infringed by the circumstance of one or more of the ministers sitting and voting in the House of Commons; only there quality of repre-

sentatives of the people gives them this right, and it is a constitutional statute of England never to pronounce the name of the king in
the deliberations of the legislative body.

There is, however, a considerable benefit that results from the
participation of the ministers in parliamentary sessions, and from
the fact that they unite in their persons the two important qualifica-
tions of members of the government and members of the legislative
body. As such, they are able to maintain their respect and influence
in the exercise of their functions; and as they could not effectually
serve the public, nor even maintain themselves in their places, if they
did not use their talents, virtues, and information, the monarch is
obliged to choose them from among the most distinguished persons
in the nation.

Here I would like to ask whether the union of all these circumstances does not give them too powerful an influence, and if that influence, in the hands of the principal agents of the royal authority, may
not endanger the constitution. This danger must be imaginary, since
the people, though warmly attached to their government, feel no such
apprehension, and since, for the period of a century, the principles of
civil and political liberty have been religiously maintained. It is not to
one single power that the protection of these principles is entrusted;
their most faithful guardian is the general happiness. Political vigilance is an inexhaustible task, if we consider everything with suspicion; and when we have done so, we resemble those jealous husbands
who, amidst all their precautions, forget that which is most essential,
the precaution of making themselves beloved.

If someone were to make another objection and said that, in general, the presence of ministers in Parliament attaches too great a degree of importance to their opinions, I would not contest the point,
but would content myself with observing that, in all affairs of administration, the influence of the heads of government is necessary to the
good of the state, serving as a counterpoise to the spirit of party, and
to that prevailing desire in people to make a name for themselves, at
whatever price it may be. Persons who constantly pursue this type of
reputation have perhaps a passion more hostile to the public welfare
than those who thirst after money; for the least applause may corrupt
them, the most trifling hopes offered to their vanity can make them

sacrifice their opinions and make them guilty of a dereliction of all their principles and sentiments.

It is indeed probable that, of the different inhabitants of the state, those who join to the quality of representative of the people the information gained by the administration of public affairs are best deserving to be heard; but they, like any other members of the House of Commons, would lose their influence, if they disregarded the voice of reason, and if they ever brought the purity of their intentions into question.

Nonetheless, the constant presence of ministers in Parliament, their capacity as representatives of the people, and their personal merits are necessary for the creation of that perfect harmony between the legislative body and the administration which is indispensable to the regular functioning of the government. And if that harmony were to disappear one day, if it were replaced by a system based on mistrust and suspicion, everything would become contest, everything would be shaken; and we would quickly discover that anarchy and confusion are the greatest dangers against which a free constitution must protect itself.

Let us compare these reflections and instructions afforded to us by a great example with the type of relations that the ministers have with the legislative body in France, and we shall clearly perceive the inferiority of their situation. They cannot be elected as deputies to the representative assembly of the nation, and have no right to appear at the sessions, except within a place appropriated for them in the meeting room. But there they only play a subaltern role; none of them can participate in any discussion not immediately connected with their office, at least till the assembly shall, by a formal deliberation, *grant them liberty to speak.** A single glance is sufficient to show us how different is the case with the English ministers. They do not have to ask for a decree of the House of Commons and have no fa-

---

* "The ministers of the king shall be heard whenever they demand it on objects relating to their administration, and when they shall be required to give information.—They shall also be heard on objects foreign to their administration, when the National Assembly shall grant them liberty to speak."—Chap. III. Sect. iv. Art. x. of the Constitution.

vour to obtain before they are allowed to speak, because they enjoy
all the rights attached to their capacity as representatives of the people, in the lower House, or as peers of the realm in the upper House.
And far from being considered in either chamber as inferiors to be
silenced or made to speak with the mere waving of a wand, they are
ordinarily expected to open the discussions on new measures useful
to the state, or to offer the first observations on the proposals made
by other members of the legislative body. Thus, the participation of
the executive in the act of legislation does not consist in the constitutional necessity that the monarch sanctions the bills of Parliament,
but in the intervention of ministers in the deliberations which precede these laws.

    This participation which leads to a normal discussion between
the ministers and the other members of Parliament is a powerful security against the use of the royal veto on the different decisions of
the legislative body; an act which must always produce a great effect,
and may easily become a source of disunion between the two powers. Finally, in England, the ministers, either by proposing themselves
new draft laws, or by familiarizing themselves with the laws drafted
by other representatives of the nation, are thus called to assist in the
drafting of each parliamentary bill, or in the discussion of all their
details. And at the moment when these bills, after having been approved by both Houses, are presented to the king for his sanction,
the deliberation of the monarch is very simple. But in France, where
all the articles of a law are adopted without the participation of ministers, the exercise of the right of sanction is attended with peculiar
difficulties. How is the king to act if, in a decree composed of a considerable number of articles, some should appear to him to be good
and others to be dangerous? The constitution obliges him to accept
or refuse the entire law, and that without making any observations.
Shall he then sanction the articles he disapproves, in consideration
of those which he deems useful? Or shall he refuse the whole to get
rid of those he fears? This is a dilemma which the French monarch
must frequently face; and this dilemma, prejudicial to the interests of
the state, is a natural consequence of the separation between the legislative body and the heads of the administration; a separation that
does not exist at all in England, does not exist in the federal con-

stitution of America, and one that we alone have confounded with the wise principle of the separation of powers.

It will be asked if the responsibility of English ministers be not weakened by the circumstance of their being members of Parliament? I answer, certainly not. The members of the House of Commons have full power to vote an impeachment against them whenever they have been guilty of any crime. They can also show their resentment in another way, by declaring the ministers to have lost their confidence, or by taking distance from their views in parliamentary debates. They are not, indeed, eager to contrive, as in France, the means of rendering the ministers the subject of a criminal prosecution; they are not spying to discover the ministers' slightest negligences and their smallest mistakes. It would, indeed, be impossible for them even to sit in Parliament, if such were the spirit of the legislative body; for if one had to pay with one's life for a single omission, one would have to be fully immersed in and occupied with the details of one's department.

Such, however, is the situation to which ministers are reduced in France.[1] The moment no doubt approaches when it will no longer be thought valiant to treat them with every possible rudeness, though enough of this propensity will, I fear, remain to render their condition incompatible with the high degree of consideration necessary to the first agents of the executive power. English ministers are in like manner liable to be attacked in Parliament; but then they are treated on a footing of equality from peer to peer, and never with arrogance and ill manners: their opinions are combated, or their principles censored, but the details of an executive measure are never made the subject of criticism. We ought also to observe that, in contests of this nature, the minister is always addressed by the appellation of *the honourable member of Parliament*, as if his quality of being the king's minister disappears from the scene.

---

1. The Constituent Assembly attempted to solve the issue of the responsibility of the executive power by trying to combine on paper the inviolability of the king with the penal responsibility of his ministers. In reality, it created a disequilibrium between the legislative and the executive powers, as Necker demonstrates here. On this issue, see Guillaume Glénard, *L'Exécutif et la Constitution de 1791* (Paris: Presses Universitaires de France, 2010), 428–45.

There is no nation so zealous in the defence of its political interests, and that preserves at same time so much respect for the head
of the state and so great consideration for government, as the English nation. This is mainly to be attributed to the judicious gradation
of the different powers, and the harmony that exists between public
opinion and the order established by the constitution. Nothing similar to this can be expected on the part of an Assembly, hastily invested with an unlimited power, and the exercise of which is confided
to men, the majority of whom are not even restrained by the stake
of property, or by an habitual regard for honour and public opinion.
There exists, indeed, a constitution, but it is only in writing, and its
precise configuration is imprinted on the mind of not a single individual; there exists a constitution, but it has placed enmity between
the powers even before they were created; and in this warfare of all
political elements, nothing is distinguishable but the prominent ideas
of liberty and equality, those undisciplined principles which extend
beyond the constitution and which every man pursues in his way and
interprets in whatever manner he likes best. Amidst this general relaxation, there was one and only one spring that could have held the
principal parts of administration together, and that, like so many others, has been broken. To preserve this spring it was necessary to give
a degree of influence to the first agents of the supreme power; it was
necessary to unite them to the new system of government otherwise
than through declamations of patriotism and all types of threats.
They would have served as a central point towards which the public mind might gravitate, in the midst of the universal dissolution of
forces; and no one had to fear that they would abuse their power, in
competition with a mass of national opinion more formidable in its
commencements than the legions of ancient Rome. But everything
was feared except anarchy, and this fear, made manifest in all respects,
is the distinctive mark of the subaltern and short-sighted character of
our legislators. They regarded the necessary agents of every department of the state in no other light than as the ministers of the king,
and they felt more pleasure in waging war against them than associating them in an honourable way to their labours. They imagined the
separation of powers derived from the separation of persons, whereas

by placing the oppressors on one side and the oppressed on the other, that was the surest means of having only one authority. Thus the degraded situation of ministers contributed, more than any other circumstance, to the absorption of all power in the hands of the National Assembly; an absorption not only imprudent and prejudicial to liberty, but even more dangerous—something they were unable to perceive—to the credit and influence of the legislative body itself. At first sight, it may appear as if an increase of its power would produce an increase of its impact; but if this increase of power makes it necessary for a representative assembly to be incessantly in action, it must lose, by attending to details foreign to its functions, the degree of consideration which it needs for general acts of legislation; or at any rate, its reputation will incur a greater number of risks. Finally, it may also diminish its credit in another way, when it assumes to itself the exercise of what belongs to the executive power, since it thereby becomes accessible to all sorts of passions. It will no longer be able to assume, at its will, the character of moderation necessary to the legislature; it will have to contend with our weaknesses, and will be unable to interfere with dignity and effect in prescribing and directing our duties; it will have quitted its central post, and our respect will no longer have a fixed point: it may seem to have enlarged its power, but its influence will no longer be the same.

I am treating then of a subject of the utmost importance when I call the attention of the reader to the different manner of constructing the government in France and in England. The question is intimately connected with the first principles of public order; and in every point of view, it is found that the Constituent Assembly, by proposing a separation of authorities, and by endeavouring to divide them between the legislative and executive branches of the state, has neglected to give to the one the necessary degree of esteem to preserve it from the invasion of the other; a precaution that ought, however, to have been constantly present to their minds; for the proportion of forces, that combination, which has always regulated the action of the elements, is equally indispensible in the conduct of political transactions; this law of nature, I think, is also a constitutional statute and the most important of all.

CHAPTER XII

The Distribution of Favours, and Nomination to Employments

After having been placed for some time at the center of public affairs, after having been, as it were, one of the axes around which moved all sorts of personal interests, I have been able to understand the activity of these interests and learn, at the same time, how people are, in turn, animated, mellowed, and always shackled by hope. They often think of themselves when they pretend not to care about their own interests, and even when they are led by circumstances to sacrifice them. During the days of parade, they have the most magnificent sentiments; but in their daily habits and in their secret confessions, we find them always occupied either with the fortune they are pursuing or the eminence to which they aspire. It must not therefore be doubted that the more we narrow the circle of patronage and rewards which the monarch can bestow, the more shall we enfeeble in his hands the action of the executive power.

In the constitutional charter the functions of this power have been brought under one particular head, and as these functions represent at the same time its prerogatives, it was doubtless intended, by uniting and collecting them together, to give them an imposing appearance; but illusions of this nature deceive only the ignorant and the superficial. The number of prerogatives is, indeed, great, but we already knew that.

I examine this ridiculously ostentacious list.* And the first thing I notice is the usual repetition of the terms *supreme* executive power, *supreme* head of administration, *supreme* head of the army, *supreme* head of the navy; but all these *supremes* only represent to me a canopy without pillars to support it. To command, to watch over, to superintend are words devoid of meaning when unaccompanied by the means necessary to inspire respect and obedience.

* Chapter IV
Of the Exercise of the Executive Power

I. The supreme executive power is lodged exclusively in the hands of the king.

The king is the supreme head of the general administration of the kingdom; the care of watching over the maintenance of public order and tranquillity is entrusted to him.

The king is the supreme head of the army and of the navy.

To the king is delegated the care of watching over the exterior security of the kingdom, and of maintaining its rights and possessions.

II. The king appoints ambassadors and the other agents of political negociations.

He confers the command of armies and fleets, and the ranks of marshal of France and admiral.

He names two thirds of the rear-admirals, and one half of the lieutenant-generals, camp marshals, captains of ships, and colonels of the national gendarmerie.

He names a third of the colonels and lieutenant-colonels, and a sixth of the lieutenants of ships. The whole in uniformity to the laws regarding promotion.

He appoints in the civil administration of the marine, the directors, the comptrollers, the treasurers of the arsenals, the masters of the works, the under masters of civil buildings, half of the masters of administration, and of the under-masters of construction.

He appoints the commissioners of the tribunals.

He appoints the chief superintendants of the administration of indirect contributions, and the administration of national domains.

He superintends the coinage of money and appoints the officers entrusted with this superintendance in the general commission and in the mints.

The effigy of the king shall be struck on all the coinage of the kingdom.

III. The king issues letters patent, brevets, and commissions to such public functionaries as are entitled to receive them.

IV. The king orders the list of pensions and gratifications to be made out, in order to be presented to the legislative body each session, that it may be decreed, if thought proper.

We should also see in this constitutional summary, a summary drawn up with a certain degree of art, that the power of the monarch has been composed only of those prerogatives that had escaped the reforming hands of each committee. No nomination has been left to the king that could be executed by the people, or regulated by rules of promotion. But to extend in appearance the exercise of the executive power, there has been inserted in the list, and in a certain pompous manner, the liberty granted to him of *issuing letters patent, brevets, and commissions, to such public functionaries as are entitled to receive them.* Thus, the monarch is reminded of the humiliating necessity imposed on him of confirming, with his seal or by some other formality, that multitude of appointments and promotions in which he has been prohibited every sort of interference.

The last article of these gaudy trappings, in which the executive power has been arrayed, is equally curious. *The king orders the list of pensions and gratifications to be made out in order to be presented to the legislative body each session, that it may be decreed, if thought proper.* Thus is it consecrated by a constitutional law, destined to remain for ages, that the king, this *supreme* head of administration, this *supreme* head of the army, this *supreme* head of the navy, shall not have the power of bestowing a recompence of a hundred crowns, without the formal consent of the legislative power.

But I am anticipating the general picture I mean to draw, that shall exhibit at one view a parallel between the prerogatives conferred on the French monarch and those enjoyed by the king of England. This parallel, I believe, may be useful; and it is naturally connected with the subject of which I am treating.

Church Dignities

The king of England in the mandates, or *congés d'élire*,[1] which he addresses to the chapters, points out of them, in cases of vacancy, the individuals whom they are to elect as bishops or archbishops, and the chapters are obliged to conform themselves to this injunction. It may

---

1. A license issued by the monarch to the dean and chapter of a cathedral of a diocese, authorizing the election of a bishop or archbishop if a vacancy arises.

therefore be accurately said that the king of England has the actual nomination to the first dignities in the church. The majority of prebendaries[2] and canons are also in his appointment, and he also chooses a considerable number of rectors.

There are no longer either prebendaries or canons in the Gallican church, and all the bishops and rectors are elected by the votes of the people.

Peers of the Realm

The peers of the realm in England are invested by the monarch, and as these hereditary titles become extinct in certain families, or the king wants to increase their number, the advancement to these high national honours forms an essential part of his prerogatives.

In France there are neither peers of the realm nor any distinctions of this nature.

Judges Civil and Criminal

The twelve judges of England are chosen by the king; he nominates also the president of each tribunal, as well as the person who fills the office of attorney general.*

In France all the judges are elected by the people, who also choose the public accuser.

The president of each tribunal is elected by the members of that tribunal.

Juries

The grand juries in England are appointed by an officer of the Crown.

The lists of small juries, regarding which the accused is allowed

---

* The municipal officers of cities have in general, in England and in France, a small jurisdiction, and are in both kingdoms chosen by the people.

2. Prebendaries are senior members of the clergy in the Anglican or Catholic Church with a role in the administration of a cathedral.

the right of challenge, are composed also by the same officer, whose title is that of sheriff.

In France the Procureur-Syndic of the district draws up the grand jury list, and the Procureur-Syndic of the department that of the small jury.

Both these public officers are chosen by the people.

Magistrates of Police

The police, through the whole kingdom of England, is exercised by justices of peace, and all these magistrates are nominated by the king.

The sheriff, another royal officer, is also invested with a certain power in the maintenance of public order.

The duty of superintending the paving, lighting, and cleaning the streets, and of inspecting the quality of provision for cases of necessity, is in England, as in France, confided to the municipal officers, and these officers in both kingdoms are elected by the people.

The functions of the police are divided in France between different administrators or magistrates, who are all without exception chosen by the people.

Maréchaussée[3]

There is no establishment of a *maréchaussée* in England. The justices of peace have subaltern officers under them, called by the name of constables, and these constables are nominated in an assembly of the justice of the peace of that county, who are themselves appointed by the king, as I have already said.

There is a maréchaussée in France bearing the name of national gendarmerie. The administrators of the departments, all chosen by the people, compile the military list of persons eligible to places in the gendarmerie, and out of that list, the colonels on every vacancy choose from whom the administrators of the departments

---

3. A type of local guard force in France, commanded by a marshal.

are obliged to select one. The king has no power of interfering except to grant the necessary provisions; and his only free function in elections relative to the gendarmerie is to nominate to the offices of colonel, the number of whom is eight, but this only on every other vacancy, and even then his choice is confined to one of the two senior lieutenant colonels. All the other promotions in this corps take place by seniority.

Collection of Direct Taxes

In England, the commissioners authorised by an act of Parliament to assess the land tax as well as the different tax collectors are appointed by the board of the Treasury with the special or tacit approbation of the king; since the minister of finances, who is at the head of that board, as well the other members who compose it, are chosen by the king and liable to be dismissed at his pleasure.

In France, the assessment of the direct taxes is made by the directors of department, the directors of district, and the municipal officers; and all the tax collectors, receivers, and treasurers are nominated by them. And these members of departments and districts, as well as the municipal officers, are all elected by the people without any intervention of the king.

Collection of Indirect Taxes

In England, the collection of these taxes is entrusted to the direction of different commissioners, as commissioners of excise, commissioners of customs, etc. and these commissioners are appointed by the board of Treasury, always with the royal consent, since, as I have said before, it is the monarch who chooses the members of that board, and who has power of dismissing them whenever he pleases. All the inferior employments are bestowed by the commissioners, with the tacit or express approbation of the minister of finances, as first lord of the treasury.

The government in France names a small number of administrators who are to control the collection of indirect imposts in Paris:

but the law requires these administrators to be selected from among the clerks who have risen to the highest ranks and have served a certain number of years in those ranks. Government is also authorised to choose the directors, but it is from among three persons who shall be pointed out by the administrators. These directors fill the office immediately under that of the administrators.

All the other positions are given, without the government having any concern in the matter, according to rules of promotion established by the National Assembly and admission into lower positions by which one's career in this department depends wholly on the administrators.

Foreigners will believe with difficulty that the legislators of France could wish to descend to such minute particulars, and thus circumscribe, as they have done in every sense, the supreme executive power.

National Treasury

The functions of the National Treasury are confined in France to the keeping a register of the receipts and expenses of the state, and to the distribution of the product of the imposts, according to the disposition thereof decreed by the National Assembly; but in England, the power of the Treasury extends much farther, and the board which directs it has properly the administration of the finances, under the superintendance of the minister or head of that department.

I have already said that the members of this board are appointed by the king and revokable at his pleasure.

The National Treasury of France, limited in its functions, in the manner I have just explained, is led by six commissioners. These commissioners are nominated by the king; but they render an account of their conduct immediately to the National Assembly, without the mediation of any minister.

The nomination of commissioners of the Treasury was not put down as one of the constitutional prerogatives of the monarch, and it has been already proposed to the National Assembly to deprive the king of this privilege: the idea has been adopted, but the decision has been adjourned.

The commissioners of the Treasury must nominate all their inferior officers, without any dependence either on the king or his minister.

Army

The admission into the army and the nomination of all the officers depend in England on the executive power. There exist, indeed, certain rules regarding promotions; but these all flow from the will and authority of the monarch.

In France, the legislative body has itself fixed the rules of promotion, and the constitution has left only to the king the nomination of one third of the colonels and lieutenant colonels, half the camp marshals and lieutenant generals, and the whole of the marshals of France, the number of which is six.

Besides, the monarch is confined by law to make his choice among the officers next in rank below.

Lastly, even admission into the service depends on an examination, the conditions of which have been fixed by the legislative body.

King's Guards

No law in England lays the king under any restraint, either in the choice or the advancement of the officers of his guards.

The National Assembly of France has in the first place fixed the conditions for admitting persons into the guards, whether in quality of officer or common soldier; and has also submitted the promotions of the officers to the same regulation as are observed regarding the troops of the line, of which I have already given an account.

Militia

The lieutenants general of the militia are chosen by the king. These officers, with his permission, appoint the colonels, and the colonels nominate the officers of the companies.

In France, the national guards choose all their officers of every rank, and are not even obliged to give any information to government of the result of their elections.

Navy

All the officers of the navy of England are appointed by the king and the rules of promotion and admission into this service depend on his authority.

In France, promotions in the navy are determined by the legislative body, and the constitution itself has confined the prerogative of the monarch to the nomination of one sixth of the lieutenants, half the captains, one third of the vice admirals, and to the choice of three admirals.

Moreover, admission into the navy is submitted to certain positive conditions, which render it independent of the will of the monarch.

Civil Administration of the Marine

In England, all employments in the civil administration of the navy are given according to the king's pleasure, by a council of admiralty, of which the minister for this department is the head. All the members of this council are appointed by the monarch, and the commission may be revoked at his will.

In France, the rules for promotion even in these kind of offices are fixed by the legislative body, and to these rules the king is obliged to conform in the small number of appointments which are left to him; and even on these conditions, according to the constitutional act, he can nominate only one half the masters of administration and of the under-masters of construction.

Invalids

The administration of the celebrated hospital at Greenwich, the rules of admission to the benefits of that institution, and the dispositions regarding the retreat of the invalids depend immediately on the authority of the monarch.

The legislators of France have converted the government of the royal hospital of invalids into an elective and municipal administration, and this important part of the public weal, with all its dependent branches, is taken from the hands of the king.

Civil Employments Regarding the Interior
Part of the Kingdom

The lord lieutenants of each county are nominated by the king of England; their principal functions concern the militia. The sheriffs also, with very few exceptions, are appointed by the monarch. Their functions are entirely civil. They ought to make the circuit of their counties twice a year, in order to execute different tasks of their administration. They form the list of juries, summon them, and are empowered to enforce their attendance. They levy all fines, recoveries, amercements, etc.[4] The sheriffs have no salary, and their office is purely honorary; but there are in the administration many posts to which very considerable emoluments are attached, among others, the place of governor of the Cinque Ports.[5]

The king also makes nominations for these positions.

There no longer exists a single office of this kind in France at the disposal of the monarch. Every part of the interior administration is entrusted to councils and to directories of districts and departments, whose members are elected by the people.

The command of fortresses and military castles are assigned

4. An amercement (from "being at the mercy of") was a financial penalty in England, imposed by the court, for small offenses as an alternative to imprisonment. The sum was not fixed but was assessed in each case.

5. Formed in the Middle Ages (beginning with the 12th century), the Confederation of Cinque Ports originally comprised five coastal towns in Kent and Sussex, at the eastern end of the English Channel: Hastings, New Romney (later replaced by Rye), Hythe, Dover, and Sandwich.

without any peculiar emoluments, to the commanding officer of the troops who shall happen to be stationed there.

Orders of Knighthood

The king of England has the right of creating orders of knighthood, and no person can be admitted into them without his will. These orders at present amount to four; the order of the Thistle for Scotland, the order of St. Patrick for Ireland, the order of the Bath and the order of the Garter for England.

There are also other national and honorary distinctions conferred by the king, as the hereditary title of baronet, and the title of knight conferred for life only.

The order of St. Louis is the only one in France which is permitted to subsist, and this distinction is obtained as a matter of right after twenty-four years of military service.

The Constitution reserves to the legislative body the privilege of granting public honors in the memory of great men, and the right to establish by laws or in a general manner the marks of distinction that should be granted to those who have rendered services to the state and are thus worthy of a great reward.

Pecuniary Favours

In England, there are a certain number of lucrative employments, of which the inutility is so fully acknowledged that they are called by the name of *sinecures;* but Parliament permits the emoluments of them to subsist, as a charge on the public treasury, to preserve to the king the power of bestowing pecuniary favours.

Nothing similar exists in France, nor has any similar prerogative been accorded to the sovereign. An annual fund is indeed reserved of two millions of livres to be disposed of in pensions and gratifications; but the participation of the monarch in the distribution of this fund is expressed by the constitution in the following terms: *The king orders the list of pensions and gratifications to be made out, in order to be presented to the legislative body each session, that it may be decreed if thought proper.* They are careful not to tell us whether this list shall include all the pensions and gratifications which have been demanded, or only those which the king has judged reasonable. They have not thought it necessary to give the king the initiative in this regard, for the most trivial solicitations are addressed directly to the Assembly, and the entire mass of pensions and gratifications recently bestowed as well as the pensions which are to be preserved was fixed in the last session of the Assembly upon the report and proposition of one of its committees.

I could easily, by entering into particulars, extend this parallel further, but I have already said enough to fulfill the goal I proposed to myself.

I remember when it was said in France that the king of England was only the principal senator in a republic. At present, however, his prerogatives are as superior to those of the *king of the French*, as those of the *king of France* were formerly superior to his.

The nomination of ambassadors and ministers to foreign courts is the only prerogative that has been granted in a similar manner to the monarchs of both countries. And here the parallel would probably have failed, if advancement in the diplomatic career could have been made subject to fixed rules. I have one other important observation to make in regard to the nominations entrusted to the king for the national utility. In leaving the consistence of the executive power imperfect, in neglecting to harmonize, so to speak, the royal functions with each other in order to create the royal dignity, in retaining the head of the state in a perpetual state of uncertain and intermittent existence, the faculty which is conceded to him of nominating people to certain employments becomes entirely null, or fails to achieve its political goal; since in exercising this faculty, the king finds himself in a situation in which he is dominated by all those who offer themselves as the temporary supports of his precarious authority. It may even be asserted without paradox that, by reducing within too narrow bounds the nomination entrusted to the executive power, they have more inevitably introduced corruption than if they had invested the monarch with all the prerogatives essential to his dignity. For having once rendered him satisfied with this royal position, they

might then expect him to be influenced in his actions only by the
public good; but dissatisfied with this situation, he must be expected
to aspire to the perpetual increase of his authority. I am presenting
here a general idea which may be derived from the character of man
and his unchanging nature, and leave aside all exceptions.

It must be admitted that there is in the French constitution a remarkable singularity. It is expected and required of the monarch that
he should dispose the people to obedience, that he should cause the
laws to be executed, that he should maintain public order, that he
should attend to the due assessment and payment of taxes, that he
should provide against and remove all obstacles in the circulation of
provisions, that he should give to every department of administration
the necessary energy, that he should regulate its motions and smooth
all its difficulties; finally, the defence and safety of the state are entrusted to his vigilance and activity. These are all the duties imposed
on him, and at the same time, in the most difficult and essential parts
of the government, he has agents assigned to him, regarding whom
he has no choice, some deriving their places from suffrages of the
people, and others from the fixed and invariable laws of promotion.
It has already been seen that the civil and criminal magistrates, the
justices of peace, the members of the tribunal of annulment, those of
the high national court, the administrators of departments, the administrators of districts, the municipal officers of the towns, all those
who preside over justice, police or administration, are nominated by
electors who have themselves been chosen by the active citizens at
large; and the intervention of the king, his consent, his approbation,
everything that can indicate the slightest concurrence on his part, has
been solemnly rejected. It is precisely in the same manner, and without any communication with the government, not even the formality
of one investiture, that the ministers of religion are appointed, those
first professors of morality and depositaries of the power of religion
over the opinions and consciences of the people. The national gen-
dermerie, whose business it is to protect by armed force the safety of
the main roads, the tranquility of markets, and all other parts of external order, is chosen by the different departments, the king having
scarcely a voice in the appointment. The national guards elect their
own subaltern officers, and the subalterns must choose the field and

commissioned officers. The army and the navy, with very few exceptions, are subjected to an invariable scale of promotions. Finally, the collectors and treasurers of the direct taxes are neither appointed in the first instance, nor sanctioned in the last by royal authority; and the individuals employed in the superintendance of indirect taxes are nominated in regular succession by those next above them, the privilege of the government extending only to the selecting those of the first order out of the persons constituting the second.

Thus, in every arrangement that has been made, the distrust towards the executive power is so conspicuously prevailing, that the necessity of its influence and esteem might be supposed to have been totally lost from sight.

Finally, never before has the project been conceived of imposing on the chief magistrate the most extensive functions, and obliging him at the same time to execute them by agents attached to him by no sort of tie; neither by the tie of gratitude, since they are not chosen by himself; nor by that of subordination, since they derive their power from the people; nor by that of hope, since there is nothing which the monarch can bestow upon them.

Could it be supposed that by leaving to the king the choice of his ministers, all the other agents of the government ought to be appointed by the nation? But the ministers of the king are a part of himself and can never be considered either as a supplement to his power or an addition to his dignity. They constitute one of the exterior wings of the royal edifice, and precisely that which the winds, hail and tempests damage most easily.

Those persons who observe with attention the progress of affairs will have readily perceived, from the last discourses addressed to the Constituent Assembly by its principal committee, that this committee began at last to be aware of the insufficiency of the means destined to the support of the executive power, and felt the necessity of giving more energy to the royal authority; but the credit of the committee was no longer high enough to persuade the Assembly to tread back its steps. For this purpose, it would have been necessary to remind it of the innumerable declamations which, under other circumstances, it had employed to express contrary sentiments. The impressions had already been given and it was too late to efface them;

the prejudices had already been formed and it was no longer possible to destroy them. A powerful lesson, which may make men aware of the dangers annexed to the language of the passions! This language delights the hearer by the promptitude of its effects, but it carries him along with it and deprives him of the liberty and power of returning to reason and truth at the moment when such a retreat is most salutary and indispensible. Thus it was seen that, in the revision of the constitutional articles, the reporter of the committee endeavoured to obtain the suppression of the decree which forbade the king to choose his ministers from among the national deputies; his arguments on the need to consider the interests of the executive power were in vain; they would not hear him, and it was impossible they should, for the constitutional committee had never fixed the attention of the National Assembly on the difficulties attending the judicious construction of the executive power and all the other implications of such a great and important question. The proposal of the committee was attributed only to personal interest, a suspicion that is always at hand, and that, by its petty nature, has more influence upon the opinions of the people than the greatest political considerations. Moreover, in returning upon its steps, the National Assembly always did it with resentment; for it pretended not only to create a political masterpiece, but to produce it at the first attempt. Alas, many virtues are needed in order to be a perfect legislator! For my own part, I would lay more stress upon these virtues than upon a lot of science.

The National Assembly, unwilling to confess it, had nevertheless a secret feeling how little assistance it could expect from the executive power, given the weak state to which it had reduced it; and it appeared that, while becoming stronger, the exercise of punishments was the most important means it wanted to use. Thus the public accuser acts a principal part both in the political institution and in all the deliberations of the National Assembly; and by an unheard of change, condemnations and executions have become at once the resource and hope of the French nation. But if, during the many ages that society has existed, punishments had been thought adequate to the regular movements of a great empire, the words government and administration would neither have been consecrated by time, nor would have found a place in any language; the apparatus of justice, destined to put in force the vengeance of the law, would have been sufficient. But it was found that nations required to be held by softer reins; it was found that the innumerable interests, in opposition to public order, demanded an active superintendence and an authority of opinion capable of restraining without effort or violence, all the active springs of the social system, and preserve the general harmony. Therefore the purpose of the executive power is not, as has been supposed, to use the sword of the law; on the contrary, its duty and utility consist in avoiding the necessity of resorting to this means of force, this means that always debases the souls and that, in a free country, could not be used without irritating the mind of the people and perverting all characters.

Nonetheless, let us not forget to point out that the accidents and vexations multiply in the same proportion as the infinite number of relations that compose human society; and it is not with a cold and unfeeling hand, it is not by the use of one instrument or one machine, that the nation can be preserved from the different ills which normally threaten it. A disorderly agitation is not without its dangers; but political lethargy is equally to be feared. Good order may be destroyed in a kingdom by the weakness, by the indifference, and by the inactivity of the administrative or other intermediate authorities. Punishments do not dispel this political stupor; it is the property of hope alone to support a continued activity; and so great is its power that can overcome even the sentiment of fear by suggesting, when necessary, those deceptions which inspire us with the confidence that we shall escape the most likely dangers.

Let us not lament this empire of hope when we consider it in general. It is milder and, in my opinion, more consonant to our nature than the stern dominion of avenging laws. In the vast range of public affairs and the various labours which they require, it becomes necessary to hold out to men different motives to action. To some, though the number is small, we may present glory and renown; to others virtue and its solitary enjoyments; to all, as a temporary motive, the love of country, together with the various modifications which the passing exaltation can give it; but to most people, hope, even the most confused and uncertain hope, can offer encouragement at all times and in all circumstances. It is therefore necessary to confide the means of exciting this hope, if I may say so, at least to a certain sufficient degree, to the custodian of the executive power, so that this power, by prudently and effectively using these means, may derive from them its vivifying force and real support.

CHAPTER XIII

Forms Observed towards the Monarch

It is not only by the aid of real prerogatives annexed to the executive power that its high consideration and the imposing dignity, so necessary to its action, are formed and maintained. It is also indispensable that the head of the state should be surrounded with all that is calculated to control the imagination. We are all liable to be influenced and impressed in various ways; a long education of our spiritual and mental faculties, the consequence of leisure and wealth, allows some of us to submit our sentiments and principles to the slow results of an enlightened meditation; but the majority of people, I mean those who are obliged to employ the first developement of their faculties in lucrative pursuits, will always remain under the influence of the most simple ideas. This is no reproach to their intellect, but the inevitable effect of their humble condition. From these indestructible truths, innate in our minds and inseparable from our social position, it is found that, to maintain in a vast kingdom the mysterious bonds of subordination and obedience, we must capture and enlist on our side the momentary passions of mankind, and their mature and deliberate sentiments.

The majority of people, attentive only to the ideas of pride and vanity with which the splendor of their rank has inspired princes, have been induced to consider this splendor as of no utility to the social interest; and the short-sighted philosophers of the day, advancing a step further, have represented as a degradation all the forms of respect destined to give lustre to the majesty of the sovereign. But

the illusions of kings regarding the origin and spirit of these different homages ought not to lead us into a contrary mistake, and divert
our attention from those primary ideas and general views, which have
converted into a political element the brilliancy of the throne and its
lenient authority over the human imagination.

The Constituent Assembly did not have these ideas sufficiently
present to its recollection; or rather it sacrificed them too easily to
passionate sentiments. Yet, as it was curtailing every day the real
prerogatives of the monarch, it became the more essential to preserve the habit of respect shown to his superior rank. As the Assembly was diminishing every day his means of influence, it was all
the more necessary not to blur his halo; but I do not know why our
legislators have always regarded the obedience of a great nation as
a simple idea, which it was sufficient to fix by an article of law. It
was decreed that the executive power should be placed in the hands
of the monarch, without paying attention to the formation of this
power; the French government was declared monarchical without
examining the manner in which the majesty of the throne should
be constituted. The utility of a monarch, however, does not consist
in his title, but in all the concomitant elements of royalty, in those
different attributes which captivate attention, impose respect, and
command obedience. Finally, and I am perhaps about to start a subject worthy of much reflection, the Assembly held in contempt every sentiment arising from custom and opinion, without perceiving
that it is by the authority of the monarch over these very sentiments
that he becomes absolutely distinct from the law, and is able to give
it energy.

The National Assembly would probably have discovered all these
truths, if it did not abandon itself so early to a spirit of jealousy. It
constantly regarded the king as a rival, instead of having the courage, as a legislator, to consider him as the principal actor in a monarchical government, and to prudently grant him, on time, his share in
government. With peculiar indiscretion, the Assembly enjoyed giving the king, during its sessions, the humble title of *first public functionary;* and it was only after having combined and dictated, as it
were, all the articles of the constitution under this term that, at the
very end of their work, it thought proper to call him for the first

time *the hereditary representative of the nation.* The Assembly was not aware that this very wise denomination alone required that the legislators go over their whole business again. What would be said of a painter who, after intending to represent on his canvas the attributes of the first of the fabulous deities, and perceiving, at the last touch of the brush, that he had forgotten to place in heaven the master of the earth, should imagine that he could repair the whole mistake by writing in large characters the name of *Jupiter* at the bottom of his picture?

The English, who are excessively jealous of their liberty and display even in the habits of social life a character of independence, have always wanted to pay the highest honours to their kings; and so far from thinking themselves debased by such homages, they feel a kind of pride in complying with them. They consider the splendor of the British throne as a sort of image or reflection of the national dignity, and they strive by their own deference to secure to the chief of their political union the respect of all Europe.

When the wise men of that nation fixed their minds upon the great principles of government, they undoubtedly readily perceived that, among all the different means of strengthening the executive power, the mildest and most suitable to the haughtiness of a free people, is the dignity with which the king, as chief of the state, stands forward as the visible interpreter of the majesty of the law. In France, the chair upon which the monarch is seated is placed at the same level as that of the transitory president of the National Assembly; great care has been taken to align them in a parallel position. In contrast, the English House of Commons, that House which makes kings and circumscribes their prerogatives, that House which with tranquil energy would, no doubt, repel the slightest attack upon the national liberties, goes in a body to the House of Lords, stands humbly below the bar, and, with a decent and unassuming countenance, listens to the discourse which the king, seated on his royal throne, addresses to his Parliament. The speaker then answers the king, preserving those forms of respect, a thousand times more honourable to the nation than that language of fellow to fellow, scrupulously constructed and laboriously kept up by the different presidents of the National Assembly. There is no greatness in this civic arrogance, far from that;

at least, it clearly demonstrates that those who use it are not yet accustomed to liberty; and we may apply to certain exalted sentiments, which we hear repeated every day, the observation once made by the chancellor d'Aguesseau on the political erudition of a man of letters: "It is evident that all his knowledge is but of yesterday."

I shall not enter into a detail of all the instances of disrespect shown to the king, of which the whole conduct of the last National Assembly exhibits a continuous example; I would like to confine my attention only to the constitution. It is not, however, less true that there has resulted from the levity of discourses held by various deputies a sort of encouragement or pretext for that multitude of pamphlets whose truly licentious language has formed by degrees a general habit of contempt for the throne and the monarch; a habit which has not been changed by the tardy penalty against those *who shall deliberately compass the degradation of the constituted powers.* The expression is itself vague, capable of various interpretations, and will never fail to be explained according to the spirit of the moment. Besides, one must wait for a public accuser, appointed by the people and often close to the end of his fixed tenure, to want to defend the honor of the Crown. Finally, the queen, whose dignity cannot in reality be separated from that of the king, their son, heir apparent to the Crown, and the other princes of the blood, are placed with respect to the calumnies they may sustain, on the same level as all other citizens; they must prosecute in their own name; they must appear in court in person, and thus expose themselves in public to the additional outrages which the defendent may employ, either as the means of justifying his first error, or merely to make himself the subject of public attention. Nothing can be more clear than that persons of this illustrious rank, or even private citizens, attached to their repose, will never want to risk entering a contentious prosecution upon such conditions.

The majesty of the monarch is still further affected by the inferior condition imposed to his ministers. They are appointed by him, they are the mediums of his will, they compose his council; therefore, everything that concerns their exterior image and prestige is of consequence to his dignity. Nonetheless, as everyone sees, they are obliged to look for support to their weakness, they are forced to fight for their life and safety, given their dependent and powerless condition. Moreover, they are delivered up to the arbitrary good pleasure of every pitiful pamphleteer; and different reasons oblige them to be respectful of this type of amusement. The penal code, which has been invented for the offences of ministers, is also, by the minuteness of its petty and ignoble details, an indirect attack upon the majesty of the king.

The Assembly took delight in trampling upon all ideas which opinion had formerly rendered sacred; and when this exaggeration is applied even to the etiquette to be observed towards the monarch and his ministers, one is easily led to a vulgar familiarity and a form of cynicism which appeal, if you will, to those who compare their present ease and impudence with their former timidity and long established practices and customs, but which inspire the strongest disgust to those who have always been firm in their courage and their pride.

This pretended freedom of principle of which they so much boast is the result of an unwise combination of republican and monarchical principles, whose incoherence is perceptible in various parts of the French constitution. How much better have these different principles been understood and clarified in the constitution of England! There both of them have their proper place and they act in harmony. Time and experience have no doubt contributed to bring about this harmony; but we have come the last, the way was prepared before us, and if we have neglected to take advantage of the circumstance, the fault is to be ascribed to the devouring vanity of our first legislators; they have preferred seating themselves above reason rather than holding a secondary rank; they have preferred becoming the masters and leaders of a sect rather than transmitting to us a happy and peaceful creed.

Shall I, to fulfil the title of my chapter, enumerate certain miscellaneous dispositions in which the royal majesty has been treated with a negligence to which we find no correspondent in any of the institutions of the free country which serves me at present as a parallel? I should then point out the entire ceremonial observed in the relations between the National Assembly or its deputies and the head of state; the rule forbidding the president ever to take part in any deputation of the legislative body to the king; the decree limiting the retinue of the monarch whenever he appears in the Assembly, and in such a manner that even the princes of his blood may not accompany him.

I should point out the familiarity with which he is treated upon every occasion; the affectation of always speaking to him in the second person; the permission given to a president, whose official existence is but for a fortnight, of writing to him precisely in the same style as he would write to a private individual; the mode of bringing into question every petty form, which has been carried to such an excess that the chief of a deputation has been covered with the applauses of the Assembly for giving an account of his mission in these terms: "When we entered, I believed the king first bowed towards us; I accordingly returned his salutation; the rest of the ceremonial passed according to usage." You think it then, gentlemen, magnificent and superb to dispute with the king even the honour of making and receiving a bow? From a heroic act to another, you will have soon proscribed all the rules of decency. I should think, however, that, in order for your courageous character to become famous, it should not have been exercised towards a king who was a prisoner, and who might see from his windows the courts and gardens of his palace, crowded with men armed with pikes and other instruments of offence. I remember to have read that Edward, the Black Prince, served King John of France upon his knees, after having taken him prisoner in the battle of Poitiers.[1]

But leaving aside the duties that superiority and magnanimity require of us, I ask once again, where is the political wisdom of deciding in favour of monarchy, while we trample under foot the majesty of the monarch? The National Assembly has always evaded this question or avoided considering it in full. It found it more commodious to refer upon all occasions to the principle it had laid down, of the equality of mankind; and this principle, applicable to an empire of abstractions and an imaginary universe, has been the chief source of the errors which have been committed in the construction of the new government of France.

But let us proceed to notice some other legislative measures, re-

---

1. Edward of Woodstock, known as the Black Prince (1330–1376), was the eldest son of King Edward IV of England. He participated in the early years of the Hundred Years War but never became king. He defeated King John II of France at Poitiers in 1356.

markable for a total forgetfulness of the royal dignity, and which do not exist in England. Among this number we may include the obligation imposed on the king of never being at a greater distance than twenty leagues from the legislative body; an obligation which we ought to compare with the liberty granted to every legislature of holding its sessions wherever it pleases, and of continuing them without interruption. So that, according to the exact terms of the constitution, a king of France may live to the age of eighty years, without ever having travelled into the heart of the Brie or the district of Chartrain.

I would also point out the powerlessness to which the constitution condemns the king, who may never take the command of the army, either without, or even within the kingdom, unless the enemy shall have approached within twenty leagues of the National Assembly; for beyond this limit he cannot go while the legislative body is assembled, and he is bound to convoke it as soon as hostilities commence. Thus have they rendered the king of France a stranger to the perils of war, without being at all aware of what they had done. Certainly such a provision, when it is made a part of the constitution, is strikingly incompatible with the diverse elements that constitute the royal dignity.

We may further remark the disrespect shown to the princes of the blood by excluding them at once from every function, both in the legislative body and in the council of the king, and by depriving the monarch of the power of appointing them either to embassies, or to the command of armies, without having previously obtained the consent of the National Assembly.

Nor let us overlook the national guard, placed near the monarch, under the title of an honorary guard, but which, being constitutionally independent of his control, seems rather to resemble a guard of inspection.

The formation of the ordinary guard will also appear upon a close examination to be equally disrespectful. The Assembly has found out the secret of degrading at once the dignity of that body, and of diminishing the interest of the officers to merit the approbation of the sovereign.

They have degraded its dignity by excluding the officers from

competition with the army of the line in military promotions, by interdicting to them all types of service, except at the palace of the king,
and by taking from them the prospect of serving in war, since the
king of France, as I have already explained, will never be able to go
to war.

They have diminished the inducement of the officers of the guards
to merit the approbation of the king, since they have applied to them,
distinct from the regular troops, the common and established rules
of promotion which limit the prerogative of the monarch, even in the
case of his own guards, to appointing only the commanding officer,
and once in three times, the colonels and lieutenant colonels, to the
number of eighteen, with this additional proviso, that the king shall
be obliged, when his turn comes, to choose them among the officers
of the rank next in order below.

The other officers could be employed to guard the king without
his consent.

I also consider as a usurpation upon the rights of the monarch
the decree by which the Assembly seized into its own hands the territorial domains of the monarch, and made itself successor to the
right he possessed of resuming his ancient domains. The Constituent Assembly, to justify its decree, was obliged to have recourse to
the ancient laws of France, which had directed the reunion of all
the royal domains in the public estate. But these laws evidently supposed, as I have observed in my former work, that the property of the
state, administered by the prince, might be confounded with his own
property and serve to increase his personal revenues; but from the
moment when, by an entire change in the constitution, the separation
of the two properties and the division of their administration were
made so complete as to preclude the possibility of confusion, there
no longer remained any legitimate motive to maintain to the profit of
the state the territorial and personal domains of the king, by substituting to them a precarious and arbitary annuity.

The National Assembly has itself acknowledged, without being
aware of it, the great extent of these properties; for in one of its decrees, of the month of November 1790, it is remarked that the ancient
domain, or as it is called the public domain, *would soon have been annihilated, if its continual losses had not been in various ways repaired,*

especially by the reunion of the particular estates of the princes, who at different times have succeeded to the Crown.

The National Assembly, however, persisted in its jurisprudence; it had recourse to the spirit of the law and despised its letter, for the purpose of changing various private properties into public property; and, on the contrary, it preferred the letter to the spirit, when it could justify in no other manner the usurpation of the landed estate of the royal family.

The king of England enjoys in like manner a civil list, granted by the nation; but no indemnification is required for this royal annuity. The English do not take with one hand what they grant with the other, and any compulsory attempt to add to the revenue of the state the private fortune of the monarch would be rejected by them as incompatible with the principles of a free constitution.

But the members of the Constituent Assembly, who wanted to install the monarch in his new capacity of *first public functionary*, were led by a sort of analogy to reduce him at the same time to the condition of a pensioner; and when, towards the close of their session, they adopted the idea of giving him the appellation of *hereditary representative of the nation*, there was no longer sufficient time to reform the various articles drawn up in the spirit of their first invented title.

Let it no longer then be matter of surprise to us that, amidst these changes and under the novice hands of so many painters of a constitution, the royal majesty should have lost its original colors. Our first legislators, astonished themselves at their omnipotence, and placing a blind confidence in it, have been daring enough to presume that their rustic authority could make up for the empire of the imagination, that empire founded on our very nature and its eternal essence. In the meantime, to how many fictions have they not been obliged to resort to maintain their sway? Illusions have been of as much use to them as realities. They feared every day that opinion would fail them; and when they were unable to gain it, they put everything in practice to tire it and oblige it to surrender. But opinion has a delicate constitution and requires to be treated more softly; and legislators who only know how to grab things ought to touch it carefully.

The National Assembly has despoiled the throne of all its embellishments, royalty of all its attributes, the king of his whole retinue, without previously considering whether, on such terms, the dignity of the head of the state could be maintained, or whether this imposing dignity, which disposes the people to respect and obedience, is not one of the principal advantages attached to the institution of a king, and the establishment of a monarchical government.

It was particularly in a government, like the present government of France, the aggregate of so many springs, that they ought to have erected a sympathy and a patriotic feeling as a main support of the exterior dignity of the executive power. They should have invented that type of superiority, if it had not already existed; they should have invented it in order to give a regular movement to such a complex assemblage. It was then an amusement worthy of children to try to diminish the majesty of the throne. Liberty grows with the age of nations while furthering their progress and making them enlightened; it will not fail to show them such an important truth.

CHAPTER XIV

Right of Peace and War

The choice that a nation makes of one of the powers of which the government is constituted, for the purpose of investing it with the right of contracting alliances, declaring war and concluding peace; a choice that is to determine in what hands the most important political function shall reside, cannot be foreign to the dignity of the monarch; but as other, still more essential, interests, ought to have their weight in so serious a decision, I have avoided introducing the discussion of this subject when examining the majesty of the throne and the various circumstances calculated to heighten or to diminish it.[1]

It is well known that in England the king can, by his sole authority, make war or peace, and enter into all sorts of political or commercial treaties.

The monarch is hereby exhibited to foreign powers arrayed in all the diginity necessary to conducting honourably and advantageously the affairs of the nation. But government is nevertheless held by two salutary checks. It can raise no funds for war or any hostile enterprize, without the consent of Parliament; and the responsibility of ministers is an adequate security for the care they will take, in all their peaceful or military transactions, to consult public opinion.

---

1. The role of the monarch and the executive power in foreign relations, including declarations of war, in the Constitution of 1791 is discussed in detail in Glénard, *L'Exécutif et la Constitution de 1791*, 193–278; also see Furet and Halévi, *La Monarchie républicaine: La Constitution de 1791*, 213–18.

We were determined to go further, and the imperfection of our law regarding peace and war has demonstrated the wisdom of the English constitution in its distribution of the powers called to decide on these important questions. That nation, in reality, has done us much harm by having found, aided by time and composure, the exactly right point in the vast system of administration; for vanity made us determined to have a system of our own, a new and untried place, and we were forced to take it on the side of reason, and often at no small distance from it.

To perceive in what manner these observations are connected with the subject of which we are treating, it is necessary to call to mind the provisions of the constitutional law of France regarding the right of peace and war.*

Chap. III. Sect. i. Art. 2. War can be declared only by a decree of the legislative body, rendered upon the formal and necessary proposal of the king and sanctioned by him.

In the case of impending or actual hostilities, of an ally to be supported, or a right to be preserved by force of arms, the king shall notify without delay to the legislative body, and shall declare the reasons thereof. If the legislative body is in recess, the king shall immediately assemble it.

If the legislative body determines that war ought not to be made, the king shall immediately take measures to stop or prevent all hostilities, the ministers being responsible for delays.

If the legislative body finds that the hostilities commenced are a culpable aggression on the part of ministers, or any other agent of the executive power, the author of the aggression shall be prosecuted criminally.

During the whole course of war, the legislative body may require the king to negociate peace, and the king is bound to comply with such a request.

Chap. IV. Sect. iii. Art. 1. The king alone may maintain political relations abroad, conduct negociations, make preparations of war proportioned to those of the neighbouring states, allocate the land and sea forces, as he shall judge most suitable, and regulate their direction in case of war.

Art. 3. It belongs to the king to resolve and sign with all foreign powers, all treaties of peace, alliance and commerce, and other conventions, which he shall judge necessary for the welfare of the state, subject to the ratification by the legislative body.

This law, without being at all more favourable to the maintenance of tranquillity than the law of England, obscures unnecessarily the majesty of the throne, throws impediments in the way of political negociations, and reduces the nation to a state of considerable inferiority in its foreign transactions.

If the different sovereigns of Europe, adhering strictly to the laws of honour, were never to engage in war till they had made their intentions known by a formal declaration, a numerous assembly, deliberating openly on the propriety of adopting or rejecting a measure of such importance, would almost be on the same level as a king meditating in secret with his council. But experience has taught us that the policy of princes can, whenever they please, dispense with these moral restraints. And, in that case, there is no equality between a monarch, who declares war by actually commencing it, and a National Assembly, openly discussing a question like this, and divulging its intentions long before the period that hostilities can begin. The assembly may indeed adopt or reject the motion for going to war with such a promptitude as to remove in some degree the inconveniences resulting from a premature promulgation of its designs; but the misfortune is that such promptitude can only take place at the expence of wisdom and of all the dictates of a prudent circumspection. Besides, how can a speedy deliberation be expected on such an important subject, unless a previous judgment should have been formed regarding it in those clubs or societies which govern the assembly of legislators? But there the objection would equally hold, and only its application would change.

Let us suppose now that two powers, after having deliberated for a considerable time on the propriety of going to war, should resolve to remain at peace. One of them has been able to share its doubts and deliberate secretly within the confines of a cabinet council, and has thus excited no distrust. The other, from the nature of its constitution, has displayed its hesitation to all the powers of Europe and evinced, perhaps, that its choice of peace was the result of a small majority in a numerous assembly; alarms are generated abroad, defensive measures are adopted; these measures produce reciprocal precautions; a quarrel ensures, and war becomes the outcome of a simple question having been publicly discussed.

I have another observation to make on this constitutional decree regarding peace and war. It prohibits the monarch from declaring war without the consent of the legislative body, and at the same time formally supposes that hostilities may be commenced by the government; and yet hostilities are commonly considered as the strongest declaration of war. It was therefore impossible to deal with the consequences of these hostilities other than in a very doubtful and imperfect manner, by reserving to the legislative body the right of suspending hostilities, and making the ministers responsible for any delay; for hostilities already commenced draw on others on the part of the nation attacked, and we are not always sure of suspending them by stopping ourselves.

Hostilities then, like declarations of war, ought to depend on the same authority, as should also the preparations that usually precede them, for these preparations are frequently sufficient of themselves to start a political quarrel.

It is not easy to explain the meaning of the constitutional act as to the right of commencing hostilities; it neither delegates nor refuses to the executive power this right, and we must search for the spirit of the law in certain loose expressions.

There is no doubt, however, that, according to the words of the decree, the government has a tacit authority to take a measure of this nature, for we can read the following words: "In the case of impending or actual hostilities, the king shall notify the same without delay to the legislative body, and shall declare the reasons for such hostilities."

It is evident that this article relates to hostilities commenced by the king, and not by a foreign nation, because the government is obliged to explain the reasons; and because in another article it is said that, on the vote of the legislative body, "the king shall immediately take measures to stop or prevent all hostilities, the ministers being responsible for delays." How could they be responsible for making hostilities end on the part of *"other nations?"*

This explanation appears to be confirmed by another article which says: "If the legislative body find that the hostilities commenced are a *culpable* aggression on the part of ministers, or any other agent of the executive power, the author of the aggression shall be prosecuted criminally." Therefore only culpable aggressions are prohibited, and not all hostilities indiscriminately.

But it was not in this indirect manner that a legislative assembly had to explain itself on a question of such a great importance; and it is even more difficult to account for such an extraordinary turn of events since, in speaking of the right of declaring war and making the necessary preparations, the Assembly expressed itself very clearly in these terms:

> War cannot be determined on, but by a decree of the legis-lative body.
>
> The king alone can make warlike preparations proportioned to those of the neighbouring states.

Why then does the constitutional decree mention hostilities only in ambiguous terms, "in case of impending or actual hostilities, etc." Such a formulation is so singular that it can only be accounted for by the embarrassment of those who drafted this decree. To have said expressly *the king has a right to commence hostilities*, after having pre-viously decreed that *war could only be determined on by a decree of the legislative body*, would have made the whole Europe laugh. And there would have been a danger that someone might rise up in the national Areopagus to ask whether hostilities are not a declaration of war and to remind that the majority of wars started with hostilities and that declarations of war changed into manifestos justifying attacks made without any formal notice.

On the other hand, taking an opposite point of view and enacting that *hostilities could only be determined on by a decree of the legislative body*, would have been giving to other nations a great advantage over us; and someone in the Assembly, recollecting that the last maritime war had started by the sudden capture of all our vessels and their crews, might have asked whether it was a good political decision to deprive ourselves in advance of the possibility of similar retaliations, and to increase at the same time the security of such aggressions to-wards us.

The members of the committee of legislation probably said to themselves, amidst their embarrassment, Let us slightly pass over the difficulty by some vague and obscure expression regarding the article of hostilities; nobody will perceive it; and by reducing the question to the empty formality of declaring war, we shall apparently be able, without contradiction, to grant to the legislative body the initiative in the transaction. The committee was not mistaken; and this decree, which authorised the monarch to make preparations and start hostilities, at the same time reserving to the legislature the right of declaring whether there shall be a war, has been applauded by all Paris as the best thing in the world.

Let us now turn our attention to the articles regarding the treaties of peace, the treaties of alliance and commerce. We notice that the constitution and the legislative decrees give the king the necessary authority to negotiate and sign these diverse treatises, but they will not be valid till they have been ratified by the legislative body.

The application of this apparently simple condition will be more complicated and the result will be that the negotiation of treaties will be more difficult and the treaties will be less advantageous to the French nation. A contracting party seldom makes known its last concession, till it is sure that concession will bring the business to a conclusion. Until then, it feared that it might give an advantage to the other party by discovering the extent of the sacrifice which its peculiar situation or its interests obliged it to make. This reserve would increase if the constitutional weakness of the negociating power afforded no moral guarantee of the approbation of the political body to which the ratification of treaties was attributed. Moreover, if you put together this disproportion of forces and the superior privilege attributed to the National Assembly, and the further influence of another right they have reserved to themselves, that of requiring the executive power to negotiate a peace, it is obvious that the legislature will demand to be informed of the progress of the negociation. And this information becoming a subject of controversy in the middle of a numerous assembly, the foreign party in the negotiation will perfectly understand the designs of our legislative body; and since the nature of its government will allow it to maintain all its secrets, its superiority will be similar to that of a merchant who possesses the magical power of knowing to a penny the intentions of the vendors and sellers, without ever being obliged to reveal his own intentions in advance. He would certainly make an enormous fortune with such a talisman.

It frequently also happens that there is only a single moment for the successful conclusion of a political negotiation; for the consent of the contracting power may depend on a variety of transient circumstances, on several circumstances entirely distorted by the mere idea of such a treaty becoming public. And then we consider that, by making it necessary for the subject to be previously discussed in a numerous assembly, war may perhaps be protracted for a whole year; when we consider that an indispensable peace may be delayed by the vain declamations of men whose only object is applause, we shudder at the danger of such a measure. And we cannot help believing that the English have acted wisely in investing the head of the state with the necessary power of conducting through the different stages, and bringing to a definitive conclusion, treaties of peace and all political negociations. And can anyone doubt that, in a free constitution, the responsibility of ministers does not offer an adequate safeguard against their treachery, or their acting in contempt of public opinion? There is then a boundary within which, for the interest and obvious advantage of the state, suspicion and distrust ought to be confined; but this boundary has been almost universally missed by our legislators, and this should not surprise us. Men, naturally inclined to extremes, are even more so when the desire to please the people becomes their ruling passion; for ideas of wisdom and moderation commonly escape the wavering mass of people who regard absent-mindedly the conduct of statesmen, people whose attention can be caught and whose suffrages can be gained only by colorful novelties and striking exaggerations.

I could defend that part of the constitution which relates to peace and war, but that would only be at the expense of the entire constitution. I must say that in the weak and degraded state to which government has been reduced, even if it invested with the prerogative, it could conclude no treaty without the concurrence of the National Assembly. There are certain proportions in the social edifice, as in works of architecture, which necessarily require other proportions;

and it would be entirely absurd to suppose that a government, having no internal influence, could possess the means or the privilege of exciting or quelling foreign political storms.

Let it be noted that the separation of powers, regardless of the subject to which it relates, can never be the outcome of an arbitrary decision sanctioned by a certain clause of a constitution. This disposition is of such a great importance that it will always be, legally or illegally, the necessary outcome of the general organization of the social system. Therefore, without giving myself the trouble of reading the particular article of the political code which determines the foreign relations of a nation, I know that wherever, as in France, such a great power has been put into the hands of the people, the latter either directly, or through its representatives or their demagogues, will be the author of peace and war.

Undoubtedly, it is of great importance that the nation should have considerable influence in affairs of this sort; but the empire of opinion, like everything else, is susceptible of abuse; and its power also needs to be subjected to certain judicious rules. Nothing is as difficult as to skillfully raise so many barriers. The English Constitution itself has not been able to simplify the prerogative of war because by entrusting it to the monarch, it reserved to itself the right of granting or refusing to grant the funds necessary to special operations. These two principles are in obvious contradiction with each other, and they are reconciled only by the strong pressure of public opinion and by the influence of the harmony established in the general system of government. Under some form or other, it is a precious advantage to a country that the national consent should be required to projects of war or their execution. It may happen, without doubt, that the representatives of the people should be the first movers in a political aggression, and England offers many examples; but the number of these enterprises dictated by the voice of public opinion cannot be compared with the number of wars that arise from the restless and ambitious temper of governments which are accountable to no one. And it is enough to open the pages of history to be convinced of this truth. It may even perhaps be true that the first and greatest benefit that arises from this wise constitution, a constitution in which the representatives of the nation surround the monarch, is the reduction, in a given time, of the number of political quarrels and the calamities which follow from them. No calculation can do justice to the benefit resulting to human nature, from the subtraction of only one war in a century; but in making this vague calculation, we feel with pleasure that a single moral conviction of the heart contributes more to public happiness than all the refinements of that political science, which is ranked in the first order of intellectual benefits by those who have taken up their residence in the middling regions of philosophy.

CHAPTER XV

The Interior Administration

I have shown in the preceding chapters that the means confided to the executive power are infinitely weaker in France than in England. What shall we say if, at the same time, resistance has been rendered more considerable? The principle of order and subordination will then appear, in a twofold sense, to have been altered.[1]

In examining this question, but certain beforehand of the result, I shall first observe that in England, there is but one single executive power, and that, till our time, no one had ever supposed that it could be differently constituted, whether it was, as in a monarchical government, confided to the king, or, as in a republic, placed in the hands of a collective body which always constitutes a simple will determined

---

1. For a brief account of the Constituent Assembly's attempts to revamp the administrative structure of the kingdom after August 4, 1789, see Furet and Halévi, *La Monarchie républicaine: La Constitution de 1791*, 199–204. They highlight the important role played by Thouret in redesigning the administrative map of France. The lawyer from Normandy gave three important speeches on November 3, 9, and 11, 1789 (reprinted in ibid., 435–61); in his last speech, he responded to Mirabeau's proposal to institute 120 departments (instead of 80 proposed by Thouret). Municipal authorities were instituted in every village, but they did not possess the necessary information and agents for acting in harmony with the general administration of the kingdom. The larger juridical implications of the administrative reform intended by the Constituent Assembly are analyzed in Glénard, *L'Exécutif et la Constitution de 1791*, 362–88.

by the majority of suffrages. The legislators of France have visibly departed from this principle of unity, so necessary to the action of government; for in reality they have divided the executive power among all the provincial councils which they had established under the name of departments, districts and municipalities, and they have attached these councils to the authority of the prince, by a thread so subtle and so slender, if I may so express myself, that the supremacy of the monarch is nothing more than nominal.

Let us examine the particular consistence of this series of powers distributed over the surface of the kingdom. The first in the order of the constitution is that which is called a department, and the deputies of which this council is composed, like the members of the districts and municipalities, owe their election to the sole suffrage of the people; the monarch does not intervene at all in this and not even his formal approval is required. Thus, from the first moment of the existence of these deputies as an administrative body, they feel their independence from the royal authority: and as, in the exercise of their functions, they act in a collective capacity, this abstract quality renders them less accessible to the empire of the imagination, and the respect which the majesty of the throne formerly inspired. Lastly, they understand that the monarch has no longer any recompense at his disposal; and the daily publications inform them of the sort of familiarity which each may be allowed to adopt in their interaction with the government. Meanwhile, they have been rendered absolute depositaries of the most important functions. To them, belongs the assessment of direct taxes; they superintend the collection, decide upon the complaints of the persons assessed, and upon every kind of remission which it may in any case be proper to grant; they nominate the treasurers and receivers, who are subjected to their orders; they regulate the public expences within the sphere of their authority; they draw for the necessary sums upon a fund which is entirely under their superintendence; and it is in the same manner that they receive the emoluments allotted to their positions. It is their business to watch over the state of repairs of roads, public edifices, hospitals and prisons. All undertakings of an extraordinary nature within their geographical limits are subjected to their orders. Finally, the supreme police is added to their other powers, and is exercised by them, either directly or indirectly, through the medium of subordinate authorities; and in support of their power, they are authorised to call in a certain species of police, the nomination of which is vested in them, and even, if it should be found necessary, to claim the deployment of all the military forces.

Let us now consider the thread which suspends their power to that of the monarch; a law which has declared the king to be the supreme head of the general administration; a law which has told the departments and districts that they were to exercise their functions under the superintendance and authority of the monarch; a law which gives the king the power of annulling, by proclamation, such acts of their administration as are contrary to the legislative decrees or his own orders; always a law, but what is a law without the union of all the means necessary to secure obedience? What is a law, if it is not placed in the midst of a general system of subordination, where all proportions are observed, and where the real forces are so wisely combined with the moral ones as to concur in the same end? In short, what is a law, and what is to be expected from its abstract empire, if we neglect to invest him who is to enforce its observance with all the prerogatives and all the embellishments calculated to elevate the dignity of his rank and remind us usually of his power and authority?

No law can be more striking and venerable than that of the twelve commandments, consecrated by religious opinion; yet, would the subordination of children to their parents be badly secured, if everything which strikes their regards, everything which influences their imaginations, everything which appeals to their reason, did not represent to them in various ways the superiority of their parents, and the necessity they are under of pleasing those who can either recompense or punish them?

Finally, had the Assembly, in detaching the provincial authorities from the real direction of the monarch, constituted them in such a manner, or subjected them respectively to such laws of order and equilibrium, that the regular action of the administration could be maintained, the degradation of the royal supremacy might have been justified, by demonstrating from experience that nothing had been taken from it but what was superfluous; but among the different authorities established in the interior of the kingdom, there exists an insubordination that weakens the efficacy of them all; and this insubordination flows inevitably from the nature of their organization. It is to persons equal by education, by rank, by fortune, and by the duration of their authority, in short, it is to equals in every respect that the law has prescribed a series of alternate obedience and command, just as the accidents of a ballot might determine. And as our legislators have, in every part of their political system, neglected the great moral spring of authority, that moral spring which compensates by its operation the power of superior numbers, the consequence of this has been that the force of resistance tends to increase under the new system. The Constituent Assembly has indeed issued its express orders to four millions two or three hundred thousand fully armed national guards to obey certain municipal officers whose authority is figured by a scarf of three colours; it has in like manner enjoined to the municipalities an obedience to the districts; and to the districts an obedience to the eighty-three departments, which on their part are to receive the watchword, or take their orders from the supreme chief of the administration; but in all this no thought has been taken to reinforce this subordination by sentiments of personal interest, and a graduated chain of hopes and fears; nor is there any ascendant power, any grand and awe-giving authority to maintain, by its means, all this discipline. They have indeed reserved to the king the right of suspending, *pro tempore*, the administrators of department; but it is previously necessary to find others willing to take their places, and who will accept the office, uncertain what may be the final decision of the National Assembly, designated as the tribunal of appeal of the administrative action of the monarch, and before which the responsible minister is bound to make his appearance. Alas! the poor minister will be singularly cautious of getting involved in such a risky quarrel, and will never express his dissatisfaction, except in flagrant and notorious instances of misconduct, if only to conceal the universal indifference with which his dissatisfaction would be regarded. It can scarcely indeed be considered in any other light than as a sort of jest to have placed in the general system of administration, on one side this firm and well-knit structure of departments, districts, municipalities and national guards, and on the other, with the title of supreme executive, a prince without prerogatives, a monarch without majesty, and repre-

sented, in his compulsory decisions, by ministers who have themselves
everything to fear and who can do neither good nor harm to anyone;
by ministers, upon whom every one performs his noviciate of heroism by allowing himself to speak of them, first lightly, and then with
more and more insolence and contempt; by ministers for whom they
have composed a specific penal code, describing in detailed language
the various punishments that may be inflicted upon them, sometimes
imprisonment, sometimes, irons, the rack,* or civil degradation, preceded, I believe, by the pillory, and who, in the meantime, are usually
treated with continuous disdain. And yet, it is these very men, the perpetual butt of criticism and ridicule, who are expected separately, for
they are not allowed to act in a body, to act as supreme commanders
of this formidable chain of small political powers, whose strength of
resistance might have alarmed Louis XIV after sixty years of sovereignty and glory. What an opposition! What a contrast! Has ever been
in political legislation a greater absence of equipoise? The National
Assembly will constantly be forced to lend its support to the administration, and this very support will render still weaker the intrinsic authority of the government.

In this place I hear myself interrupted by the pamphleteers, the
orators, and even the ministers themselves. You may criticise the constitution, they say, as much as you will, but under this constitution
everything would be marvelously well, if you were only willing to
obey it. My friends, you are perfectly right; but great politicians like
you, gentlemen, ought to know, that if obedience is the pillar of social
order, the inclination, the necessity to obey, must be the result of that
order. Obedience is a means, the obligation to obey is an outcome. Be
so obliging as to reflect for a moment on this distinction. And if I had
to make myself even clearer, I would say that a young man, just out
of college, might build an admirable system of government, a system
under which it would be pleasant to live, if people were made to obey
the laws which derive from the moral principles of this young legislator. It is in this very point, the generation of obedience, the combining of the necessary means to secure general subordination without
despotism and tyranny that the whole science of politics and the dif-

---

* *La gêne*, a sort of iron yoke placed on the neck.

ficulty of social organization consist. When therefore, in order to justify the epithet of sublime, so ridiculously bestowed upon the French
constitution, you hear it said again and again by the august representatives of the nation, that with obedience this constitution would be
perfect, the august representatives of the nation are saying and repeating a truly foolish thing.

Among the different kinds of resistance to which the action of
the government is subjected today, I could mention that multitude
of authorities dispersed over the kingdom, authorities which are not
established by the constitution, but are the result of its imperfection.
Everyone is familiar with those clubs which have become so famous
both on account of their extensive affiliation, and their odd interference in public affairs. Our first legislators wished to suppress the influence of a society which began to bother them; but they wanted this
when it was too late, and hereafter people will remember only the
long association between their principal members and a dictatorship
which they themselves had created.

To this picture that has no model, this heterogeneous mass of so
many authorities, let us add the immoderate use of petitions, amidst
a people who are now all philosophers, all familiars, all equals and
comrades; let us add the liberty of the press, restricted by a single article of law, which may in a thousand ways be evaded; let us add the
further liberty of giving speech to the walls, by covering them with
every sort of placards; some within the tolerated limits, others pervaded with all the licentiousness which is inevitable where the police
operates constantly under the influence of fear. Let us moreover add
the general relaxation of manners and that emancipation from every
sort of respect, the natural consequence of a systematic equality, and
we will see that so many liberties, in addition to the political independence introduced by the constitution, must oppose a continual
resistance to the establishment of order and the regular exercise of
the supreme authority.

Finally, and this last reflection is of all others the most disconso-
late to me, there is a type of irregular authority which has risen up
in the midst of us, and has justly been made a subject of complaint,
which has perhaps become an indispensible ingredient in a constitution that does not include in its nature any spring of motion; such a

government cannot be maintained without passion, and whenever this passion shall subside, the French constitution will fall into decrepitude, just as the human body appears destitute of motion and life when the unnatural activity of a fever has subsided.

I must now compare the actual state of the administration of France with the institutions of a nation which, though its love of liberty is ardent, and though it has twice within a century imposed conditions on a new dynasty of kings, invited from the continent into its island, has never lost sight of that civil and political harmony which secures the tranquillity of the state and gives to the laws the necessary vigour for ensuring to all classes of citizens the happiness that they oought in their oocial union.

I have already said that in England, there is but one single executive power, and this unity has not only been determined, as in France, by certain legislative phrases, but care also has been taken, in regulating the exercise of that power, to maintain a principle whose importance was universally acknowledged. The laws, once sanctioned by the wisdom and maturity naturally to be expected from the union of three wills, the task of executing some and of enforcing the observance of the rest is confided to the head of the state, and the constitution has neither established a division of this part of his authority, nor provided any resistance against it. Let us look, for example, to the assessment and collection of taxes by this important branch of public administration. It is not by a long chain of deliberative councils, elected by the people, that the monarch acquits himself of his functions. A board of treasury instituted by the king, whose members are all nominated by him and removable at his will, conducts, with his tacit or formal approbation, the whole business of the finances. A prince cannot do everything himself; but when he chooses and delegates the agents whom he employs to fulfill the duties of royalty, the unity of the executive power is preserved.

The commissioners who must determine the land taxes, those who ought to collect the customs and excise taxes as well as all the indirect taxes, are chosen by the board of the Treasury, and the nomination of receivers and all the subordinate agents depends equally on its authority. Refusals of payment of legal taxes and other contentious opposition experienced by the collectors are adjudicated in the first instance by a justice of peace, an officer of royal investiture; with the right of appeal to the court of exchequer, the members of which, not removeable at pleasure, have been raised to their appointment by public esteem and the nomination of government; and lastly, it is the sheriffs, a species of public officers appointed by the king, who are nominated by the board of Treasury to direct the execution of these judgments. Thus the authority of the monarch appears in a manner more or less direct, through all the details of this capital article of public administration, the collection of the kingdom's taxes.

We equally find the traces of this authority in the dispositions adopted by the English nation for the maintenance of civil order. The functions of police are confided to the justices of peace, and these justices, as I have already said, derive their appointment and functions from the government. The justices of peace appoint the constables, a sort of inferior officers of police acting under them. Finally, the twelve judges of the kingdom, whose office it is to direct the juries, as well as, when the juried have decided upon the nature of the case, to declare the sentence of the law respecting it, are all appointed by the monarch.

Moreover, there is in each county a lord lieutenant deriving his appointment and functions from the prince. One of his functions is to command the militia when they are assembled, and attend to their regular organization. The officers of this body destined to the preservation of internal peace must have a certain qualification, proportioned to the ranks that are to be occupied, of from fifty to four hundred pounds per annum landed estate. The king chooses the principal of these officers, either by formal nomination, or by his approbation required to the nomination of the lord lieutenant.

In short, we do not find in England a municipal body in every village, a body deliberating and deciding without possessing the necessary information for acting in harmony with the general administration. Yet, this is what has been invented for France, where we see no less than forty-four thousand conventicles, invested with municipal authority, and which form so many links in the vast chain of government.

The cities and boroughs of England have alone municipal officers, and these officers are nominated by the people; but their functions, within the limits that I have already described, are very different from the functions of police, which devolve on the justices of peace; and they are the justices of peace, and not the municipal officers, who, in case of popular commotions, are empowered to call in the assistance of the army, and to warn the people, by reading the *riot act*, of the dangers to which they will be exposed by the vigorous exercise of the law. These justices of peace, uniformly chosen from among the most esteemed citizens, are numerous in every county; so that there is no necessity, as in France, to confide the maintenance of order in the country to the municipal officers of a village, to officers obliged to resign their places after a two-year apprenticeship.

The abbreviated explanation I have given suffices to show what means the English have employed to facilitate the action of the executive power; and yet, notwithstanding all the support given to it, all the authorities are so fettered by the laws that the government is only very imperfectly able to preserve public order and tranquillity. Its task would be still more difficult, and its success still more precarious, if the people of England were less happy, and if those contending principles, those various centres of resistance, which agitate us in France, existed to the same degree in England.

For example, we may observe that in England, the very arms of the militia are deposited and placed under the protection of an officer in each county, and that no individual is permitted to have a musket in his own house without an express licence, at the price of a guinea per annum.*

The liberty of the press also, partly by the express letter of the law, partly by the vigilance of the officers of justice, and partly by the empire of mores and public opinion, is confined within such limits as to prevent the fatal excesses of which we are witnesses.

---

*The author is mistaken; every Englishman has the same right to have a musket in his house, as a lock or bolt on his door. There is indeed a law, and to this Mr. Necker probably alludes, that will not allow him to employ that musket, even in his own field, in the destruction of game, without an express license, at the expence; not of one, but of three guineas a year; and this licence only exempts him from one penalty, and leaves him exposed to another, unless he possess landed property to the amount of a hundred pounds per annum. [This note was written by the English translator of the 1792 English edition—A. C.]

The idea of a daily communication of all the good and bad citizens with the lowest classes of the people by means of posters displayed in the streets, this idea, as dangerous as it is odd, is absolutely unknown in England, or indeed in any civilized country, and probably would meet with a very bad reception. But in our new political system, it has been laid down as a principle, and built up as a maxim, that that part of the nation which is destitute of all instruction and condemned by its indigence never to acquire it, is capable of understanding all political questions, and has the faculty of distinguishing truth from the most specious falshoods, a faculty which is so rare even among the most educated of the people. Base and unworthy flattery, more extravagant than the flattery of courtiers themselves! It will hereafter be seen that, even after the establishment of primary schools, it is easier to mislead the people by an incendiary phrase than to use the power of words to bring them to reason, either by the systematic addresses of the legislative body, or the homilies that are issued from the offices of government.

Finally, they are equally unaccustomed in England to the immoderate use of petitions and the violent domination of republican clubs. They have thought there, and with reason, that liberty is of all moral ideas the one most susceptible of variation, and that, accordingly as we fix it high or low, the nation itself will be happy or unfortunate.

CHAPTER XVI

Military Force

In the course of my plan, I have continually gathered new proofs of the truth that I have tried to investigate; but at present an objection may be raised which I must try to resolve.

The kingdom of France, on account of its central and Mediterranean location, is under the necessity of keeping up a more considerable standing army than England; and as the monarch may make bad use of the military force, of which the constitution has declared him the supreme commander, did not the legislators act wisely in counterbalancing this inevitable danger by weakening all the other branches of the executive power?

This is, in its greatest simplicity, the question which I must clarify; and in order to do this, it will be necessary first to call to mind a few primary and fundamental ideas.

In forming a social compact, the end men had in view was not the obtaining a system of liberty, that should not only be complete in all its parts, but also secure from every imaginable accident. Had their ambition been thus limited, had this been the sole object of their wishes, they would have remained, what they originally were, hordes of savages, without a chief, except at intervals, and capable whenever they pleased of emancipating themselves from this transient authority. But in proportion as they perceived the benefits to be derived from industry and the exercise of their mental and spiritual faculties, and particularly as they felt the delightful experience of this, the desire to preserve the fruit of their labor gave them the idea of laws of justice; and to maintain those laws against the invasion of personal interests and hostile passions, a political force was soon found necessary, a force that, placed in judicious hands, might preserve social conventions, and assure to every individual a security, which has naturally become, since the acquisition of their new fortune and new ideas, one of their dearest wishes. Undoubtedly, in resigning their original independence, mindful of the various satisfactions that accompanied it, they were anxious to limit the sacrifice of their liberty, and accurately proportion it to the precautions which the maintenance of order and the safety of the state demanded. Usurpations, conquests, abuses of every kind, and the complication which time has introduced into human associations have frequently obscured the first principles of their political union; but these ideas have undergone no variation and are found to exist in their primitive simplicity, whenever circumstances allow nations to study them anew, or whenever, called to reconstruct the tottering edifice of their felicity, they seek a fixed point which may serve as an anchor to their wandering thoughts and their uncertain speculations.

From these reflections it would follow that the absolute sacrifice of order to liberty should be considered a way of upsetting the natural succession of social ideas. This would amount in a certain way to making the human mind perform a retrograde course and returning it insensibly to the savage state, by the same paths through which it had arrived at civilization.

Let us also observe that the savage state, in the midst of society itself, that state which is represented by anarchy, is of all conditions the most unfortunate. Barbarism and ferocity can only be softened in their effects by the distance at which men live from each other; but when their habitations are contiguous, when they reside together, and at the same time suffer their claws and their talons to grow, this situation becomes dreadful, and the isolated life of families and individuals in the midst of woods and forests is infinitely preferable.

Everything then leads us to conclude that public order, this guardian idea that preserves the moral world, is the first condition of every social institution. This principle should ever remain unalterable amidst the arrangements of legislators; but at the same time, it is expected from their science, that they should be able to reconcile it with all the other blessings which men desire, or of which they know the price.

Among these blessings, liberty will, no doubt, be of the first rank; but it requires, more than any other of our enjoyments, to be united to ideas of order and subordination, since, in the midst of a society without discipline, we perpetually see the most despotic authorities spring up on every side.

Why should we dissimulate it? This union of liberty with public order can never be perfectly cemented but in countries which, because of their location or small size, can dispense with maintaining a standing army; for this army is a moving force whose direction may disturb the equipoise established by the legislator. But of all imaginable political projects, the most inconsiderate is that of wishing to remedy the inconveniences, or possible abuse of such a force, by depriving the executive power of the necessary means for preserving interior order, guaranteeing public security, and watching efficaciously over the maintenance of liberty itself. It is creating a certain evil, an evil that will be felt every day, for the sake of avoiding an uncertain danger and which may be more wisely avoided by different means. By the same system of precaution, if we were to govern the world, we should modify the elements and alter their healthy influence and fertile action in order to prevent the vapors of the earth, by raising up into the atmosphere, from producing sometimes terrible thunderstorms.

Is not the responsibility of ministers and other agents of the executive power a real security against the danger of a standing army? Is not the constitutional obligation, imposed on all military commanders, of never employing an armed force in the interior of the kingdom but at the demand of a civil officer, another real precaution against the same danger? Finally, is not this fundamental law by virtue of which no supplies can be raised without the consent of the representatives of the nation, a very effective provision against any ambitious projects of the head of the state? And if the legislative sanction necessary to the collection of the taxes, instead of being renewed in each legislative session, was extended over the space of a year, if the sanction was accompanied with an imposing solemnity, and if the mode of doing it included the announcement that the confidence in the constitutional powers was still entire, this additional precaution would not affect public order at all. In like manner, no inconvenience would result from the adoption in France of another constitutional statute of England, which makes the validity of martial authority and all laws relative to the discipline of the army to depend on the passing annually an act of Parliament, known by the name of the *Mutiny Bill*. Lastly, I will go further and assert that, rather than sacrifice the prerogatives necessary to the civil action of the executive power to the mistrusts and fears caused by the existence of a considerable standing army, it would be better to reduce the extent of that army; for the loss may be supplied by means of the militia; and with a prudent conduct towards foreign powers, a kingdom such as France will never find its tranquillity in danger from their enterprises; but nothing can compensate, in the interior of a vast country, for the annihilation or the extreme reduction of a power whose function it is to protect the property and personal safety of the citizens, and to watch constantly over the maintenance of public order.

Meanwhile I must be allowed to doubt whether, even if we were to completely leave aside the above important considerations and attend only to the interest of liberty, whether it would be politically wise to try to counterbalance the necessity of a standing army in France by degrading and throwing contempt upon the executive power and the majesty of the king? Let us pay attention for a moment to the particular features of an army subjected to the yoke of discipline, features that so strikingly contrast with the philosophical principles of government. We will see that in the first place, the whole secret of military operations lies in the unity and rapidity of their action, and unity and rapidity can only flow from the absolute obedience to a will that may not be questioned. One must still make sure that soldiers will constantly entertain a strong admiration for this organization which subjects the most powerful force to a single will. They are the more attached to the empire of force, because this empire is their particular business; and they will always find themselves somewhat uncomfortable when they will want to connect their habitual ideas and sentiments with the independence of civic opinions. How can it be expected that, when they enter the political clubs, they should be subjected to mixed and complex ideas, and in the camps, to the simplest idea of authority that people have ever conceived of? The Romans, indeed, reasoning like citizens in the forum, were at the same time the most rigid observers of military discipline; but before going out to war, they entered into a solemn engagement implicitly to obey the commands of their general; and we know also the deep impression which the religious obligation of an oath made on their minds. Besides, the political sentiments of the Romans had no connection with ours, nor with those maxims taught in the clubs of Paris and in the provinces. This nation, so renowned in history, was apparently still too close to the infancy of the world to be able to understand the great principle of absolute equality and its utility in a vast empire.

I'm coming closer to my subject, I will confess then that, for a time, it will indeed be possible to introduce the soldiers in the midst of our political clubs; it will be possible to make them share for a moment the ardour of our ruling passions; but when these passions decline, and everyone will draw their feelings from their situation, either we shall have no army able to cope with foreign forces, or this army will be circumscribed by the rules of discipline. And this organization which acquaints the soldiers at every step with the notions of rank and influence, will sooner or later bring back their attention to the most striking of all authorities. The state of obedience, when our obedience can neither be reasoned, nor reasoning, this state is softened for most people only by respect and veneration for him who commands. There will always be a kind of secret affinity between the spirit of an army and the supreme authority of a monarchy; and it is in vain that we may expect, by stripping the monarch of all the prerogatives of his throne, to turn aside his thoughts from the only means by which he may one day restore himself to his original authority. Hence, the necessity of a considerable standing army, so far from offering a plausible motive for rigorously restricting the civil prerogatives of the monarch, this necessity itself should recommend an absolutely contrary proceeding; for the existence of such a large army and the habitual discontent of one of the powers of which the government is constituted will always go badly together and will always be fraught with danger. It was therefore necessary to obviate one of these circumstances, when it was not possible to dispense with the other; and I have shown, from the example of England, that neither the welfare of the state, nor public liberty, nor general happiness required that we should alter, as we have done, the rights, the prerogatives and the dignity of the throne. It is by having overlooked this truth and having followed directly opposite principles that the National Assembly has been the author, so to speak, of its own alarms, and has voluntarily engaged in a system of precautions, in consequence of which it has found itself under the daily necessity of making new sacrifices.

It is not with chains, the offspring of mistrust, that the different branches can be maintained in their constitutional limits; if that were the case, all these chains would be crossed and interwoven around different authorities in such a way that the activity of the administration would always be blocked. Why have we not thought of employing that great and admirable chain, contentment; a chain so flexible, a restraint so pleasing, as to retain every one in his place, without fettering the energies of any? The English, however, have given us an idea of this type of government; policy and morality have equally recommended to them this well-adjusted proportion, by which the king, the people, and their representatives are each satisfied with their share of rights, functions and privileges. Admirable harmony, which at once conceals and displays all the science and wisdom of the legislator!

A very simple reflection might have suggested itself to the mind of the authors of the French constitution. Public opinion had for a long time acquired, under the ancient government, so much vigour and energy, as to be capable of itself of restraining all excesses of authority. What ground then would there have been for reasonable suspicion of the designs of the monarch, if this power of opinion had been reinforced with those political precautions that would not have affected the activity of government? The entire nation, without being constrained or hypocritical, would have served as the rampart of a liberty which would have not demanded the sacrifice of public order; and the admiration of Europe, the universal approbation would have formed a kind of second fortress around our happiness.

CHAPTER XVII

Of Executive Power
as Connected with Liberty

No nation has shown itself more constantly jealous of its liberty than the English, and this is not with them a novel passion; they fought for it when the other nations of Europe did not so much as consider it as a good, and their success in this noble ambition has been consecrated by history. The efforts and triumphs of despotism have taught them to know the supports which they needed, to preserve with safety the rights that were disputed; and the revolutions which have happened, between the Magna Carta, the statutes of Edward and the *Habeas Corpus* act, have but served as lessons to instruct them in the science of freedom. They were only missing the opportunity and power to consider in times of tranquillity the remaining imperfections of their government. This favourable opportunity presented itself after the flight of James II.[1] The representatives of the nation, prior to raising a new king to the throne, made, in a certain sense, a revision of the constitution; and the Bill of Rights, that celebrated act of the revolution in 1688, became the

---

1. James II (1633–1701), King of England from 1685 until 1688, the last Stuart male monarch. In December 1688, he fled for France, and in February 1689 the Parliament offered the Crown to William of Orange. The Bill of Rights signed by William in 1689 became a cornerstone of his rule and of English constitutionalism in general.

complement of English liberty. Finally, as if it were still not enough
for the political fortune of that nation to have applied the observations of a succession of ages and the lessons of their own history
to the harmonious combination of all powers, a particular circumstance further gave the English the means of examining and reflecting whether anything had escaped their restless attention; and, after
a twelve-year experience, they once more revised their work. Queen
Mary died without leaving a successor, and the princess Anne[2] had
just lost her last son. The English then employed themselves to regulate the right of succession to the Crown; they took advantage to
add certain clauses to the convention of 1688, which were favourable
to national freedom; and the solemn act was passed in 1701, a memorable era in the annals of Parliament. Since that epoch, the English
have imagined they enjoyed all the happiness which liberty can procure, and have never spoken of their government without testifying
by some epithet the love which they feel for it. *Our happy constitution*
is their habitual phrase, their familiar expression, not only among
their representatives, but in their distant provinces, at the extremities
of the kingdom and in their towns and villages. Yet to this nation, enlightened by so many events, and whose constitutional vigor is fortified like forest oaks by winds and strong tempests, to this nation
our politicians of yesterday, our cold theorists and our tumultuous
legislators have wanted to pass on their hasty and recent innovations
as a replacement for its old and mature ideas. May heaven eternally
preserve that nation from such an exchange! To me, it would seem a
crime even to conceive this idea. You, who are the ardent propagators
of novelties not yet proved, respect this cradle of liberty; respect the
country in which freedom was born, the country destined perhaps to
remain its sole asylum, if ever your own exaggerations should drive

2. Queen Mary II (1662–1694) was the joint monarch of England, Scotland, and
Ireland with her husband, William of Orange, from 1689 until her death. Daughter
of James II and sister of Mary II, Anne (1665–1714) became queen in May 1707, under the Acts of Union that created what is now known as Great Britain. She was
the sister-in-law of William of Orange and the last monarch of the House of Stuart. Anne's sole surviving child, the Duke of Gloucester, died at the age of eleven in
July 1700.

it from among you. And you, generous nation, you, our first instructors in the knowledge and love of liberty, continue long to preserve the good of which you are in possession! May this freedom be ever united to your grand moral qualities, and may it ever be defended by your prudence as much as by your courage! Alas, the abuse of which we have been guilty will perhaps be more dangerous to freedom than our long indifference. To you it belongs to maintain its renown, and religiously guard that sacred fire which, among us, has but become the instrument of conflagration.

It may, however, be asked whether, since the passing of the Bill of Rights and the Act of the Parliament 1701,[3] the English have not had cause to repent their decision not to limit any further the prerogatives of the executive power, and whether the monarch has not used his means of influence to limit the national freedom? He would have attempted it in vain; for that freedom is under the guardianship of both Houses of Parliament, the peers and the representatives of the people. No law can pass without the joint consent of these branches of the constitution, as well as that of the monarch; and were it possible that all three should agree to effect some essential change in the constitution of the state, they would have to combat the will of the whole nation, which they would never dare to do. Besides, I have already said it, the perfection of the English Constitution does not merely consist in this just combination which secures liberty without being harmful to the action of the government; it has the further peculiar merit of having attached to itself all the powers and orders of the state in support of the established government. Indeed, one of the best guarantees of that constitution is the happiness of all the contracting parties; a happiness which is not speculative, is not theoretical, but has been submitted to the proof of time, that grand test from which reason only can acquire new force.

Some will perhaps alledge that, since the year 1701, changes have been made in the laws of England, whose motive may relate to the influence of the Crown; from which it may be inferred that this influence is too extensive.

3. Also known at the Act of Settlement of 1701, this act made sure that the Crown of England would only go to a Protestant monarch.

The two remarkable examples used or which may be used to support this reasoning are, on the one hand, the lengthening of parliaments from three to seven years, and, on the other hand, the power granted to the king of subjecting military offences to martial law. But if these dispositions can be justified as means of promoting the good of the state, and especially if they do not infringe on freedom, it is not well founded to suppose them proofs of the dangerous influence of the royal prerogatives.

It would be difficult to determine whether the most rational duration of a parliament would be five rather than six years, or six rather than seven; and I have already shown in a preceding chapter the principal inconveniences attendant on the too frequent renewal of legislative assemblies. Those reflections will find here their proper application, but I should avoid to repeat what has so recently been said. Neither is the possibility of continuing the same Parliament for seven years offensive to freedom; it is only the abuse which the king may make of this prerogative. But if liberty in England is sufficiently guarded by those precautions with which it is environed, the privilege of dissolving Parliament, which has been granted to the king, does favour public order without affording any cause of uneasiness.

Let us, however, remember that the long duration of parliaments in England could not be maintained, if the possession of property were not necessary in order to become a member of the House of Commons; for otherwise the number of candidates to this dignity would be so great, as in France, that their impatience would never bear to wait for long; and they would wish to have more frequently the chance of being nominated as representatives of the people. Hence, it may be conceived how a vain nation, three times as populous as England and Scotland combined, is inclined to think as too long the interval of twenty-four months between the periods of elections. The patience of French vanity is visibly exhausted before these two years are about to end. And thus among other unfortunate consequences resulting from that law of the constitution which allows men without property to be elected deputies of the National Assembly, must be listed the frequent renewal of these assemblies, which is the necessary consequence of the multitude of candidates.

I return to the particular subject of this chapter.

The Act of Parliament which, in the year 1718, invested the king of England with the necessary authority for subjecting military crimes to martial law cannot be criticized in the name of freedom. The result was nothing more than greater subordination in the army, and freedom cannot be found in a relaxation of discipline. Such an idea would be a strange one, since it is discipline which prevents the abuse of force. And supposing that the existence of a standing army in a free country would generate a certain anxiety, it would be better to diminish its numbers than to weaken its action.

I have referred to the two bills which, in a remarkable manner, have augmented the royal prerogative posterior to the Bill of Rights and the Act of Parliament of 1701. I now ought to mention that, since the same era, there have been bills evidently unfavourable to this prerogative. I will cite that by which all persons, in possession of offices under the Crown, which have been created since the year 1705, have been disqualified for members of Parliament; and the bill under the present reign, by which all excise and custom house officers, who are nominated by the government, have been deprived of the right of voting for members of Parliament; an act which has evidently restrained the influence of the Crown. The true increase of this influence should be attributed to the progressive increase of taxes, expenses, and colonies; circumstances which, by multiplying the branches of the administration, have increased the number of positions appointed by the monarch. But it has not hitherto been proved that the combined prerogatives of the king have given him the power to infringe, in any respect, on the national freedoms and the laws of the constitution.

These laws are more favourable to freedom than ours and yet, public order has not been sacrificed to them. In England, as in France, we see a national body from which all laws originate and which alone has the right to initiate legislations; a national body which determines all taxation, fixes all expence, examines all accounts, and which annually renders a public statement of the finances; we see there ministers responsible to the nation, and liable to be impeached by this legislative body; we see there the army remains inactive until the moment when the civil magistrates demand its mobilization; and we see there freedom of the press extended to the point where it would be in absolute contradiction with morality. We see there personal freedom secured by a constitutional proscription of all imprisonment, except according to law. We find there the salutary establishment of juries applied not only to criminal but to civil prosecutions. Finally, we see there all the essential foundations of civil and political freedom, such as we have taken them in great part from a nation worthy to serve as an example to others. But this nation has raised two ramparts more than ourselves in favour of that freedom of which she is so jealous. One is the constitutional statute, in virtue of which the discipline, and in some manner the existence of the army, are necessarily maintained by an act of Parliament which must be renewed every year. The other, truly precious, because it is in continual use, is the right granted to every man arrested, or unjustly detained, to sue the civil officer for reparation who has abused his authority. There is no French citizen who would not exchange for this single bulwark of English freedom half the advantages of our constitution; for there are at present in the kingdom so many powers invested with the right of imprisonment, and which is exercised on occasions so trivial that, although the old name of prison has been exchanged for the gentle but new expression of *lieu d'arrestation*,[4] the locks and bars remain just as they were, and the people are terrified at the facility with which departments and districts, municipal officers, sections, justices of the peace, and others, seize on the persons of individuals, and prolong their captivity, without being themselves exposed to any personal danger.

I suppose now that, after these diverse reflections which undoubtedly may be extended further, someone might ask, however, whether it is not true that the National Assembly has invented for the French a freedom superior to that enjoyed in England. We would then be forced to reply that this pretended advantage, this apparent triumph, is entirely composed of the spoils of the executive power and the remains, as it were, of public order. We are obliged to receive as an increase of liberty the new social mobility, the rights of elections constantly renewed, and all the subdivisions of the executive power. We are obliged to receive as an increase of liberty the absolute reign of the lowest class of the people and the displacement of all author-

4. Literally, place of arrest.

ities; we are obliged to receive as an increase of liberty the disregard of all decorum, and a release from those ties which are most necessary for the support of domestic manners; finally, we are obliged to receive as an increase of liberty all the mockeries made of ministers and all those legislative acts which have despoiled the throne of its support, or stripped the monarch of his majesty; nonetheless, an increase of liberty like this has served only to overthrow the balance of government, a balance whose most important goal is the preservation of liberty itself.

Continual attempts have been made to present the defeat of the executive power as a victory gained by liberty. Nor was this conduct devoid of personal motives. The English having discovered and laid with a firm hand all the cornerstones of freedom, it was necessary, in order to surpass them in fame, to open a field for glory bordering upon this. It is easy to confound the total degradation of the executive power with independence, and independence with freedom. And this degradation presented itself as the means for acquiring an absolutely new splendor and glory, a means left, so to speak, by all the preceding legislators entirely in the hands of the National Assembly. But wise men are not to be so misled. They will perceive that the English have applied themselves to support the activity of government, and prevent at the same time its abuses; while we, legislators without any skill, and blindly striking at everything in front of us, have destroyed the power of administration in order to protect ourselves against its mistakes.

I do not therefore know why the National Assembly has been reproached with usurping the functions of this power; for it is absolutely necessary that the only real force established by the Constitution should be put in action and exert itself wherever there is danger. Government must function; obstacles will inevitably arise, and difficulties must be removed; and to use a word which has become constitutional, as there is in administration always *urgency*, the public business cannot wait till the executive power shall have acquired respect and means of acting. Therefore the National Assembly, though it should have no such desire, would be obliged to act and give aid. In vain may ministers cry aloud—*Efficacy to the law, Respect to the law, Homage to the law*. Their too feeble voices would be ill understood, amid the noise of departments, districts, municipalities, national guards, and a whole people put in motion by the word equality.

The National Assembly ought not therefore to be blamed when it is seen to interfere in all things; the fault is in the lawgivers who laid it under the necessity of exercising such power; it is that incomprehensible Constitution which is blameworthy, and which has placed, on one side, a single permanent assembly, the numerous members of which, limited to an existence of two years, need the multiplied labours of the legislative body so that each may play his part; and on the other side, an executive power, without prerogatives, without the means of doing either good or ill, while it is stripped of all exterior splendor, by changes of every kind, which have deprived the throne of majesty and its ministers of respect. Such arrangements could only produce the very effects we witness. What forgetfulness, or what mistake prevented this from being foreseen!

In like manner, after having led the calm and gentle waters of a rivulet, without depth or descent, near an impetuous torrent, uncertain in its course and falling from the mountains in huge waves, it might perhaps be supposed that, by the aid of some magic words, these different streams would ever remain separate.

There exists, no doubt, in the book of the constitution, two powers entirely distinct; but the lack of proportion in their respective strength must inevitably lead to their confusion; and this lack of proportion became inevitable when our lawgivers, as I have shown in the beginning of this work, had so long forgotten both the executive power and the rank it ought to assume in the combination of the Constitutional articles.

It is, however, a maxim which has become almost proverbial, that the union of powers is an attack on the principles of liberty. It is indeed often repeated in a thoughtless manner by those who can give no reason for what they say. But I will not repeat that which all intelligent people already know. I will only remark that the chief objection made against the old form of government related to a union of powers in the hands of the monarch; yet the obstacles he had to encounter in the inconsiderate exercise of these various powers were public opinion, the influence of manners, the opposition of parliaments, the rights of provinces, and, for sometime past, the enlightened resistance of provincial administrations. No doubt, the immoderate power of an assembly composed of national representatives is not so formidable as the despotism of a single individual; but it has inconveniences peculiar to itself, and which ought to be particularly felt by certain characters.

A numerous assembly, when it exercises the executive power, can never act by nuances, and everything that is mild, indulgent, or accomodating to the weaknesses of human beings will ever appear to it effeminate; and if that assembly is composed of legislators, its habitual course of thought will bring it back to general and decided principles. This spirit is most conspicuous in such an administration, in the mode and rigor of its punishments. A collective assembly, obliged to renounce that foresight which prevents faults, that penetration which discovers their origin, that mixture of indulgence and firmness which is better adapted to human beings than to principles, and that prudence which artfully wrestles with difficulties; such an assembly, unacquainted by its legislative capacity with the temporising and modifications which are so often necessary in government, is continually obliged to exhibit itself armed with the exterminating sword: yet the simple union of severity and power, though it may not be despotism yet, presents so lively an image or resemblance of it, that noble minds sometimes find it difficult to endure the spectacle.

There is another consideration which obliges a large assembly to seek for every means of action in the sentiment of fear; for it can neither afford hope, nor promise gratitude. And yet these are the only emotions which influence, with mildness, the conduct of men. An assembly, renewable every two years, can neither observe the successive efforts, nor remember the zeal, nor encourage the obscure talents of individuals. It has many rewards to offer, but candidates for them must arrive at a certain and uncommon degree of perfection, before they can be perceived by, or obtain marks of distinction from such an assembly; at which time public opinion, which grants the highest distinctions, has anticipated its applause. Besides, if the brilliant favors, those mingled with the sentiments of respect, receive additional value from the free and voluntary approbation of the representatives of a nation, it is very different with favours of another kind, and especially with pecuniary rewards, the only ones which can maintain the habitual motion of the administration; they too plainly announce, on the part of those who grant them, an air of superiority; and so far as relates to collective numbers, people love an assembly of benefactors less than a mass of admirers.

Finally, we may be certain that a legislative assembly, whether from the spirit inherent in its functions, the abstract character which it insensibly acquires by its habitual examination of general questions, or the simple progress of opinions and sentiments as existing in large bodies of people; such an assembly, I say, can never conduct, neither with mildness nor with moderation, that part of public business which is understood by the word government. It will soon come to hate the temporising of which it is itself incapable; and it will then incessantly be told of oaths, of public accusers, high national courts, responsible ministers, dismissal from office, death or ignominious punishment, and every other invention of revenge. All the stores of tyranny, so to speak, are displayed to its view, and finds itself obliged to have recourse to it, not from the love of despotism, but to provide itself with the only instruments it can employ, when it quits its legislative functions to seize on those of government. Yet benevolent and wise people are equally offended by this proceeding; and that freedom of sentiment which ought to reign in all hearts is then obliged to be sacrificed to this abstract freedom, this liberty which, having no central point, fills an indefinite space in the fantastic declamations of orators and writers of romance.

There is no real liberty, or at least there is no secure freedom, if there is an authority without balance in the state.[5] And what power can be the counterpoise to the power of an assembly, which combines in itself, not only every legislative right, but every dominion it shall please to assume over internal administration, over foreign affairs as well as over judiciary function? What power can be a counterpoise to the independence of an assembly which, avoiding only those few faults calculated to agitate public opinion, finds itself above censure, and which, by continually calling the attention to new objects forces the oppressed people to think only of the problems of the

---

5. This is the fundamental idea underlying Necker's theory of constitutionalism. For more details, see Grange, *Les Idées de Necker*, 255–331.

day, and seems to stifle by beat of drums their murmurs and complaints? Lastly, what limit can be fixed to the confidence of an assembly which, being renewed every two years, and having accomplished, unrestrained, its momentary reign, far from being subject to any responsibility, suddenly disappears from the scene and, like lightning, disperses itself in invisible particles?

How can we not be terrified by the authority of an assembly which, in a moment and without appeal, decides on the honour, the fortune, and the freedom of citizens; an assembly which, proscribing by a small majority of votes the appearance of opinions presupposed contrary to the sentiments of this majority, thus secures, by its tyranny over the opinions of the people, its despotism over their persons? How can we not be terrified by the authority of an assembly which, on the report of one of its members, and without deigning to hear the accused, or their advocates, fill the prisons with its victims?* Who will not dread the authority of an assembly, ever ready to obey popular opinions, and which afterward employs these very opinions to force the compliance of the monarch, and thus to destroy the feeble dike which the constitution had raised to the omnipotence of the legislative body? Finally, who will not dread the unbounded authority of a collective being which, passing in a twinkling from a living to an abstract nature, has no need of compassion, nor any fear for itself either of censure or condemnation? If a country can be called free which is under the yoke of a power so absolute, in which the secu-

---

* Thus they have lately sent to Orléans the minister for foreign affairs, on an accusation, of which no deputy could give any clear account, so entirely was it composed of subtleties. It resembles the riddle of the Sphinx and is accompanied by equal danger. The minister has not been heard, nor has the diplomatic committee: the moment appeared favourable for the ruin of a prudent man, and it was seized. Never was judgment pronounced in Turkey with so much levity. We have not, they say, passed sentence, we have only issued a decree of accusation. True; but such decrees are followed by imprisonment the end of which is unknown, and which perhaps delivers up a father, a mother, a tender wife, and a whole family, a prey to the most terrifying fears. An accusation therefore is a most severe condemnation, since the consequences are so terrible, and nothing can excuse the haste with which it is carried into effect.

rity of person, the respect for property, and the maintenance of public tranquillity depend on the talent of an orator and on the moment which he may artfully choose for gaining votes; if a country can be called free in which no balance of authority exists, where the executive power is an empty name, where its rights are all imaginary, where the opinions of the wise are no longer listened to, religion is powerless and manners have no influence over the laws; if a government thus composed can be called free, one has no idea of the first principles of social organization.

Again, if the authority exercised by an assembly freed people from every other kind of despotism, its inconveniences would be felt less; but this unparalleled authority is not the only one made possible by the extreme weakness of the executive power. The eighty-three departments, all named by the people, perceive each day more and more two incontestable truths; first, that they have nothing to hope or fear from the government, and that they are generous when they act with good manners towards it; and next, that a numerous assembly, continually mutable, is incapable of watching over them with steady perseverance. Thus, by merely keeping certain terms with it, they will be, whenever they please, absolute masters within their jurisdiction.

It will be asked, what then? They will then resemble republican councils, which govern as well as other councils. But we forget that these councils are situated near the legislative body, and in the centre of the various active and reactive forces, intended to form the complete organization of a government. We likewise forget that the authority of these councils, in small states, is at once guided and moderated by the active superintendance of the whole community.

To this the French constitution offers nothing similar. The departments do not resemble separate states, except by being limited, and have nothing of a republican government left to them but the right of election. They can possess neither laws originating with themselves, nor laws which are guaranted by the various authorities and censors which compose the whole of a constitution, and which may be said to render the principles of order and liberty indigenous. Neither can they have laws appropriate to their manners and customs, nor laws calculated to give them a distinct character; and being obliged to assume the name of some river or some rock, as the distinctive mark of their political existence, they have not even that species of tie which stamps a more interesting designation and which, being applied to the citizens formerly, maintained a common sentiment among them of honour and fame in the provinces. Different indeed from the States of America, which have only joined together their political interests, everything must come to them from the universal regulator of the French empire, such as laws, manners, opinions, taxes, and the whole as well as the details of their internal policy.

We are not, however, free from inquietude when we reflect that several of the departments, thus constituted, are at the distance of two hundred leagues from the sovereign legislature; and we could conceive a just diffidence of their constant subordination, were the National Assembly to persist in neglecting the active mediation of the executive power, and in discrediting the authority which ought to connect the obedience of the people with the abstraction of law. Let there be time enough, and we shall see that, deprived of this imposing mediation, the progressive domination of a single assembly will necessarily favour the absolute empire of the administrators of departments, or the popular chiefs to whom these administrators themselves shall be subject; for they will secure themselves from every kind of particular censure, by pleading responsibility only to that great central authority whose superintendance will not terrify them, and which will always have to deal with them.

We cannot make the tour of a kingdom like France, in a chariot with seven hundred and forty-five wheels; its pace would be too slow and too much embarrassed; more rapid motion is necessary everywhere to maintain order and freedom.

The beginning of all disturbances and insubordinations will elude the attention of a numerous assembly situated in the centre of a vast kingdom. It can neither act suddenly enough, nor discover with sufficient accuracy the first guilty leaders. It receives information when the intricacy of events has already obscured the truth, and when the passions have disfigured all the facts and rendered testimony suspicious. Yet, it will not be less willing to judge both people and things; and its commissioners, to whose reports alone it will listen, becoming its sole guides, it cannot, except by chance, guard itself against the highest forms of injustice, or the most dangerous forms of imprudence.

We continually find that the limits of the different political powers are fixed by laws, inherent both in the nature of these powers, and in the first principles of reason and morality. No doubt, they can be extended or tightened, according to the scale of a theoretical government; this can be done in system, or in revery; but when the social impulse is given, and when this immense rotation ought finally to move by itself, the merit of proportions discovered by a long chain of observations will then be perceived; and people will regret, but too late, that more respect had not been paid to experience, and that her noble origin should not have been discovered under a garb worn and tattered by time.

Finally, and this shall be my last reflection, I ask the legislators of France, from what motive, while following unconstrained their system of innovation, have they deprived the departments of the inestimable advantage of forming themselves separately, and then no doubt in more extensive proportions, into distinct states, united like those of America by a political, financial and commercial federation, of which the monarch would have been the hereditary chief? From what motive did the Constituent Assembly, having released itself from all ties, deprive the various sections of France of the inestimable advantage of each concurring in the passing of their laws, with all the plenitude of their own consent, instead of subjecting their individual accomodations to the hazard of a decision by a majority of votes given by the deputies of the whole kingdom? Why did the National Assembly deprive these same sections of the right of fixing their own legislative constitution, their forms of administration, their order of judicature, their ecclesiastical regulations, and their fiscal system? Why have they not been permitted to possess each a legislative body, and to contain within themselves that balance of powers which guarantees order and freedom? Why have they been forced to yield up even the particular titles in which the inhabitants formerly gloried, and which continually recalled to their mind the fame of their native country or the high deeds of their ancestors? Lastly, I ask the lawgivers of France, what was the motive for so much hardship imposed on all the ancient provinces of the kingdom? I shall no doubt be answered that the intention was, by mingling every interest, and by a more intimate federation, to secure more fully peace within and power without. But while they do well to fix so high a value on these two social conditions and political advantages, and while to obtain them they have not scrupled to demand, from every section of the kingdom, the sacrifice of their most essential interests; how could they resolve to render this sacrifice ineffectual, by weakening the power destined to be the protector of internal order, the tie of public force, and the moderator of all hostile passions, amidst an immense political society, regulated and directed by one sole law?

CHAPTER XVIII

Whether Absolute Equality Is a Necessary Condition of Liberty

The watch-word in France, at this moment, is equality; and upon the faith of a small number of sectarians and their commentators, it is regarded as an established axiom that without absolute equality, there can be no liberty, and that this equality is the fundamental idea, the true spring of the French constitution. The architects of that constitution will also tell to whoever wants to listen to them that the principle of quality was the polar star by which all their labours were guided and of which they never lost sight. Therefore, in order to enter into the discussion of this subject on an equal footing with them, it is necessary to begin by annihilating the advantage they would like to derive from their steadiness of opinion and the accord between their earliest ideas and all their subsequent legislative reflections.

We know the date of birth of this opinion on absolute equality, the period when it first made its appearance among us; there was a kind of artifice in the attempt to connect it with the words of the *Declaration of Rights* which says: *Men are born and remain equal in rights.* The same phrase may be used to order the equalization of all properties. Moreover, when the first article of the philosophical *Declaration of the Rights of Man* was adopted by the National Assembly and became the general topic of conversation, it was objected by some that the people might construe the principle into absolute equality; to which others replied that such an interpretation was too absurd to be presumed.

The rigorous principle of absolute equality did not take birth till the epoch of 19 June 1790, and upon the passing of the decree suppressing all orders, titles and liveries.[1] The attachment of the Assembly to this innovation was at that time so feeble and wavering, that it is probable it would have modified its decree, if the king had adopted the critical memoir upon the subject which I read in the council;[2] and in support of this opinion, I might cite the well-known sentiments of various members of the Assembly, ardent admirers of liberty and the constitution. Nor should it be forgotten that, when the memoir I have just mentioned was made public, a committee was nominated by the Assembly to revise the decree of 19 June; but the opinion in favour of this law having insensibly gained ground, the committee never tried to fulfill its mission, or at least never issued a report, and the Assembly did not think proper to remind it of its mission.

Let us examine now whether, prior to this epoch, the principle of absolute equality, regarded as the true spring of the French constitution, had ever entered into the imagination of our legislators, or appeared in any of their deliberations. There is not a single debate of the National Assembly that announces it, or that contains the most distant allusion to it. The proper opportunity for bringing forward a principle, without which it was affirmed there could be no liberty, this natural occasion was undoubtedly when the constitutive articles were drafted, articles generally known and presented to the king at the same time with the declaration of rights.

I would cite another memorable period when honor would have

1. On June 19–20, 1790, the Constituent Assembly passed an important decree, abolishing the nobility and noble titles in France. Among other things, the decree stipulated: "No one whosoever shall use or be addressed by the titles of prince, duc, comte, marquis, vicomte, vidame, baron, chevalier, messire, ecuyer, noble or any other similar title. Every French citizen must use only the real surname of his family. He may no longer wear livery or cause it to be worn or possess armorial bearings. In church, incense will be burned only to honour the deity and will not be offered to anyone, be he never so high. No body or individual will be addressed by the titles monseigneur and meisseigneurs nor by those of excellence, altesse, eminence or grandeur." (http://alphahistory.com/frenchrevolution/decree-abolition-nobility-1790/).

2. The full text of Necker's memoir can be found in *Oeuvres Complètes de M. Necker*, ed. Auguste de Staël (Paris: Treuttel and Würtz, 1821), vol. 7, 520–31.

dictated to the deputies of the Assembly the open avowal of the principle of absolute equality, had that principle really been their original thought and the fundamental idea of their legislative initiatives. That moment was the famous night of the fourth of August,[3] when they were so content with the sacrifices proposed by the nobility and clergy, that they received them with the liveliest satisfaction, with loud and universal acclamation, with the most touching enthusiasm and expansion of heart, which consistently increased to a point, that it was at last unanimously decreed that the remembrance of such a happy day should be consecrated by a *Te Deum* and perpetuated by a medal. Now I ask, had the design been formed of reducing all ranks of men to the same level, would there not have been something perfidious and dishonourable in these demonstrations of joy and gratitude on the part of the commons? Should not their language then have been: *These are the sacrifices you offer us; we want much more than that?*

How many discourses also, delivered by the most distinguished speakers of that Assembly, could still confirm the truth of my claim! But I prefer to cite the exact words of a decree. It is the one from 11th of August, therefore posterior to the period designated as the era of the revolution; we can read in it these words, in article XI:

> All citizens are admissible to employments and dignities of every kind, ecclesiastical, civil and military, no profession being allowed as a disqualification.[4]

---

3. The decree of August 4, 1789, put an end to the feudal system in France, with its feudal dues, tithes, and privileges; it was followed by a week of intense debates leading to the decree of August 11. See François Furet, "Night of August 4," in *A Critical Dictionary of the French Revolution*, 107–14.

4. The decree of August 11, whose principal author was Duport, was passed a week after the famous night of August 4. It confirmed the total destruction of the feudal regime, and abolished the sale of offices and all dues involving personal servitude. Among the abolished rights were the tithes of all kinds along with the private rights attached to various bodies. As a result, all citizens became equally subject to the same general laws and eligible to the same offices and dignities, as stipulated by Article XI quoted by Necker here. For more details, see Furet, "Night of August 4," in *A Critical Dictionary of the French Revolution*, 110–12.

These last words evidently suppose the existence and preservation of the nobility.

It would still be easy also to prove, by a multitude of small examples, that absolute equality, that pretended cornerstone of the French constitution, ought to be included among the principles to which the National Assembly came in the course of its deliberations, and which was conveyed to it, like so many others, by the tide of popular opinion.

Now, regardless of its date and origin, let us examine the principle itself and see whether this absolute equality is really a necessary condition of political liberty, as so many repeat it today, without having at all reflected on this subject.

Such a doctrine can be advanced only in direct opposition to the lessons of experience; for the example of England proves diametrically the reverse, and it might easily be shown that, in a great kingdom, there can be neither public order nor general liberty with an absolute levelling of all ranks.

Nonetheless, it is proper to say something regarding the type of gradation which must be considered necessary in a monarchy, when that monarchy is joined to a free constitution. It is not the separation of the nation into two orders, the nobility and the commoners, that can serve any useful purpose in such a form of government; still less is it a type of nobility that might be purchased with money, as it was once the case in France. There is nothing like this in England. The only type of gradation necessary in a free and monarchical constitution is the one of which that kingdom furnishes the model. This gradation requires only the existence of a body whose dignity is secured by its union with the general political body, whose splendor accompanies the throne, and whose rank represents a sort of transition from the immense multitude of the people to the singular unity of a king and a crown. The effect of such an intermediary or middle power derives its value merely from opinion, or, if you will, from imagination; yet this does not prevent it from being the absolute condition of the respect we have for the supreme rank, a respect without which kings would become useless and the spirit of monarchy would no longer exist.

We can see how previously, with warlike nations living, as it were, almost entirely in the midst of camps, the gradation of rank was not necessary to the consideration of the supreme head of the state; military discipline was sufficient to his authority, because this discipline was itself the strongest and most expressive of all hierarchies. We can also see how the caliphs of the East can maintain in their subjects a respectful and awe-inspiring idea of their grandeur without the aid of any gradation of ranks. Shut up within their palaces, and having no communication but with their visir or their slaves, their mysterious withdrawal serves to picture them to the multitude as an unknown power, which the eye is unable to circumscribe, and of which a vague imagination magnifies all the dimensions. And provided that in those ceremonies in which they appear in public, a triumphal pomp attends them, and that, at certain intervals, their authority is announced, like the explosion of thunder, by striking acts of vengeance, the minds of the people are held in a continual state either of astonishment or of respect.

The examples that I have just mentioned bear no relation to the temperate monarchies of Europe. It is not in the midst of camps, nor in the obscurity of a seraglio, that the supreme chiefs of such governments are called to reside. The civil administration constitutes the essential part of their duties, and they can reign neither by the sword of the military nor by a blind enthusiasm. It is therefore necessary, with us, that the authority and the magic influence of opinion, so indispensible to him who is appointed to watch over the execution of the laws in a vast empire, should be differently secured; it is necessary that the founder of a social and constitutional order should skilfully unite to the real prerogatives of the monarch, the exterior of dignity and splendor which must constitute the supreme authority, and should enable him to render those important services that are expected from him.

Next we should consider whether the majesty of the throne can continue to exist when no gradation of rank prepares the people to respect the imposing supremacy of the head of the nation; whether the majesty of the throne can exist where the king appears alone and isolated, surrounded by a large mass of people, placed on the same level and boasting loudly of their perfect equality.

Respect is a disposition of mind that needs education, and the ties of habit are equally necessary to it. It is with this sentiment as with every other feeling, and there is a secret connection between the deference we show to a superior and that which we ourselves expect from men placed below us in the social order. Thus, when by the absolute destruction of all ranks, the respect for the royal dignity, being supported by no personal interest, by no habit of opinion, would cease to have force, it would no longer be felt and would shortly appear foreign to our new manners. A monarch, a throne, a crown, would astonish us without imposing respect, were we led to the idea of such supremacy by no gradation, no intermediary steps. We should be certain that our perspective would be changed, if ever that levelling scheme without any example in the history of mankind, designated by the name of equality, should establish and perpetuate itself, and entirely change the moral foundation of France.

There exists but one being in the universe whose supreme majesty we can constantly adore, without the intervention of any idea between his power and our weakness, between his greatness and our insignificance. But in the case of God, his very infinity and absolute omnipresence bring him, as it were, into contact with every particle of our mind and our soul, and thus furnish a sort of perpetual ladder by which we may ascend to himself through our thought; and such is the nature of this spiritual conversation, that the further we advance and the closer we get to the sovereign master of the universe, the higher is our respect for Him.

If we search, under another point of view, for another proof of the importance of gradations and the various applications of this truth, we shall find it in the religious philosophy of paganism. That philosophy, having despoiled the first author of nature of his spiritual essence, and having continually represented him under a corporeal form, it felt at the same time the necessity of captivating the respect of men by a hierarchy of deities which, descending from the sovereign of the skies to the mysterious powers of the earth, aggrandized, in the eyes of mortals, the God whom a fabulous religion had dared to assimilate to their nature.

The reader will pardon these digressions; they are, in my opinion, not unimportant; it is the characteristic feature of great truths to exist everywhere under a variety of forms; and this august quality has always fascinated my attention in every moral or philosophical investigation to which my thoughts have been directed.

But to proceed further with my subject in a more direct manner, when I look forward to the effect that will be produced on the majesty of the throne by the suppression of rank, I behold a whole people, weaning itself daily from all attachment to every kind of superiority, and insensibly arriving at the disavowal of the only one that remains; I behold a whole people, carried away by the waves of equality, approaching so near the monarch, that the throne, that last vestige, no longer strikes with awe; and who will shortly, perhaps, consider it as an irregularity in that general levelling plan of which they have become such admirers. Furthermore, I behold a nation, always extreme in its sentiments, exacting of the king of the French the forms and manners of a private individual, and demanding, as a proof of his patriotism or his love for the constitution, that he should abandon his exterior dignity to the point of forgetting his greatness. But let him guard himself against giving in to these ephemeral desires. It would be sacrificing to the popularity of a moment that empire over the imagination which constitutes a part of his power and is one of the instruments of his authority. What then, it will be said, was Louis IX not respected when he dispensed justice at the foot of an oak? Was Henry IV[5] not respected when, in an edict of the Hôtel-de-Ville, he gave himself the title of first citizen of Paris, or when he partook of a rustic repast at the table of a peasant? Yes, certainly, they were both respected; but it is easy to perceive that it was the brilliant contrast of their omnipotence that gave to the simplicity of their conduct its greatest lustre. In like manner, we admire Catinat[6] for joining in the games of his soldiers; he did it after a victory. But when, by a chance of constitution, a monarch

5. Louis IX (1214–70), King of France, also known as Saint Louis.

6. Henri IV (1553–1610), King of France from 1589 to 1610 (also King of Navarre from 1572 until his death). He restored Paris as a great city and was a major patron of arts.

7. Nicolas Catinat (1637–1712) was a popular French military commander and Marshal of France under Louis XIV. His memoirs were published posthumously in 1819.

has been divested of his greatest prerogatives, and when the rights of the nation have been increased in every way, the general interest requires that no popular familiarity may ever jeopardize the respect due to his rank and his person. How many ideas are connected with that respect, and how many realities depend on it! Either we must renounce monarchy, or invest the monarch in all the imposing attributes which constitute his dignity; this condition is impossible to fulfil when all ranks have been entirely annihilated. Let us affirm then, to sum up, that there can be no liberty without public order, no public order without executive power, no executive power, in a great kingdom, without the support of royal majesty, and this majesty cannot subsist without an intermediary rank between the throne and the people. Thus, the system of equality, when carried to an extreme, instead of being favourable to liberty, in a monarchical government, appears to be diametrically the opposite.

Now, after such refined considerations, should one descend to say that the existence of two, three, or four hundred peers of the realm, in such a country as France, would be so limited a superiority that it would interfere very little, in my view, with the vanity of twenty-six millions of men? Must we be obliged to negociate with such a petty and ridiculous sentiment, when it has been already proved that the idea of a king cannot subsist alone, that we must have a gradation of steps leading from the vast plains of equality to his supreme rank; that these abstract considerations, these apparent fictions constitute the very essence and soul of a monarchy; and that a great country, whose law and administration are one, needs this type of government? Nonetheless, since in all its excesses and extravagance, vanity must be considered as the origin of all our misfortunes, since we see this vanity and recognize it, in every point of our system, through the heroic mask under which it hides itself, let us represent to it with mildness, and if necessary, with humility, that the sentiment of superiority arising from holding a political office is of a totally different nature than the pride inspired by noble rank. The latter is compelled by many artifices to maintain that respect which philosophy refuses to it; the former is clearly defined and does not need to resort to any illusions. The demarcation line for political superiorities is set by national interest; and the country has a part in all the homage that is paid to those dignities which it has created or which have been invented for the good of the state. The peers of England are created by the king; but they know very well that the reality of their rank depends upon the preservation of the constitutional laws established in their country. They never pursue with restlessness an imaginary opinion, but cultivate with tranquility an opinion which is part of the entire structure of government.

Everything is moral in these political dignities, everything is in accord with the general utility; and it is not possible to confound them with those distinctions which benefit from others without paying back anything in return.

Nonetheless, are we allowed to judge and weigh the important issues to which all these reflections are attached by using the capricious criterion established by vanity?

I will allow myself to add only one more observation in the same direction. People were right to stand up against the multitude of titles that existed previously in France. But the indignation which was suddenly felt at hearing the words counts and chevaliers did not limit itself to appellations which nobody was obliged to use; it looked further to the ideas of superiority perpetuated by distinctions of birth. Yet, in spite of our efforts, these ideas will always reappear in a thousand disguises; and the tone, the forms, and the manners will serve as a supplement to the public registers. Therefore the Assembly would have been more successful in reaching its goal if, by imitating the English and creating a House of Peers, it had raised those giant oaks which smother all smaller shrubs instead of attempting to extirpate by fire and sword that vegetation whose nature is to be perpetually reborn.

As I am speaking here of the interests of vanity, I must also recall an observation I made in my last publication,[8] that the institution of a House of Peers would have given new splendor, in the eyes of Europe, to the quality of French citizen. Moral esteem, subjected to the same laws as relief in physical objects, will never fit with a vast uniformity. Vanity had an ingenuous idea to associate the numerous rep-

8. Necker refers here to *Sur l'administration de M. Necker par lui-même* (1791).

resentatives of a great people to a class of men resplendent by their dignity. In vain may we seek to supply this effect upon the imagination by becoming stiff, by addressing to one another the exhortation *to assume a becoming loftiness and an imposing attitude*, and by employing various bombastic phrases which prove much more clearly the efforts of vanity than its success. I remember having once heard a witty fellow say: For my part, I despise the public, above all because I am one of them myself. An interesting lesson may be inferred here from these words; they teach us that we will always need some political contrivance in order to institute respect for the multitude and their numerous deputies; that monotony must be broken in a certain way if we want to establish, in the midst of a large political society, a system of reverential obedience which can impress and keep its constant hold upon the imagination.

These skillful contrivances are of no use in small countries; not because perfect equality is established there, but because the distinctions based on merit are sufficient, where the state is small enough, to make these gradations visible; and as in small spaces all the public actions can easily be brought under the laws of reason, the government borrows from this august authority all the influence it needs. Neither of these circumstances exists in large states; they must therefore be organized in a different way. But when people have not yet received the lessons of experience, or when they disdain them, they foresee only in a faint manner the disparities which result from differences in size and number; they take them for mere variations of one principle, whereas, in the social system, they form, if I may say so, two entirely opposed things.

We may then affirm without hesitation, and after having examined the question in all its different relations, that the principle of equality cannot be adapted to a vast country, subjected to a single law and a single authority. Either this principle will necessarily destroy monarchy and its government, or monarchy will bring back gradations of rank. In instituting therefore this sort of government, absolutely indispensable to France, an intermediary body ought at the same time to have been established between the throne and the people, and that body ought to have been judiciously united, as in England, to the political constitution of the state.

I would also wish that someone should explain to us how the heredity of the throne can be reconciled with the destruction of every species of intermediary ranks between the monarch and the people, and with the annihilation or weakening of all prerogatives which are the essence of royal majesty. This hereditary succession, which leaves to the accidents of nature the personal qualities of the prince, cannot subsist without the perpetuity of those sentiments of respect inherent in his supreme rank; and it is the uninterrupted transmission of these sentiments that constitutes, in a political state, the true hereditary succession. Hence it follows that, to preserve the crown in the same family by right of primogeniture, this disposition so important to public tranquility cannot be separated from the conditions necessary to secure to the royal authority a respect independent of the personal worth of the monarch.

Men capable of reflection could easily understand the various truths I have presented; but from the moment when legislators, who were called upon to instruct their contemporaries, chose rather to enlist themselves under the standard of all the passions and to pursue their fortune in the applauses of the hour, they perceived that, in their attempt to establish perfect equality as a maxim of policy, morality, and philosophy, they were going to find many supporters; for there is no man in the daily course of civil life who does not regard a superior as an inconvenient being. As soon as they were allowed to transform this petty sentiment into a principle of government, the multitude were bound to listen with enthusiasm to these new lessons. The crowd cannot analyze a complex truth; the many can do no more than associate themselves, by an effort of feeling, to the opinions that are taught to them. Thus those who feel destined to lead the many attempt no more than to present to them one or two ideas, and they flatter their arrogance by telling them that the whole science of government is to be found in the development of a single axiom. It is thus that, in the name of equality, they have convinced them to believe that the most free, the happiest government in the world, the government of England, is tyrannical. It is thus that, in the name of equality, they have taught them to apprehend danger from a division of the legislative body into two houses, an institution that had been adopted in our time even by a republic, the United States of America. It is thus that they have inspired the people with an irrational contempt for all intermediary ranks, philosophically indispensable to support of royal majesty. It is thus that, in the same name of equality, they will order, when they please, a partition of landed property, and from one levelling to another, they will establish by their plan of uniformity the most complete anarchy. But look at the universe, and see whether gradations and distances have been rejected by its wise architect: on the contrary, it is by them, it is by a general system of subordination, that everything holds its place, and that the general harmony of the world is maintained.

Hear the words of a celebrated writer of antiquity:

> The Supreme Being separated the elements to place them at peace. Fire, the lightest of all, was sent to shine in the regions of heaven; the air had the second place, and next came the earth suspended by the laws of gravitation in the midst of the abyss; water had only the fourth rank, yet was it to constitute the limits beyond which the world might no longer pass. Thus did the author of nature, by assigning their different situations to the elements, organize the universe.*

* Hanc Deus & melior litem Nature diremit:
Nam coelo terras, & terris abscidit undas;
Et liquidum spisso secrevit ab aëre coelum.
Quae postquam evolvit, coecoque exemit acervo,
Dissociata locis concordi pace ligavit.
Ignea convexi vis & sine pondere coeli
Emicuit, summâque locum sibi legit in arce.
Proximus est aër illi levitate, locoque:
Densior his tellus, elementaque grandia traxit,
Et pressa est gravitate sui. Circumfluus humor
Ultima possedit, solidumque coercuit orbem.
                    OVID. METAMORPH. *Lib.* I.[9]

9. "God—or kindlier Nature—composed this strife; for he rent asunder land from sky, and sea from land, and separated the ethereal heavens from the dense atmosphere. When thus he had released these elements and freed from them the blind heap of things, he set them each in its own place and bound them fast in harmony.

Oh! how happy is it for the human race that our political Quixottes are unable to dissolve this harmonious system and make its elements similar! Before the end of the year they would renew the ancient chaos; and, to complete the unfortunate catastrophe, the memory of their genius will perish with them and with us.

The fiery weightless element that forms heaven's vault leaped up and made place for itself upon the topmost height. Next came the air in lightness and in place. The earth was heavier than these, and, drawing with it the grosser elements, sank to the bottom by its own weight. The streaming water took the last place of all, and held the solid land confined in its embrace." Ovid, *Metamorphoses*, Books I–VIII, trans. Frank Justus Miller and G. P. Goold, Loeb Library (Cambridge, Mass.: Harvard University Press, 1994), pp. 4–5.

CHAPTER XIX

The French Constitution Has
Introduced the Greatest Inequalities

Distinctions which consist in mere appellatives of convention do not constitute in the social order upsetting distinctions and inequalities; in order to offend the vanity of some and flatter the pride of others, it is necessary that these signs of distinction remind of real advantages or present the image of certain honorary rights consecrated by opinion.

Inequalities may therefore exist, susceptible of no precise designation, and which yet may be more burdensome and oppressive than those decorations and titles which have excited such a great jealousy. I shall explain how the French Constitution has multiplied this type of inequalities and show how it has managed to do it.

The ancient lawgivers of nations, in order to balance the terrible effects of the power of numbers, a power always possessed by the people, placed the moral force in the hands of governments, and tried to restrain in this way the rise of passions engendered by ignorance and misfortune. We have subverted this prudent equipoise, have at once destroyed the authority of administration, weakened the empire of wisdom, and after consecrating, by an abstraction, the sovereignty of the people, have conferred on it every species of power. At sight of this new master, every one has inquired by what means he was to be seduced, and what address was necessary to obtain the first rank in his court. To obtain from him a municipal office, a seat on the bench of judgment, a church dignity, and to contest these places with an infinite crowd of competitors, was too petty a sphere of ambition. A universal passion was excited of directing the opinions of the despot and of influencing his sentiments. Some have nourished his suspicions, others inspired him with jealousy and distrust, and all justified his rage. The daring partisans of sedition, eager above all others to exercise their sway, have held consultations at taverns, or have mixed with the groupes which assemble in public places; and there, according to their pleasure, according to the ruling passion of the day, have irritated the people against the king, against the queen, against foreign monarchs, against ministers, against magistrates, against every man holding rank in the social order, and lastly directed its fury against property and all those who possess it. At the same time, another class of people, who had the ambition to achieve a greater influence and the ambition of a more extensive domination, have composed pamphlets, suited to the taste and understandings of every class of society; and mixing, in their account of events, the most libertine maxims and most dangerous principles, they have disseminated through the kingdom a spirit of independence and irreligion. They have given the name of fanatism to piety, the name of vexation to the laws of order, the name of tyranny to the most feeble authority, and the still more terrible name of aristocracy to every opinion contrary to their own doctrines and teachings. And among these men, some, writing their pages with the dagger's point, have knowingly calumniated the most virtuous citizens and denounced them without scruple to the vengeance of a blind people.

Such are the new authorities which have risen in the state, such are the different superiorities which the constitution has produced, such are the actual inequalities which have replaced the vain distinctions, the suppression of which has been celebrated with so much ostentation. What titles shall we invent to express the supremacy of those who can, with impunity, stir up the people against the opinions and persons of public men; who can, with impunity, draw insults upon the monarch and all who are connected with him; who can, with impunity, cut down my woods, ravage my estate, set fire to my castle; who can, with impunity, recommend a traveller to popular outrages, or can themselves constrain a peaceable citizen, by menaces, to fly his paternal abode, and become an exile from his family? What titles also shall we invent to express the supremacy of those who have engrossed exclusively to themselves the public ear, who by their daily publications occupy the whole of the few precious moments that peasants and artisans can devote to reading; who thus govern the people by lies, inspire them with whatever passions and sentiments their base purposes may require, and insensibly weaken in them every tie necessary to the maintenance of social subordination? Yes, what titles shall we invent for all these powerful people? Oh! let us call them dukes, archdukes, princes and viceroys; let us promise them solemnly to treat them with the utmost deference, provided they will engage in return to leave our property and our lives secure, and to respect morality and religion, and we shall make a happy exchange, we shall sign, at the present moment, the best of all possible contracts. For, I repeat it, these are the masters which have been given to us by a constitution that has placed the sceptre in the hands of the demagogues of the multitude; this is the terrible aristocracy which that constitution has generated. And yet, we dare to talk about equality! We dare to boast of our so-called system of equality that places everyone upon the same level! It is true the superiorities which heretofore existed are no longer to be seen; but those which have succeeded them are a thousand times more terrible. We have destroyed the parchments which conferred on the ancient chevaliers of France their honorary prerogatives; but we have given commissions of audacity and impunity to men strangers to every generous sentiment. We have taken down the weathercocks upon the castles of the nobles, but we have introduced on all sides the torches of incendiaries. We have destroyed the pigeon-houses of lords of manors, but we have populated the plains with bloodthirsty tyrants. We have broken to pieces the sumptuous tombs that covered the ashes of the dead, but we have sealed, we have surrounded with a dreadful silence the abysses destined for the burial of the living.

Menace has been everywhere substituted for the mild law of respect, and sanguinary vengeance for the efficacious interposition of a respected authority. Government has been sacrificed to the fear of despotism, and there has immediately sprung up a multitude of tyrants who, celebrating hypocritically the charms and blessings of equality, have extended their yoke over the property, over the persons, over the opinions, and over the consciences of people. Meanwhile, they are not descended, as one might be led to imagine, from the land which Cadmus sowed with the teeth of serpents;[1] but they owe their origin to those fatal germs of anarchy, which have corrupted the vegetation of the moral soil of France, and rendered it prolific in malevolent demons and savage spirits.

1. Necker refers here to Cadmus's slaying of the serpent-like dragon, the son of Ares, the god of warfare. At the advice of Athena, Cadmus got the teeth of the serpent and planted half of them in the ground; after that, several fierce warriors appeared out of the ground and a ferocious battle ensued among them. Five of them survived and subsequently submitted to the authority of Cadmus whom they helped found the city of Thebes.

CHAPTER XX

Concluding Reflection on the Parallel
of the Two Constitutions
# of France and England

The National Assembly, which wanted to obtain glory at whatever price and which now finds itself so confused, had an open path before it to achieve this goal, the first object of its wishes. What a splendid role it could have played in the middle of nations if, when occupied with drafting a code of laws for a great people, it had concentrated its scattered ideas around a center and had ranged itself, in a certain way, around the most distinguished political constitution of Europe, with the noble design of taking it for a model in all the measures that could have been suitable to France and which had not been contradicted by experience! The English, for it will be presumed that it is of their government I speak, would themselves have been eager to point out the corrections which their political system needed; and every nation of the earth, attentive to the scrutiny which would have preceded the most august of adoptions, would have been convinced that it was their interests that were discussed in advance, since a similar political liberty, once established among two rival nations, the first nations in Europe, this double example of liberty without disorder would have acquired such an authority that, forcibly conveying with it the tide of opinions, would have influenced the destiny of the world.

Every one of us ought to have fallen prostrate at the feet of legislators who would have adopted this plan. Would a sage and prudent spirit of imitation have injured their renown? No; the whole earth would have rendered homage to the morality of their intentions and the happy outcome of their generous cares. What ingenious novelties, what traits of originality could have been compared with such a success! It is always by the outcome of their labours that the wisdom of legislators is appreciated. In the exercise of their power, they address an immensity of interests, and it is impossible to separate them from the latter, or to give them a renown apart from the misfortune or happiness of nations.

Furthermore, not every sort of ambition or glory is proper to a collective body. The honors of a primitive metaphysics can never become the common property of any assembly; for nobody supposes that the great number could penetrate into these sanctuaries, where the space shrinks as one goes up; and it is for this reason, among many others, that success is the only type of glory that can suffice and be shared by many.

The legislators of France then ought to have surrounded themselves with positive and practical ideas; they should have attached themselves to the realities of the human life. Many travelers had described the long road that begins with the origin of things, and the National Assembly did not have to take the same road to bring it to our knowledge. The Assembly would have better informed us and would have served us more effectively if, with the English Constitution in their hand, the deputies had asked themselves openly and publicly: What additions can we make to this constitution to secure more firmly public order? What changes can be made to its different authorities to perfect the system of liberty? What new institutions shall we have to prepare in order to strengthen more effectively the influence of morality on the people? These questions would have led to others; the executive power, instead of being totally forgotten, would have been scrutinized in all its parts, and it would have been discovered whether, among the prerogatives conferred on the English monarch, there were any that the maintenance of public order and the activity of government might dispense with. It would perhaps have been seen that, from the size of the standing army, the number of promotions in the power of the monarch ought to be limited. It would perhaps have been seen that, in a kingdom as vast as France, collective administrations were attended with considerable advantage, but that it was indispensible to subject them to the executive power by all the ties and connection which constitute true dependence. It would perhaps have been seen that these administrations were capable of enlightening, by regular communication, and even of restraining, within certain limits, the discretion entrusted to the authority of the sovereign. It would perhaps have been seen that a middle term, between the short life of our legislatures and the long duration of English parliaments, was advisable. It would perhaps have been seen, that the number of peers of the realm ought to have been limited, and their nomination subjected to certain conditions. The unequal distribution of the rights of representation might have been prevented by the judicious plan which has been devised by the Assembly. In like manner, turbulent elections, of which England often furnishes examples, might have been remedied by the same means that are employed at present, or others of greater efficacy. Finally, without trampling upon those important principles, or neglecting those powerful springs which constitute together this connection, so difficult to obtain, between order and liberty, between the firmness of authority and the moderation of power, it would have been easy to introduce the various amendments upon the English Constitution which truth and experience might have recommended. What a superb monument we would have raised, if we had not wished that everything should be new or should wear the appearance of novelty! if we had not wished every stone in the edifice to bear some characteristic mark of our imagination and be dated with the era of our genius! Alas, what a great injury has our vanity done us! There was a government in which tranquillity, confidence, public order, and the regular movement of administration were united to the most perfect civil and political freedom; and we have instituted a government in which disorder is everywhere prevalent; in which all the world commands and no one obeys; in which liberty is only a simple device, morality a mere maxim, and happiness a vain boast. But before I fix my attention more particularly upon the sad effects of our faults and our errors, before I take a last view of the state of France, I would consider in a new light the important subject we have undertaken to examine.

AN

ESSAY

ON THE

TRUE PRINCIPLES

OF

EXECUTIVE POWER

IN

GREAT STATES

TRANSLATED FROM THE FRENCH OF
M. NECKER

And if each system in gradation roll,
Alike essential to the amazing whole;
The least confusion but in one, not all
That system only, but the whole must fall.
POPE's *Moral Epistles*

VOL. II

LONDON
PRINTED FOR G. G. J. AND J. ROBINSON,
PATERNOSTER-ROW
MDCCXCII

The Constitution of the United States, as Connected with the Subject of This Work

America Does Not Require so Considerable an Executive Power as France

I should but imperfectly fulfil the end I proposed to myself, were I to confine my attention to a comparison between the constitution of England and the new government of France. Moreover it would gratify the wishes of our political metaphysicians to let them enjoy, untroubled, the glory which they desire the most, that of agreeing in principles with the legislators of America. This pretension may be just, and may yet be no conclusive argument in favour of their work; for even adopting all the speculative opinions of an ancient or modern legislator, we may nevertheless execute poorly what he has executed well, if we avoided imitating at the same time his genius and his prudence. These two qualities are the only ones which apply equally to all the infinite diversity of circumstances, the only ones which can be brought into general use, in a science composed entirely of links and connections; and such is certainly the science of social order. Thus the wise and enlightened legislator who, on a new continent and far from the errors of the old world, would adopt the principle of perfect equality and place an implicit confidence in the sole empire of the law; this same legislator would change his thoughts, were he to find himself amidst our French manners and in the most ancient country in Europe as to its customs, wealth, and knowledge.

Our National Assembly, or if you please, its supreme guides, deceived themselves, therefore, in supposing that they had taken possession of all the legislative virtue of the sage Americans, when they had only embraced certain general ideas, carried them to extremes, and applied them forcibly to a nation totally unprepared by its character or disposition for their reception. While trying to appropriate to ourselves the political philosophy of the peaceable inhabitants of a new hemisphere, we should have extended further our acquisitions; we should have taken possession of their houshold gods, their morality, their religious spirit, their domestic virtues; and in this manner we should have been able to build a well-proportioned edifice, which the hand of time will respect. But no sooner had we thought of copying the American declaration of rights, than we imagined ourselves to be republicans. Something more, however, would have been necessary to complete this transformation.

The Americans have placed their declaration of rights[1] at the head of their constitutional code; and from this circumstance we were led to imagine that it was in a manner the commencement of their political nature; whereas in reality it was rather the extract and result of it. Their continental position, the nature of their exterior connections, their manners, their customs, and their modest fortunes, all these important circumstances which determine the character of a nation existed prior to their declaration of rights; so that their profession of faith was found, as all words ought to be found, in the relative dependence of things, and in perfect harmony with the absolute empire of facts. Our political legislators, however, have regarded this declaration of rights as the efficient cause of American liberty and as a universal principle of regeneration equally applicable to all nations. They

---

1. Some of the state constitutions did have such declarations of rights. The most famous example was the constitution of Virginia, which was well-known in France in the 1780s, through the translation of the liberal-minded Duke de la Rochefoucauld d'Enville in 1783 (he translated eleven state constitutions in total). Yet, the original text of the US Constitution did not have a Bill of Rights. The latter was adopted as the first ten amendments to the Constitution in June 1791. The influence of the American Constitution in France is analyzed in Marc Lahmer, *La Constitution américaine dans le débat français: 1795–1848* (Paris: l'Harmattan, 2001).

have also, without taking into consideration the moral and physical nature of the kingdom of France, without reflecting on the fact that a declaration of the rights of man would be putting an offensive weapon into the hands of the people, or at least would be a kind of political emancipation whose solemn ratification would require the utmost circumspection, surpassed the Americans themselves and, observing no bounds, have subjected the grave and prudent approach of the legislator to all exaggerations of philosophy.

It would be easy to illustrate this proposition by comparing the different declarations of rights adopted by the individual states of America with the profession of faith which serves as a preamble to the French constitution; but such a long discussion would present no interest today. We no longer think of measuring a river at its fountain head when, having increased in its course, and descended like a torrent on the plain, it floods the country or intersects it in every direction. I shall, therefore, avoid all useless inquiries and delve into the important subject which I must examine now.

We may imagine to ourselves a nation possessing such moderation of sentiment and such gravity of character, that it doesn't even need written laws; but in proportion as the people depart from that spirit of temperance and moderation, whether from their natural dispositions or other circumstances, a more active authority must be given to the power that protects the social harmony.

I shall doubtless be told that, by destroying existing prejudices, and erecting a new government on the ruins of old laws, the manners of a people are changed, their characters modified, and, so to speak, another nation is created.

Such is the language of men who attach all their ideas to a single leading axiom, and who, justly doubting whether they could reconcile different principles, would like to give an exclusive authority to the principle which they have chosen. No doubt, the nature of a government has an essential influence on the morals of a nation; but how many other circumstances take part in that influence! It would be a flagrant illusion to imagine that liberty, equality, and the rest of our new institutions will assimilate us to the Americans and render us like them obedient to the sober counsels of reason, or the simple yoke of the law. Separated by an immense ocean from the passions which agitate Europe, they peacefully enjoy their political youth and can freely exercise the virtues peculiar to that age. A soil, still new, offers the richest rewards to their industry; and its vast extent everywhere inviting cultivators, the dispersion of their habitations compels the majority to seek their felicity in domestic life, that constant source of all the milder sentiments, of every pure affection, and the best school of mores.

They are also called to the exercise of similar virtues by all the duties of hospitality imposed upon them by the nature of their country and the distance at which they reside from each other. But one of the happiest effects of this peculiar situation is that there is less rivalry between the passions of men, and the mind is more securely guarded against the sentiments of envy and jealousy, the common source of so many troubles. Finally, placed in the midst of a continent where there exists, as yet, no sort of proportion between the state of population and the multiplicity of useful employments, the citizens of every class feel no inquietude from the growth of their families; and they are kept by every tie within the boundaries of virtue, far from those rocks of temptations to which older nations are exposed.

No doubt there is also in the character of different peoples, a disposition, inherent in their nature, or of which the principle is at least unknown, that makes them more or less inclined to social harmony. I examine the constitutions of the individual states of America and I feel the most pleasing sensations at the simple view of a title, instinctively assumed by a considerable body of delegates whom their fellow citizens charge with the important work of legislation. *We the representatives of the* GOOD *people of Virginia.* What emotions does not this simple denomination excite! A title like this offers by itself a great lesson, being at the same time an honourable testimony of national character. Oh! could our National Assembly have assumed it, could a sentiment of truth have suggested the idea, France would have been less unhappy, we should not have shed so many tears, and the torrent would not still continue to flow from our eyes. But when our declaration of rights was drawn up, nobody could any longer take up the august denomination of representatives of the *good people* of France. The time, alas, had passed! deplorable remembrance, sad and lamentable reflection! Had the Assembly adverted to this, it would have felt that, in reminding us of our rights, it was necessary at the same time to remind us of our duties; had the Assembly adverted to this, it would have been deterred from weakening, as it has done, the power destined to maintain justice and the observance of the laws.

I have not indicated yet all the circumstances, peculiar to America, which, while they tend to support social order, are nevertheless totally foreign to the nature of government and its influence. There is probably not a single American, even among the lowest classes of society, who is not able to read, write and calculate, and who has not had leisure to learn and retain by heart the first principles of religious and moral truth. And when a merchant, an artisan, or any other industrious citizen takes into his service a young man without property, it forms an express article in their mutual agreements that the domestic or the apprentice shall be allowed and enabled by his master to acquire, within a short period of time, the elementary instructions which I have just pointed out. Now, such a contract can exist only in a country where, from the multiplicity of employments offered to industry and the limited number of inhabitants, labour is so advantageous as to permit men of every denomination to consecrate, from their youth, a portion of time to the acquisition of knowledge, however little connected it may be with the particular duties of their station. Our legislators, therefore, when they imagined that they should attain the same end by the establishment of a new hierarchy of schools and colleges, only showed how ignorant they were of the first causes of national instruction. This instruction cannot be universal, it cannot exist, no matter what we do, in a country whose population is so immense as to reduce the price of labour to so narrow a limit, as to be barely sufficient for acquiring the necessaries of life.

Let us now observe, and this is still connected to my subject, that of all the obstacles capable of hindering the proceedings of administration, undoubtedly the most serious ones are directly connected with the burden of taxes, or the scarcity of provisions. We are then as in presence of the strongest passions of the people; and so limited is the circle of their hopes and wishes, that they are fixed almost entirely on these two great objects of inquietude. To make the people, therefore, a party in any political dispute, all that is necessary is to hold out a real or fictitious connection between the subject of that dispute and the only objects that interest them. In this consists the art of intrigue, and an adept person knows the precise measures he has to take.

In the United States of America, burdensome taxes and fear of food shortages are causes of commotion hitherto unknown and in the order of probability, that will continue to be so for a long time. The Americans have neither fleets nor armies to maintain, and their public debt is very moderate; thus, all things considered, their expenses can bear no proportion to the expenditures of France. And they are less exposed than us to those events which produce extraordinary expenses and needs; for being situated far from the troubles of Europe and separated from its politics, they may preserve, as long as they please, the happy peace which they enjoy.

Their situation also, as to the means of subsistence, places them equally above all those inquietudes, those alarms and commotions, from which a kingdom like France is never secure. It will be long before their population will be equal to the produce of their crops, and at present their only care is to sell the great quantities which they do not need.

It has frequently been asserted that the harvest of all the different parts of France taken together is at all times adequate to the demands of the kingdom. Admitting the truth of this assertion, which, however, may justly be called in question, the utmost freedom of circulation would still be necessary to supply the scarcity of one district by the excess of another; and it is the maintenance of this circulation that particularly requires the aid of public force. No doubt it should be used judiciously and with caution; but this prudence ought never to be carried so far as to make the government weak.

Let us now take a different view of France, and we shall perceive the inhabitants elbowing each other, continually interfering with all their motions, and yet all of them resolved to run the career that is open to interest, vanity, ambition, and glory. We shall see them playing with the rules of civility and observing in an ironical and mocking way the last barriers of order overturned by the fashionable philosophers of the times. We shall see them, for the most part, crowded together in these corrupted towns, where ingenuity combined with idleness successfully propagates the vices and honors them; where luxury, inseparable from the maturity of a rich and commercial nation, regulates labor, and renders dependent upon the landed proprietors that immense multitude that lives by their caprices and is corrupted by them. Finally, it is easy to demonstrate, from certain general truths, with how much difficulty the laws of order can obtain respect in such a kingdom as France. Public commotion and private discontent usually originate in, and must derive from, the unexpected disturbances and changes in the material situation of the majority of the inhabitants of a country; and this situation is so closely linked to our social laws and the compelling rights of property, that the slightest variation in the price of provisions or the price of labor quickly affects the feelings of the masses and their real interests. Nonetheless, if one seeks to find where this type of commotion must be most frequent, one will undoubtedly discover that this happens in a country where the course of industry and agriculture in which a numerous part of the nation is employed depends to a great extent on the fluctuations in the transactions with other countries, and the uncertain trends of luxury in all parts of the world. It will be discovered that these commotions must be more frequent in a country where the population, equal or nearly equal to the consumption of the average crop, often provokes alarms and uncertainty which disturb the relations established between the price of grains and the price of labor.

Not one of these circumstances exists in America, where there is employment for everybody, and an employment that is likely to exist for a long time, since it depends neither upon the arts of luxury, nor the exterior commerce with industrial goods, but on a cultivation of land that will long be susceptible of the greatest improvement.

Why then compare with France a country so dissimilar? It would be easier to govern America by the single tie of its mores, than to maintain order in a kingdom like France by laws without number, if those laws have no support but that feeble executive power, the chance result of the patchy combinations of the National Assembly.

The day will perhaps arrive when the present government of the United States will no longer be found sufficiently powerful, and that day will be when mores will have changed. That will be a still distant epoch when their continually increasing population shall grow to the point when it will consume all the crops of the land. That will be the

epoch when the landowners, after having become absolute masters of
the price of labor, will reduce to the lowest necessary those who live
from the labor of their own hands. That will be the epoch when, by a
continual accumulation of wealth, transmitted from age to age, luxury
shall increase and shall render the difference of situation more conspicuous between those who inherited the fruits of the earth and that
multitude of men forever condemned, by the rights of property, to acquire only a mere subsistence by the unremitting sweat of their brow.

Then, when all these revolutions arrive, the inevitable outcome
of the passage of time, there will be a numerous class of citizens who
will enjoy, without labor or exertion on their part, certain territorial
revenues, the inheritance of their ancestors; another class will exert
itself in various ways in order to acquire by commerce a part of the
annual increase of personal wealth; finally, a third class, more numerous than either of these, will constantly surround them and will offer
them the fruits of their labor and industry in order to earn or deserve
a salary or reward; and art will develop every year in order to excite by
its novelties the taste and fantasies of the indolent dispensers of the
goods of fortune. Then at the same time, for the purpose of enjoying
more commodiously these daily and diverse conveniences, people will
generally assemble themselves in towns; the tribute of the plains will
be collected thither, and will there be consumed in dissipation and
luxury. A relish for frivolous enjoyments and the need for emulation
will imperceptibly weaken the authority of reason and subject people's tastes and sentiments to the empire of factitious ideas. Finally,
luxury and penury being intimately joined together, by multiplying
the passions and rendering them hostile to each other, will introduce
new mores, and the simplicity of ancient times will serve only as the
ornament of poetical description. Nor is this all; for with a change
of situation, religion, that sweet consolation amidst a domestic life,
religion, all the duties of which constitute a chain of felicity, will not
fail to become troublesome, and a new type of artist will appear, who,
under the name of philosophers, will invent other systems for the
times. And after these philosophers shall have relaxed all ancient ties,
after they have broken them, they will replace them with other ones,
more commodious and easier to bear; and after these philosophers
shall have relaxed and weakened everything, they will be replaced by

political metaphysicians, who will trace the plan of a new world to be established on the ruins of the old. Alas! while I have thus suffered my fancy to rove through all the vicissitudes and revolutions to which the hand of time will subject America, the spectacle of France has, I fear, been too constantly present to my mind; but in all affairs of importance, the history and experience of age is the book of destiny for youth.

I ought however to remark, that the Americans have adopted the only form of government capable of opposing resistance to these ever active causes, the only one that for any length of time can defend national mores against the daily influence of increasing wealth: and as this form of government has not rendered it necessary to invest the executive power with a degree of force proportioned to the vast extent of their dominions, a double motive engages me to treat the subject more at large; and this I shall do in the following chapter.

The Nature of the Government of the United States

That part of the continent of America, forming the dominions of the United States, presents to our view an immense surface, of which the circumference is approximately seventeen hundred leagues. But the government of these new regions is divided into fourteen states, of unequal population, varying from four hundred thousand down to sixty thousand souls, and of which the aggregate number of inhabitants is still short of four millions.

Each of these states forms a particular sovereignty, having a legislative body, an executive power, a judiciary order, together with all other institutions that constitute a free government and an independent society as a whole.

These states form therefore so many small republics, separated from each other, but united by their political and commercial interests, and their mutual defence. They have agreed to use the same coin, and a uniform standard of weights and measures. The debt contracted in the acquisition of liberty is a burden which they have agreed to share in common, as well as to contribute in a determined proportion to, whatever new expenses the safety of America may require. Lastly, the regulations and measures that are the necessary consequence of such a federation are committed to the care of a Congress, composed of delegates chosen by the fourteen states; but the power of this Congress and the authority of President do not extend beyond the circle of objects and interests that the different sections of America have decided to place in common.

From a political organization like this it results, however, that the vast extent of the American continent has no destructive influence on mores. By its division into small states the citizens are placed immediately under the eye of their respective magistrates, are restrained by the yoke of opinion, and are encompassed by all those chains which maintain in republics a general propriety of conduct and stability of principles.

Without doubt the population of each state, and particularly that of some, will progressively increase, and when arrived at a certain level the security of public manners will inevitably diminish; but the sage policy of the Americans seems already to have taken precautions against the effects of this inevitable circumstance. It appears to be their determination to form new states, as their population shall advance, that they may never exceed the limits most conformable to social happiness. They have calculated, as it were, how far the vigilance and care of government can extend, and by one of the wisest resolutions that ever entered the mind of a people, have determined to inaugurate a new independent authority, as soon as they shall be able to confide to it a dominion proportioned to its means. We shall thus behold, what has never been seen in the history of mankind, a sovereign state freely detaching itself from a part of its empire to secure more effectually the happiness of its citizens and the preservation of order and mores.

The conception alone of such a plan would have a just claim to our homage; but with the Americans this is no simple speculation. Already have they admitted the state of Vermont into the Confederation, and have further proposed, though I am at this moment unable to say what has been the result of the proposition, to separate Kentucky from Virginia, and Maine from Massachusetts. In proportion as these new divisions shall take place they will form so many integral parts of the general Confederation.[1]

---

1. The Commonwealth of Kentucky became the fifteenth state to join the Union in June 1792. Maine remained part of the Commonwealth of Massachusetts until 1820 when it was admitted to the Union as its 23rd state.

If we combine these explanations with the circumstances enumerated in the preceding chapter, we shall see the main cause of the
preservation of mores in America. We shall also perceive that their
purity is not, as has been supposed, the simple result of perfect equality, and that finally this equality is not the only secret of the Constitution of the United States. And though the members of the National
Assembly of France, by adopting and exaggerating this principle of
equality, may have imagined themselves to have trod in the steps of
the American legislators and to have laboured, so to speak, under the
guidance of their genius, it is not sure that they have been acknowledged by their masters. Before they detached a single principle from
a general system of government invented for another country, they
ought to have examined with attention whether, stripped of its ac-
companiments and hastily transplanted into a foreign soil, it would
be equally productive. In particular, they ought to have examined
how far this principle would agree with the immutable part of our local and peculiar circumstances, with our twenty-six millions of men
to be governed from a single central point, with the necessity of a
disciplined army, with our national character, that work of ages, and
which it is easier totally to subvert than to subject to any transformation. Oh! of how many various elements is the science of politics composed; and who is there that is able to penetrate the depths in which
those elements are combined and where their relations develop?

But it is alone by securing to the different governments of America the support of public mores that the Constitution of the United
States has facilitated the action of the executive power, or rendered
it less necessary; there are other ways in which it has accomplished
this essential goal.

The government of America, considered as a whole, is divided
into two parts. Each of the individual states, sovereign master within
the limits of its dominion, regulates, by its magistrates and the influence of authorities it has established all the branches of civil order; it
unites within itself all the necessary powers for the maintenance of
subordination; and as these powers have only to act in a narrow circle and are also closely seconded by opinion, they stand in need of no
great energy to fulfil their purpose. In a certain way, theirs is a gov-

ernment of a family, similar to that of all republics. So much for each individual state.

But they have placed in common all their political interests, all their commercial interests, together with certain other interests; and, as I have already explained, they have invested their respective delegates, assembled in Congress, with the necessary authority to decide on those diverse interests and guide them. It is easy, however, to perceive that an administration like this, always occupied either with negotiations abroad, or with general regulations at home, and which does not have to fight against the pretentions of individual states, does not require an executive power perpetually in action and endowed with extraordinary means.

Thus, by the plan of the political separation established in America, the difficult part of government, that which must at all times be in action, that which is destined to contend with the various passions of mankind and fight against their resistance, that government is given to an authority whose obligations extend no further than the boundaries of the territory to which their functions in this respect apply; and the only government whose superintendence comprehends the interests of all America has been rendered easy by the nature of the functions reserved to it.

It is impossible then, in treating of executive power, to establish any sort of parallel between a country containing only three or four millions of inhabitants, and a kingdom whose population amounts to twenty-six millions, between a confederacy of fourteen small sovereignties, and an empire where all the laws ought to proceed from a common centre, and all the layers of administration must derive from a single point; finally, between a people in the flower of its age, animated and sustained by the opinions and sentiments appropriate to that period of political life, and a nation arrived by progressive steps at the extremity of its course, where morality no longer operates, where religion itself is discredited, where all ideas of respect are obsolete and obedience is reduced to a metaphysical abstraction; where everything is old, everything is in decay, except, however, the spirit of vanity, that spirit so predominant in France which never dies, and which at present reminds us more than ever of the mythical phoenix, at the moment when, from the middle of the funeral pyre which it had built itself and which is composed of odoriferous shrubs and perfumes, is suddenly reborn from its own ashes.[2]

But patriotism, we are told, will make us young again, and thus compensate for all our losses. Be it so; but this sentiment also exists in America, and yet the Americans have never thought of making it the sole mover of the machine of government. For some time, we have painted everything with our own colors and thus we have made our own judgments uncertain. When time shall have effaced our light colors, we shall no longer be able to recognize anything, and shall then be convinced that it is not enough to call oneself *patriot* in order to know the real interests of the state, much as the names of *brothers* and *friends* are by no means the pledge of a permanent affection. All these appellations have hitherto served more as pretexts for hatred than as bonds of love. We must exchange a part of our exaltation for a little common sense, or our affairs will succeed very poorly. But in imitation of the National Assembly, individuals are anxious to distinguish themselves, to go beyond what their predecessors have said or have done; and thus every man continually strains himself into an unnatural attitude and oversteps the line of his real opinions.

2. According to the mythical story, the phoenix is a legendary Arabian eagle-like bird. As it approaches the end of its long life, it sets fire to its nest of twigs and is reduced to ashes. A new bird is then born from the ashes of the old one.

CHAPTER III

How the Executive Power in America Has Greater Force Than the Executive Power in France

In the preceding chapters we have seen the principal circumstances which impose the obligation of imparting to the authority of government in France powers of action and a degree of energy of which the republic of America has not experienced the necessity.

Suppose then it should be found that the proportions adopted by our legislators are the reverse of this?

To examine this question, it becomes necessary to draw a double parallel, and to compare the executive power of France not only with the executive power instituted in the individual states of America, but also with the executive power established for the maintenance of the federation. These two comparisons can shed new light on several important truths.

I shall first call the reader's attention to the executive power vested in the president of Congress,* and the different institutions which tend to assist the exercise of that power.

The laws enacted by Congress, like those of the Parliament of England, have this important advantage over the laws of France that they announce to the nation the united sentiments of two Houses,

---

*Congress is the name given to the Assembly of delegates of all the United States; and the president of the Assembly is the celebrated Washington.

and thus present a character of maturity and reflection which commands additional respect and renders obedience more certain.

The delegates who compose the upper House, or Senate, are elected for six years, and this circumstance serves as a counterpoise and security against the versatility of principle to which the lower House, or House of Representatives, is exposed, by a change every two years of its members.

Senators must be at least thirty years old; it is required that they shall have been citizens of the United States for at least nine years; and it is recommended in the entire country to choose these delegates from among the wisest men of the nation. These circumstances tend to secure a degree of consideration to the Senate, and dispose the minds of the people to honour the legislative body, of which this Senate forms a part.

Only the fools, the mere theorists, or the novices in moral philosophy estimate opinion to be of little worth in their political combinations. Its assistance is absolutely necessary to all governments. It serves tyrants by assuming the form of fear; and it is by borrowing the milder image of respect and confidence that it assures to the magistrates of a free nation the deference which they need.

This deference, so indispensible to the upper House of the legislative body of the American federation, is further augmented by the constitutional statute declaring it to have the sole power of trying impeachments, voted by the House of Representatives, whether for treason or other public misdemeanors.

Lastly, the senators owe their election to the enlightened will of the legislature of each individual state; an essential point, since the experienced character of the electors, the knowledge they have acquired of the difficulties of government, and the interest they already have, in virtue of their own positions, in preserving the consideration given to public persons are so many factors which make sure that the electors are prudent in their choices; none of these conditions are secured by the forms of election established in France.

A particular regulation contributes also to the maintenance of order and unity in the deliberations of Congress. The two Houses do not have, as in France, a perpetual succession of presidents removable every fortnight: the House of Representatives chooses a speaker who officiates during the whole session; and the president of the Senate the Constitution has decreed shall be the Vice-President of the United States, an officer appointed to assist the chief President in his functions and in case of necessity to replace him. By this institution the first link is formed of a chain connecting the legislative with the executive power; and such seems to have been the intention of the legislator.

Now if we add to these circumstances the information we may readily acquire regarding the character and reputation of the people called to form the Congress, we shall probably think that a legislative assembly like this would, by the sole weight of its consideration, give more power to its laws than an assembly armed, like ours, with the authority of the nation and perpetually surrounded with menace and proscription.

But it is not only by the wise formation of the legislative body that the action of the executive power is aided and facilitated, the prudent organization of the judiciary order contributes also to the same end; for while in France all the magistrates of that order are chosen by the people, and for a limited time, two circumstances unfavourable to the independence of the judges, the tribunals of the American federation are filled by men appointed by the Senate and the president of the United States, and no period is fixed for the termination of their functions.

Let us now direct our attention to the authority granted to the depositary of the executive power in the American federation, and we shall find that it surpasses, in various respects, the prerogatives of the French monarch.

No law can be complete till it has received the sanction of the President. It is true that this sanction cannot be purely and simply refused, like that of the French king during the existence of two legislatures; but as it is in neither government applicable to constitutional laws, I conceive the veto of the French monarch to have less force and efficacy than the right of opposition granted to the President of the United States. In order for everyone to be able to judge of this question, it is necessary to remind the particulars of that right.

These particulars are extremely simple. When a bill has passed the two Houses, it must be presented to the president of Congress, and if he refuses his assent, he is bound to give his objections in writing. The bill is then reconsidered by the two Houses that still meet separately, and if still approved by two thirds of each House, the opposition of the President becomes null. I ought to add that the names of the persons voting for and against the bill are entered on the journals of each House respectively, as well as the objections of the President which shall have formed the subject of debate.

It is easy to perceive how small is the probability that a memorandum on the part of the president, the head of the executive power, should not prevail upon the minds of one third of the members of one of the two Houses; and we can also observe the weight that must obtain the judgment of the President in defending the motives upon which his decision is founded, and explaining himself fittingly and with dignity. Alas! on many occasions, only the exercise of such a right of remonstrance on the part of the French government was needed in order to prevent the National Assembly from making many errors; but in its quality of Constituent Assembly, it obliged the monarch to give his negative only in a simple form, and thus it deprived him of the approbation he might have obtained in the eyes of public opinion. Nonetheless, as a result of such a separation, when a decree is presented to the monarch for his sanction, it is not enough for him to examine whether this law is contrary to moral justice or the public good; unfortunately, he must also consider whether it is safe for him to reject it, without being permitted at the same time to inform the legislature and the nation of the reasons of his rejection. The Constituent Assembly, influenced by a miserable jealousy, has always refused to the king the authority of reason, nor would it ever have been brought to admit of a veto similar in all its circumstances to the right opposition vested in the President.[1]

A further important remark ought also to be made. The American Constitution, very different from that of France, has not interdicted the sanction of the supreme head of administration as to certain legislative proceedings, and particularly that most important one of all which relates to the fixing, the continuing and the collecting of taxes.

---

1. In original *Président du Congrès*. Obviously, Necker refers here to the veto power given to the President of the United States.

It is not laws alone that require the sanction of the President; the constitutional charter has subjected to his sanction, in a general manner, such votes and resolutions to which the concurrence of the two Houses is necessary; and the only exceptions to this rule are the deliberations regarding adjournment.

We thus see that the sanction of the chief of the United States has more numerous and extensive applications than the sanction of the French monarch.

Lastly, since the American legislators did not declare constitutional many articles admitted as such in the French code, the resolution of those different dispositions is the function of the legislative body; and as the exercise of those functions are subjected to the sanction of the President, his influence is greater in proportion as the articles invariably fixed by the national convention are fewer.

One of the most striking prerogatives vested in the President is the right of pardon; and this prerogative extends to all offences committed against the United States, with the exception of the criminal prosecutions instituted at the request of the House of Representatives. It is otherwise in France, where the monarch has been deprived, almost inhumanly, of this right, the most precious, honourable and imposing of all the ancient privileges of the Crown. But I have already treated this subject in the effusion of my heart; and I shall forbear, therefore, to make use of the new weapon which I might at this moment derive from the conduct of a people jealous of its rights, and glowing with all the fervour of liberty.

The President of the United States is empowered, with the approbation of two thirds of the Senate, to conclude treaties; and as this council consists only of thirty-two delegates, it is easy to perceive that the President, in his transactions with foreign states, is little exposed to retractation and inconsistency, and is therefore able to inspire confidence into those states. The case is very different in France, where no treaties can have force without the approbation of an assembly of seven hundred and forty-five deputies, who are for the most part wholly unversed in political affairs, and little able to acquire the necessary information in a short reign of two years.

The President is empowered, with the approbation of the Senate, to nominate to all offices without exception, and these include the judges of the Supreme Court. To this article it will no doubt be replied that the king of the French is empowered of his sole authority to nominate ambassadors and some other public officers. But it is known that the French government is subjected to the empire of opinion; it is thus obliged to consult the inclinations of a master very hard to please, inclinations that must be guessed when they do exist, and that will be feigned when they do not exist; and thus one is forced to serve a mysterious divinity, equally to be feared whether it speaks or is silent. Which would the government prefer, this slavery, or the guarantee of a Senate over which it would necessarily have considerable influence as long as it acts with propriety and reason? We must also note that if the President is obliged to act in concert with the Senate for the small number of nominations which, in France, are attributed to the sole authority of the monarch, his prerogative, thus limited, applies indiscriminately to all employments in the service of the United States; while on our part the king has been deprived of all participation in the choice of the majority of public officers, such as judges, directors of the police, directors and administrators of the provinces, and even in the offices left to his disposal, there are certain rules of promotion established which, for the most part, reduce his functions to an empty formality.

The President is also solely empowered to fill up all vacancies that may happen during the recess of the Senate; and the commissions which he thus grants are not to expire till the end of its next session.

From the preceding explanations the following truth is discovered that, by the obligation imposed on the President of acting in concurrence with the Senate, one of the two Houses which form the general Congress is connected with administration and united to its interests; and the consequence of this measure is a more complete and certain harmony between the legislative power and the government.

This was the original intention of the legislator in the organization of Congress. It forms indeed an exception to the common principle of the separation of powers. Does it really matter as long as this exception serves to better achieve the common good?

But is not the responsibility of the executive power hereby diminished, it will be asked by certain of our new politicians, and by those in particular whose happiness and glory consist in the hope that they shall one day exercise that responsibility, and who are unwilling to consent to the slightest renunciation of the thousand and one modes in which they can attack or harrass the first agents of government?

I answer that the prudent legislators of America have prefered the general harmony to these petty amusements of jealousy and envy; and men of sense of every country will not fail to applaud and honour them.

The President, obliged to act in concert with the Senate as to the nomination of public officers and the negociation of treaties of commerce and alliance is nevertheless sole depositary of the executive power; he can even convoke the two Houses, or one of them separately, before the expiration of their adjournment; and though the period of adjournment be usually fixed by themselves, the president has the right of determining it in case of a difference of opinion between the two sections of the legislative body.

Every mark of honour is also bestowed on this first magistrate of the United States. He alone gives audience to foreign ambassadors and ministers; he enters the legislative assembly accompanied by a numerous retinue; and so far from his exterior dignity being exposed to those small annoyances which are the glory of our infant politicians, the Americans, with pride and pleasure, respect in the chief of their union the majesty of a free people.

I should make one last very important observation. Were we to confine our attention to a comparison between the constitutional charters of the two nations, we should form a very erroneous judgment of the respective prerogatives of the French monarch and the President of the United States. The American original code indeed contains all the restrictions to which the President's authority is subjected; whereas the French code gives but a very imperfect picture of the political situation of the king, at the moment when the Constituent Assembly ended. Let us explain the reason of this difference.

The legislators of the American federation had no further authority than that of preparing, by common consultation, a good constitution. This was the sole object which occupied their attention; and the government they created did not begin to exist till their project of a constitution had been adopted by the United States. Thus, no anterior law, no law connecting legislation and constitution served to join its authority with that of the national convention.

It is not thus in France. The National Assembly has taken its constitutional code from a multitude of laws it has made and enacted during the course of its session, and those which are not comprised in this code are still in force and govern the state like constitutional laws. The only difference between these two sorts of laws is that the constitutional laws are immutable for a given time, whereas the others are not; but if to change the latter an express vote of a legislator is required, their duration is similarly uncertain, and may be as long, as indefinite, as the duration of constitutional laws.

I shall take an example or two from among a great number to illustrate the very important remark which I have just made. The constitutional code fixes no term to the functions of all the judges established in the kingdom; and yet this term cannot extend beyond six years, if the law which has thus regulated it should undergo no change. The constitutional code does not fix the number of municipalities; but there will be no less than forty-four thousand, as long as this institution, decreed by the first National Assembly, shall remain unrepealed. How very imperfect then would be our idea of the obstacles opposed, in France, to the establishment of order and the activity of the executive power, were we to decide in this respect merely from reading the constitutional code?

These is inevitably a striking difference between a constitution grafted upon ancient laws and a constitution antecedent to the existence of a government; and the effects of this difference are perhaps unalterable, since, in every country where the legislative action must depend upon several powers, it becomes infinitely difficult to abolish or modify the preexistent laws relative to one of those powers.

The brief details I have given about the organization of the different powers in America and the prerogatives attributed to the President are sufficient to show that the United States have secured the activity of government in a more firm and respectable manner than we have done in France. Let us now consider and appreciate the small number of circumstances that seem to contradict this truth.

The chief of the United States is liable to be tried before the Senate upon an accusation of treason or other capital crime, brought by the House of Representatives.

In France the person of the monarch has been declared inviolable.

Here there is no doubt a great difference; but the circumstances are extremely rare and improbable that can lead to such an extreme situation, so that in reality the executive power is neither aided nor constrained by it. The situation is different with the regard to the responsibility placed in France, not upon the king, but upon all his ministers; that responsibility is continually applied, and people tend to use it as a weapon of attack to such a degree that it becomes, in the hands of restless and envious individuals, a source of continual agitation. It would be better, no doubt, for the maintenance of government, that the king should be inviolable and his ministers open to prosecution; but considered only in relation to the executive power, the inviolability of the monarch does not compensate for the inconveniences deriving from the extremely precarious position of his ministers.[2]

The hereditary nature of the throne, compared with the transient reign of the chief of the United States, is also a circumstance favourable in principle to the stability of government. But let us not dissemble that the consideration attached to an hereditary authority is frequently balanced by those unlucky throws of the dice inseparable from the chances of birth. Washington possessing, by descent, an authority like this, would probably enjoy a much greater power than Washington temporary chief of the United States; but it is for geometricians, skilled in the science and calculation of probabilities, to inform us in how many ages a man, endowed with such eminent qualities, would become the chief of a nation by the simple succession of the laws of nature.

In America there is no standing army, so that in case of necessity the executive power could not avail itself of their assistance; but it can call in the aid of the militia. To assemble this military force, a decree of the legislative body is necessary; but the Constitution has vested in the general president the right of commanding it. In case of war also he is commander in chief of the army and navy; a pre-

2. On the responsibility of ministers, see Glénard, *L'Exécutif et la Constitution de 1791,* 427–65.

rogative that is not rendered nugatory, as has artfully been contrived in France, by interdicting the monarch from removing to a greater distance than twenty leagues from the legislative body, and by obliging him to convoke that assembly the moment hostilities shall have commenced.

In America, the organization of the army and its rules of discipline are subjected to the legislative authority; but the sanction of the President forms a part of that authority; and thus, the chief of the state will not be prevented from giving his opinion regarding admission into military service and promotions, as has been the case in France, where these military regulations have been included among the articles of the Constitution.

I cannot conclude the parallel I have undertaken without adding to the list of advantages secured to the executive power one very remarkable circumstance; that is the fortunate distance at which all the chiefs of the federative government are placed from the first movement of individual passions, a movement always dangerous, but against which they are protected by the mediation of the authorities that exercise, in each particular state, the normal duties of sovereignty. This happy distance will long maintain the entire respect for Congress; and perhaps the wisest feature in federative constitutions is this, of erecting, in the midst of many governments, a supreme power which, without being involved in the petty hostilities and daily disputes to which these governments are exposed, is able to come forward with dignity and effect, when events render its intervention necessary. Such a power becomes a sort of *corps de réserve* in the midst of internal divisions; it makes judicious use of a credit which has not been rendered cheap, it exerts a firmness that has not been compromised, and it displays a generosity that has never become familiar; and thus great political ideas are always related to the morale of the people.

CHAPTER IV

Of Executive Power in the Individual States of America

England, in its unity, America in its system of federation, present to our view two admirable models of government.

England shows us in what manner an hereditary monarchy may be maintained without alarming the partisans of liberty; America, how a vast continent may be subjected to republican forms without giving umbrage to the friends of public order.

England shows us how a single executive power can secure in a large state, without the aid of despotism, the regular activity of administration; America, how a diversity of sovereign powers may attain the same goal, but without confusion.

England teaches us how a small number of large springs may be made regularly to act within their proper bounds; America, how a great number of small springs may be united to form a single force.

England shows us how far unity of interest may be the result of inequalities of rank in society; America, how this unity may be reconciled with inequalities of strength in a political federation.

England demonstrates that the advanced age of a nation is not incompatible with the preservation of public manners; America, that a people may prolong its youth and keep itself for a considerable length of time free from the most seductive and dangerous vices.

England shows us how from a single source of intelligence may be derived all the knowledge necessary to the happiness of a nation;

America, in what manner perfection may be attained by the subdivision of political discussions.

England also presents us with the view of a government in which, from its very perfection, the slightest innovations are dangerous; a government whose principles of existence seem to touch, to correspond, and to depend on each of the laws by which it is organized; while in America, on the other hand, the centre of union is at such a distance from the radii as to be capable of performing its action even when some movement might be felt on some part of the circumference.

Finally, the government of England and the government of America, though strikingly and materially different, compose nevertheless each of them a system in which the eyes of observers may discern evident traces of the genius that presided in the formation of these two great political societies.

We perceive nothing similar in the French constitution. Our legislators have been desirous of placing the entire administration of the empire in the hands of a single authority, and by weakening that authority in every possible manner, have subjected it to the opposition and annoyance of an infinite multitude of powers. Meanwhile they have neither diminished its task, as in America, nor given it additional energy, as in England. And notwithstanding the National Assembly of France had these two grand models of government continually before its eyes, we can trace nothing in its work but an amphibious creation, the result of the incongruities and perplexities of its own mind.

The National Assembly has moreover been under a continual restraint, both from the fear of appearing as an imitator, and from its limited circle of political combinations. It has seen itself reduced to the necessity of borrowing details, here and there, from all the existing social constitutions. Happy would we have been, if, like the bee, that Assembly had possessed the necessary instinct to form from its thefts a perfect hive! But the spirit of propriety and proportion are among the first best gifts of nature.

The federation of America, being composed of fourteen small states, each possessing a constitution to itself, and a constitution very little known, a certain portion of good might have been extracted from it, without the plagiarism being perceived. But our legislators, in their selections, have always given the preference to articles the least favourable to public order. And, if it would not engage me in too long a discussion, I could prove that each of those small states, many of which do not contain more than fifty or sixty thousand souls, has given greater force to its government than we have done to the supreme administration of the largest kingdom in Europe.

I shall remark however, in general, that if we examine the various constitutions of the American states, we shall find in them a difference of opinion upon several important questions of government. For example, in some of these republics the judges hold their offices for life, and are nominated by the depositary of the executive power. The chief of the state has in like manner the nomination of all the other civil magistrates, militia officers, officers of the federative army, and the different agents of administration. Whereas, in other sections of the continent, the nomination to these employments, and which are held pro tempore, are given for the greater part, either to assemblies of the people or to the legislative body. And we may observe, what is indeed reasonable, that the smaller is the state the fewer are the prerogatives conferred on the executive power; but in none of these republics, not even the smallest one, do we behold anything equal to the total destitution of the king of the French, divested of every privilege that gives ascendancy and influence to the supreme authority.

A circumstance still more remarkable and truly astonishing is that all the states of America, without a single exception, have granted to the chief of the executive power the right of pardon, while we have wrested from the hands of the king this august prerogative.

We see also, though not generally, yet in several states of America, a number of other privileges enjoyed by the executive power, and which have been refused to the French monarch. The constitution of Massachusetts, for instance, empowers the governor to convoke, by circular letter, the elected senators; to prorogue the legislative body, if he shall think proper, for the space of eighty days; and to participate with the executive council in judging certain causes. A part of these prerogatives exists likewise in other states.

But the most important political regulation, whether considered in itself, or as connected with executive power, is the formation of the legislative body into one or two Houses. This is a truth which I have frequently illustrated. Meanwhile, among the different states of which the federation of America is composed, there exist but two, Georgia and Pennsylvania, in which the plan of a single house has been adopted. And let us remark that these two republics seem to have distrusted the inconveniences resulting from such a constitution of the legislative body, since both of them have tried to temper them with the aid of particular provisions, not to be found in any other state of America.[1]

In Georgia, the single House of Representatives, after the second reading of every new bill, is bound to send a copy of the projected law to the executive council, which must examine and return it to the legislative body with its opinion.

In Pennsylvania, the plan of every intended law is printed and published, and its preamble must contain the reasons inducing the legislative body to adopt it; and that a freer course may be given to its public discussion, and advantage taken of the light thrown upon it by such discussion, the decree cannot be made definitive till the following session of the legislature. There is also established in Pennsylvania a council of censors nominated by the people, whose function is equally to watch both over the proceedings of the legislative body and over the conduct of the executive power. It is empowered to recommend the repeal of laws contrary to the good of the state and the principles of the Constitution; and it is invested with a number of other prerogatives.

It is easy to perceive in what manner the absence of a second house of legislature is indirectly supplied by these regulations.

Let us further remark that, in the eleven states whose government is formed of two chambers, the upper House, known by the name of Senate, is the constituted judge of all public misdemeanors and state crimes, prosecuted by the House of Representatives. Pennsylvania, by composing the legislative body of a single chamber, has been obliged to confide to a particular tribunal the functions attributed to

---

1. On the eve of the Philadelphia Convention in 1787, eleven states (out of thirteen) had bicameral legislatures; yet, the Continental Congress had been monocameral. Those who embraced the principle of bicameralism did so out of different theoretical and political considerations.

the Senate in the other states. And, could one believe it? the Constitution has decreed that this tribunal shall consist of the executive council, together with its president and vice president. If such be the necessary result of a single chamber of legislature, little cause will the other states of America have to regret the system they have adopted of two chambers. Nor will their regret be increased when they shall reflect upon the mode of proceeding in France relative to state crimes, and shall examine the singular institution of our high national court.[2]

The Americans have not determined by constitutional laws the forms of consideration and respect that shall be observed towards the elective chief of the state, and I do not know all the particulars of their ceremonial. But I observe, in the convention of Georgia, that when a mere committee of the executive council is deputed to confer with the legislative body, the persons of whom the committee is composed must be seated and covered, while it is prescribed to the members of the legislative body, the speaker excepted, to remain uncovered as long as the conference shall continue. It appears, from this circumstance, that the Americans have a just idea of the exterior respect that should be paid to those on whom the important and difficult task devolves of maintaining the respect for the laws and constraining the people to obey them. Let us compare this political decorum with those forms, more than familiar, with which the ministers of the king of the French are received, with that impertinence practised in general towards the executive power, with that code of etiquette invented for the monarch, with that systematic bluntness in which we foolishly pride ourselves. No longer the Americans, it is ourselves who become Quakers, and the French, thus travestied,

2. According to Chapter 5 ("Of the Judicial Power"), Article 23 of the Constitution of 1791, "A National High Court, composed of members of the Court of Cassation and Grand Jurors, shall have cognizance of offences of ministers and principal agents of the executive power, and of crimes against the general security of the state, when the legislative body had rendered a writ of indictment. It shall assemble only upon the proclamation of the legislative body, and at a distance of at least thirty thousand toises from the place where the legislative body holds its meetings." (*A Documentary Survey of the French Revolution*, ed. John Hall Stewart [New York: Macmillan, 1951], 257).

are objects only of ridicule; for their ancient forms of dress are seen through these new modes, and the whole exhibits an accoutrement so bizarre as must excite the laughter of all Europe. Alas! we ought to have taken from the Quakers their scrupulous morals, their sentiments of humanity, their religious veneration for the sovereign Author of Nature; and wanting to imitate them, we should not have contented ourselves with the rigid observance of *thee* and *thou*, in violation of all propriety, and with being blunt and familiar on every unseemly occasion. But exterior forms and modes of speech are easily copied; and beside it has ever been the character of the French to fall at once into extremes; for which reason they frequently go backward or are stationary, while others are still marching forward.

Never was there a more serious or more important instance of the display of this national character than in the blind veneration we have shown for certain American principles or American usages. It would have been natural to have modified a little the ideas of liberty and equality when taking them from the bosom of those small republics, situated at the extremity of the world, and still simple in their mores and in their fortune, in order to transplant them in the midst of a great and old monarchy, surrounded by all the passions and all the vices of Europe. It was necessary at least to have tinged them lightly with our ancient political principles, with those features engraven by time, and which the effort of a day would be incapable of effacing; but far from pursuing this method, our legislators have drawn from every individual constitution of the American States the most democratic articles; and after having exaggerated them, as I have demonstrated in the course of this work, have then negligently adjusted them to the words king, throne, monarchy, leaving to future revolutions the care of separating, in whatever manner, that which could not remain united.

It is unfortunate for France that the leaders of the National Assembly, in composing their theme from the various elements of which the American state constitutions had been formed, carefully concealed their mode of proceeding. There are few of their political ideas regarding which we should not have formed a better judgment, had we been acquainted with the origin of those ideas and the systems from which they were derived. We should then have asked early if the usages of a small number of republics, among the fourteen states of America, were better suited to France than the misguided ways followed by others of the same continent. We should have asked, if certain details ought to have been copied literally; if certain principles of a particular republic ought to have been adopted, while its form of government was rejected by us. Finally, we should have asked if certain American ideas were more analogous to a great kingdom than institutions the merit of which the happiness and prosperity of England have consecrated. The nation would have more securely participated in the examination of great political question if they had been placed in parallel with models, and if the attention of the public had been limited to a small space, instead of being left to wander in the boundless region of metaphysics and abstraction. But the legislators were determined to attribute to themselves all honour and to pass for inventors. With this view, they sometimes exaggerated known truths, sometimes arranged words in a new order, and sometimes called things by different names, thus giving an appearance of originality to the most literal imitations. In a word, they broke in by night, with a dark lantern, into the great magazine of American political ideas, instead, as they ought to have done, of filling it with light and calling all the world to judge what they borrowed from them and what they rejected. It is true that the people of France would then have been less astonished by so many dispositions which they thought to be novel; by the famous declaration of rights, by the Constituent Assembly, by the election of magistrates, administrators and priests, by popular ballot; by religious toleration, by the systems of equality, by the constitutional code, by national conventions, by the feast of the federation, by the era of independence and liberty;[3] lastly, by so many particular details, all borrowed from the various American constitutions, and often so poorly adjusted to the unchanging circumstances of the French empire.

The principal object of consideration ought to have been the suitableness of this application; but our legislators have considered prin-

---

3. Necker refers here to the new calendar introduced in October 1793 during the Terror and the habit of dating public acts from what was considered as the beginning of a new era of liberty. The new calendar was abolished by Napoleon in September 1805, and the Gregorian calendar started again on January 1, 1806.

ciples as a form of spiritual entities that existed everywhere and have not paid attention to the fact that these principles have significant consequences in reality. No doubt, abstractions can be applied universally; they are like a large compass that you may open as wide as you please, and by which you may bring together in imagination distant points of extension; but in practice, everything is connected, everything moves down to earth, and it is then that we face obstacles that were overcome in our speculations and are confronted with numerous problems ignored by theory.

CHAPTER V

Of Executive Power in the Small
Republics of Europe

Dare I say it? The executive power of the small republics of Europe has greater efficiency and vigour and experiences less resistance than the authority which is placed in the hands of government in France. This assertion is not a vain paradox; it would be quite easy to justify it, by explaining the constitutions of Geneva, Basle, Zurich, Scaffhausen, and other republics, considered at present as the most popular in Europe;[1] but should it enter the head of one of our journalists, who are listened to as oracles by all the novices in politics, to give the name of aristocracy to any of those states mentioned as an example, he would be taken on this word and I could expect to make no impression but upon the few, the very few persons who still have the time and habit of thinking for themselves. I shall therefore take an extreme example and place my point of comparison in the very centre of those small cantons of Switzerland, whose excessive democracy is universally acknowleged.

The legislative body there is composed of the whole nation, and it is in a general assembly of the citizens that the most important affairs of the state receive their sanction, that laws are debated and decreed, public contributions established, and war and peace resolved

---

1. These are some of the cantons and cities that would later form what is today known as the Swiss Confederation, with the capital in Bern.

upon. Finally, it is this assembly also that elects the councils, the principal officers of state, and the chief of the republic, distinguished by the appellation of *landaman*. Such is in abbreviated form the popular authority in these small cantons; and their political differences do not deserve to be mentioned.

This authority of the people is quite great, but it leaves to the executive power room for its action; and perhaps the prerogatives that still remain vested in government might appear as a principle of despotism if established in the middle of a kingdom, or transplanted into the center of a vast region.

We must first observe that a legislative body, composed of all the inhabitants of a country without distinction, and in which every one has the right of suffrage from the age of fifteen or sixteen years, can never remain long assembled. Thus its presence does not annihilate the consideration of the executive power, as it happens, and must necessarily happen in France, where the sessions of the national legislative assembly are perpetual, unless it should think proper of its own accord to adjourn; and as it is representative, and its members are renewed every two years, it feels no inconvenience in residing constantly in Paris and enjoying the salaries annexed to the functions of deputies. The inhabitants of the small cantons are given no salaries when they meet in general assembly, and their meeting commonly lasts only two or three days.

The landaman, elective chief of the state, surrounded by his council, places himself in the midst of the general assembly, known by the appellation of *lands-gemeine*. There he presides and opens the business which is to occupy the attention of the citizens. What would our politicians think of an initiative like this, confided to the executive power, and called into action, amidst a legislative body, tumultuously assembled for the space of two or three days? What would they think also of another prerogative of the executive power, the strongest one that the imagination can conceive, and which nevertheless exists both in the smaller cantons, as well as in the other republics whose form of government is most democratic? I refer to the union of the judiciary power to the executive; there is certainly no greater and more effective means of consideration than this.

Moreover, the difference is in every sense so great between the small republics formed in the interstices of the Alps and a large monarchy erected, so to speak, on the vast plains of the world, that there is a kind of absurdity in comparing them; yet it was tempting to show in a few words that, even in these narrow corners of the earth, where the government is a sort of paternal administration, it has never entered the imagination to sacrifice, to liberty and equality, that executive authority, without which, simple and uncontaminated as may be the general manners, there would exist neither peace, nor tranquillity, nor political society. I am ready to admit and I must repeat that the French constitution, just like any other constitution, would perfectly fulfill these conditions if the constituted powers were respected and the laws obeyed with common consent. And people are right to incessantly repeat that it is time for subordination to begin to appear. It is time; but it is really stupid to present this subordination, to solicit it as a compliment of the Constitution, as an homage which we are required to pay it, while in reality it ought to be fruit and result of the Constitution. What is in reality the obligation imposed, by the nature of his office, on the institutor, the first founder of a social system? It is not to convert, like a mere framer of laws, obedience and submission to the best possible use; this would be too common a task; his duty and destiny call him to higher functions; and we expect from his genius that, by a profound knowledge of men and their passions, by a skilful organization of powers and forces, he should create that obedience, should guaranty that submission, and should succeed therein without offering to liberty the smallest degree of violence. These are the two objects which he is bound to accomplish; and if he fails in either, he will in reality have done nothing, and we shall clearly perceive either that he has not understood the extent of his mission, or has lacked the energy necessary to its completion.

CHAPTER VI

In What Manner the Weakening of the Executive Power Has Favoured Republican Systems

Different motives have, no doubt, given birth to the opinions in favour of republican government, which have appeared, and are still making their appearance in France. I shall not seek to fathom the individual interests which serve as a stimulus to the intriguing and the ambitious ones. We must leave in the darkness what they want to hide; even so, there will still be enough actions of which some are very proud that could make the age blush. But there is one very natural cause of the favourable reception that many people give these new systems. It is seen that royalty, in the state of degradation to which it has been reduced, can no longer maintain public order, and it is asked if a king, if his ministers, are not too great an expense when compared with their utility. It is further asked if an elective senate, if a president of that senate would not be able to exercise an authority as efficient as the feeble means of a monarchical government, when that government is constituted as we find it at present among us. These doubts are the natural result of the extreme weakness of the executive power, and the authors of the new social order in France have no right to take offence at them. They have acted towards the royal authority as they have acted relative to money; they have changed the nature of both, and they are angry at all those who no longer estimate them at the same value. Let us pursue this comparison a little further. They have deceived the nation after having first been deceived themselves; they have left the name of king at the head of their political institution, after having previously stripped that name of every idea that entered into its formation; and led on by this logical manoeuvre invented by a small group among them, the entire France and the majority of the National Assembly have been led, without knowing it, to the very confines of republicanism, and monarchy no longer consists but in the hereditary possession of a vain title. In the same manner they have reminded of the French loyalty and have professed its doctrine; they talked with great parade of their unwavering fidelity to the obligations that had been entered into in the name of the state; and to discharge these engagements, they have introduced a fictitious currency which no longer represents the same values,[1] and by means of which every foreign creditor suffers the loss of half the principal. Strange and unfortunate abuse of words, which favours every species of perfidy, and of which we have never witnessed a more terrible example!

How many other faults, how many other errors might not be accounted for by the same explanations? It might be easily shown that the words liberty and equality, by being wrested from their meaning, have become a source of disorder and confusion; but this investigation would carry me too far out of my way; I shall therefore content myself only with a single general reflection. In the whole domain of human knowledge, the science most exposed to misunderstanding, the science in which the language is less adequate to convey the diverse modifications of ideas is, no doubt, the public science.[2] And we should not be surprised by that, since, being practiced for a long time only by men of genius or deep thinkers, they were able to represent and convey many ideas in a small number of words, while separating the same ideas in their application both to government and legislation. But when the mob of school children or half informed men, mingled with party leaders, have rushed at once towards this science, each laid hands, as he could, upon one of the mixed ideas that composed the words liberty, equality, sovereignty, monarch, and monarchy; and mis-

---

1. In the sense that it represents a value much greater than its intrinsic worth.

2. In original: *la science publique,* that is the science that deals with issues concerning the public sphere, political science in the broad sense of the term.

taking the fragments thus pilfered for the whole, these small conquerors have made and unmade in their imagination the governments and the constitutions and spread themselves throughout the entire Europe in expectation of the moment when they should be called upon to become legislators. They would have had less confidence in their mission, had they not, with the aid of the words liberty, equality, and a few others, been able to register their whole political baggage under two or three labels. Let us conclude from these reflections, addressed only to thinking people, that arranging a multitude of thoughts under a few simple signs is practice suited only to sage and experienced nations; but the division and dispersion of all the ideas united under a general denomination create true confusion and have devastating effects in countries where every man suddenly becomes a politician and a philosopher, and especially when there do not yet exist any words in the language capable of clearly expressing all the parts of this universal decomposition.

CHAPTER VII

Reflections on Republican Systems
as Connected with France

Those who are continually calling out for a republic render an essential service to the men who fear the reproach of having introduced such a form of government in France; thus the authors of the Constitution must observe with pleasure the growth of extravagant opinions, which have prevented us from seeing the striking resemblance that exists between their political work and the most popular systems.

The appointment of an hereditary chief to the first office in the state is one of the elements which distinguish monarchies from republics; but it is by no means the most important one, and it would probably be ranked last, in the order of differences between the two sorts of constitutions, were it not that it has been selected, on account of its conspicuousness and simplicity, in order to signal the complex idea that had to be represented.

Meanwhile, such is the authority of language and its hereditary influence on mankind that, by the aid of a Greek derivation serving to justify this meaning of the word *monarchy*, the lawgivers of France have conceived that they should keep themselves clear of republican government, by maintaining only the institution of an individual chief; and it was thus that the National Assembly, amidst the ruins of all sorts by which it was surrounded, and while destroying every ancient tenure, subjected itself nevertheless to the empire of words, an empire the least legitimate of all and the least respectable.

Can anything, however, more nearly resemble a republic, and a republic of the most democratic kind, than the right vested in the people of choosing all the legislators, all the magistrates, all the judges, all the clergy, all the militia officers and all the administrators of the state, a choice taking place, at stated periods, without the interference of any superior authority whatever? Can anything more nearly resemble a republic, and a republic of the most democratic kind, than a continual renewal of elections, and the almost daily exercise of the power of the people either by primary assemblies, or assemblies of district, or assemblies of department, or municipal assemblies, or assemblies of section, or political clubs and other associations, presenting petitions, three times a week, to the whole representative body of the nation, and every day, every hour, every moment to all the inferior authorities? Can anything more nearly resemble a democracy, and a democracy of the most free and unrestricted sort, than those political discussions in the streets and public walks, than those communications, by means of advertisements posted in every corner of the streets, communications authorised by our discreet legislators, for the sake of avoiding the danger of every man's proclaiming his opinions by beat of drum and sound of trumpet? Finally, can anything be more in the style of popular government, more tyrannically democratical, than that armed authority which is transferred, *de jure* or *de facto*, from the prudent hands of the wise ones into the blind hands of the multitude and which, proscribing all individual wills, subjects to the plurality of voices and to the vote, so to speak, of the first mob, the personal liberty and private property of every member of the community?

And what remains of monarchical government in France, as the word is commonly understood by nations? It will be said, an hereditary executive power. But if the hereditary quality be still the same, the heritage itself has totally changed its nature; for so much has the executive power been weakened, that it has become almost nominal. They have also surrounded the heir to the throne by responsible ministers, whose ephemeral existence depends on the will of the representatives of the people.

There is more reality in the right of the suspensive veto, a right fortuitously saved from the general wreck of the prerogatives of the Crown; but it is not unknown in republics, where it exists under other forms, since the initiative in legislation is there usually blended with the executive power; and the necessity of this initiative is the most powerful and unequivocal check upon the undefined privileges of the representative assembly.

Be this as it may, all the dispositions adopted by the National Assembly are so truly democratic that to complete the transformation of France into a republic, nothing is wanting but to confide this executive power to a council, or a senate, nominated by the people, and to grant this suspensive veto to the same senate, or some other similarly elected body.

The question being thus reduced, let us see in what manner we are to discuss it in order properly to judge whether this system of democracy is or is not suitable to France. And considering in the first place the executive power, it appears to me that there are two doubts which require to be solved and we must ask the following questions.

First, whether the executive power, with such prerogatives only as the constitution has vested in it, would have greater force and efficiency in the hands of an elective senate, than when exercised by the monarch.

Secondly, whether admitting the necessity of increasing the prerogatives of the executive power, in order to enable it to fulfill its functions, the interest of freedom would advise that this power, with all its increase in strength, should be lodged in an assembly of men, elected pro tempore by the people, rather than confided to a permanent and hereditary monarch.

Though I might be misled in the examination of these two questions, I shall yet have done some service in reducing so important a discussion to its simple terms, and thus having allowed a greater number of people to take part in it.

The first idea that presents itself in favour of a senate charged with the exercise of the executive power is that, elected by the nation, it would have more confidence in its strength, and would be more respected than a monarch, possessing the supreme rank by the sole claim of birth.

It might further be supposed that if the members of the executive senate and those of the legislative body were allied by a common origin, the suffrage of their fellow citizens, no disputes would prevail between them, and they would mutually derive assistance from each other.

But their being children of the same bed would be no pledge of unanimity. Competitions are never so active as between men separated from one another by the most trivial differences; every jealous feeling is then awakened, and the first and slightest offence changes instantly into irritation and war. The elevation of the one above the other is not a circumstance indifferent to the harmony of the two powers; and it is not sufficient that this gradation be the effect of a law, the universal regulator of every rank in the state; it must further be guaranteed by the most powerful of all statutes, that of opinion. Two assemblies in every respect parallel would never pardon the reproaches addressed by the legislative body to the executive power in France, and still less the forms with which they are accompanied. Such assemblies can only exist in small states, where each feels alike the necessity of order; nor am I sure that the exception is applicable to republics where vanity is constantly present; for the paths cross each other especially where the passion for applause and the love of distinction are most eagerly cherished; there are so many open roads, so many ways that lead to an encounter with vanity!

Let us suppose, however, a legislative assembly reproaching the executive senate for not causing the laws to be observed; and the executive senate, in its turn, upbraiding the legislative assembly, and ascribing the disorder of which it complains to the incongruous nature of the laws themselves. Such a controversy between equals would shortly become a subject of general scandal and derision, and government, by losing its consideration, would not fail to lose at the same time all its respect and authority. It is the elevated station of the monarch that dignifies the attacks of the legislative body; and it is the splendid coat of mail of the throne that blunts the darts levelled at it by all the petty archers with which the National Assembly is constantly filled.

But moral considerations have almost always escaped the view of our legislators, or have at least occupied but a small share of their attention; and this is the main cause of our misfortunes. They have studied the body politic as simple anatomists, and have therefore never perceived the spirit that gives it motion and life.

I have placed among the circumstances favourable to republican systems the confidence which a senate, elected by the nation, could have in its own strength. But without putting this article out of the question, I would ask whether it is not balanced by the perpetual strategies to which the members of this senate would resort out of the desire to please, the ambition to be re-elected, or the hope to obtain some future office from the votes of the people? Enough has been seen of the dangerous effects of the sycophantic spirit in the midst of the legislative body. We have seen how many opinions, how many laws have owed their birth to the modest desire to obtain the applause of the tribunes. Respect is a plant of slow growth; men who have but two years given in which to exhibit themselves will often neglect to cultivate it. Much less time is needed to please and become popular; you may sow one day and reap the next. But if legislators have condescended to be governed by these motives, men whose functions led them to consider people only as a mass, and who cannot hope to survive but through the benefits they confer; how shall we expect more independence on the part of a senate whose office extends only to the execution of the laws and which must perpetually struggle with the interests and passions of individuals?

Let us also remark that the mobility and temporary tenure of offices, that condition congenial to republican government, cannot be extended to the administration of a great kingdom without further weakening the executive power; and that weakening would arise not only from the variation of principles inseparable from a perpetual succession of people at the helm of affairs, but also from the additional indifference that would be felt by all the agents of government, the moment they receive as a superior a collective body whose members constantly change. Such an administration has such a character of abstraction that the people do not know how to link it to the ideas of memory and gratitude.

I have therefore no doubt that if anything can supply the constitutional weakness of the executive power in France, it is the shadow of royalty, it is the impression that remains of the ancient splendor of the throne, it is the calculation of all the chances which may augment the authority of the sovereign, it is, finally, the idea that a single individual not removable from his place, and the small number of persons who are the agents of his will, are capable of a certain stability both in their gratitude and their resentments.

There is another circumstance which must be taken into account. The discipline of the army is one of the conditions most indispensible to the security of public order and the maintenance of respect abroad; nonetheless, in order to achieve this goal, one cannot compare the awe-inspiring supremacy of a monarch and the mediating authority of a collective senate, holding its office for a time and chosen by the people. I have already said it: the idea of unity is essential to an armed force, unity of will, unity of command, united temper, interest and movement. It is by means of one of the most powerful operations of the imagination that an armed force submits to the yoke of obedience, and exposes itself to all dangers. It would therefore be absurd to expect an army to be indifferent to the greatness and majesty of the head of state. Ages must elapse before the idea of one's country can be expected to assume that live force which was the object of adoration in ancient Rome; it would require a consistency and firmness in the principles of morality and virtue, of which our times are perhaps incapable.

It will probably be said that notwithstanding the annihilation of royalty, the unity of temper and action, so necessary to the government of a large state, might nevertheless be preserved; and that nothing more would be required, to obtain this object than to confide the principal part of the executive power in a republic to the temporary president of the senate, or to some other transient chief, appointed, as in America, by the whole nation. But where is the man whose qualities and virtues would be sufficiently known, sufficiently extensive so to speak, as to be thought worthy of such a situation, in a nation consisting of twenty-six millions of inhabitants? Nothing is less obtrusive than wisdom, nothing less apparent than moral character; yet these two qualities are absolutely indispensible in the administration of public affairs. I will, however, suppose that once in a century, an individual should so far unite the suffrages of his countrymen as to be sufficiently entitled to general confidence; how long will he preserve that confidence in the midst of a perpetual conflict of opinion, and of the numerous Areopagi[1] with which France is covered? How shall he surmount the obstacles which arise from the inconstant temper of the nation and from the jealousies that a restless vanity will not fail to instil?

We feel no great difficulty in accepting the superiority of our equals when they are only called to fulfill the role of legislators; their authority acts upon us only in mass, and we can regard them as accredited moralists or philosophers in action. Green-eyed envy consoles itself for the homages that are paid them, by calculating the number among whom those homages are shared, and the slender portion that falls to the lot of each. The executive authority appears under a very different aspect; particularly where it is unreservedly confided to a single individual who is one of our equals. No abstraction takes off its edge; everything in the application is precise and particular; and this superiority, by the various forms it assumes, becomes only the more sensible and irritating. For this reason it is that political institution, when it made birth a condition of supreme power, in reality practised a necessary indulgence to the weakness of human beings. It extinguished rivalship and ambition, while it defined the right of the Crown by immutable laws; it forbade resentment and enmity, while it made chance the only principle of exclusion; finally, by placing at a greater distance from the rest, him who presides over the rest, it softened the splendor of his dignity and the apparel of his dignity. I will admit, however, that a long and prosperous reign would give to a mere citizen, raised by fortune to the higest rank, the power of inspiring confidence and gaining general admiration and respect; but when the authority is confided for no more than two or three years, none but the most unprecedented circumstances can insure to the temporary chief of a great nation the consideration and respect which he would essentially need. One must still consider what would be required of a simple citizen called to represent the French nation in its relations with the ambassadors of

---

1. A metaphor for a significant obstacle. The Areopagus was a prominent rock northwest of the Acropolis in ancient Athens where it functioned as the site of a court.

foreign powers. It is much more incumbent upon him than upon a king to maintain respect and to strike an awe even into the legislative body. Talents and virtues, however eminent, will not in this case be sufficient: he would still need that native dignity that keeps others at a distance without parade, and that impresses respect almost without being perceived. If, on the contrary, ill formed for his elevated rank, he should have any trivial familiarity in his manners, any ignoble weakness in his behaviour, or should afford any handle to ridicule and satire, it may be unfortunate to have to admit that it would be impossible for this man in France, in these conditions, to obtain and keep up that political authority which is always inseparable from personal importance.

Here it will perhaps be asked if nature, blind in her gifts, does not expose to the same dangers, does not subject to the same contrasts those who owe their crown to the chance of birth. Rarely, one could answer; for forms and noble manners derive, in great measure, from a sort of confidence in one's situation and a temperate desire to please, two circumstances inherent in the education of princes and the habits of exalted rank. There is moreover a conventional greatness for kings, which outweighs their actual weakness. I do not know by what accident, or what habit it is, that they appear to us surrounded with a magic brightness that makes it impossible for us to see them as they really are, and our imagination, incapable of defending itself, is the first to bend the knee before its own creation.

The history of modern times has preserved the remembrance of a republican chief who carried the glory of his country to the most exalted height, and who knew how to maintain internal order with equal success. Cromwell, that singular character, obeyed and respected more than a king, owed his situation to his own efforts; and it is to be doubted whether he would have had the patience to have waited for his advancement, from the gradual operation of our absolute pluralities and relative pluralities, from our ballots by list and individual ballots, and from all that gradual ascent of reputation of which the primary assemblies form the first round. Cromwell, not sufficiently known before he started into celebrity, and too well known when he extended his yoke over England, would never have obtained by election the rank to which he raised himself by his own forces; and woe to the country, in which a man of this character and this genius should have the direction of public affairs!

The example of Washington may be adduced with more advantage to combat the various reflections presented in this chapter; for the authority enjoyed by this renowned chief of the United States is the result of the most free and regular choice. But what man was ever so well seconded by nature and by events? Prudence, moderation, fortitude, courage, an unimpeached morality, a commanding figure, adorned in peace with the memory of his military reputation, he seems to have had all the qualities; all these, together with the magnanimous indifference he feels for his high dignity, and the general sentiment that his inherent greatness is nothing inferior to the splendor of his office, moderate the unhappiness of the ambitious and the envious. No doubt that this unhappiness is less known in a nation where virtues are commonly respected; for this type of esteem equally honours them that give and him that receives it. Another good consequence that flows from the general respect for principles of morality is to link self-interest to the public good, to show the governors that their office derives its authority from the public good and the governed that their obedience acquires dignity, at once from its object and the motives that inspire it. In this case, rank does not look like a ladder, but like a circle; and the place of honour perpetually reminds the person that occupies it of the importance of order and unity which must be preserved. Finally, and though I have before made the observation, it is worth repeating here, these sentiments, these principles of morality, the beginning, the end, and the sum of all, and which could maintain social harmony on their own cannot be applied, with similar hopes, to a country of twenty-six million of souls, to a nation whose character is fixed, whose habits are rooted, and whose ancient forms constantly reveal themselves, in spite of the wide and flowing robe which it has been forced to wear. It is a country of three to four million inhabitants of which Washington is President, and his authority is limited to the circle of interests, placed in common by the federation of the fourteen states. How great the difference between this government and that of the whole kingdom of France! It would require a colossal stature, a stature that should be everywhere visible, a stature that does not exist, to render possible, and of permanent effect, the election of a temporary chief of a kingdom like France; and in all countries, men qualified to unite the suffrages of a nation are thinly scattered in the course of ages. From this point of view, it was a great idea to try to replace the real imperfection of human nature by that beauty of convention attached to throne and empire; in a word, it was a most ingenious scheme to avoid the effects of our reluctance to admire by committing into the hands of nature, so to speak, the choice of object which we should admire and which all our pride and vanity would have such a hard time to select.

Nonetheless, there is no senate, no council, no individual chief, or chief among many, elective or nominated by the people, that did not possess the faculty of exercising effectively the executive power, provided the most extensive prerogatives be added to their authority; for these prerogatives may be carried to a degree of despotism, but such combinations could not serve the cause of freedom. Let us never then forget that, in France, monarchical authority will better protect public order and give to the national consideration stronger support than any other form of government. This principle being once established, would it be reasonable to infringe it in order to gratify a chimerical jealousy and mistrust? I have demonstrated that the executive power, as composed by the first National Assembly, was inadequate to the purposes for which it was instituted; but I have also shown that an increase of this power, far from being a violation of freedom, would become a safeguard to it; and the example of England alone would be sufficient to confirm this truth. Nonetheless, if we were to quit reality in order to enter upon a calculation of all possible chances, it is not among the least probable that all the various dangers inseparable from republican government and all the unheard of excesses to which it may give rise may find their place in the midst of a country like France. We have only to recollect the disorder and agitation that at present pervade every part of our social system; we have only to consider this terrible spectacle in order to imagine to what height confusion would rise, if the supreme administration and executive power were once to become the property of the people at large, if this last game table were thrown open to a nation fermenting with a thousand passions, and which at present directs its energy and desires to enjoying or distributing all the officers and the positions of author-

ity. The end of government would be thought to consist in the pleasure of governing, and every one would contend for his share, either
as elector, deputy, or eligible, either as censor, satirist, or petitioner,
or as a menacing member of those parties which are everywhere to be
found in our clubs, our coffee-houses and our public squares. There
would no longer exist a single sentiment, a single thought that was
not allied to intrigue or faction; and in the midst of this general commotion, we would see rise an ambitious individual, more fortunate,
more skilful, or more daring than the rest who, presenting in his turn
the hopes and chimeras of the future to men always disaffected, on
account of their condition, to the existing order of things, would inspire the multitude with the desire of a revolution. He would also
gather around him all those who, tired of the disorders of anarchy,
might wish, in the secrecy of their hearts, for the return of an unlimited authority, and look to it as the only refuge. In short, he would
seek to overturn the government in order to elevate himself on its
ruins, or to dispose of his influence to the best advantage to some
person more favourably situated than himself, to realize the usurpation he desired.[2] An intestine war would signal the commencement of
such an enterprise, and the establishment of the most tyrannical despotism would probably be its final result. Then we would regret the
disdain with which we had treated the counsels of wisdom; then we
would regret the abuse we had made of our fortune. Then we would
regret that, while we had within our reach every blessing and felicity,
we wantonly sacrificed them to the most imprudent exaggerations.
Then we would ask ourselves by what stubborness we had refused to
acknowledge that a monarch, surrounded by the representatives of
the nation, restrained by judicious laws, and subjected to the empire
of opinion, was the true point of union, the connecting tie of order
and liberty. Then we would lament, too late, that in the necessity of

2. A prophetic statement by Necker that anticipated the rise of Napoleon, a few
years before the events of the Thermidor and the Directory. Necker's staunch opposition to the First Consul drew Napoleon's ire, especially after the publication of
Dernières vues de politique et de finances in 1802, in which Necker provided a thor-
ough critique of the Constitution of Year VIII. On this issue, see Grange, *Les Idées
de Necker*, 477–94.

confiding the executive power to an individual and distinct authority, and in the further necessity, not less indispensible, of fixing invariably the limits of that authority, we did not perceive that it was
safer for all to render it hereditary and patrimonial than to expose it
to the continual invasions of the ambitious, or to the turbulence of
demagogues. It requires but a moderate portion of wisdom on the
part of legislators to hold within the boundaries of the law the man
whom the law makes happy, and to attach him to the constitution,
who owes to this national compact his rank and greatness; but usurpers of the rightful authority break through so many duties to arrive
at this point, that no discretion can be expected from them; and too
frequently the most extravagant projects, the most violent and compulsory measures are the inevitable consequence of a first violation
of social order.

CHAPTER VIII

Continuation of the Same Subject

The vesting of executive power in an hereditary monarch is not, as I have already observed, the only circumstance that distinguishes the French constitution from a republican government; there exists another, equally remarkable particularity, I mean the right granted to the prince of refusing his sanction to the decrees of the legislative body; a right of the greatest importance, but which cannot prevent these decrees from passing into a law, if approved by three succeeding legislatures. Let us examine whether this royal prerogative be injurious to the welfare of the state; let us examine if it ought, or if it can be made an argument to justify the ardent enemies of monarchical government. And in the first place, a most essential observation presents itself to the mind while occupied on this question, which is, that in the political annals of no modern republic do we find an example of a National Assembly, composed of a single house, and possessing the supreme right of making laws without the participation of any other power. This participation, indeed, has not been determined and adjusted in a uniform manner; but in the majority of republics it is more striking and effective than in the French government.

The federative constitution of the Americans has made the concurrence of three wills necessary to the making of national laws; the assent of the House of Representatives, the assent of the Senate, and the sanction of the President. Of these, only the last condition is subjected to certain restrictions, but the restrictions are of less force than the limits fixed to the right of opposition, or veto, with which the French monarch is invested.

The particular states of America, in spite of their small size, and notwithstanding the deposit they have made, in the hands of Congress, of a part of the functions of sovereignty, have also subjected to the deliberations of two houses the decrees which relate to their interior affairs; and New York, as well as New England,[1] further require that these decrees should be sanctioned by the chief of the state; the form of which sanction is in all respects similar to the mode adopted by the United States.

All the other republics of Europe, and those most distinguished for their democracy, have vested the legislative function in the people or their representatives; but the proposal of decrees must originate, either with the executive council, or the chief magistrate; and by this formality, to which the name of *initiative* is given, the executive power has a participation in the laws prior to their being debated and approved by the legislative body.[2]

Thus even in republics, it has never been supposed that the right of legislation could be lodged in the people or their representatives, without a division of houses, or some restriction, some modification, some precaution, which should secure the state from the danger of hasty and inconsiderate measures. And were we to examine the constitution of every free government that exists in Europe, we should find that, among the different limitations prescribed to the exercise of a single legislative body, the suspensive veto, established by the French constitution, was the weakest of all. It is not then this right of opposition, considered in the abstract, but only its delegation to an hereditary monarch that can be described as alien to republican ideas.

This essential distinction being once established, the question that is to occupy our attention reduces itself to very simple terms, for

---

1. Necker refers here to the individual states from New England.

2. According to the Constitution of the United States, the right of legislative initiative is divided between the Senate and the House of Representatives. An important caveat is stipulated by Art. 1, Section 7: "All Bills for raising Revenue shall originate in the House of Representatives; but the Senate may propose or concur with Amendments as on other Bills."

we have only to examine whether the interest of the nation does not imperiously require that the right of opposition to the resolutions of the legislative body should be confided to the executive power of the state, in preference to every other constitutional authority; and it appears to me that diverse important considerations leave not a shadow of a doubt in this regard.

It would, in the first place, be condemning the executive power to the lowest abasement, to make it the blind agent of the will of another power; and on such a condition it could not exist; for in vain would it attempt to fulfil its high functions, unless it were supported by public opinion. But it will be said that it does not need this aid? The means which the laws place in its hands are sufficient to enforce universal obedience. Such, I am aware, is the austere language of the day; but if we are to trust solely to these means of constraint, an usher of the black rod or a sergeant at arms would be the proper depositary of the executive power. The great art of the legislator consists in the creation of authorities which may serve to dispense from a perpetual recourse to means of severity, a resource, whose frequent use is an offence to the dignity of man. The National Assembly wished to have governed mankind by decrees and it would have gladly tried to do it; but after decrees have been made, the execution remains to be provided, and obedience to be secured, and here the real difficulties begin.

A second reason for vesting the right of sanction, or of opposition to the decrees of the legislative assembly, in the executive power is that we could never rely on the active zeal of government, if we had no mode of ascertaining its real sentiments regarding the laws whose execution is entrusted to it. In a large kingdom there are numerous ways of creating difficulties, or assigning plausible reasons for intended delays; and whenever the opinions of the legislative body and the sentiments of administration should strikingly differ, public affairs would stagnate and become a perpetual subject of quarrel. It is an egregious mistake to imagine that to establish perfect concord between the two parties, it is sufficient to remind ministers of their responsibility, and to dazzle them with the glittering sword of justice. They must be very ignorant of the world who can depend only upon this precaution; punishment has relation only to major faults, the avoiding of which is easy; it is in the detail of actions difficult to be noticed that enmity and ill will are exerted without danger. But the National Assembly has hitherto shown a strong attachment to rigorous means; they have constituted the support of its systems, while it has neglected to appreciate the aid that might be derived from moderation and prudence. Arrived unexpectedly and without preparation to the enjoyment of a considerable authority, it has swelled with pride; and in its state of exaltation, it has taken for granted that its commands, which have proved all powerful to destroy, would be equally capable of building, sustaining, and perpetuating a new edifice. But between these two operations the distance is incommensurable. The one often requires only the aid of circumstances, to the other the deepest reflection and all the sagacity of genius are necessary; the one has all the passions for accomplices, the other has them all to contend with.

A third argument proves the propriety of joining the right of sanction to the legislative power. In all political questions, the government will always possess a knowledge that will be unique; not a knowledge that derives from the personal merit of its agents, but from the nature of its functions. The government must be particularly acquainted with the means of executing the laws; and there are also ideas which will be neglected by an assembly whose authority lasts for two years; these ideas must not and cannot be neglected by a less transitory authority. Thus, by conferring upon the executive power the right whether of initiative or of sanction, we obtain not only an additional stock of knowledge, but a joint reasoning that flows out of different ideas.

It is not then by chance, but in the name of the good of the state, that the legislators of every republic in Europe have made the executive power to participate, in some mode or other, in legislative resolutions.

Nor would the effect of this observation be destroyed by alleging that the liberty given to the king of England to refuse his assent to acts of Parliament must be considered as of no importance to the interests of the nation, since he has never made use of this liberty. To this objection I would answer that the mere possession of the right is sufficient to support the dignity of the executive power, and that the presence of ministers, either in the House of Commons, or House of Lords, the essential part they take in Parliamentary measures, and the initiative which they usually exercise, associate government, in the most efficient manner, to the deliberations of the legislative body.

There exists, however, a practical exception to the principles established in this chapter; for the majority of the individual states in America have granted neither right of sanction, nor right of opposition to their executive power, and the joint will of the two Houses of which their legislative body is composed is sufficient to the formation and adoption of laws. This disposition, however, has been adopted neither by New York, nor by the states in New England, nor by Georgia, and even if there resulted no inconvenience from it, it would not amount to the authority of a precedent, on account of the peculiar circumstances that accompany it. It is not necessary for me to mention over again the total lack of analogy between the small states of America and a great kingdom like France; but I will remark that these states have divested themselves of many essential parts and functions of sovereignty, to confer them upon the general Congress of the federation; and that in Congress, the consent of the executive power, with the reserves I have specified, is absolutely necessary to the validity of laws. The legislation of the particular states of America therefore is limited to their interior affairs; and thus circumscribed, as well as supported by the principles of morality and order, still respected in those small states, all types of free government would be adequate to their administration. We should also note that in a society where there is not only an equality of fact, but also an equality of opinion, the deputies to the legislative body have a constant and familiar communication with the head of the executive power, a communication which palliates and modifies the inconveniences attached to the entire separation established between the two powers. Finally, let us suppose, which is very likely to happen, that the particular states of America should aggrandize themselves, that their interests should become involved and complex, that the simplicity of their mores should be corrupted, that enmity should break out, and political divisions be fomented, I will then venture to predict that the legislative and executive power will begin to quarrel with each other; at least, that they will become disunited to such a degree as to annihilate all relation and concourse of opinions and wills between them.

Let us recapitulate. I have shown in this and the preceding chapter:

I. That the delegation of the executive power and suspensive veto to an hereditary monarch constitute all the difference between the French constitution and republican government.

II. That a legislative assembly, exercising by itself, and without modification or limit, the right of proposing, discussing, and determining all the laws, would be an institution contrary to the true interests of the nation, and to the instructive examples which surround us.

III. That, given the real necessity of choosing an authority distinct from the legislative body to which to confide either a right of assent, or a right of initiative, the preference was due to the executive power.

IV. That in a kingdom like France, the executive power must be lodged in the hands of an hereditary monarch, otherwise public order and freedom would be endangered.

From this set of propositions, we may infer that granting the right of opposition to the decrees of the legislative body to the king of the French can no more justify the inconsiderate wishes of the partisans of republicanism than the appointment of this monarch to the executive power and the supreme administration.

CHAPTER IX

Concluding Reflection on the Same Subject

In entering upon an investigation of new republican systems, I should, at any other period, have first examined whether they were practicable; but at present, nothing is real, nothing at least acknowledged as such, but abstract reasoning. Possibilities, like examples and precedents, are no longer considered as authorities of any weight; and in this country of theory, in this newly enclosed land of metaphysics, it is boldly presumed that anything can happen, that all plans can grow; and they are in a manner excusable in entertaining such an opinion, seeing what we have seen and continue to see. Now, however, after having paid my respects to general ideas in a long discussion, I hope I may be allowed to draw forth from their obscurity two particular truths, two observations, far indeed from novel, but still important; the one is, that the majority of the French nation will never consent to a change of its monarchical government into a republican one; the other, that foreign powers would not acquiesce in this political subversion; and as a result, that a civil and foreign war would be the only result of such an attempt.[1]

1. Necker wrote these lines in early 1792. Subsequent events confirmed his intuitions and prediction. In April 1792, when his book was released, the Legislative Assembly declared war on Austria, with the Prussian army also engaging in the hostilities soon afterwards. In September 1792, the French defeated the Prussians at Valmy. A few months later, in February 1793, the French Republic declared war on Britain and Holland, which triggered the formation of an anti-French coalition between Britain, Austria, Prussia, Holland, Spain, and Sardinia.

But why, it will be asked, should we suppose that the very same people, who have so highly approved and celebrated in such vociferous strains the daily degradation of the authority of the prince, would rise up against the absolute extinction of royalty, particularly as this dignity at present, stripped of the power that is its peculiar attribute, appears as nothing more than a vain pomp? The grounds of this contrast are easy to point out. The successive degradation of the royal authority, the gradual disarming of the executive power, these ideas sufficiently conspicuous to an attentive spectator escape the slight and careless observation of the majority of the people. Nor can anything appear more natural than this, if we recollect a truth established in the commencement of this work, and remember that the prerogatives of the executive power were fixed in an accidental and unsystematical manner, without any timely observation of the point to which the scattered provisions of the different members of the first National Assembly would lead. Nevertheless, if such were the mistake or absent mindedness of the constitutional committee itself, can we be astonished that the nation should not have perceived all the consequences, with respect to the royal authority, of these miscellaneous decrees, adopted by starts and by accident through the course of a twenty-eight month session of our first legislators? Remembering the former abuses of authority, they could not but observe with joy the reduction of a power, the idea of which was still terrible to them; and having never reflected, either upon the degree of force necessary to the government of a vast empire, or the multitude of connections which form the basis of obedience and subordination, they were absolutely ignorant whether the prerogatives of royalty were too much or too little retrenched. They still saw the name of king at the head of the government, and they never conceived the idea of calculating at what distance we were from a republic. But should this last barrier, which separates us from such a form of government, be suddenly broken down, the old partisans of monarchy would be awakened from their slumber, and the change of names would make a deeper impression than has ever been produced by the general disruption of things.

The sentiments of the people, in spite of all the instructions we may imagine ourselves able to give them, will always be formed in a manner opposite to the opinions of the philosopher. The latter proceeds from general ideas to their consequences, and from these consequences to particular and individual results and facts, words serving no other purpose than as a register of these facts. On the contrary, the people proceed, so to speak, from words and symbols to opinions and sentiments, and passions frequently begin to lead them at the very moment when enlightened individuals have already reached their conclusions and made up their minds.

In vain, then would the partisans of republican government attempt to prove that such a government differs but little from the existing constitution; in vain would they insinuate that there would be an inconsistency in having acquiesced, without regret, in the transformations which have brought forth that same constitution, and afterwards opposing a mere formality destined to complete the *system*; the names would no longer be the same, and the efforts of the innovators would be useless.

It is not unimportant also to observe that the felicity promised by these systematic republicans would consist entirely in the future, while the most deplorable divisions and calamities of the first magnitude would be our immediate portion. Meanwhile should we not have reason to doubt of this felicity, constantly adjourned, and of which the present generation can know nothing but from the terrible harbingers that announce it? The genius of our benefactors deals almost exclusively in injury to ourselves, reserving the fruits for a distant posterity. Alas! my mind, no doubt, is prosaic and short-sighted in comparison of theirs; for it rejects the most flattering prospects when they must be enjoyed amidst the groans of the unfortunate and the tears of the oppressed. Could the skill of man, however, guarantee to us this future destiny, which is to be purchased by so many sacrifices, we might resign ourselves to such an exchange; but we are required to renounce the present, and the future is guaranteed to us only through simple abstractions.

These reflections may seem to be merely an affair of feeling, but they are of the highest importance in the investigation of all political questions; and if we want to accurately observe, we shall soon have occasion to see that the lively affections of the soul have a secret analogy with the great moral truths; nothing is clearer than those who spring from a common root and lead us back to the same author. Let us illustrate this observation by a recourse to the subject that suggested it, the transmutation of the French monarchy into a republic.

I have just expressed the feelings of a soul oppressed with the image of all the calamities that hang over us, and which must be seen as the pledge of a future happiness guaranteed only by theoretical speculations. At the same time I seem to myself to have discovered a train of arguments, so to speak, correspondent to these feelings, and which rests upon a first principle of the highest importance. I ask myself what social power there could be, lawfully invested with the right of subjecting or exposing the present generation to all the calamities of civil war, in deference to the imagined interest of a future race; and contrary to the general opinion, I could not comprehend how so lofty a prerogative can be delegated to sovereigns, the masters of a single moment in the succession of ages. For such a purpose it would be just to call in a perpetual arbiter; a monarch, so to speak, of ages and centuries, to whom we might, without exaggeration, attribute the right and the capacity of regulating such a difficult controversy between the present and the future. Emboldened by this thought, I ventured to doubt the plenipotentiary powers even of the people itself to subvert at will the principles of government. The bounds of its understanding ought to bound its pretensions; and because it is capable of no unity but of feeling, purely speculative changes should be out of its province. It is only by a fiction that in such affairs anyone can pretend to act in its name. In great revolutions, in circumstances in which, by a subversion of principles, the fortune of a nation may be overturned from the foundation, it is not sufficient to obtain the approbation of its temporary deputies, it is necessary to consult the immovable representative of its true interests, rights, and duties, and this immovable representative is no other than absolute, perfect morality. The sovereignty of the people, in a kingdom consisting of twenty-six millions of souls, is a pure abstraction; for the innumerable wishes and sentiments of a master like this can never be known by the small number of persons appointed to be their interpreters. Under such a reign, therefore, every plan, every measure, every system, in whatever legal form it may be clothed, will always be usurpation, if they do not bear the stamp of reason, justice, and sound policy.[2]

These, I know, are truths which imperious demagogues do not love to hear. Their object is to erect a sovereign whose authority should be independent, whose despotism should have an appearance of legality, in order that they may reign in his court, command in his name, and have a sanction for their own excesses, their spirit of animosity or revenge. With what dissimulation do they ascribe to these sovereign ideas and wishes that he does not possess! They recreate him as best suits themselves, and profess a most sacred respect for the sentiments they put into his mouth. All on one side is artifice, and on the other credulity.

I have said that a second obstacle to the conversion of the French government into a republic would spring from the opposition that would be made by foreign powers to such a revolution. It could not with justice be expected that they should remain indifferent to such an important political event; and it could not be imagined either that they should remain entirely uninterested in the destiny of a royal house, seated for eight hundred years on the throne of France, and united, by ties of blood, to all the sovereigns of Europe. In vain would our polemical writers hope to detach them from the cause, by telling them that the representatives of the sovereign people had, in a national convention, determined this change of constitution, by a majority of three hundred and ninety-nine voices against three hundred and forty-seven, or in some other proportion, and that therefore the revolution was perfectly legal. Precisions of this sort are proper, and even necessary, in the usual course of things; but in circumstances out of the common order, they become pedantic and absurd, and we should never conceal the fact that the principles themselves are no longer of the same nature. Reason, august reason, which laid the foundation stone of all truths, has reserved to itself also the power of marking out their boundaries, and of intervening again in those occasions in which, by exaggerating these truths, their original sense is

2. For more information on Necker's views on sovereignty, see Grange, *Les Idées de Necker*, 267–76, and Craiutu, *A Virtue for Courageous Minds*, 146–54.

lost. Thus, the will of a sovereign people is legally expressed, in the ordinary course of affairs, by the majority of its deputies, even though each deputy should, as in France, represent the interests of thirty-five thousand souls; for reason tells us that, in political deliberations, we must adopt the best means of achieving results without trouble; but the sovereignty of a nation can no longer be thus represented when the question relates to a subject so grave and so immense as an absolute revolutionary change in a government. Reason refuses to allow an affair of this importance to be decided by such forms, and the empire of method to be so extensive. It is therefore necessary that the desire of a revolution should be attested in a stronger manner, and this is necessary not only to render this revolution legitimate, but the better to ascertain that it is the national will. This will, when the object is an absolute change of the social order, ought to be guaranteed by the publicity of the motives that produced it, by the state of oppression of the people, the tyranny of their chiefs, or by whatever other striking sign, that admits of no dispute, and which reason can consecrate.

Hence it follows that, according to the character of a nation, to the degree to which knowledge is spread among its members, to the stronger or weaker degree in which it can be subjected by declamation, or rendered the object of intrigue or turbulence, we must employ greater precaution seeking to know its will, and a solemn formality in recording it. Thus, in a nation like the American people, where the multitude are not condemned by their poverty to absolute ignorance, where men have more character, where vanity, self-love, and the other motives of the imagination have not established their empire yet, where morality has a fixed authority among people, and reconciles sentiments and reason, there, I say, the general will is less obscure and ambiguous than in France, and a small number of sages may be sufficient to express it and guarantee its reality.

It cannot then be concealed that there exists no simple way, no means compatible with legality, with internal tranquility and external peace, by which to introduce into France an entirely republican constitution. The attempts made to this effect would bear such a striking character of violence and usurpation that it could not fail to excite general alarm.

There are contagious calamities which interest other nations much more strongly than a violation of territory. It cannot be imagined that they should look with indifference and on the establishment of a source of disorder and anarchy in the very centre of Europe, on the continual encouragement granted to systems of insurrection, and on the subversion of principles which, in all countries, serve as pillars to the social edifice. Our first demagogues would, in a very short space of time, overturn governments. They would excite the people to discontent by secret manoeuvres and false promises; they would then say that they heard its voice; and proclaiming this murmur as a sovereign law, terrifying by violence all who should dare to object, they would become the tyrants of the earth, while pretending to be its liberators. Alas! such friends of liberty do more injury to its cause than despots; and in whatever republic they should reign, lighthouses ought to be placed at the four corners of the territory to caution travellers against approaching it.

Let us then repeat while it is yet not too late. France has greater need of its king than the king has need of it. I do not know what portion of happiness an individual may derive from rank and fortune, for habit, even in times of the utmost serenity and composure, soon extinguishes the charm of this kind of superiority; but France, abandoned to the empire of all the hypocrites of liberty, France, subjected, under the name of a republic, to the successive yoke of every daring spirit, France, without any point at which to rally, the object of every vanity and torn by all the passions, France would exhibit a most terrible and heartbreaking spectacle; and the final result would perhaps be that, from one end of the earth to the other, the question would be raised, whether men, for the greater part without property and by the sole privilege of having drawn their first breath on the banks of the Seine or the Loire, would possess the right of rendering uninhabitable, by any but themselves, a country consisting of twenty-five thousand square leagues, situated in the most charming climate in the world, and favoured with the most precious gifts of nature. There is no idea, however absurd, that the abuse of force and the exaggerated use of its rights may not sustain, and the ground of this is not the will of individuals, that reason is the eternal law, the first and the last, and that her empire is everlasting.

Let me not be told that a republican government is the wish of the patriots, and that its establishment will be the work of patriots. Who is there that can deserve the title? Who will dare to assert their claim to it, at the time that they plunge their country in all the horrors of anarchy? Patriots are those who love order and the laws, as much as liberty; patriots are those who wish to render liberty the portion of all men, and not the exclusive privilege of a cast of factious spirits and demagogues; patriots are those who desire to place it under the guardianship of a well-ordered authority, and refuse to put it under the dangerous protection of every popular tyrant; patriots are those who wish to see their country as the refuge of the oppressed, the sacred asylum of persecuted virtue, an honour in the midst of nations for amenity of manners, splendour of talents, and the glory that is attached to every generous proceeding, and not the school of ingratitude, or a place of terror to every honest and peaceful citizen. These are the only genuine patriots; history and future generations will acknowledge no other; and time will efface all those false colours with which the traits of our fantastic heroes are at present disguised, and by which they vainly hope to mislead the incorruptible posterity.

CHAPTER X

Of Federative Government

By federative government is understood a union of small states which, without renouncing their rights of sovereignty, or their particular administration, submit themselves, as to their general interests, to the authority of a representative diet, or a supreme chief, or to the authority of both these powers combined. These general interests consist in commercial regulations and treaties, offensive and defensive alliances, resolutions of peace and war, the apportionment of expenses, contributions and loans necessary to the defence and safety of the united states, to the execution of hostile projects, and every enterprise of general utility. These common interests further include the different precautions relative both to the maintenance of each individual government and the constant observance of all the duties of the union. Finally, federative legislation may be extended to a uniformity of money, weights and measures, to the direction of public roads, and to such other dispositions as are for the equal convenience of all the contracting states.

A convention of this nature may be established between republics of very unequal population, as in America; and may even exist, as in Switzerland, between republics which differ not only as to their extent, but also in the principles of their respective governments. Meanwhile the complete harmony of these constitutions would no doubt require that, between the different states united by a political contract, there should be an entire parity.

Federative government, considered in its perfection, and abstractedly from circumstances that may oppose its establishment, unites advantages of the greatest importance and the highest consideration. It secures political force, without giving to the depositaries of the different powers a task above their strength, and by preserving all the means of defence which result from a commanding association. It circumscribes the civil government within the limits which the weakness of human beings renders so necessary and proper. Finally, while the people derive from it the security, which is the particular apanage of great states, they enjoy at the same time all the fruits of that wisdom and those vigilant cares that essentially characterize the administration of small republics.

Could we then, by any supernatural means, divide all Europe into republics consisting of three or four hundred thousand souls, and out of these republics form fifteen or twenty particular federations, more or less similar in their organization to the federation of America; could we further, by the same act of power, give to these new nations a moral character, still pure, and a spirit congenial to such a mode of government, I have no doubt that the peace of the world and the happiness of mankind would rest on more solid foundations, and that a thousand other salutary influences would derive from this political transformation. But constitutions of this kind, though they were to depend on the most perfect freedom of choice, could not be made to accord with the interest of the people, without the uniformity I have supposed; for if placed amidst powerful kingdoms, amidst governments subjected to the authority of a single individual, they would never have more than a precarious existence, unless, like the Helvetic cantons, defended by their situation, or, like the states of America, by their distance from Europe.

In the meantime, such is the imperfection of the French constitution that, were it not susceptible of change, a federative government would be preferable; and of the two innovations there would have been more genius in risking this last, than in giving us, by way of experiment, a bastard republic, a constitution of parade, a government without solidity, a body without a solid appearance.

It would at least be possible to have alledged many strong arguments in support of the federative system. It might have been said that to secure liberty and order, and above all to promote healthy mores, it was necessary that the task imposed upon governments should not be beyond their strength, and that they should not be kept too much at a distance from the majority of their pupils. It might have been said, and that with strong philosophical arguments, that one legislation, one executive power, one supreme administration, one public opinion, must ever promote, in a very imperfect manner, the happiness of twenty-six millions of men. It might still have been remarked, with the sagacity characteristic of the moralists, that the only sure means of subduing the influence of rank and fortune was to narrow the social theater in order to diminish the effects of imagination by bringing the perspective closer together, which would at once render talents and virtue more conspicuous, and enable all real superiorities to engage in a hopeful contention for the distinctions of opinion.

Lastly, in the midst of the anarchy which we are witnessing, and while so many citizens are divided between the interests that retain them in France and the fears that general insubordination inspires, it might be regretted that France was not divided into so many independent states, that might have felt the necessity of maintaining peace and order within their borders, and that should, in this respect, have emulated each other in order to invite among them rich owners and the inhabitants of every country, who rank personal security as the first of blessings.

Undoubtedly, it would have been more difficult to show how political force and activity could be reconciled to a federative government; but France has so many means of defence, when she is prudent and does not invite all Europe to make war upon her, that those difficulties would not have been invincible. The great obstacle to such a constitution would not, in my opinion, have arisen from the impossibility of uniting federative government and political strength, or from the impossibility of achieving this goal without endangering general liberty; but from other considerations, less visible, but still more insurmountable.

The indivisibility of monarchy is as dear to Frenchmen as monarchy itself. Our legislators, however, either with their consent or without their knowledge, have contrived to alter this indivisibility, by the nature of the powers that have been instituted in all the departments, as they have struck at the subversion of the monarchical government, by the degradation of royalty; but a visible change, both in names and in forms, a change that should have impressed the imagination of the people, would have experienced the most general opposition. The French, after having constituted for so many ages the integral part of a great nation, the image of whose glory is present to their minds and lives in their hearts, would never consent to partitions that, in their view, would diminish the splendor of the kingdom and replace its complete unity with a simple federative unity. France, it is true, by adopting such a system, would be in the same situation as America; but the political procedure of the two nations in this respect would be extremely different. America already existed, divided into separate states; it therefore only received a greater consistence, and as it were a sort of moral extension, by the federation of these states. France, on the contrary, would pass from the most complete whole to sections and divisions; and though these sections might remain united, it would still be a sort of decline, and a movement directly the reverse of the progression of the Americans. Now a nation would not easily content itself with a retrograde course, even with the certain prospect of a better government. This struggle of reflection against the power of the imagination is almost always a useless attempt.

The large American states, as I have already observed, have manifested a disposition of dividing themselves into two parts, of which each is to be an independent state, when their increase of population shall have established a disproportion between the duties and power of their government; and, should they execute this project, they will give an example unique in the history of the world. But a political morality of the highest perfection would be necessary to induce men to reject the ideas of greatness established by opinion, and to sacrifice them to the mere desire of maintaining social order. This morality is, however, absolutely required for the discharge of the strict duties of a federative constitution. I call then upon the French themselves to determine whether this is what they are capable of, whether they have the calm determination necessary to live in peace in a nation of forty or fifty federated republics and to be preoccupied, in all occasions, only with their internal happiness. We may justly doubt of this. They are too fond of distinction, too fond of acting, in every sense, to be able to contain themselves within the sole limits of felicity. Formerly, it might have been practicable, but it is otherwise now. They resemble, at the present moment, men escaped from a long captivity, and who search everywhere for space; in vain should we recommend to them to form themselves into separate states in order to taste the goods enjoyed by the Americans, they would believe that it would reduce them to the condition of anchorets. A great number among them, it is true, wish for a republic, but they would have it as large as the universe; for when they form to themselves a pleasing idea, it is more from a desire of reigning, in their turn, than from any natural attachment to the austere empire of mores. They speak with affection of the law, but it is rather to dictate than to obey it; and if they profess equality, it is much more from personal and ambitious motives, from a student disposition to laugh at their former masters, than for the sake of enjoying, like the English, the sentiment of a tranquil pride.

In truth, the character of the French nation is not yet fixed; everything is in flux as are its politics; and this is the language that its true friends should embrace. But one of the most severe reproaches that can be cast upon its first legislators, is that of having obliged it perpetually to go out of itself, and perpetually to appear in the offensive; for such is inevitably the effect of a constitution in which every consent is forced, in which all powers, all authorities are mutually jealous and mistrustful of each other, in which nothing is connected by the tie of happiness, in which practice and theory, maxims and their application, realities and appearances are in a state of war.

There are also circumstances peculiar to the kingdom of France, which it would be no easy matter to reconcile with the establishment of a federative government. I will cite the two principal ones. France, by its central situation in Europe, needs a great number of fortified places for the defence of its immense frontiers; and the protection of these places, the expense that their maintenance requires, and above all the military powers that must be established therein, would become so many subjects of controversy between the federative authority and the particular authority of each of the states in which these fortified towns may be situated.

Another obstacle to the establishment of a federative government in France would derive from the magnitude and splendor of the city of Paris. This capital of an undivided kingdom would then be only the chief town of a federated state, and the other parts of France, ceasing to participate in its lustre, would not fail to become jealous of it. Beside, as it would no longer be in an equal degree the centre of affairs and of general circulation, the liberal arts, those companions of fortune, the liberal arts, which require a vast theatre to arrive at perfection, would insensibly lose their renown. The inhabitants of Paris, therefore, foreseeing this decay, would avail themselves of the superiority of their credit in the kingdom, to combat a system essentially contrary to their interests.

Finally, it is not possible to make two successive attempts at the introduction of a new government; for the passions, whose co-operation is necessary to the success of such an enterprise, cannot be turned out of their course; on the contrary, it is necessary, in order to maintain their first impulse, that we should continually smooth the way before them, and to retain the multitude on our side, we must always guide it in the same direction. Various considerations then might be adduced to show that, even were we to regard a federative government as the best of all political systems, we should today attempt in vain to establish it in France, and to substitute it in the place of a temperate monarchy. And let us here call to mind a reflection, already illustrated in another part of this work, but which is perfectly applicable to the present question. The hereditary nature of the throne and every kind of supremacy by right of birth would be incompatible with a federative government, composed of republics subjected to the principles of absolute equality. The office of Stadtholder, the succession to which is by right of primogeniture, could not be maintained in the United Provinces, if there did not exist in each a body of nobles, a preeminent body, serving as a mediator between the chief of the state and the rest of the nation, and which thus keeps alive that respect for opinion, that reverence which is able to resist, to some extent, the capricious laws of nature and preserve the power and action of an hereditary authority, regardless of the character of the prince by whom that authority is exercised.

It will now be asked if the National Assembly, by dividing France into departments, and by confiding to the free choice of the people the nomination of the administrators, the judges and the clergy of each of the different sections of the kingdom, have not borrowed from the federative government of America all that was most valuable, and have not thereby displayed the labor of the bee and the instinct of genius. The legislators of France would doubtless assent to this *conclusium:*[1] but, for the timely prevention of remonstrances, let us examine a question that has before offered itself to my notice, but whose importance is such, that the discussion necessarily demands a more than cursory attention.

No doubt there are traits of resemblance between the constitution of republican governments and the constitution of our departments; but in politics, as in all sciences that have relation to life, similarities that lead to contrary results are actual differences. Social organization is not a cabinet rarity, destined for the amusement of the curious ones; to judge of it properly we must see it in motion and applied to the use for which it was intended. And setting aside, for the present, every kind of social organization, what should we say about an artisan of Paris, or any other great town, who, after having made a common village clock, but a clock that would not work, or that played the chimes at the wrong hour, should answer the complaints of the parish officers, by proving, wheel by wheel, and pin by pin, that his clock was exactly similar to that of Notre-Dame or Saint-Sulpice? Observe, he would say, the crown wheel and pallets which form the escapement and give motion to the balance; observe also the verge and pendulum spring; observe all that. Mr. Artisan, one of the parish officers would say, we see that your story is all very plain and very distinct, but still our clock does not work.—What do you say, it does not work? You think perhaps that I have not made the balance sufficiently large to possess the requisite centrifugal force?—No, I do not say that.—That I have neglected to adjust the wheels and the pinions?—No, I do not say that.—And in God's name what do you say?—I say nothing, Mr. Artisan, but that our clock does not work, and we must have another.

In like manner, in the organization of two political societies, of which one should achieve its end and the other widely deviate from it, the ingenious legislator might easily find, between the different

1. In Latin, in the original. The literal meaning is acceptance or conclusion of a treaty; also a decree.

parts of the two constructions, a multitude of similitudes, and yet the ignorant public would be right to say, with the parish officer—We do not doubt your skill, *but our clock does not work.*

I am aware that this coarse mode of reasoning cannot but be very unpalatable to the legislators of France. They have, indeed, been abundantly careful regarding all the figurative part of the political machine; and if men were not so stubborn as to attach considerable importance to a single fact, its exact and regular movement, neither the artificer nor his work would be liable to the slightest reproach. Let us now see if we can add anything to the arguments of these sensible people.

The individual states of America as well as the majority of republics perceive that order is established among them, the laws are respected, and their public administration is conducted without effort and violence.

The departments in France are founded in appearance upon similar principles, and, as I have said, elections are determined therein by the voice of the people. Why then do they present so different a spectacle? The levying of contributions experiences resistance; the rights attached to manorial lands, and which have been sanctioned by the national representatives, depend for payment solely on the will of the debtor; the circulation of corn is obstructed; property is imperfectly secured; the tribunals are intimidated, and personal safety often exposed to the violence of the people; finally, the departments, uncertain of being obeyed by the subordinate authorities, feel in their turn a sentiment of independence in all their relations with the supreme head of executive power. Whence this contrast between our departments and the individual states of America? Why are two constitutions, resembling each other, productive of such dissimilar effects? The reason is not difficult to indicate.

Each American state possesses within itself, if I may be permitted so to speak, the whole apparatus of government. It has not only elective judges and administrators, like our departments; it has also a distinct legislative body; it has an authority of opinion peculiar to itself, and every institution suited to its mores or its genius. They are these means united, and united within a limited circle, which, forming in a manner the spokes of one of the same wheel, give to the whole administration a certain and regular movement. The close connections between the legislative power, the executive power, the judiciary power and the power of public opinion, make them act together and with a common accord; all the citizens become then so many agents of the same principles and the same authority, so many judges of the common interest, so many inspectors of the observance of the laws.

There certainly exist in America a legislative power and an executive power, placed at a considerable distance from the different parts of the continent subjected to their authority; I mean the power of Congress; but this power has no influence over the civil order and interior administration of the individual states; it reigns, as it were, at the circumference of them all, since its empire is restricted to external affairs and the maintenance of harmony between the federated republics. Thus it diminishes the functions of each particular government, without occasioning any disagreement between its will and their domestic determinations, between its opinions and their respective interests, and without risking at least, by its daily exertion, to jeopardize the respect due to its supremacy. And this is one of the many great advantages of federative government.

Not one of the important circumstances I have enumerated, so auspicious to liberty, so favourable to public order, is applicable to the departments of the kingdom; so widely does their organization differ, in essential points, from the Constitution of the individual American states. They have, in the first place, no proper legislative body: the decrees by which they are to be governed depend on the majority of voices in a National Assembly, where the same laws are instituted for them, as for the other eighty-two sections of the kingdom. This legislative body which must serve all the departments, is situated at a very considerable distance from many of them, and they have no influence over its sentiments but by means of a small number of deputies. These deputies also receive no mandate, no instructions, and are at liberty to prefer their individual opinion to the general will of the citizens by whom they are elected. Hence it appears that the national laws cannot obtain, in the different departments, that force of consent which belongs to laws conceived, digested and adopted in the midst of small states, whose interests they must regulate. The will of an assembly dictating, by its sole authority, the obligations and duties of twenty-six millions of men, cannot correspond, either generally or habitually, to the prevailing opinion in each department; and it will frequently happen that, along with the law, will arrive in the different parts of the kingdom an account of the dissentions that attended its formation, and which by this means are calculated to weaken this legislative will. There is therefore no comparison between the authority of laws made for the government of a moderate population, at the centre of a republic of modest extent, and the authority of laws issuing from a single place in the empire and designed to extend over a vast kingdom.

Let us add to these remarks an important reflection, entitled, I believe, to particular attention. It is that legislative authority, to be exercised with effect by a single assembly, composed of our equals and representatives, must be adapted to a theatre infinitely circumscribed; for, devoid of all the attributes which strike the imagination, it is necessary, in order to give it relief and obtain for it the support of opinion, that the conformity of its decisions with the principles of morality and reason should be easily perceived; and that its laws should thus appear, in the eyes of all the citizens, stamped with the image of the most august of authorities.

It is further to be observed that in the individual states of America, as in all republics, the real executive power is located close to the legislative, a condition absolutely necessary to render it judicious and give it the strength that it needs. Legislation and execution must be kept separate, but in spirit they must be blended with each other; a fundamental point which, I believe, has never been made, perhaps because the opportunity has never arisen to do it; for never till now did any of the different founders of political societies think of placing the mere form of the executive power in the vicinity of the legislative, and scattering its reality in all the provinces of the empire. What is the consequence of this division? It is that the executive power is nowhere what it ought to be; it is nowhere properly balanced; it lacks the force at the head of government, and is unbridled elsewhere. And yet, between these two divisions of the same power, the supreme administration and the departments, people constantly contend with the one that is less powerful and treat the other one with forbearance; they valiantly fight against the lion's shadow, while they shrink from the real lion himself.

It is true that the departments, independently of the consciousness they have of their own power, a power stronger and less exposed
to accident than that of the legislature itself, have another means of
defending themselves against any form of responsibility; and this extremely valuable means is the power of resistance placed below them,
under the name of districts and municipalities.*

Every day then we shall perceive better that no comparison is to
be made, either with regard to public order, or liberty, between the
executive power of republics, and that which our legislators have invented for France. That the one is preserved in all its plenitude and its
unity, the other divided, partitioned and dissected in every possible
manner. That the one is under the superintending eye of the legislature, and that the other has only its figurative part subjected to this
inspection. That the one is surrounded, supported and restrained by
opinion, and that the other has no such central position, because it
exists fully nowhere. That the one is responsible for its inaction, while
the other can always exculpate itself by appealing, when it thinks fit,
from its conduct to its means. Finally, that in republics, the executive
power is always accountable to all citizens for the abuses of its authority, but in our government, the departments can exercise various
acts of despotism at the same time that they can rebuff the first complaints by pretending that they are only subordinate, and referring
the complainants to the supreme executive power, that administra-

---

* The departments may act as they please, when not at variance with a municipality more powerful than themselves, or with the political society of the canton. In
that case the department says in vain: It is my province to command.—The municipality replies, it may be so, but I will not obey your commands.—But the constitution rejoins the department, the constitution for which you have promised to die;
this is the moment of trial.—Not at all, answers the municipality; you indeed may
thus interpret it, but I understand it differently: I will, therefore, with your supreme
permission, continue to live, and yet will not obey your injunctions. Great embarrassment, big controversy; and after having been a subject of scandal and derision for
a considerable period, the affair comes before the National Assembly, which takes
cognizance of every circumstance, even the respective credit of the two parties, and
afterwards pronounces its decision, but with as much tardiness as possible. And the
king! alas, he is all the while the supreme executive power; no one denies it, no one
feels sufficiently interested in the question to dispute it.

tion devoid of real substance, obliged to plead indulgence to conceal its nullity. Thus, one of the numerous absurdities of the French constitution is that the right of appeal, in the hierarchy of the administration, conduces less to restrain the inferior authorities than to provide them with an excuse and justification.

Thus I have sufficiently demonstrated that there exists but a half resemblance between the individual states of America and the constitution of our departments. They are these half resemblances, these partial imitations, in politics, which reveal the uncertainty of the legislator. We hereby perceive that his desires and fears have been at variance, and that, by a sort of accommodation with himself, the legislator has mysteriously copied the outlines of such governments which he dared not take in all points for his model. Their spirit and unity are of consequence lost, and after much labour and study he has produced but an irregular and counterfeit work, composed also of so many shreds, that resembles a book of patterns rather than a well-wrought cloth. And it is for this reason, perhaps, that the French constitution, monarchical in its title, republican in its forms, despotic in its means of execution, confused also in its principles, variable in its march, uncertain in its end, presents to our view an imperfect mixture of all forms of government and political ideas.

CHAPTER XI

The Moral Effect of the French Constitution

The science of political legislation is similar to a labyrinth of thought; and yet, the study of moral man is a still more intricate labyrinth. We conceive it to be easy, because the observer and the object of his attention, the spectator and the spectacle, seem to touch themselves and become one; but it depends on laws of vision of which few of us possess the secret. So many paths lead to happiness, so many lead away from it, that amidst such a complicated picture, the most attentive philosopher can with difficulty fix his judgment.

How then expect to discover the moral effect of a civil and political constitution, if we have not long meditated on the nature of man, if we are ignorant of the cravings of his soul and the secret propensities of his heart, if we do not relate to him with respect to both his virtues and vices; finally, if we have constantly enjoyed ourselves and lived in perpetual distraction, so to speak, undisturbed by reflection?

Nonetheless, if a knowledge of man be essentially necessary to the legislator, we may be led to infer that a political system, all the parts of which should be perfectly adjusted and disposed, could never be the work of a numerous assembly; for the refined ideas and subtle observations which constitute the science of the human heart can never be put into common property; they are essences too thin to support the shock of debate, or to serve as a focus of attention. Vulgar and common people, in all great assemblies, bring down the tone of reasoning to the level of their comprehension, just as deaf men give the tone of speaking in all companies where people want them to be able to understand them. Let us not then be surprised if the chief leaders of the National Assembly, in their intention to impose their will, have brought forward only two perfectly distinct and emphatic principles, liberty and equality. They were perhaps forced to do this, in order to hold under the same yoke a great diversity of characters and dispositions. But the National Assembly is not the less reprehensible for having submitted itself to such laws, is not the less reprehensible for having thus narrowed our interests and excluded all our other desires. The study of our different sentiments might have embarrassed it, but it has circumscribed them by a fiction; the study of the various elements that make up human happiness might have multiplied its combinations, but it has reduced them by an arbitrary supposition, and acknowledging only two of these elements, has counted the rest for nothing. Thus all that constitutes human beings, all that is necessary to them in a thousand ways, either it could not see or did not take into account. One would suppose that, in imitation of the iron bed of Procustes, it wished, by a similar invention, to proportion to its narrow system our moral nature, and to retrench from us all that we were by our habits, our characters, the diversified qualities of our minds, our imaginations, our hopes, our rooted ideas of honour and glory, and particularly by our principles of education, our duties and our religious opinions. Liberty and equality would thus become our unique fortune, and by a singular combination, our destiny would be made to depend upon a mere philosophical summary.

There is something strange in this manner of discerning both our wishes and our interests; and such an approach shows how shortsighted are our legislators, as well as the real limits of our moral domain. Let us restore to this domain its rightful scope, and considering man on a more comprehensive scale than our legislators have done, let us examine, in this point of view, the utility of their work, and the wisdom of their principles.

Man is happy, no doubt, in the enjoyment of civil and political liberty; but as his faculties are limited, as he sojourns in a land sown with good and evil, as he is not placed in an enchanted garden, where he may without effort, without labour, without the help of others, gather, at his will, either nourishing fruits, or odoriferous flowers, liberty, to be a blessing, must be accompanied by all the virtues necessary to guide and assist him in the toilsome paths of life.

Filled with these thoughts, if I take a view of the discourses and decrees of our legislators, I perceive them continually occupied with reminding men of their rights, but talking only lukewarmly about their duties and obligations. But this amounts to proceeding in an opposite direction to the one dictated by a morality of perennial renown, and which, by its twofold character of wisdom and holiness, has preserved for so many ages a memorable influence over all the nations of Europe. The author of this admirable legislation had perceived that mankind being called to increase and multiply upon a globe the productions of which are limited, the sacrifice of a portion of our desires was imposed upon us by one of the immutable laws of nature; and that thus the most sublime philosophy would be able not only to soften this sacrifice, but to present it as a form of happiness, by associating with it the idea of duty and all the encouragements that accompany it in an admirable moral system.

It is to this idea of duty that a perpetual homage ought to be paid; and when it is treated with contempt, when the attention of the people is directed to their rights, they are fed with illusions, and even dangerous ones; for the multitude once forced out of its limits, soon meets, in its random and inconsiderate march, with the numerous barriers by which our happiness upon earth is surrounded everywhere.

We deceive ourselves then when we consider duties as only useful to those who have rights. This proposition can at least never be made applicable to social organization taken in all its extent; for it will soon be perceived that duties and the morality which prescribes them serve as consolations to a great number of men, by aiding them to live contentedly within the sphere which lot has assigned them. And when people are forced to leave that sphere, by talking to them in vague terms about their rights, their opinions are upset but their destinies are not improved. But it is easy to weaken their faith in these truths; and when the legislator himself refuses to acknowledge them, when his political strategy is to favour and support illusions, it is to the empire of falsehood that mankind are subjected.

Nonetheless, it is not only the happiness of the people that is essentially affected by telling them so much of their rights, and so little of their duties; the respect for justice is also violated in an essential way; for when legislators disseminate a general spirit of pretention among those who possess more strength than knowledge, the boundaries which separate right from wrong are easily overlooked; and these boundaries once passed by some, will shortly be so by others, from the mere force of imagination, which is necessarily great in a populous nation. Justice also begins to be contaminated in its principle, when it is not observed with a common accord; for it has for its basis a general compact; and it is only by favour of such a compact that each thinks to find in the universal order the compensation for his individual sacrifices.

It was the work of time and the task of ages to establish the different barriers destined to restrain the turbulent passions of mankind; but their destruction may be the result, not only of a political constitution badly arranged, not only of a law imprudently made, but also of a false maxim, when considerable eclat is given to that maxim by the rulers of the nation; and such has been the unfortunate effect of the first principle of the Declaration of Rights.

Justice ought to be the principal object and interest of government; but justice must be looked after and ought to be guarded with double care; we must, as it were, secure it with an additional defense when legislators have placed the civil and political authority in the hands of the people; for thus placed, it will naturally ferment all the sentiments of jealousy and envy, of malice and resentment, which are inseparable from misfortune; and instead of serving as a consolation to those who have reason to complain of their lot, it will only wound and irritate their souls. They expect that a new power should better their condition, and disappointed in their first hopes, they run after other illusions, till at length events and changes of scene become for them a necessary amusement. They reflect on the means of acquiring credit, and the advantages that may be derived from it; and distracted by the ever varying ideas that present themselves, they regard unconcerned their usual occupations. Then we see those tranquil and domestic virtues, the companions of industry and a settled interest, either languish or totally disappear. A confused ambition, an uncertain restlessness usurp their place; nobody gains in happiness, every one is a loser with regard to morality, and the state derives from the countless multitude of authorities only so many sources of resistance.

Another immoral effect of a constitution that vests too much power in the hands of a people is that it weakens the majestic empire of wisdom and reason, and aids the triumph of artifice and hypocrisy. The multitude can never be gained but by means proportioned to its mass and extent; in order to capture its opinion and to engage its suffrage in a populous country, we must put on passions that we do not have; we must exaggerate their symptoms to the degree necessary to produce the intended effect even upon the most distant spectators; and we are almost obliged to imitate the players in the vast theatres of Rome, who elevated themselves on buskins and were dressed with gigantic costumes.

The National Assembly itself felt this necessity, and trembling, as it soon did, before an authority of its own creation, it has had recourse, in order to charm and gain the favor of its new master, to factitious sentiments, gaudy measures, and formal discourses. It has puffed itself, as it were, into size; and individuals, borrowing its spirit, have quitted the language of nature and the expressions of truth; every one has chosen his part and selected his mask; and so effectual was the disguise, that it was no longer possible to recognize anyone. In the courts of princes, men whisper their flattery; in the midst of a democracy, they flatter the people to the sound of a trumpet; that is all the difference.

Alas! that noble simplicity, the characteristic feature of elevated souls, is lost, I fear, forever. Men are drawn out of themselves with too great a force, and the equilibrium necessary to sustain the true virtues and the modesty of virtue is totally destroyed. All this is the fruit of a constitution which, by overturning all hierarchies and subjecting government to the domination of the people, the reflections of the wise to the impetuosity of the multitude, has confounded the powers it proposed to separate.

How many other virtues, how many other ornaments of human nature have in like manner been sacrificed to this new political order! I lament particularly those sentiments of generosity, which seemed to be the inheritance of the French nation, those sentiments that afforded a sanctuary to the oppressed and made misfortune an object of worship. But how would it have been possible to preserve them while we are constantly obliged to submit to force and respect violence, and while, the better to disguise to ourselves the baseness of our submission, we excuse the persecutors and incriminate their victims? How would it have been possible to preserve them while we applaud the revenge we could not prevent, and the conflagrations we could not extinguish; while we put on the colours of the tyrant, in order that we might leave it in doubt whether he had not put on ours? Shameful compound of weakness and servility to which the soul has been debased, instead of having maintained it independent and proud, under the tranquil protection of a better ordered government and a constitution better understood! We are told of liberty, while the noblest part of man is put in slavery, that which brings us closest to the divinity, that which renders us compassionate and generous, and gives to all sensible people the chance to taste the sweetest enjoyments of which, on earth, their nature is capable. Go, with your popular adulations, prostrate yourselves before those who, ere long, will disdain your abject caresses; go submit yourselves blindly to the capricious will of the multitude. Tell us if its yoke be easy and its empire light; tell us particularly if you have been free, in giving it a government which does not govern it; if you have been free, in extinguishing, for its pleasure, the signals which wisdom and science had lighted up; if you have been free, in so often renouncing your inward convictions, and in forming the rash project of subjecting the present generations, and generations yet unborn, to laws dictated by ephemeral wills and the passions of the moment.

Be it further observed, that this injudicious distribution of powers suffices to subvert the public manners; for when we give to the people a sentiment of their strength, without being able to communicate to them, at the same time, the knowledge that would dispose them to temperance, the sentiment easily degenerates into ferocity. No period of history affords an example of twenty-six millions of men, united into one republic, so that no part of this immense population was placed, as before, beyond the sphere of the political movement by the laws of slavery. Rome herself, at the late period when the nations of Italy were admitted to the right of citizens, never presented any such thing; since in Rome the mechanical professions were never exercised by free citizens. The degree of political influence then conferred on the people in such a country as France is a true phenomenon in the annals of the world. And when every nation joins in reproaching this people for the excesses and barbarities of which it has been guilty since the revolution, I would ask men capable of reflection, with a view of extenuating its faults, what would be the fate of other societies of very considerable population if, by the establishment of a similar imprudent constitution, the authority of reason and the credit of government were suddenly to be weakened; if the imagination of the multitude were to be inflamed by philosophical maxims of equality and the acquisition of every type of power, and if we were thus to rouse it to a sense of its physical vigour, without diminishing its needs or improving its education. Under these circumstances, men would generally resemble each other. Great political changes are only attended with additional danger when they are introduced in the midst of a nation whose character is incompatible with gradual progress and incapable of balancing by its sagacity the errors of the legislators.

It is a truth that can scarcely be too often repeated. When, in a country infinitely populous, we are unable, like the governments of antiquity, to place out of the social order all the industrious class of the people; when we are unable to exonerate them from the necessity of owing their subsistence to their labour; when this very circumstance, inseparable from the laws of property, opposes an insurmountable obstacle to the general acquisition and sharing of knowledge; and when, of consequence, ignorance and barbarity, from the lack of education, must be the inevitable portion of the multitude, it is contrary to mores, it is against the lessons of philosophy to weaken, in every sense, the government and to give to the people an influence which reunites in them the moral forces and the material ones. The people themselves would not wish for this; they would stop, they would moderate their pretensions, at least if they were competent judges of their own happiness. And we, who are better informed, but tired of the antiquated precepts of reason, and under the spell of false glory,

we have preferred the honour or eclat of an extravagant system to
that wisdom which, while it equally secured liberty, would have maintained public order and all the virtues that follow in its train.

There was a shield which would still have guarded the mild mores
and manners of the French nation; those laws of civility and politeness, which were not written upon tables of marble or of brass, but
which, by the mere power of opinion, recalled men to the reality of
those sentiments of which they were constrained to assume the appearance. But civility and politeness, having acquired like our other
ideas, a sort of refinement from time, became, in their perfection, the
particular privilege of individuals of good origin. Nothing more was
necessary to render these qualities suspected; they were supposed to
be allied, in some way or other, to gradations of rank, and they were
quickly included in the general proscription exercised against every
form of aristocracy. It was not perceived that they flowed from very
different principles; it was not perceived that they owed their origin
to ideas of equality; it was not perceived that, invented to protect
weakness against strength, they were associated with the most generous ideas. Their first employment was to draw around age a magic
circle that should protect it from the insults of the imprudent youth,
at the moment when its reign is about to begin. Their next use was
to afford a safeguard to the weak and timid sex, whom the laws of
nature had subjected to our prideful dominion. Lastly, these same
sentiments were destined to support the power of imagination, and
thereby to maintain the authority of the rulers of nations, against the
force of number and the disorderly excesses of the multitude.

These laws then of exterior demeanor bear the stamp of a profound wisdom; but our superficial philosophy has regarded them as a
code of slavery. Our legislators have been the first to break these pretended ties; and the contempt which they have affected for all forms
has communicated itself to their very principles. They have insensibly habituated themselves to a spirit of irreverence, which has caused
them to overlook what was due to the first magistrate in a monarchy,
and has obliged them, in order to support their own dignity, to have
recourse to frequent acts of power. They wanted perhaps to prove to
us, by their rude manners, their austere language, and their slovenly
costumes, that, in giving us laws, they had no communication with

the goddess Egeria,[1] and were indebted for their genius to no inspiration. But they need not have feared the accusation; there was no circumstance that could have given rise to it.

While they attempted to apply even to exterior forms their doctrine of equality, they have erected the greatest and most disgustful of all supremacies, that of audacity and insolence. They thought to level everything, and they have subjected, with a rod of iron, the mild to the audacious ones, the discreet to the violent, and goodness was made the plaything of the ferocious souls. Finally, while they have suppressed all ideas of decency, while they have abolished all the differences, and always endeavored to level to the lowest denominator in order to amalgamate the manners of the people, who are forever distinct from each other both by fortune and by education, the consequence, I fear, of such a system of familiarity will be nothing more than an additional opportunity for more hatred. In its magnificent spectacle, nature tells us everywhere that there can exist no harmony without shades and gradations. The moral world, by its striking disparities, had no doubt deviated too far from this model; through another extreme, we are converting today the moral world into a vast plain, where every man will cross and elbow his neighbor, and all the advantages will fall only to the most rustic and robust ones.

None of our old opinions were wished to be retained; and if, in the passion that has shown itself for a general renewal, the principles of morality have not been altered by express statute, they have at least undergone considerable transformation. Accusation was made a subject of honour, calumny a proof of patriotic zeal, ingratitude to the living the very extract of philosophy; compassion was treated as weakness; clemency as an insult to the law, and the voice of conscience as jargon and cant. The desire of obtaining notice and the love of glory have saved from shipwreck the few virtues that could have been made to appear gigantic, as well as those which it was thought necessary to impose on others; thus our innovators have talked of sacrifices demanded by the country to all those who were deprived of their rights or their property and they held up Brutus as an exam-

---

1. Egeria was a fountain nymph who advised Numa Pompilius, one of the founders of Rome. She subsequently became a symbol of wise and secret counsel.

ple to the king when, before his eyes, and regardless of his sufferings, they decreed the accusation of his two brothers. Frenchmen, who no longer wanted to be French! Romans, risen from the grave, you are still pale! would it not, alas! have been much better, if you had cultivated the qualities congenial to your nation, instead of perpetually endeavouring to metamorphose them; if you had aimed at their exaltation or embellishment, by the happy influence of a wise liberty, instead of giving them, by absolute independence, a savage and severe character; if you wanted to remember that it is a vain attempt to leap over twenty centuries, and to transport, in a circle of one single year, a modern nation into the forum of ancient Rome, and that, in so rapid a course, everyone would be injured or maimed in the attempt? But supposing we were to succeed, how ridiculous a figure should we make with our corrupted mores, our luxury, riches, misery, and inequalities of fortune, with our vanities, pretentions, and refined philosophy? Every people has its own virtues, appropriate to its situation, and specific to the period of history in which it is placed; these are the only virtues that can be given to it; and it would be a true anachronism to wish to adapt simple laws and principles to an old and established nation.

What a magnificent spectacle would not France have exhibited, if her inhabitants, already distinguished in Europe for their genius, talents, industry, literature, sociability, courage and military ardour, had added to so many predominant attributes that vigour and stability of principle given by a free government; that general dissemination of knowledge, the necessary result of a people's participating in the institution of laws; that elevation of thought, that dignity of character, formed amidst great interest and events! To make this picture real we only have to join to the brilliant qualities of the French nation all that is most excellent in the free genius of the English; and it is impossible for the imagination to go further without losing its way. This mixture of the social spirit and the moral and political character of two people, who had each, in different ways, arrived at celebrity and glory, would doubtless have constituted a beautiful association. Alas! it was my delightful revery, it was my secret hope; but I have seen the splendid vision escape, I have seen my fond expectation blasted. Our legislators have rejected a form of perfection and happiness to which we might have reasonably aspired; through their imprudent ideas, they have thrown all sentiments and all principles into confusion; they aimed at a liberty that had no model, and they have produced a disorder that had no example; they have constructed a system of government in which all is exaggerated, and they had no method of raising themselves to its level but that of pomposity; they have imported virtues from Sparta and from Rome, they have canvassed and talked them all; but not one of them could suit either the men or the situation. Finally, after having drawn up a philosophical constitution which in its vast abstractions and outrunning all realities, could meet with no obstacle, they have commanded the nature of things to conform to it, they have commanded mores to obey, opinion to submit, and reason to surrender; like all chiefs of sects, they have measured virtue and vice, merit and demerit, according to the opinion that was entertained of their doctrine; and the Mahomets perpetually cried out, long before their Saïds had learned the lesson, *the constitution, prosperity to the constitution, nothing but the constitution.*

Moreover, they proscribed under the name of prejudices all ideas that threatened to resist in any respect the universal innovation. In the very first instance, they laughed at honour, treated it as an old-wives tale, that could not flourish, nay that could not even exist in the middle of civic virtues. It would have been well to have tried these virtues, to have experimented them in tranquility, before weakening and extinguishing a sentiment, the delicacy of which has often served as a supplement to morality, and the energy of which has produced so many sublime things; a sentiment that so well accorded with the French character, and displayed itself in every page of their history. Virtues are not in the nature of a tontine stock, one does not gain by the extinction of its rivals; thus honor, this brilliant idea, honor, the parent of innumerable acts of heroism, deserved to be treated with more respect, and a republic, yet in its infancy, had no right to employ against it all the rigors of ostracism.

We do not have too many props to our moral system. Honour among us is a necessary support to probity, modesty to chastity, politeness to kindness; and never has it before been attempted, under any government, to bring into discredit the assistant virtues; but our new political instructors have such distorted ideas that they believe in their hearts to be able to govern the whole world by liberty and equality.

Nonetheless, among the various innovations of the present time, the most fatal perhaps to our character is the contempt that is affected for every idea of leniency and compassion. I have already shown how a numerous assembly, assuming to itself not only legislation, but the reins of government, would be under the necessity of resorting continually to numerous punishments. It can employ none but absolute and general means because its mass does not admit of any flexible movement. As legislator, it can try to prevent the commission of evil, but as administrator, it would be in vain to try to do so, because its progress is always too slow and heavy, and it has only law as an instrument at its disposal. Nonetheless, the main duty of government is prevention; by wise precaution, it must supersede the necessity of punishment; it must be just towards human frailty, before being severe with regard to persons.

Legislative bodies, even if they were competent to the task, would conceive the majesty of the law to be degraded if they tried through indirect means to elicit obedience; and this consideration alone is sufficient to prove that administration would be improperly placed in their hands. We have been persuaded besides, by certain democratical writers, that harshness of manners is the characteristic of liberty, and this harshness we have immediately assumed; for in our eagerness to be republicans, we resemble M. Jourdain[2] who, wanting to become a gentleman, asked his tailor how a man of quality ought to be dressed.

I would like to ascribe the new manners of the French to a temporary wandering of the mind; for when a hardness of character derives its source from the heart, there is no more remedy. Moreover, this hardness of character is favoured by a constitution which perpetually obliges us to pay our court to the people and to do homage to their omnipotence; for unfortunate as is the condition of the mass of mankind, the people always derive a secret gratification from the humiliation of others and the infliction of severe punishments; and this

---

2. Monsieur Jourdain, main character in Molière's play *Le Bourgeois gentilhomme* (1670).

sentiment appropriate to the situation of the people, is augmented in the present instance by their independence. Oh! How could we not say anything about a constitution which has produced at once both the excesses we have witnessed and the indifference with which the report of those excesses has been heard? How could we not say anything about a constitution which encourages the strong ones, intimidates the weak, and blends the ideas of liberty with the most odious practices of tyranny? An enlightened nation, a nation of the eighteenth century, cannot be conducted by decrees of accusation and the perpetual menace of punishment. It was necessary at least to prevent or to moderate the hatreds and aversions; it was necessary, with intelligence and kindness, to conciliate different interests. Social order consists of fixed ideas and nuanced ideas; the first can be perceived in theory; the second are unknown except by experiment; but the lessons they teach have been comprised in our system of proscriptions, or adopted as motives of accusation before the high court of our pride.

Gentleness and politeness of mores and manners, the inseparable companions of indulgence and kindness, have other affinities not less remarkable; and composed of various ingredients, they are more intimately connected than we are apt to imagine with forms of language. We owe to the most fine and delicate impressions a portion of our sentiments and even of our ideas. Often, while the mind is occupied in reasoning, we are already carried away captive by our imagination. Placed, as it were, at the exterior of our spiritual nature, and having the first communication with our senses, it takes us so much by surprise, it exercises over us such a rapid authority, that we scarcely have time to defend ourselves. Thus, when the language of a nation, when its habitual expressions become rude and harsh, the character of the people will partake of the same savage nature; and as the lyre of Orpheus animated the rocks and rendered them sensible, the language of the times, by a contrary effect, hardens our hearts and petrifies our feelings. One would suppose whole centuries had elapsed between the polished age of France and the present period; and I find a considerable analogy between the new eloquence and the new politics. It has neither measure nor harmony; it sets no bounds to its liberty, it pays no attention to decorum; its force is in the wrong place, its enthusiasm is harsh, its boldness is entirely dictated by the head; it is agitated without action, emphatic without elegance, didactic without clarity, monotonous without unity; finally, it is extravagant in all its parts, and stupid as a whole.

I quit this comparison to make another observation upon our new language, an observation which may be thought to belong only to grammarians, but which really indicates a modification of our moral character. Every day we coin new verbs, altogether barbarous, and substitute them instead of substantives. Thus we say, *influencer, utiliser, exceptionner, préconiser, fanatiser, patriotiser, pétitioner, vétoter, harmonier, &c.* This remark may appear as too subtle or insignificant, but it indicates that we no longer feel the necessity of sweet and measured expression; for it is not by verbs, whose sense is always positive, but by the union of adjectives to substantives, that ideas acquire nuance and gradation.

I shall now be asked how the new French constitution can, not *influence* our language, but have upon it an *insensible influence.* I answer that exaggerated sentiments and a certain manner of speaking have a very intimate connection; that this manner of speaking is connected with the desire of captivating popular favour; that this manner of speaking is connected with the multiplication of our ephemeral scribblers and journalists; that this manner of speaking is connected with the growth of oratorical vanity through the frequent assemblies of all types; finally, that this manner of speaking has a very intimate connection with the real situation of the people.

Taste is no longer necessary when deference of every sort is entirely lost, when there is no longer any limit, when all ideas and principles are confounded; when there is but one single thought in the whole country, and when, by a blind enthusiasm, that thought is supposed to have universal application and be all-sufficient.

Taste is no longer necessary when the people have become the sole master, and when the grossest incense gratifies this newly-chosen god.

Taste is no longer necessary when the empire of opinion is under the guidance of impassioned writers and corrupt instructors, those new shepherds who desire not to lead their flocks to the flowery vallies and the green meadows, but to throw them into torrents and precipices, imbuing them with the spirit of demons and hurrying them along with incantations and enchantments.

Finally, taste is no longer necessary, and must become every day more and more perverted, when everyone wants to speak and write, and in the midst of this universal rivalry, each endeavours to surpass the other by using the most savage expressions and the most repulsive images.

I fear having dwelled too long upon a subject that will appear perhaps insignificant, in the situation in which I have introduced it; but a secret sentiment has impelled me. I turned a melancholy eye to those brilliant periods when the divine eloquence of Racine and Fénelon, when the celebrity of so many other writers, worthy of being their rivals, gave splendor to their country, and stamped with the seal of their genius the glory of the French name. I reverted to that wonderful period when the most harmonious of all languages served to convey the purest sentiments and most sublime ideas to the soul. A multitude of masterpieces, the triumph of the human mind, had rendered French the language of all Europe. What will it become when it shall have passed the forges of our new cyclops, who will have smashed it into pieces on their terrible anvils? Its sole use will then be to express the chaos and combat of all the elements.

The moral subject which I have treated in this chapter grows larger as I proceed, and it could by itself constitute the object of a great work. In order to conclude, I must therefore gloss over a variety of observations that could still be of interest, if an excess of ideas could ever be interesting, while everyone today is so focused on getting forward in their journey. I cannot, however, prevent myself from adding one more reflection on the immoral effect of the French constitution. Hitherto it has been obliged to be supported by rigorous means, and by committees of research and committees of surveillance. A mysterious inquisition has been the consequence; encouragement has been given to informers and spies, letters have been intercepted, and other mean practices of a similar nature, all contrary to the laws and to the principles of morality. This conduct has been justified by the supposition that party spirit rendered such precautions necessary. But is this party spirit likely to cease, when a considerable part of the nation are dissatisfied with the constitution? And with what feelings are we to regard the sad necessity of confiding the maintenance of a political system to a spirit of inquisition and intrigue? Everything appears to be lawful, when the legislative body itself has deliberate recourse to dishonesty. The consequences of such an example given from above are infinite.

The purest atmosphere should ever encompass the sanctuary of the laws. When we direct towards it our regards, we ought to feel ourselves attracted by an unknown influence, by a sort of moral beauty, to which our opinions should submit without restraint. When we approach this sanctuary, we ought to experience as it were a new soul, and to become more deeply impressed with that love of virtues which guarantee social order. What gratitude would not have been due to the legislators of a great people, if, while employing their thoughts on those political interests which divide nations, they had shown themselves at the same time the preceptors of that morality which unites them; if instead of making themselves the servants of the multitude, they had become its guides and instructors; if instead of seconding its tyrannical will, they had assembled with fortitude around the standard of reason and justice; if, instead of following its tyrannical will, they courageously stood on the side of reason and justice; if, instead of perpetually reminding themselves that they must assume *a proud attitude*, they tried to be great through the simplicity of their actions; and if, instead of running themselves out of breath to catch the nimble fame, they had calmly waited for her or had given her rendezvous at the temple of Truth.

CHAPTER XII

Continuation of the Same Subject

There is a moral effect of the French constitution that has been constantly present to my thoughts and my heart, but I have on purpose avoided combining its discussion with the miscellaneous reflections of the preceding chapter. The subject I was there handling demanded, on account of the variety of its relations, a great variety of style; but undoubtedly, there is only one style, and that of the most respectful sort, that can accord with the grave sentiments and important considerations which I am now about to present.

It seems that our legislators, while they weakened the authority of government and sapped all the foundations of public order, should have taken the greater care to preserve the salutary influence of religious opinions which would be sufficient by themselves, in the plenitude of their power, to maintain the entire social system in harmony. But religion had long found a rival and an enemy in that imperious philosophy, which wanted to have all the honours to itself of instructing and governing us, and which still retains the same pride amidst the ruins which surround us, amidst those devastations which cannot but remind it of the exploits of its blind sectaries and the glorious feats of its numerous militia. Every day, by the active interposition of these ardent missionaries, some link of the moral chain is broken, and we are reduced to the necessity of waiting patiently the operation of an universal system, which is once more to begin afresh the education of the human species.

The National Assembly has observed the same conduct relative to religion, which it observed towards the executive power and the royal dignity. It declared the executive power to vest in the chief magistrate, but it neglected to grant to the depositary of that power the requisite means for enforcing obedience. It decreed the French government to be monarchical, and it stripped royalty of all the attributes that constitutes its essence and utility. In like manmer, the National Assembly considered public worship as in the first rank of state functions; but instead of cultivating in the minds of the people the respect for this worship and all the sublime ideas connected with it, it has tolerated a contempt both of religion and morality; it has countenanced and applauded speeches in which this contempt was unblushingly displayed; it has imagined that, after having composed for France a philosophical government, it had entered into a league with every daring spirit, and was bound to treat with disdain all common opinions.* Finally, the National Assembly, diverting its attention from the intimate union that subsists everywhere between respect for religion and deference to its ministers, has introduced an intestine war into the the church; it has set conscience and interest at variance; and loading with the most opprobrious epithets such members of the clergy as were wicked enough to be governed by their inward convictions, has rendered them the objects of popular outrage. Morality and decency, however, the boundaries established by religion, once broken down, the distance is short to the last stage of disorder; and presently will be brought to the test that catechism, purely political, to which, on the perilous faith of certain speculative minds, we are anxious to confide the instruction of the human race. Such is the substitute we are to receive for religion, such the last blessing which our present sages have in reserve for us. Philosophers of yesterday, children of presumption, we shall see what will be the effect of your reasonings on the mass of the people; we shall see how you will contrive, in the midst of its un-

---

*In a French newspaper, that has invariably given a favourable account of the debates of the National Assembly, I have read the following passage. "It is impossible," observed M***, "for a society to exist without an immutable and eternal system of morality (loud and repeated bursts of laughter)." *Moniteur,* 15 *November,* 1791.— We have here an abstract of the spirit of the times. I have selected the passage from a thousand others, which all Europe has remarked.

fortunate condition, to reconcile its interest with the respect due to justice; we shall see by what means it will be made to understand your incomprehensible jargon; we shall see how you will create leisure for those to listen to your cold lessons, who, from the earliest acquisition of physical strength, are obliged to have recourse to labour for their subsistence. But you tell us, there will be no class of citizens reduced to such a condition, they will not exist under the reign of liberty; indigence was the work of despotism. Deceivers as you are, to talk in this manner, when you well know that indigence depends on other circumstances, which are indestructible in the social order. Or if you are uninformed of this fact, which may possibly be the case, descend from the chair of instruction, quit that lofty situation in which your ignorance forbids you to remain. I have frequently explained these laws of social order, but I must repeat, since complex principles, and such in particular as are not to be expressed by simple terms, have need of long cultivation, in order to be deeply impressed on the memory and rooted in the mind. And yet, would one believe it, it is by such abstract ideas as these, which the teachers themselves are unable to retain, that the people are to be educated and their morals to be formed.

Let me then repeat, since it is necessary. Indigence in the context of political societies derives from the laws of property, those laws which are essential to public order, which gave birth to these societies, and which still are the fruitful cause of labor and the development of all types of industry. Nonetheless, one of the outcomes of these laws is that, in the midst of the successive growth and diminution of all types of property, in the midst of the continuous fluctuations of fortune which are their necessary effect, two very distinct classes have appeared; the one owns the fruits of the earth, the other is simply called to assist, by its labor, the annual renovation of those fruits and riches, or to exercise its diligence in order to offer to the owners commodities and objects of luxury in exchange for their superfluous provisions. These universal transactions, these constant transactions constitute the social movement; and the laws of justice prevent these motions from degenerating into quarrels, confusion, and war.

Nonetheless, one of the inevitable consequences of this relation between the two classes of mankind is that in the midst of this general circulation of labor and production, of necessary goods and objects of luxury, there is a perpetual struggle between the contracting parties; but as they are of unequal force, the one is invariably obliged to submit to the conditions imposed by the other. The conveniences which the landowners derive from the labor of those devoid of property appear to them as necessary as the soil which they own; but, favored by their competition and the urgency of their needs, the rich are able to fix the price of labor; and, provided that the recompense be adequate to the daily demands of a frugal subsistence, no insurrection disrupts the exercise of such an authority.

It is not then the despotism of government, it is the operation of property that reduces the lot of the mass of mankind to mere necessities. This law of dependence is almost equally valid under every different kind of political authority. Everywhere the wages of those workmen whose skill does not require any previous education are subject to the same proportions. The little variance to which this rule is exposed only serves to confirm the rule; since this variance directly depends upon the commercial value of production, or upon the number of articles ranked among necessities, which perpetually fluctuate according to habits and climates. Happily for us, the empire of property over the price of labor does not constitute the measure of happiness. The wise and prudent nature has placed under the limits of no authority her most precious benefits, and the poor and the rich partake of this fortune in equal manner. All enjoy the advantages of public order, the ones in connection with labor, the other in the midst of the anxieties generated by the lack of occupation.

Nonetheless, what is the result of these principles inherent in the very nature of society? What is the result of the rights of property, of those rights upon which the smallest infringement cannot be made, without throwing the state into confusion, of those rights which it would be necessary to establish anew the very instant after their destruction had taken place? The inevitable result is a greater truth: that it is out of the power of legislators, and more especially legislators of an extensive and populous kingdom, to contrive for the multitude sufficient leisure to acquire a long and proper education; and that therefore all instructions which are purely political, all instructions founded on abstract ideas, will eternally fail in attaching a whole people to the duties of morality; and one of the strongest proofs of mediocrity is to entertain such a hope. Let us then preserve, protect, and respect the inestimable advantage of religious opinions, and consider them as the strongest tie of social order. They are surrounded by whatever can strike the imagination; and, as simple in their influence on the human heart, as infinite in their alliances with our reason, they are also adapted to our infancy and our maturity, to our weakness and our strength, to our habitual ideas and our most elevated reflections. All the political and civil laws reach us only in certain portions of our lives; and their empire seems to end where our solitude begins, when the first shades of night cover our actions from the view of others. Thus, the person who is not influenced by religious morality has no other motive than interest, no other law than personal gratification. Such limits cannot be imposed to the authority of religious ideas, and the latter are never more active and dominant than when they get hold of us, in the midst of our most intimate moments and in the private retreat of our thoughts. What can be more arrogant then, in the legislators of a state, than to suppose that the contrivances of their genius shall be omnipotent, that order and happiness can flow from the single efforts of their wisdom! No; there is no human science that will ever equal in our destiny one single moral idea, appropriated to the whole of our singular nature, our nature compounded of reason, imagination, foreboding and hope, and all that is most wonderful in the wonders of the universe! Of all moral ideas, however, that is unquestionably the most magnificent and sublime which religion implants in the human heart, which takes possession of us from our first sentiments and follows us through every stage of existence as our comforter and our guide. Oh! No doubt, this idea is great and magnificent, this idea the impression of which is kept alive and strengthened by the contemplation of the universe, an idea that inspires us in happy times with the sweetest emotion, and calms us in adversity by affording us a glimpse of the sunshine of a fine day, through the thick shades of death. Thus this is an idea equally auspicious to social order and the happiness of man; equally applicable to our external relations and our intuitive sentiments; restraining us in the ebullition of our passions, and relieving us in the languors of melancholy; rendering us severe towards ourselves, and indulgent towards others; exact in the performance of our duties, and moderate in the exercise of our rights. Finally, this is an idea equally adjusted to motion and to rest, to the bustle of the world and the stillness of solitude, to the charms of our hope and the tranquility of our memories. This universal application of one idea and of one sentiment would represent the most remarkable feature of the religious morality. How many other features, not less important, would it be my business to describe, if I had not already written upon this majestic subject, at a time when the dangerous progress of a presumptuous philosophy had excited my alarms! Alas! who could have supposed that the period would arrive when legislators themselves would manifest an indifference for opinions essential to the maintenance of social harmony? Who could have supposed that the period would arrive when, amidst our sins of ingratitude, forgetfulness of the political blessings of religion would occupy the first rank? Who could have supposed that the period would arrive when the rulers of a great nation would debate whether they ought not to abandon public worship to the caprices of liberty, and whether the era of the most intolerable license might not be made choice of to deprive public morality of its firmest support? Worshippers of new opinions, illustrious champions of philosophy, where will you stop? And what future are you preparing for us, as a sequel to the excesses which we are witnessing at the present? You want to prove by abstract reasoning the intimate connection of private with public interest; and yet the former was never so ardently pursued, the latter was never so differently interpreted. What will become of us with no other safeguard than your instructions? Observe the confusion that prevails, look at the tumult and chaos which the licentious overthrow of political principles has caused, and judge whether religion was ever more necessary! Oh, finally, calm down, and leave us in possession of something appertaining to the past. You will be sufficiently celebrated for what you have already done, if the genius of destruction opens the gate to the Temple of Memory. Do not then sacrifice our only remaining blessing to your renown and be contented with the conspicuous situation which you think you have secured to yourselves.

Alas! had these legislators been less covetous of glory, or had they made a better choice of it, a tranquil and prosperous day would now shed on us its benign influence, and our tears would have been less abundant!

Heureux si j'avois pu, pour prix de mes travaux,
En chrétiens verteux changez tous ces Héros;
Mais, qui peut arrêter l'abus de la victoire?
Leur cruautés, mon fils, ont obscurci leur gloire;
Et j'ai pleuré souvent sur ces tristes vainqueurs,
Que le ciel fit si grands, sans les rendre meilleurs.

VOLTAIRE[1]

Nonetheless, I still hope that these religious opinions, so indispensible and so consolatory, will escape the destructive pruning knife; will retain their influence in the midst of those ruins of all kinds that are heaped together, notwithstanding every effort to the contrary; and that the same power which bestowed them to us, will protect and preserve them for us. Presumption itself, while it misleads us, will give salutary lessons. We shall see that patriotism, the motive from which everything is at present expected, is not strong enough to bind together so many diverse interests. I speak, however, of patriotism in all its purity, such as it exists in the heart of a great number of French citizens. For I have nothing to say to you who pronounce this name with enthusiasm, that, by generalising your sentiments, you may dispense yourselves from the practice of every private virtue; to you who are suddenly smitten with the love of your country, after having never loved anything through the whole course of your lives; to you who are now so unalterably united to the good or ill fortune of twenty-six millions of men, after having never thought of an interest beyond your own. It is not easy to believe that your affec-

---

1. A fragment from Don Alvarez's opening remarks in Act I, Scene I, of Voltaire's play *Alzire ou les Américains* (1736).

After a life spent in my country's service, / Could I have formed these heroes into men, / Could I have made them virtuous, mild, and good, / I had been amply paid for all my toils: / But who shall stop the haughty conqueror? Alas! my son, their cruelties obscure / The lustre of their fame; I weep the fate / Of these unhappy victors, raised by heaven / To greatness but to be supremely wicked.

Alzire, in *The Works of Voltaire, A Contemporary Version* (New York: E. R. DuMont, 1901); http://oll.libertyfund.org/titles/2197.

tions and your sentiments are all centered in your country, merely
because you were born within the circumference of this vast kingdom, at the same time that, surrounded with the rays of that great
luminary the sun, admitted to behold the wonders of nature, and gra-
ciously allowed to partake of her bounties, you scarcely ever think of
that magnificent country, of which the vaults of heaven form the vast
circumference. We will ask you by what singular perverseness you
feel yourselves thus filled with a respect for a boundary of convention, while your philosophy teaches you to overturn all the barriers of
nature, and would like to convert the admirable intentions of the sovereign Master of the world into an eternal and uniform vegetation?
Your patriotism is a banner which you ostentatiously display in order
to draw around you all those whom you want to govern; it is a signal
by which to move at your will the passions of the multitude. It is by
means of this false patriotism that you can hate and persecute, with
cold composure, those who differ from you in opinion. It is by means
of this patriotism that you can transform your savage tempers and
your rude and unaccommodating humours into civic virtues. It is by
means of this patriotism that you can vindicate the most chimerical
accusations or defend the most unjust principles and the most atro-
cious actions. It is by means of this patriotism that you can overlook
the insults offered to those pious nuns who consume their lives in
charitable sacrifices, and can hold out a friendly hand to the murder-
ers of Avignon, chanting their canticles on the borders of the abyss
into which they had thrown, piecemeal, the palpitating limbs of their
innocent victims. Thus it is by one and the same principle, one and
the same sentiment, that you convert into crimes against the state the
most trivial offences, and look with an approving eye upon the most
inhuman villainies. Finally, it is by means of this false patriotism that
you can be everything and nothing. This participation resembles the
creed of Spinoza[2] and reminds us of the God of that celebrated athe-

---

2. Baruch Spinoza (1632–77), prominent Dutch philosopher, author of, among
others, *Ethics* and *Theological-Political Treatise* in which he embraced *avant la lettre*
key principles of the Enlightenment. His critics took him to task for his rationalism
which was sometimes seen as a disguised form of atheism.

ist, the God of his deranged imagination, which was a representation of all existing things, without existing anywhere itself; which was at once both the heaven and the earth, the angel and the serpent, the inanimate tree and the furious tiger; and which, possessing neither centre, nor perfection, nor determined attributes, appeared an aberration of the imagination, the illusion of an exalted mind, a mind ambitious of preserving a word, the sense of which was destroyed by all the explanations and definitions that were attempted to be given of it.

CHAPTER XIII

Why Has the National Assembly Been Unable to Form a Good Constitution?

There are so many correspondences between men and their works, so many affinities between the circumstances in which they are placed and the result of their actions, that in studying the legislator after having examined the legislation, our attention is still employed upon the same object. This truth applies with still greater force to the founders of a new social order; and it is not illogical to try to know what were their means after having investigated their labors. For a political constitution is a kind of moral region or an abyss, if I may so express myself, into which so few minds are able to penetrate, that we ought to judge of the wisdom of this constitution, as we appreciate the recitals of distant travellers, by examining at once both the true and the probable.

I shall first direct my attention to one of the principal causes of the faults committed by the National Assembly: I mean the passion it displayed, from so early a period, for praise and applause. This passion, when it exists in all its vigour, must necessarily lead astray the legislators, since it will give them a distaste for wisdom whose fruits arrive late; and by inspiring them with an ambition to please, will render them the slaves of all popular opinions, the only ones which vary every day, because they are at the mercy of every prejudice and every impulse. Finally, the love of applause, when it rules like a tyrant over a numerous assembly, presents to every eye a fortune that has no limits, a fortune divisible into a thousand parts, and the conquest of which being jealously disputed by each individual, a petty spirit of rivalship takes place of that unity of interest, which is alone capable of giving firmness to the steps of the legislators, and directing them in the way of true glory.

Meanwhile, to what lengths have not the effects of a single passion been extended! But in France, vanity is an indigenous plant, and everywhere finds a favourable soil. Envy and jealousy also spring up by its side, and becoming inseparable, they unite in spreading their dangerous vapours.

Who would have believed that? The first painful sentiment which the National Assembly experienced came from the idea that the monarch had assumed too large a share in the regeneration of public happiness. It was indeed the king who, when in the full plenitude of his liberty, and by a generous sacrifice at least of his rights, if not of his power, had made a solemn declaration that in future all laws should be the work of the national representatives; that none should be valid which had not their consent; no burthen be imposed without their express will. It was the king who also submitted to their determination the measure and distribution of public expences, without excepting from this general rule even the revenues destined to the support of the royal dignity. It was he who recommended to them to consider by what means the liberty of the press could best be reconciled with public order, and personal liberty most effectually secured against every attempt of despotism. Finally, it was he, the august depositary of a power consecrated by the authority of ages and the prosperity of France, who voluntarily resigned into the hands of the representatives of the people the glorious task of hereafter defending the happiness of the nation against the errors of government, and of adding to the lustre of the French name all the real enjoyments which arise from the wisdom of laws and from political liberty. And it was not merely for a moment, it was not during his own reign only, that he invited the nation to the exercise of the most precious rights of sovereignty; he wanted that the throne should be forever surrounded by the faithful interpreters of the needs of the people, and that, for the common good, an indissoluble alliance should be formed between all wills and all powers. At the view of such a noble design, in light of such a generous concession on the part of the king, the National Assembly, one would have supposed, touched by so many virtues and benefits, should have celebrated them, should have, as it were, emulated them in order to achieve with mildness, with confidence, and under the tranquil auspices of an enlightened reason, the work of public happiness and the immortal monument of French regeneration. Far however, from yielding to such a natural sentiment, they were impatient to bury in a general system of subversion every distinctive trace of the first origin of French liberty; and even at this very moment, every art is practiced to efface the remembrance of it.

Such an unexpected conduct saddened the heart of the king. When he came forward thus disinterestedly, he felt himself discouraged and repelled; and he frequently found no alternative left him but to enjoy his beneficent intentions in the privacy of his thoughts and the solitude of his conscience. It soon became manifest that the participation of the king in the great work of national reform, the concurrence of his ministers and the co-operation of government, were so many thorns to an assembly, which aimed above all things at celebrity, and proved to be intolerant as to every reputation but its own. Particularly it was remarked that those of its chiefs, still novices to the profits of glory, and as yet having no experience of it, were on that account only the more eager to acquire this new coin, this brilliant and sonorous money, which they vaguely hoped to be able to convert into every species of enjoyment. The public soon perceived this ardent rivalship, and were careful to feed a disposition which, without any effort on their part, would bring them into power, and raise them above the representatives of the nation. An action and reaction were then established between the candidates for glory and those who conceived themselves to be its dispensers; and in observing the anxiety of certain orators to captivate the tribunes, we might, nonetheless, have fancied ourselves to be in a salon among courtiers, rather than in a council of lawgivers.

The flatterers of the people are made of the same stuff as the flatterers of kings; and the people, in one respect, are very easy to serve, unlike certain despots, who require not only to flatter them, but also to anticipate what they like. There was no doubt that they would be pleased with the humiliation of the powerful; and instead of opposing limits to this sentiment, instead of tempering it in the name of wisdom and reason, the legislators were zealous in encouraging it and subscribed to all its different exaggerations. In this system of complaisance and caresses, they offered daily, as a holocaust, the great and their greatness, the rich and their riches, property and its possessors. But it was particularly by the sacrifice of ministers and of authority that they signalized their courtesy. The opportunity was singularly favourable; for while they allowed it to be believed that the supreme power was still alive, and carefully concealed the certificate of its death, they could appear courageous without any danger, and for the first time give to flattery an air of heroism. Finally, by one step after another, always paying court to the opinion of the moment, and endeavouring to enhance their popularity, they made a jest of all those ideas to which royalty had always owed its veneration; they urged its fall; they laughed at its splendor; and pulling down, one after another, all the ornaments of the throne, threw them into the public arena to entertain and please the multitude.

It must, however, be observed, in justice to the sensible people by whom the Assembly was directed, that many of them, in the midst of all the applauses they received, saw clearly enough the extreme to which they were hurried; but fearing to be outdone by their rivals if they ever stopped, they advanced on the same path well beyond the point where they would have liked to end; and since every stranger guest in the court of the people needed, in order to be remarked, to bid ever more to gain the favor of the public, or at least to add some exaggeration to the last definition of liberty, from these rivalries resulted a series of unnatural sentiments, in the midst of which all truths were confounded, and which made impossible, in a certain way, for reason to discover them.

Now, I ask, how from such a mixture of real and speculative sentiments, of serious and of counterfeit ideas, how, from this chaos of pretensions and vanity, it was possible for a system of government, with all its proportions, and in all its majesty, to arise?

Nonetheless, among these different forms of vanity of which I have given an image and exposed the danger, we saw emerge one of the highest stature and which, bearing the name of the genius of metaphysics, has served more than any other to create a general confusion of ideas. Those who had talent or taste for this sort of science, and who regretted being able to exercise their skills only on vague speculations, felt a secret pleasure at the arrival of the moment when it might be brought into practical use. No sooner did they perceive the first blow that was given to the cornerstone of the edifice, no sooner did they hear the crackings of the joists and the rafters, than they were seen to descend from their cabinets, with their compasses, their rules and their squares, with their crayons and their drawing paper, blessing, in their hearts, the chaos which afforded them an opportunity of sketching the plan of a new world. Immediately all those who possessed the art and felt the need to destroy, but who feared the consequences, eagerly ranged themselves under the direction of these architects, who promised, upon the word of men of genius, to rebuild and reconstruct all that was overthrown. These two sets of men were united by mutual interests. The former did nothing other than fulfil their mission; only the others have yet to give an account of their actions.

Metaphysicians, who draw all their figures in the void, are easily misled by their own imagination. Nothing is so captivating as the liberty of which they hold out to us the picture; but they frequently experience the lot of the unfortunate Ixion;[1] they embrace the cloud instead of the goddess, and they are obliged, like him, to turn away their eyes from the monstrous fruit of their loves.

The metaphysical spirit and the spirit of vanity are not, however, the only ones whose pernicious effects we have experienced; there is a third frequently united to these two, and which has proved equally inauspicious to the formation of a good constitution in France; it is the spirit of exaggeration. Nothing is more difficult than to stop when one is possessed by the immoderate desire to boast; nor does anything hint to us the necessity of doing so, when we have established the workshops in the land of abstractions. The National Assembly still further put reality at a distance, as soon as it created an

---

1. In the Greek mythology, Ixion was the King of the Lapiths, who went mad after pushing his father-in-law into a bed of burning coals. He lived as an outlaw ever after that.

indefinite sum of paper money; and I call upon the reader to remark here, among so many unfortunate consequences of this measure, one more fatal than the rest; I mean the tendency it has displayed, by rendering administration too easy, to convert government into a mere game, and to make France like a chess-board, a scene in which you can move all the pieces wherever you please. This convenience will exist as long as there shall be lands to answer to new creations of assignats; but these extraordinary means once exhausted, real difficulties will again make their appearance; unless, by a disloyalty that is without example, we sacrifice the entire fortune of the creditors of the state to our speculative ideas.

It is not only in great constitutional questions that the National Assembly has manifested a spirit of exaggeration; the same feature is visible in the majority of its legislative dispositions, which I could easily prove if I tried to discuss this immense subject. I have sometimes asked myself to what it is owing that a nation so long celebrated for gracefulness, decorum and purity in the arts, in elocution and in manners, has displayed so little of these qualities in its new capacity of legislator; and the most favourable explanation I would give was that a free and easy deportment were allied to a certain degree of confidence, and that this confidence the French had not yet acquired in a science, in which they were beginners and wanted to distinguish themselves before their strength was at its maturity. They were also fearful of losing themselves in their new career, they were fearful of going out of their depth, if they quitted for a moment the chain of reasoning; but with this compass, proper enough when we have to steer a direct course, we shall never arrive at those miscellaneous and scattered truths of which the science of moral man is essentially composed. Lastly, the deputies of the National Assembly, astonished at the greatness of their mission, rejected sentiment as a common idea, incompatible with their extraordinary dignity and their supreme rank. It is sentiment nevertheless, and sentiment alone which can delineate the transitions and shadings of ideas, connected by some point or other, with the weaknesses and passions of mankind.

Having thus explained the several sorts of talent and disposition which concurred in the great work of the French constitution, I shall now call the reader's attention to such positive circumstances, as prevented the National Assembly from acquitting themselves with honour in this memorable enterprise.

One of the most decisive, in my opinion, is the resolution they so early formed of treating all public affairs indiscriminately in general assemblies, thereby renouncing the plan they had first adopted of dividing themselves into different committees for the examination of great political questions. Such a division was unnecessary and improper in discussing objects of legislation; but it was perfectly applicable to the work of the constitution, and this difference is worth explaining. The subject of a civil law, or law of administration, has doubtless a certain number of relations and dependencies; but the circle is sufficiently limited to be within the comprehension of a numerous assembly; the multitude of rays therefore which, in this case, illuminate a single point serves only to exhibit it under all its different aspects, and it is sure of leading to a full deliberation. With a political constitution it is otherwise: a political constitution is an immense work, composed of an infinite number of parts, the union of which ought to be considered in all its harmonious proportions, if we would form a right judgment of it. The business is less to discover the circumjacent ideas of each article, than to regard them as a whole, and to estimate them by one and the same spirit, one and the same interest, one and the same rule. It is necessary, in examining and composing a political code, that we should have continually in our view the first, the last and the intermediary thoughts to judge well of the central ideas; it is like a fan mount, that must be kept perfectly extended and have all the parts of the drawing exposed to the same light.

The National Assembly had indeed instituted a constitutional committee; but this committee made its report by piecemeal, frequently at considerable intervals, and always in presence of the whole legislative body; and accordingly as the Assembly was more or less numerous, according to the prevailing disposition, a disposition often determined by exterior movements; finally, accordingly as the principal speakers and leaders of parties found it necessary to enhance their reputation with the people, the declamations against the executive power, and the royal authority in general, were more or less animated. And thus did the sentiments of the moment alone preside in the construction of a work destined to last for ages. The same passions, and others of a still stronger nature, displayed themselves also at the period when the constitution was revised; and this second labour could repair only but imperfectly the faults of the first. Besides, it was now too late to think of correcting the elementary principles of the constitution; it was too late to guide opinion; it had been rendered independent of reason, by being employed as an hostile force, and to place it under its former yoke was no longer practicable. In short, all the passions were in such turmoil that it was no longer possible to speak or act with calmness; and the Assembly was less than ever in a condition to revoke the testament *ab irato*,[2] which now serves us as law.

All these inconveniences and misfortunes would probably in a great measure have been prevented, if the constitutional committee, after having finished its work, had submitted it to the examination of the different sections of the National Assembly. They would not then have had to calculate perpetually the opinion of the moment; they would have ceased to watch with a jealous eye their daily small crop of applause and praise; they would have seen everything in its true place against a vast horizon, and they would have adapted their system to the comprehensiveness of genius that was capable of estimating it as a whole, and not to the narrow conceptions of men who were able to see but a small part at a time. Divided into sections, the Assembly would have been more free in its opinions than it was possible to be in its deliberations, as it was the case, amidst the tumultuous waves that incessantly agitated it. The Assembly would have taken a large view of the constitutional code, before it had chained itself down to each of its particular articles. It would have been able to hear the many wise and discreet reasoners, who from weakness of voice, prudential fears and the timidity of their character, were struck dumb in the midst of an assembly, where only the bold ones had an advantage. In the same manner, the Assembly would have subtracted from personal contests and vehement declamation all that part which had no other object than to make impression upon a numerous au-

2. A Latin expression which literally means "by one who is angry." It refers, in legal terms, to a gift or bequest that is made adversely to someone's interests, out of anger or hatred.

dience, and to gain a name in the small memory registers kept by the journalists. Reason would have gained all that vanities would have lost, and we would have been almost forced to perceive the essential vices of the constitution. Each man would have inquired, without fearing to pass for courtier or coward, what degree of power ought to be vested in the royal authority, to maintain order and insure the activity of government in a kingdom like France. Each man would have asked, in a moment of courage, what was executive power without the necessary prerogatives to secure its ascendency? What was a king, without the attributes essential to his dignity, without gradations of rank which serve as the connecting tie to opinion? Finally, every one would have been prompted to consider, in all the calmness of meditation, all the questions which I have endeavoured to gather imperfectly in this work.

We find in the conduct of the Americans a sort of model which I regret was not imitated, and which I have just outlined.

Each particular state of the continent nominated delegates who met at Philadelphia to compose together the Constitution of the United States. These delegates showed themselves more jealous of meriting than impatient to enjoy the glory reserved for wise legislators; and they conceived that it was not their duty to discuss, before the lowest classes of the people, the vast and complicated questions of which every political constitution is necessarily composed. As good patriots, as we pretend to have been, and acquainted sooner than we with all the common places, which have been so emphatically developed to justify the presence and empire of the tribunes, they judged that true wisdom, that a work calculated for duration, a work destined for the future as well as the present, ought not to be drawn up under the influence of that part of the nation which, of all times, is never acquainted but with the present time. They believed that honest legislators could not receive, without blushing, partial applause, article by article, while they were composing a work whose true merit must lie in the whole. They would have been ashamed of being extolled by men without property, while all those who had property observed a fearful and mournful silence; in like manner, they would have been ashamed of the praise of the rich, if the other classes of society could have found something to reproach them.

Nonetheless, there does not exist in America, the same differences of fortune and education as are observable in France and the other countries of Europe. And of what consequence is that? Those differences are to be regarded as nothing, since the law has declared that all men are equal. Such I am aware is your language; but it does not express the most intimate sentiments of your hearts; for you well know that the law is not sufficiently powerful to level the inequalities of our physical and moral nature. You well know that education alone establishes disparities between men, which no decree, no jury, no high national court are competent to remove. A plant preserves the same name in botanical dictionaries, whether it has been watered with assiduous care, or has withered by neglect; and yet its properties and virtues are materially altered by these circumstances. It is the same with human beings: all the constituent assemblies of the universe might proclaim them equal, they would still remain otherwise, as long as there should be differences of education; and these will always exist, since disparities of fortune and patrimony are the inevitable result of all social laws.

Nonetheless, the French constitution, and this is one of the reproaches that can be made to it, the French constitution, by its singular nature, renders the presence of the people in the national assemblies absolutely necessary; such is this constitution that it would fall into decay, if it were not continually supported by popular will. But supposing this principle to be just, we are not to conclude from it that the constitution itself ought to have been debated with all doors open and voted under the domination of the galleries. The true conclusion is opposite to this: for if the presence of the people, at the deliberations of the legislative body, can be considered as one of the elements of the French constitution, it was certainly wrong, while composing that constitution, to admit among them spectators, whose more or less expressive influence could not fail to operate upon the constitution itself. This is like in a controversy referring a question to arbitration, and admitting one of the parties to vote among the arbiters.—But the people are the true sovereign; they have a right of entry to the assembly of their mandataries, whether the debates relate to civil or political laws, since the nation is equally concerned in all. What a confusion of principles! The sovereignty of the nation is nothing more than an abstraction, till it has been determined what are the forms according to which the national will is to express itself; and this is the main goal of a political constitution. Thus, when a part of the people, through its actions, exercises an influence over the construction of this constitution, it commits a great irregularity; for this amounts to acting as a sovereign before the sovereign is known and recognized, before at least the *active* sovereign is determined, before it has come forth from the night of abstractions in order to clothe itself in a visible and definite form.

The delegates who assembled at Philadelphia to prepare in common the federal Constitution of America, transmitted their plan not article by article, not chapter by chapter, but in its complete form, to the legislative body of each individual state; and these legislative bodies, composed in general of few members, examined it with mature deliberation, and in the same manner as the National Assembly could have done if, for this purpose, it had divided itself into several sections; and by following the example of a wise nation, it would have given to France a constitution in which we would have recognized at least that character of maturity and temperance without which every government must fail to inspire general respect.

One thing in particular that has never been tried before, by any institutor of social order or by any founder of political government, was to leave in a certain manner the executive power out of the question, to abandon it, in detached parts, to the determination of each of the committees entrusted with the task of organizing the different branches of the constitution; to the committee of war, the committee of marine, the committee of jurisprudence, the committee of pensions, the committee of contributions, the committee of finance, and a multitude of others; and to admit only into the constitutional code the prerogatives which remained in the hands of the government after all these partial dispositions had been made, the prerogatives that escaped the rival emulation of the young stoicism of our modern censors. But I have already exposed this capital error at the beginning of my work and shall not therefore dwell upon the same idea here.

I am thinking of other circumstances which were hostile to the formation of a good constitution. And I do not need, no doubt, to remind anyone that this constitution was constructed in the midst of discord and antipathy, an antipathy carried to such a great length, that reason herself seemed to lose her authority on one side of the hall the moment it was supported by the deputies on the other side. How was it possible that a social legislation, that work of which harmony is the principal beauty, should be the result of such an intense contention among our legislators? It is to the same source that we are to ascribe that hatred which has so often hardened all the hearts, that we are to ascribe in part the forever to be regretted change that has taken place in the national character; it is to the intestine divisions that broke out in the very commencement of the Assembly, that we are bound to refer the early and fateful repudiation of all means of conciliation, the resolution that was formed never to unite, by the benign influence of morality, the different parts of the political system with each other; so that everything remained rugged and unformed both in the constitutional laws and the means chosen for their execution. All that we see is so many abstractions chained together in an artful or unartful manner, never that auspicious union of judgment and feeling, in which the strong and the weak persons, the ones led by the heart and those led by reason, the friends of order and the partisans of liberty might equally agree.

We may include also, among the causes of the discordance apparent to every one, between the different parts of the constitution, the new principles embraced by our legislators during the course of their session. Such, among others, was the principle of absolute equality which suddenly made its appearance, in contradiction to the constitutional security which had been accorded to property, and the solemn admission of monarchical government as one of the foundations of the political system of France.

I have shown in a preceding chapter that this principle, such as it was understood in the course of the discussions of the National Assembly, had no share in the earlier proceedings, and if the Assembly felt inclined to grant it a retroactive epoch, it was only that it might give to successive ideas the external honours and form of consistency. Nonetheless, the maintenance or abolition of an intermediary corps in a great kingdom was a political circumstance the effects of which were so important, that it was impossible to construct with prudence the first elements of a monarchical government, while a question of this importance was left uncertain.

There is another question equally important and which, after having been left unsettled by the National Assembly itself for some time,
was finally presented as evident and placed out of doubt when it was
finally considered; I refer to the question whether the consent of the
king should be included among the conditions necessary to give an authentic character and complete authority to the political deliberations
of the National Assembly. Now we read in the minutes of its proceedings that, on the eleventh of September 1791, and posterior therefore
to the epoch distinguished by the name of the Revolution, the question was raised, whether the king could refuse his assent to the constitution; and the National Assembly, after a debate upon the subject,
decreed that there was no necessity of coming to a decision upon it *at
present.*

It may further be mentioned that the deputies of the commons in
particular departed greatly from the sentiments expressed by them
in their first addresses to the king. "Your majesty shall be convinced,"
they said in one of them, *speaking of themselves,* "that they will not be
less just towards their fellow-citizens through every rank of society
than devoted to your majesty."

But the most important remark, on account of its numerous applications, that I have to make is that the representatives of the nation were in the beginning far from thinking themselves dispensed
from paying all attention to the instructions and mandates of their
constituents. This idea suggested itself in a gradual manner, and their
proceedings must have been influenced by such a great change in
their first combinations.

It cannot be disputed then that, in the discussions upon the fundamental basis of the constitution, many essential principles were
yet undefined, in the opinion of the National Assembly, which were
afterwards given and admitted to be the parent ideas and the original thoughts of the French legislators. It is therefore with sufficient
reason that I have placed the fluctuation of their sentiments among
the circumstances that contributed to the imperfection of their work.

Nor must it be concealed that certain extraordinary events, over
which it is my duty to throw a veil, inspired the representatives of the
commons with just suspicion, and that this suspicion contributed to
the frequent changes in their proceedings. In the sequel of their la-

bors, they could have resumed that unity, that comprehensiveness of plan that well becomes the victors; but they did not do it.

In short, and this shall be my last observation, the innumerable multitude of objects which distracted and fatigued the attention of the Assembly prevented it from uniting and fixing all its thoughts on the important work of the constitution; and as among these objects many irritated and inflamed its passions, it was the more difficult to preserve the impassive or temperate character so essential in all great legislators. This consideration alone is sufficient to excite doubts regarding the perfection of a political code, that should harmonize in all its parts, in the midst of this agitation and such a conflict of circumstances.

It was not thus that the legislators of America conducted themselves; they assembled for the purpose of constructing a constitution, and they confined their attention only to that object. The French Assembly, on the contrary, took under its survey, destroyed and remodelled everything: political laws, civil laws, criminal laws, laws of administration, ecclesiastical laws, maritime laws, military laws, forest laws, rural code, statutes of mines and miners, statutes of commerce and high roads, system of taxation, of coinage, of finance, finally every article that ever entered into political deliberation, the Assembly attempted to change. It seemed resolved to place its own glory in causing to die of a broken heart all personal vanities past, present and to come; not suffering itself to consider, that any one of these branches, properly digested, would have done them more honour than a thousand rude and half made outlines. Nor was this all, for after having totally weakened the executive power, the Assembly found itself obliged to take the real functions of this power into its own hands; and from that moment on, the constitution was merely one of the many articles that made up its task. How then could it have been possible, amidst so many obstacles, to combine in the right proportion all the parts of such a difficult and complicated work? Or how could it have been possible, amidst so many distractions, for the Assembly to carefully attend to this task and complete it? Probability contradicts the supposition even more than reality; but probability and reality unfortunately agree in the present case, to attest the imperfection of the political constitution of France.

It is nevertheless to this constitution and the whole of this constitution, to nothing more and nothing less, that vows of eternal love are paid; it is for this constitution that men are ready to sacrifice their lives, to shed every drop of their blood. Alas! if they knew it better, they would be less prodigal of such declarations of attachment. Of all men in Europe, the persons most astonished at its success are its first parents; and I cannot but believe that, when they observe the blind zeal and fervid homage of its adorers, they say to themselves, with a Roman pontiff, *quando quidem bonus populus vult decipi, decipiatur.*[3]

3. "Since these good people insist on being deceived, let them be deceived." In Latin, in the original French text. The phrase is attributed (by J. A. Thuani, in his *Historia*, 1733) to Carlo Caraffa (1517–1561), a nephew of Pope Paul IV, who noted cynically the acclaim he received as he entered Paris as Cardinal Legate in 1556. A slightly different phrase appears in Saint Augustine, *The City of God*, book 4, chapter 27.

CHAPTER XIV

Of the Public Assent to the French Constitution, and the Inferences which May Be Drawn From It

It is much easier to direct the public judgment than to form a good constitution; and on this account the National Assembly, or those by whom it has been governed, has been more successful in the first than in the second task. The opinions of the people are particularly easy to subjugate; it is sufficient only to be acquainted with its few predominant passions, and to connect with these, either by a real or an illusory tie, such ideas as we may wish to instil. Men of a superior class often allow themselves to be led in the same manner, so flattering is it to have the spontaneous effusions of their souls honoured with the glorious appellations of thought, meditation and reflection. It was then an artful contrivance, the success of which was certain, to attach the constitution to two principles, two words, liberty and equality. Wise people would perceive that between these ideas and the just conception of a political institution there was a vast, and, as it were, a desert space to be filled up. But while the mind of genius, in its comprehensive view, continually turns its eye from the centre to the circumference, it is by a direction absolutely the opposite that opinion is to be governed. The people are to be acted upon only by reduction, and it is by restricting their ideas to the narrow circle of their feelings, and absorbing their passions in a conventional phrase, that we become their masters. This object accomplished, a watchword, or in its stead, an outward token, a mark of distinction, the colour or fold of a ribbon, has greater efficacy than the wisdom of a Solon, or the eloquence of a Demosthenes. Such are the many, such is the description of empire that may be obtained over them; and guilty indeed are those who, knowing their weakness, take advantage of it, and love, by the practice of every art, to deceive them rather than, without any guile, render them happy by the sole authority of reason and morality.

The diminution or neglect of this authority is one of our greatest misfortunes; the power of the wise, that power which, in all ages and in all empires, has alone proved to be an accurate counter-balance to the irresistible force of the multitude, has thus been destroyed. There is not a single one of our faults that has an equal influence both on the present and the future. The very first elements have in this case been corrupted, and the law of gravity of the moral world has been reduced to nothing.

By fixing the attention of the inhabitants of France only upon these two simple ideas, equality and liberty, the legislators were able to direct their opinions to whatever point they pleased; they were sure at least that a veil would thus be thrown over the vices of the constitution; for it is then only when public order is represented as the essential end of social compact, that men feel, with the force of conviction, all the importance of the power destined to secure the observance of the laws and maintain the regular movement of the public administration. It is then also that political ideas begin to be complicated and cease to be adapted to the capacity of inattentive and superficial observers. We are all of us but too prone to forget social order, in the same manner as we forget the order of the universe; it is the impression which everything, carrying with it a stamp of permanence and uniformity, makes on the human mind. But while political harmony, that great and admirable result of the work of genius, escapes the observation of some, to others, and these are by far the greater number, it is incommodious and troublesome. Dissatisfied with their lot, curious about novelty, anxious for a change, they feel no admiration for those laws of equilibrium which preserve men in their mutual relations and respective places. The words liberty and equality convey a charm which strikes their ear in a more agreeable manner. They thirst after the revenges of envy and jealousy, because they feel all the chagrin arising from those passions; and, cut off from perfect happiness by the immutable decrees of nature, they imagine that the salutary bonds of society alone prevent the attainment of that end, to which the illusions of their thoughts continually bring them closer. Thus, when legislators themselves, these guides and instructors of nations, support themselves the errors of mankind; when these sworn champions of reason, called upon to fix the limits of every principle, overturn with their own hands all the barriers opposed to the usurpation of general ideas; finally, when political philosophers speak of liberty and equality with the impetuous zeal of novices, and dissemble truths which the wisdom of ages has consecrated, it is no longer astonishing that the people should abandon itself to every type of exaggeration. To the national representatives then must we ascribe all the mischief which the continual cry of liberty and equality has occasioned. These absolute expressions, supposed to comprise all the multifarious ideas of politics and philosophy, resemble the burning glass of Archimedes, which was capable of being employed either to set fire to the enemy's ships, or to reduce Syracuse to ashes.

How then can the assent of the people be adduced as proof of the excellence of the constitution? Can the multitude be a judge of such a complicated work, a work composed of so many different elements? Can even the nation be a competent judge, a nation that has never before during the lapse of so many centuries, employed its thoughts on political questions and difficulties? The very men who have been selected to prepare this constitution, in all the calmness of deliberation, have themselves been deceived; and how to expect an enlightened judgment from others amidst the distractions and the passions of the world?

Moreover, it is well known that the majority of the inhabitants of France still confound with the political constitution all those great acts of simple legislation which have been the work of the National Assembly;[1] and great pains have been taken to support this error. It

---

1. On the achievements of the National Assembly, also see Madame de Staël, *Considerations on the Principal Events of the French Revolution*, 186–93. She concluded: "We are indebted to the Constituent Assembly for the suppression of the privileged castes in France, and for civil liberty for all; at least, we owe them liberty, such as it exists in its decrees" (ibid., 190).

was in reality the best possible way of attaching the people to the new government, since among these acts of legislation, there are not a few whose utility to the state are by no means equivocal. The suppression of the *gabelles* and the *aides*,[2] the removal of the custom houses to the frontiers, the simplification and equal assessment of the taxes, the destruction of the corrupt spirit that attended their collection, the fixing of the amount of the expenditure by an authentic public act, the irrevocable proscription of every type of prodigality and abuse, the institution of juries and justices of peace, and various other regulations equally wise and benevolent, are all included, in the opinion of the multitude, in the constitution, and no attempt has yet been made to rectify this mistake.

To the constitution also has been ascribed, in all the provinces, the long delay of substituting other taxes in the place of the abolished ones, a delay which has proved so injurious to the public treasury. What is certainly due to the new government is the liberty each man enjoys of contributing according to the degree of his patriotism.

Care has likewise been taken to embellish the constitution, by incessantly comparing it, not with a better constitution, not with a constitution more wisely contrived, and at the same time equally free, but with the former political state of France, with the ancient government, taken at some distant period, and represented in a point of view that cannot fail to make it detestable. The constant object with which it is contrasted is despotism; as if there were no free governments, as if the English and the Americans were slaves; and as if, in short, there existed but one way of becoming free, invented or discovered for the first time by the National Assembly.

Lastly, by the constant use of the term conquest, it has been attempted to obliterate the recollection that all the essential foundations of liberty, all those of which the importance is universally

---

2. Two unpopular taxes during the Old Regime. The *gabelle* was an unpopular salt tax; the *aides* were excise taxes levied on the sale of items such as wine, tobacco, and iron.

acknowledged, had been laid by the king on the 27th of December 1788, prior to the meeting of the Estates-General.[3]

Meanwhile, the word conquest may certainly be applied with more propriety to the various stratagems which have been formed to usurp public opinion than to liberty; for never was the plan of a campaign more skilfully and artfully conducted; and there have been employed, without scruple, as auxiliaries, every act of violence and means of terror that could second it. Those French citizens who, from the commencement of our political disputes, supported the old government, or defended the privileges of the clergy and the nobles, were designated under a particular appellation; and this appellation, after being converted into a term of war, has been employed, at pleasure, to let loose the vengeance and hatred of the people against all those who have presumed to differ, in the smallest point, from the opinions of the chiefs of the National Assembly. Thus, whoever in the sincerity of his heart and from the dictates of his judgment wished, for the good of the state, that the legislative body should be formed of two houses; whoever was concerned about the degradation of the royal dignity and the extreme weakness of the executive power; whoever deemed it essential to the interest of France that the national representatives should possess a certain degree of landed or other property; in short, all those who coincided with Europe in opinion regarding our principal political questions, have been branded with the name of *Aristocrates*. As a term of Greek derivation, it was happily chosen, since it might be made to comprehend whatever its inventors should think proper, without danger of objections on the part of the people; and accordingly it has been familiarly employed, sometimes to bring under suspicion, but more frequently to devote to proscription, those who dared perceive any spots on the

3. On December 27, 1788, at the recommendation of Necker, Louis XVI agreed to double the number of deputies for the Third Estate. The King's decision overruled the Paris Parlement's previous decision from September 23, 1788, that maintained that each order should have exactly one third of representatives, and thus gave the majority to the privileged orders (the clergy and the nobility).

planet of the constitution. And it has sometimes happened that the most moderate censors, gaining credit with some because of their moderation, have incurred the greatest share of odium.[4]

Nor is this all; for the same purpose of usurping and conquering public opinion, societies were established in every part of France, whose object was to support the glory and celebrate the perfection of the constitution, long before the constitution was finished. These societies had to add to their political creed every new article of political symbol, as so many additional beads to their rosary; and woe to him who should hesitate to follow the example; woe to him who should doubt the inspiration of the prophets; he would have to contend with missionaries who, now arguing and now tyrannising, employed every expedient they could devise to render their lessons persuasive.

Nonetheless, after having confounded, in the public mind, acts of simple legislation with the political institutions of the National Assembly, so that the new system of government might be more successfully defended; after having constantly brought into discredit the well informed men among them, by carefully concealing this fact, that, though they disapproved of various articles of the constitution, they were the warm advocates of every principle essential to liberty; and after having employed all the other means I have pointed out, they fell on a new type of stratagem. This was no other than adroitly confounding the revolution itself with the constitution; and accordingly whatever methods were taken to secure the one became favourable to the other. Thus, in the name of the revolution and profiting of the universal wish for a change in the old government, two oaths of fidelity to the constitution were imposed before the constitution was brought to its conclusion, a circumstance without precedent in the annals of history; and the wise deference that, from prudential motives, all peaceful citizens paid to the predominant authority was afterwards construed as a general approbation of the constitution.[5]

4. On the role of the moderates who defended bicameralism, (absolute) royal veto, and balance of powers during the first phase of the French Revolution, see Craiutu, *A Virtue for Courageous Minds*, 69–109.

5. Louis XVI took the oath to respect the Constitution on September 14, 1791.

Nor did they stop even here. They brought into action, and that at every possible risk, the two great instruments known to everyone, the multiplication of assignats and the requisition of an oath from the clergy. The one would attach to the new order of things all those who possessed paper money, and the other alike offered the revolution as the only refuge to those who should desert from the laws of the church to enlist themselves under those of politics.

They have resorted also to promises of every kind, chimerical or ostentacious, to influence public opinion. They foresaw that this opinion, once elevated to admiration, would there remain fixed, or that, at any rate, it would be easy to cut off its retreat.

It was in this manner that the National Assembly first gained over the state creditors, by assuring them that they should receive the interest of their capital without the smallest deduction; by proscribing, in all its acceptations, the word bankruptcy; and by loudly trumpeting forth the fidelity of the French nation to its engagements. These creditors, however, are now paid with paper money, the precarious value of which enhances and must necessarily enhance the price of goods and merchandise of every sort; as a result, though they receive their nominal interest, they can no longer procure with the sum paid them the same amount in real objects. It is true, indeed, instead of assignats, the lands and houses forfeited to the nation are offered in payment; but as this property is sold by public auction, its price increases progressively, not according to its effective value, but in proportion to the decrease in the value of the assignats; so that the state creditors, in this way, sustain the loss they meant to avoid by the purchase of national property; and it is always the public treasury that invariably profits by their loss. The situation of foreign creditors is still more deplorable; since, whatever sacrifice they may be willing to make, it is not possible for them to convert the bills they receive into money, the exportation of money out of the kingdom being prohib-

---

Yet, his acceptance of the new Constitution did little to convince his critics of his real intentions. The royal family's flight and capture at Varennes in June of that year had rendered many skeptical toward the attitude of the king and his entourage.

ited. They are therefore obliged to submit to all the disadvantages of
the price of exchange, and to receive for a hundred pounds due to
them from France probably not more than fifty. Such to them is, at
present, the result of French loyalty. What a strange loyalty! No min-
isterial maneuver had ever created for them such a great mischief!

Let us remember another deception of the same kind, or at least
in the same spirit. Great emphasis has been laid on the diminution of
public expences; meanwhile in the estimate that has been published, a
circumstance of the highest importance has been carefully concealed,
namely, that the annual produce of the taxes falls short of the fixed expenditure; and the difference is by no means small, since it amounts
to upwards of a hundred and sixty millions (6,666,666l.*) In congrat-
ulating the nation then on the amelioration of its lot, it would have
been but just to have apprised it of this considerable gap, and in what
manner it was to be supplied. By permitting a deficit in the finances to
take place, it is in the power of every government to give a temporary
relief to the people. But the intention here was to gain the goodwill of
the taxpayers, in the same way as the state creditors had been seduced;
and to accomplish this goal, those rules of sincerity were abandoned
which the politicians regard as so many fetters upon their actions.

I might also mention under the same point of view, and as no ordinary form of affectation, the publicity given to the pretended destruction of all the privileges which were formerly annexed to certain
provinces of the kingdom, a destruction which has been presented as
an example to follow regarding all citizens possessing any particular
advantage. Everyone has taken upon credit the story of this full destruction and it is still believed to be true. It is, however, greatly mis-
represented; the most essential and remarkable of these privileges in
the provinces in question is not annihilated, I mean their unequal
share in the burthen of taxation. The privileges relative to the gabelle,
the aides and others, are gone, because these taxes have been abolished; but the partial favour that certain provinces enjoyed has considerably influenced the distribution of payment to the direct taxes.†

---

* See the First Note at the end of the volume. [See pp. 350–52.—Ed.]
† See the Second Note at the end of the volume. [See pp. 353–54.—Ed.]

To the other resources which have most eminently contributed to hide the defects of the French constitution, it is my duty to add the daily accusations against the executive power, and the perpetual custom of imputing to that power the disorders of the kingdom. The idea was ingenious, and no one will have anything to reproach to the leaders of the National Assembly for using these kinds of stratagems. It is obvious if we attend to the origin and history of opinions, that the more we circumscribe the supposed causes of great events, the more impression does our representation produce. Thus, he who talks of the imperfection of a political system, that source of disorders so vast, so irresistible, but at the same time so complicated, has much less hold upon the general attention than he who talks of the supposed duplicity of a minister, a being who has a name and a face as well as distinct and precise traits.

It is by a kind of connection with these same principles that an excellent opportunity has apparently been gained of imputing to stock-jobbing[6] the great loss sustained by assignats. But this loss is the natural effect of the great abundance of this new type of currency, and of the superiority which money everywhere must gain over an exchange with paper, unless the paper, as in England, can be converted into money at the will of the holder. This loss is the natural effect of the different value which must necessarily be stamped on money, that is current throughout Europe, and on paper that is only current in one kingdom, and not even there without exceptions. Finally, this loss is particularly the natural effect of the sale *by auction* of the territorial domains, on the security of which the assignats were at first issued and to which they must finally revert; for these domains increase in numerical value, in proportion to the fears of the holders of fictitious currency. Thus the state, by not having set a fixed price on the national domains, and by reserving to itself the power of profiting by the terror of purchasers, has become from this speculation the chief cause of the fall of assignats. The National Assembly, while introducing an immense quantity of paper money and assigning, as a unique fund for their repayment, the purchase of national domains, ought

6. *Agiotage* in the original French. It refers to speculative buying or selling of stocks.

not to have subjected that purchase to an *indefinite* bidding. Such a
kind of auction is contrary to justice, which supposes the payment
to be in real money, the received value of which is invariably fixed.
Morality is a species of philosophy that is applicable to everything.
If we study it deeply, we shall find that it is at once a most common
and most abstract idea; a most individual thought and a most universal principle. It is perhaps these two qualities, these two functions of
morality, that have caused our novices in politics, fixing their attention solely on its private application, to refuse it as a guide in public
affairs. I return to stock-jobbing, to that frivolous operation which
has been assigned as the cause of the discredit of the finances, much
as the disorders of the kingdom have been attributed to the executive power. I have already shown the true origin of the loss sustained
by assignats, which could neither be caused nor prevented by any effort of stock-jobbing, the influence of which is confined within very
narrow limits, and its effects are very soon counterbalanced by the
interests of opposing parties. Some speculators contribute to lower
the stocks, others to raise them, and all must buy after having sold, or
sell after having bought. The movement of these particular interests
favor the general price of the public funds, because they are thus rendered more easily negociable; but it cannot alter the grand principle
and source of the intrinsic value of things. That stock-jobbing should
be proscribed as an immoral and often dangerous speculation, is reasonable; but to attribute to its influence the discredit of the assignats
or public funds, is to take a very confined view indeed of the subject.
In the meantime, the greatest act of stock-jobbing ever yet conceived
is that of which the National Assembly has afforded the example, by
issuing an immense sum of paper money, and afterwards profiting
by its discredit to sell the national domains at a higher price. The occasion obliges me once more to repeat what I said to the legislators
themselves when the plan was first proposed which they have since
carried into execution: "It does not become a nation to transform itself into a stockbroker, and avail itself of the apprehensions of individuals to make its own fortune."

I only wanted to remind the great political manoeuvres which have
been employed to enlist public opinion on the side of the constitution. How many others, less remarkable, might I not cite, if I wanted

to prolong this list! Art has everywhere been practised, and in all its diversity of forms. Nonetheless, and in spite of so many precautions, in spite of so much knowledge, the constitution has been regarded in a light distinct from the revolution by the majority of the French nation; and while the wish for a change in the old government has remained almost general, nothing is more equivocal than the sentiments of the majority in favour of the constitution. Of this we shall have a striking proof, if we observe the small number of citizens who make their appearance in the assemblies of election. This tacit censure, the only one which can be exercised with impunity, clearly speaks for itself.

We ought to pay attention to the various means used to calm down the fears and which gave hopes of a favorable change. It was first announced that the formation of the municipalities would put an end to internal disorders; it failed however of producing any such effect. The goal was delayed until the establishment of the districts and departments, and the events contradicted this conjecture as well. It was next promised that the winding up of the constitution would be the era of the regular functioning of administration, and this assurance has by no means been realized. Finally, the restoration of order is now referred to the dispersion of the emigrants; and if a disappointment should again happen, the entire destruction of party spirit will be taken as the final term. But this spirit of party is not merely the result of the oppression exercised by one part of society over another, it is also the necessary consequence of a bad system of government; and the moment in which this part of society would prove most dangerous, would be that in which it should seem no longer to belong to any particular class of citizens, and in which, less striking, it would cease to afford a point of union, pro and con, to the doubtful, the wavering and the irresolute. When the Romans could no longer say: *Delenda est Carthago*, Carthage must be destroyed, all the intestine divisions were engendered which brought about the ruin of the republic.

The people have been kept ignorant of the true merits of the constitution by an exaggerated account of the evils of aristocracy on one side, and of the virtues of republicanism on the other. It has been taken for granted that reason must lie between two extremes; but it has not been observed that these opposite errors have been produced by the impossibility of remaining in the middle point fixed by the Constituent Assembly.

And what is the present object? Alas! it is but too apparent that a last political resource is hatching, not less artful than the preceding ones, but certainly more condemnable. It is wished to blend external troubles with the disorder of the kingdom so that in the ensuing general confusion, the true source of our public misfortunes may no longer be known, and that, occupied with a single interest, the public may be diverted from every other thought. By what a monstrous series of illusions have the people of France been led on so far as to desire a war! First, the people have been made to believe that liberty lay in the exact dimensions that our philosophical legislators had marked out to her, and that a hair's breadth more or less would replunge France into slavery. Next they have undertaken to persuade us that a constitution founded upon such a sublime and novel theory was the object of universal admiration; and certain deputies of the human species have been ushered into the Assembly to announce the sentiment that was present in the whole world. Imperceptibly, they went farther and have not hesitated to assure that, if the nation were to rise up majestically, it would impress that small number of aristocrates who occupied, *ad interim*, the different throne of Europe, and that French liberty, that liberty which the citizens of peaceful states contemplate with horror, would become the treasure and future bank of the world. From these absurd ideas and opinions the distance was short to an open declaration of war against all sovereigns, and foreign nations will not be much encouraged to confidence by the cry War *against the mansions of the great and peace to the cottages of the peasant*, because all civilized nations still think that the owners of mansions are citizens as well as other men; because they would fear lest, in setting fire to these mansions, our incendiary hordes should neglect to give timely notice to the master, or his family, to his steward or his servants, and that their escape from the flames would be a matter of uncertainty; because they would fear that the old servants, pensioned by their lords, and preserving an unconstitutional respect for them, might be forgotten in their beds, or in the obscurity of the night become the victims of blind ferocity; because they, these nations, would fear that the zeal of these destroyers might cause them to mistake for mansions, the houses of the middle class, and that, from one gradation to another, every habitation with a chimney might be thought a fit sacrifice to the exclusive love of cottages. Similar mistakes have already been witnessed in France, and little confidence can be placed in the prudence or accurate discrimination of those who undertake to burn houses.

Be that as it may, it is certain that foreign nations, with whom we want to share, as friends and brothers, our sublime constitution, are so little disposed to receive with grateful acknowledgment the blessing that it is offered them; consequently, all the reports which have been propagated to inspire the French with an ardour for war are stratagem and deceit. The French, however, are fond of events, hazards and glory; and this trait in their character has been made the instrument of misleading them and perpetuating their error. Such is at least the tendency of the nefarious policy meditated and prepared by the chiefs of the nation who are totally unworthy of its confidence. They would subvert the whole world in order to promote their image a day longer or to protract the triumph of a single of their opinions. Alas! they dread no remorse; and there lies our misfortune. Their philosophical consciences will leave them in the most unruffled tranquillity amidst all the disasters which they shall cause; they will calmly listen to the recital of ravages and conflagrations of which their armed cohorts would dispute the glory; they will calculate without emotion the comparative number of dead, dying and mutilated, and in their small portative notes, represent these numbers by the letter X or some other algebraic sign, to abridge their calculations. Great God! in what hands is the destiny of a nation placed! And it is to the authority of inanimate ratiocination, it is to the yoke of lifeless reasoning that a whole nation consents to submit. O, virtues of former periods, virtues so long honoured by us, have you then quitted us forever? Certainly you could form no alliance with our pedantic ideas and our systematic abstractions; but you might have been united, you might have been reconciled with the noble sentiments of a generous freedom. You could form no alliance with those severities by which the legislators of France have become the oppressors of a numerous body of citizens, with those barbarities by which they have rendered themselves the accomplices of their despair; but you might have been brought to unite, you might have been perfectly conciliated with the dignity which a true emancipation from every arbitrary authority inspires in all mankind. You could form no alliance with that upstart language, those insulting declamations by which, without ceremony or reserve, all the sovereigns in Europe have been wounded; but you might have been allied, you might have been reconciled with that majestic tone, that dignified retenue, which never fails to command the respect of nations. Yes, these ancient virtues would have served us more effectively, would have been ornaments more graceful than all our heroical exaggerations, than all our daily additions to a complex nature, which is not our own, but the personification of which we have nevertheless been urged by all sorts of expedients to support. Alas! the present and the future equally terrify me; and when I see the finest country in the world, a country so dear to my heart, a prey to all the distractions of anarchy and threatened by new disasters, I weep over the passions which have heaped on France so many calamities; and recollecting a beautiful expression of Bossuet,[7] I exclaim, sorrowfully contemplating her lot: "Behold her, such as she has been made by her vanity and pride."

7. Jacques-Bénigne Lignel Bossuet (1627–1704), prominent French bishop and theologian, famous for his sermons and orations during the reign of Louis XIV. Among his best-known works were *Politics Drawn from the Very Words of Holy Scripture* and *Funeral Orations*. Bossuet was an advocate of the doctrine of the divine right of kings.

Inferences which May Be Drawn in Favour of the French Constitution, from the Speech of the King, Delivered on the Fourth of February 1790

Towards the close of January 1790, fresh disturbances, accompanied by personal violences, plunder and conflagration, laid waste several of the provinces, and a considerable agitation prevailed in the capital itself. The whole of this agitation, the further progress of which was dreaded, was ascribed in general to certain suspicions regarding the king's political intentions; and it was openly declared that, without a particular manifestation of his sentiments, the tranquility of the kingdom could not be re-established. It was by these considerations, so worthy the attention of a monarch, that the conduct of his majesty, on the fourth of February, was governed. At that period, it was impossible for the king, or any other person, to form an enlightened idea regarding the merits of a constitution of which there had yet been seen only the first immature fruits. The king sincerely and generously wanted that a free government should be established in France; but he felt, in common with all wise men, that the care of liberty should never divert the legislators from the maintenance and security of public order, and that the welfare of the state demanded that these two objects should equally share their attention. Convinced of these truths, the king avowed his sentiments in the most unambiguous terms; nor did he express more than he felt when, declaring anew his attachment to the general principles of the constitution, he delivered these remarkable words. "I shall therefore defend and maintain that constitutional freedom, the principles of which the general wish, according with my own, has rendered sacred."

In this manner he expressed himself upon the subject of liberty; but immediately after, he called the attention of the National Assembly to the care they ought to take of the authority destined for the maintenance of order:

"I cannot entertain a doubt that, in finishing your work, you will seriously employ yourselves, with wisdom and candor, to strengthen the executive power. It is a condition without which no durable order can exist within, nor any respect outside of the kingdom. You can have no reasonable doubts remaining on this issue. It is therefore your duty, as citizens and as faithful representatives of the nation, to secure, for the good of the state and public freedom, that stability which can only be derived from an active and tutelary authority. You will surely remember that, without such an authority, every part of your constitutional system will be disjointed and incongruous; and while employed on the liberty you love, and which I also love, you will not forget that disorder in administration, introducing a confusion of powers, degenerates, by acts of blind outrage, into the most dangerous and alarming tyranny."

The Assembly, on the fourth of February, when his majesty delivered this speech, had yet time to confer on the executive power the authority necessary to the effectual discharge of its functions; and an assurance had been given that this should be done, the moment they were satisfied with the sentiments of the monarch. But after the royal declaration, the first thing they thought of was to take advantage of the public disposition, and exact an oath of fidelity to a constitution not yet formed. And since that period, far from employing their thoughts on the executive power; far from reflecting how, by the mediation of that power, public order and the activity of government, were to be secured; far from completing in this way the political constitution of France, they pursued principles of a diametrically opposite nature. For it was *subsequent to the fourth of February* that the following measures, all destructive to the majesty of the throne, and the royal prerogatives, were constitutionally decreed.

The judiciary organization has deprived the monarch of every kind of influence in the nomination of civil and criminal judges, and justices of the peace.

The organization of juries has entrusted to public officers, named by the people, the privilege of filling up the list both of small and of grand jurors.

The organization of the high national court has entrusted in like manner the choice of the jurors of that tribunal to electors named by the people.

The monarch was left no share in the nomination of the public officers who are to exercise the function of the police.

The new ecclesiastical constitution has deprived the king of all participation in the choice of bishops and other ministers of religion.

The organization of the National Guard has also excluded His Majesty from exercising any influence in the discipline of that body and the appointment of its officers.

The intervention of the monarch in the formation of the *gendarmerie*, destined to supply the place of the ancient *maréchaussée*, has been reduced almost to nothing.

It was also *subsequent to the fourth of February*, that the military constitution circumscribed within the narrowest limits the royal prerogatives, by allowing the king only a small number of appointments, and by rendering admission into the sea and land services independent of his will.

The constitution of the marine has extended the same principles to the civil administration.

The decrees relative to the finance department have deprived the king, without any exception, of the entire choice of the receivers and treasurers of the direct taxes; and as to the indirect taxes, the nomination of the revenue officers has been subjected to rules of advancement which leave few options to the authority of government.

It was still *subsequent to the fourth of February* that the order of the noblesse and titles were suppressed, a measure which weakened the executive power in two ways, by depriving the king of a mode of bestowing favours, and by destroying an intermediary rank favourable to the majesty of the throne, without supplying the loss by the institution of any other political dignity.

The same observation may be applied to the abolition of the orders of knighthood, which was equally *subsequent to the fourth of February*.

It is also since that period that the king has been deprived of the power of bestowing the smallest gratification or the most trivial pension, without the approbation of the National Assembly.

It is since that period that he has been interdicted from making peace or war, treaties of alliance or commerce, without the consent of the legislative body.

It is since that period that his sanction has been rendered unnecessary to all laws relative to the establishment, reduction and assessment of taxes.

It is since that period that he has been stripped of the most ancient, most august and most precious of all the prerogatives of the Crown, the prerogative of pardon.

It is since that period that he has been denied the liberty of choosing any minister, any agent of government, from among the deputies of the National Assembly, a prohibition that has even been extended to a period of two years after the end of the legislature.

It is since that period that the royal authority has been in a manner brought into disrepute, by the king's being obliged to sanction, in consequence of popular tumults, the most severe measures against ecclesiastical owners, and other decrees of the Assembly contrary to his opinion.

Lastly, it is since that period that the royal majesty has been degraded in every possible way, by the various regulations enumerated in a former chapter of this work; and to crown the whole, the entire constitutional code has been made subject to such a form of revision that, in three years, reckoning from the present time, there is nothing which can prevent a legislature from proposing to succeeding legislatures the entire subversion of monarchical government.[1]

It may then be said with perfect truth, that the dispositions of

1. During the first session of the Convention, on September 21, 1792, the newly elected deputies unanimously voted to abolish monarchy and proclaimed the republic as a new form of government in France. This vote recognized *de jure* a *de facto* situation that had existed since August 10 of that year.

the National Assembly, after the fourth of February, have essentially destroyed the executive power; and that, had a different course been pursued, this power would have existed, and France would have enjoyed a constitution, not indeed without defects, but in which public order and liberty would not have been found at variance; and time and experience would have perfected that work.

Meanwhile, if, as I have proved in so many different ways, executive power forms the keystone of a political edifice, and if this power has been destroyed since the period of the fourth of February, instead of having been confirmed and invigorated, in keeping with the promises which were held out, it is clear that no inference favourable to the French constitution, such as it now exists, such as we have received it from the genius and munificence of our legislators, can be drawn from his majesty's speech. The king's speech on the fourth of February was prudently restrained in its expressions, and by no means overstepped the circumstances. It was the Assembly that wrested it into a false meaning, by immediately building upon it an oath of fidelity to an incomplete constitution not yet finished; and this proceeding on its part, at a time when the executive power was yet unconstructed, was yet, if I may be allowed the expression, unsketched, shows, in a very striking light, the inattention of our legislators to the laws of social order and the fundamental principles of public order.

I was bound, no doubt, to examine, as I have done, the inference which might fairly be drawn from the conduct of the king on the fourth of February; for this measure, however urgent might be the serious reasons that dictated it, had nothing in common with the king's acceptance of the constitution on the fourteenth of September 1791. The circumstances which preceded this last acceptance, that accompanied and that followed it, were of such a nature, that no person in Europe needs any help to be told what opinion he must form in this regard. People may differ in their language upon the subject, but their sentiments are the same. Moreover, the freest assent on the part of the monarch could be regarded only as the opinion of an individual; and political subjects are too serious to allow us to form a judgment regarding them from anything but the relation they bear to the interest of nations, and the sacred principles of order and morality.

CHAPTER XVI

The Conduct which the Second National Assembly Ought to Have Observed in Receiving the Constitution

Two roads were open to the National Assembly at the time of beginning its legislative career; the one pointed out by wisdom and moderation, the other by those extravagant ideas which had so constantly misled the Constituent Assembly. It may seem at first sight that in this second mode there was no longer an opportunity left for extravagance, and that our first legislators had reached the goal; but upon closer examination, we noticed that they had not reached yet the endpoint of their exaggerations, and their successors hastened to fill in that void, certainly not as a reasonable place, but as the most conspicuous, the most glaring and that which led to the loudest applauses. Goaded by jealousy, panting after fame, the second National Assembly wished to cover their foreheads with such splendid crowns as should entirely obliterate those of their predecessors; but the laurels of the one will fade as suddenly as those of the other, and they will all appear to posterity with unadorned heads.*
They aimed at glory, and they obtained only a transient popularity;

---

*I do not conceive it necessary to cite in this place the exceptions which occur to me on recollecting the honourable character and distinguished talents of several deputies. I sacrifice the pleasure I should feel in naming them to the sentiment, probably too generous, which prevents my pointing out others of a contrary description.

and as they have been indebted to the frivolity of the nation for their triumphs, so will they owe their fall to its inconstancy. They were unable to alter their stature, but they have contrived to be called great by the multitude, whose eyes they have covered with a double and a triple bandage. One single action, supported by reason and morality, would have acquired them honours infinitely more durable than the fictions which so delight them, and which will prove evanescent like every other chimera. Truth, powerful truth, whose empire nothing can subvert, the time will come when you will be avenged of all that fantastic celebrity, of all those false reputations, which have been gathered in the regions of falsehood.

I would not have had the courage to point out what ought to have been the conduct of the present National Assembly, if I directed my attention to what it has done. I shall therefore confine myself to that moment of hope when it received the constitution from the hands of its precursors. The eager and enthusiastic homage which it rendered to this work excited the admiration of everyone; nor will I allow myself to censure with severity this instance of its behaviour, knowing, as I do, better than any man, the empire of circumstances and the deference we are obliged to pay to them. Avoiding then all particular considerations, I shall, in the discussion of the question before me, look only to general ideas.

In the first place, I must remind that, in another part of this work, when pointing out the defects of the decree relative to the revision of the constitution, I demonstrated that there would have been as much wisdom in rendering immutable a small number of articles, as there appear to be imprudence and folly in subjecting the multifarious dispositions, of which the constitutional code is composed, to an impracticable mode of amendment. The present is the moment to develop a little further my claim.

In my opinion, it is impossible in a great state to secure liberty while omitting at the same time any of the following articles.

1. That the representatives of the nation shall have the exclusive right of making laws, subject to the sanction of the monarch; comprehending under the term laws, without exception, all that relates to the selection and regulation of taxes.

2. That the representatives of the nation shall have the exclusive

right of fixing the amount of the public expenditure; there being evidently included in that right the amount of the military expenses and forces.

3. That all articles of receipt and expenditure shall be accounted for to certain commissioners appointed by the representatives of the nation.

4. That the taxes shall be annually renewed by the representative authority, excepting those taxes which are given as security for the payment of the interest of the public debt.

5. That all arbitrary authorities be proscribed, and that every citizen shall have a right to bring his civil or criminal actions against all public officers who might have abused of their power.

6. That military officers shall not be allowed to be active, within the kingdom, without the previous requisition of the civil officers.

7. That the mutiny bill, or the law for authorising the discipline, and of consequence that gives existence and force to the army, shall be annually renewed by the legislative body.

8. That the press shall be free, as far as is compatible with the interests of morality and public tranquillity.

9. That the taxes shall be equally laid, and that no citizen shall labour under disqualification to the exercise of any public office.

10. That the ministers and public agents of government shall be responsible.

11. That the throne shall be hereditary; a condition indispensible to prevent factions and to preserve the tranquillity of the state.

12. That the executive power shall be given full and entire to the monarch, together with every means necessary for its exercise and for the securing public order; a provision absolutely necessary to prevent all powers, united in the legislative body, from introducing a despotism not less dangerous than any other.

To these provisions it would be necessary to add the most inviolable respect for the rights of property, if this respect did not constitute one of the elements of universal morality, under whatever form of government people may be united.

These twelve articles I have enumerated must appear to every enlightened mind as the fundamental basis of the civil and political liberties of a nation. They ought therefore to have a distinct place assigned them in the constitutional charter, and not be confounded with those numerous regulations subject to continual discussion.

Why has this not been done? It is because, by giving these articles a prominent place in the constitutional charter, two truths would have become visible which the Assembly wanted to conceal.

The one, that the fundamental principles of French liberty were all contained either in the letter or spirit of the king's declaration of the twenty-seventh of December 1788 and its subsequent explanations.

The other, that all orders of the state, every class of citizens, after the first agitation and uncertainty had subsided, would have acquiesced in these principles, and would probably still give their assent to them if they were invited to do so.

The Assembly had therefore a deep political view in confounding the fundamental articles of liberty with all the other details of the popular government which it sought to establish; since a way was thus provided of denouncing, as enemies of the principles of freedom which occupied a place in the constitutional charter of France, all those who disapproved of any part of the new political system.

Add to this, that the first National Assembly conceived the design of converting these principles into its own property, these principles universally admitted and dear to the heart of every person, by mixing with them its own exaggerations and bizarre inventions; and as the Assembly never afterwards separated the false jewels from the true ones, few other persons attempted to do it.

Nonetheless, let us remember what fatal consequences resulted from this strange blending of incongruous articles under the general name of constitution.

The Assembly was right to be suspicious of the rectitude of the majority of these regulations and could not refuse to subject them to the test of experience. But, in so doing, it could not avoid applying the same method and plan of revision to all the constitutional articles without distinction; and thus, it became evident that, while the Assembly reserved to the succeeding legislators the means and power of correcting and improving various articles that were too easily admitted under the denomination of constitution, it exposed those very principles which form the basis of social order and the essence of public liberty to a continuous discussion.

Finally, as I have shown in a former part of this work, the Assembly generated a system of revision so absurd as to make all improvement legally impossible;* articles which no one ought to have been permitted to question, were declared to be fluctuating *de jure*, and articles which cannot be too soon superseded unalterable *de facto*.

Can anything, I demand, be more unsuitable and unwise?

It was immediately upon the blending of these incongruities, upon this strange combination, that the new representatives of the nation arrived in Paris from the different parts of the kingdom. The constitution had been completed during their journey, and they had no opportunity to read and contemplate calmly the three hundred and twenty-nine articles of which it is composed, when they suddenly met together, expressed their unanimous approbation of this political code, and pronounced with enthusiasm the oath imposed upon them by their equals, by an Assembly which had arrogated to itself the right of giving immutable laws to France.

That the whole nation should have sworn to submit to the constitution decreed in 1789 and the two succeeding years, to that constitution which some understood but imperfectly, and others not at all, ought not to astonish us; since it may easily be accounted for by the dangers that would have been incurred by a contrary proceeding. Moreover, as this constitution gave to every person the liberty of declaring one's sentiments on the new system of government, nothing more was necessary than to possess a sincere intention not to violate the established order, to be sure of remaining faithful to his engagement. But the deputies of the second National Assembly were in an entirely different situation. As representatives of the nation, like their predecessors, and warned by the disorders of the kingdom of the defects of a constitution which began to be experienced, it was incumbent on them to consider whether they ought to consecrate in the most solemn manner and without any previous examination, the immutability of a system of government, constructed during the tumultuous sway of the passions, and evidently incompatible with public order, with the internal peace of France, with the regular functioning

---

*This subject will be found discussed at large in the sixth chapter of the first volume.

of administration, with true liberty, with all the laws of a wise policy and sacred morality.

Had the deputies of the present Assembly allowed themselves sufficient time to perceive these truths, or at least sufficient time to study them before they bound themselves by a rash oath, this is what they could have told themselves.

The greatest political misfortune is a social state without government; and to this situation have our predecessors reduced France, by unconstitutionally depriving the executive power of the required force for the accomplishment of its important goal.

Another equally great political misfortune would be a social state in which, by the sole will of its founders, a government new in all its parts should be incapable of modification and obliged to subsist with all its defects, precisely as it was shaped at the first rough cast. This, however, is what our predecessors have unintentionally done, by subjecting the revision of the constitution to exceptional conditions which could never be fulfilled.

If then our predecessors have struck the political organization of France with two distinct palsies, two palsies, of which one is destructive of every blessing, and the other of every hope, does it become us, representatives like them of the nation, to accept the constitutional charter on the conditions they have imposed, and to sanction and perpetuate its defects by the solemnity of an oath?

Such unquestionably would have been the reflections of the second National Assembly, had it been at liberty to listen to the suggestions of reason, or had it not been itself under a kind of spell at sight of a constitution blindly celebrated from one extremity of the kingdom to the other.

I will admit that, considering the disposition of the public mind when the present Assembly began its sessions, it would have been difficult to make in peace a comment on a work accepted both by faith and hope; it may justly be doubted whether distinctions strongly recommended by the sound reason would have been favorably received; but to consecrate at once by an oath, the total annihilation of government in a kingdom like France, and the impossibility of applying any legal remedy to this order of things, was surely the most fatal resolution. Such, however, was the dangerous alternative, such the inextricable dilemma to which the Constitutional Assembly reduced its successors. It has involved in every possible way a system of government, which, lacking sufficient means for the preservation of public order, thus leaves liberty defenceless, and supplies fresh arms to its numerous calumniators.

But what the Constituent Assembly did not enjoin the assembly that succeeded it was to surpass it in exaggerations; it did not enjoin it to be more eager than itself in the pursuit of popular favor; it did not enjoin it to cringe and tremble more before the savage power of the multitude; it did not enjoin it to sacrifice to that power a greater number of victims, and to accept, out of compliment to it, the servile office of the *lion's purveyor*. Lastly, the first National Assembly had never imagined that new means would be devised of weakening the executive authority; that the royal majesty would be degraded still further; that the monarch would at length be reduced to a mere phantom, to lend his name to public measures, while his power was without action, and his government without dignity. And yet people continue to dispute about monarchy and republicanism! What a vain controversy! Was ever democracy more unmixed than that at which we have already arrived? Some continue to dispute about names while others have already gone beyond all limits. But how indeed could anyone acknowledge any truth in the midst of so many fictions, in the midst of such a general conceit and universal discord? How could it be otherwise when a garrulous philosophy has been promoted above everything else, a philosophy which, while it appears to set out from a certain principle, continuously leads us into a false path? And there are so many such principles, and on the same scale, in the vast circle of political science! Nonetheless, we proceed with such hasty strides in the route of illusions that it cannot be but we shall soon be obliged to turn back, because our road goes no further and there is not room to take another step. God grant that the kingdom of France may rise superior to all these disorders, and still be able to profit from the return to moderation and wisdom!

CHAPTER XVII

Concluding Reflection

In reviewing the various reflections contained in the present work, I do not despair that, more deeply investigated or better developed by other friends of reason, they might contribute to deter the nations of Europe from admitting in their midst a government similar to that of which the legislators of France have transmitted to the universe the bizarre model. We might, perhaps, allow ourselves to consider this government as an amusement of the mind, as a work of the imagination, had it not led to the most fatal consequences, had it not produced the saddest effects. We might regard that innumerable multitude of commanders whom nobody obeys, of sovereigns who excite no respect, of *friends and brothers* between whom there prevails no understanding, no harmony; all these images would be only a curious phenomenon if, amidst the general dissolution that we have witnessed, we had not seen vanity, in every shape, rise its head, and, striving for the mastery, transform itself into devouring passions; if amidst this general disorder, we had not seen envy, hatred, malignity, and all the ferocious attributes of savages display themselves; if amidst this general decay, we had not seen in particular a constitution make its appearance, a constitution which engendered anarchy and which, substituting systematical ideas in the place of the common principles of social order, has loosened every tie of which the nature of man has so long attested the importance and necessity. No constitution has ever excited so many disorders! No constitution has ever caused so many tears! Adopt it then, this constitution, adopt it without change or modification, ye nations of the earth, that may be indifferent to the maintenance of public tranquility; that can look with calmness on the confusion of all authorities, the progressive despotism of a tumultuous assembly, and the degradation of the power destined to watch over the observance of the laws. Adopt this constitution, you who wish to bend your neck to the yoke of the multitude, who wish to have its servants for your masters, its flatterers for your tyrants! Adopt it, if you are weary of cherishing goodness, compassion, charity, mercy, and all the virtues which embellish and dignify human nature! Adopt it, if you want the philosophy of the present day should triumphantly establish itself on the ruins of religion! Finally, give the preference to this constitution, if calm reason, manly independence, liberty without ostentation, and morality in all its vigour, which appear to be the fruits of the English government, do not inspire you with greater veneration than our complex ideas, or extravagant principles, our factitious sentiments, and all those spontaneous productions of a systematical legislation and a government devoid of every tie and connection.

The greatest attraction possessed by the new French constitution consists in its inexhaustible fund of gratifications given to all types of vanity by the public administration; in the general banquet that is prepared, to which every type of vanity is invited. But which is the purpose of the social system, to govern ill, or to be governed well? The most required thing is that we should be all conscious of liberty, and that we should all partake of peace, order, and security; but these goods are committed to perpetual risk by the political anarchy to which our legislators have given the name of constitution. The great traits of this anarchy are known to all the world; but its innumerable details are so carefully disguised, that few men are able to form a proper idea of them. All France is at present divided into two classes, the oppressors and the oppressed; and no man possesses a secure tranquillity. Travel through the kingdom in all directions, or inquire of those who have done it: if your informers be men of veracity, they will tell you that, down even to the smallest municipalities, you must not look to the law for protection, but to certain persons in power. Violence against property and restraint upon personal liberty depend upon the decrees passed in the marketplaces. Were the examples less numerous, the terror they excite would be equally frightening. Disorders which derive from a moral principle are different from the revolutions of the universe; the latter can be subjected to the calculation of experience, and we can normally know their timing. No doubt, we do not take our seat in the councils where the elements hold their stormy debate; nor where the flames of Etna and Vesuvius prepare themselves in subterraneous caverns for future eruptions; but we are able to discover, by long observation, the limits which even the fury of their burning lavas respect. Trees are planted, cottages are built in security almost upon the line where their violent power ceases. It is not thus with the disasters whose cause is a moral one, and above all, it is not thus with the excesses that derive from a bad system of government. They regenerate themselves in every direction; they have no determined circumference; the moment, the day in which their fury shall burst forth cannot be predicted; we are always in terror, always in alarm, and the tyrannous exertions of today can by no means guarantee the tranquility of tomorrow.

I would like to explain myself without reserve. I shall, perhaps, be pardoned for that, for if frankness must be held in esteem, it is at the moment when we are perishing as victims of all the hypocrisies and personal speculations. Moreover, I am far from wanting to adopt any political opinion as a party man; I speak only from that pure and untainted affection with which I have long loved and still love France. I have united myself to her destiny, and I feel in the utmost degree depressed by her misfortunes.

It is no longer time to conceal a truth foreseen by a small number of sages, and that experience is every day confirming in the most terrible manner. The constitution of France is a bad constitution; and it is in vain that, out of respect for the persons or genius of its authors, we perpetually struggle against the opposition of reason, that representative of the eternal nature of things and which can neither be vanquished nor dominated. It is impossible to maintain a political constitution in which the executive power is forgotten, in which all legitimate authorities compete against each other, in which the people alone can preserve their sway, can increase it every day and exercise it with the most formidable tyranny. It is impossible to maintain a constitution in which public order is left defenceless, when sur-

rounded by such numerous enemies. It is impossible to maintain a
constitution in which the deputies of the legislative body, dispensed
from giving proof of their possessing any property, are in a great measure, and before long perhaps will be completely false representatives
of the interests of France. It is impossible to maintain a constitution in which all power will necessarily be concentrated in an assembly obliged to bend to the will of certain favourites of the multitude.
It is impossible to maintain, it is impossible to attach oneself to an
order of things, in which lying will have its utility, calumny its triumphs, hatred its gratification, and in which all kinds of vices will
serve all types of ambition. It is impossible to maintain a constitution
in which punishments must form the principal, and perhaps only resource of administration; a constitution, in which the science of government is reduced to two principles, so that every man may believe
himself competent to the talk, and rudeness and insolence are in perpetual honour, so that all may suppose themselves worthy of the honors destined to great characters. And how many more efforts are not
necessary to maintain the integrity of a constitution to which there is
no other way of gaining partisans than that of continual proscription;
a constitution which, instead of being the centre of a generally felt or
generally hoped happiness, appears to be the rendezvous of all hostilities; a constitution which, by the infinite multiplication of passions
and pretensions, keeps up in France such a dreadful agitation that it
is impossible for the French today to move around without coming
up against each other. Finally, and above all, it would be impossible
to maintain a monarchical government in which the majesty of the
throne is guarded by no prerogatives, by no intermediary rank, by no
opinion able to preserve that respect without which royal authority
is nothing more than an empty title.

I believe I have clearly demonstrated these truths, and others have
already done it or will still do it. I have further proved, and this is the
principal source of my despair, that the constitutional means which
have been devised for the purpose of altering such a defective system
of politics are totally chimerical. These are, no doubt, sad truths, but
the longer we divert our attention from them, the more will the confusion increase, the greater time shall we have to advance to the last
extremity, and to flounder against all the rocks which lie in the way.

To save ourselves it is no doubt necessary to oppose a vast mass of opinions to the errors and agitations which prevail; and this force must be made to act in a manner diametrically the reverse of the impulse which is given to the public mind by those who wish to arrive at a republic by means of anarchy, or at anarchy by means of a republic. For if, in departing from the constitution as framed by our first legislators, as many steps had been made towards a regular government, as the current Assembly has taken towards democracy, we should at present have been at no great distance from the end that ought to have been kept in view.

This end, in my opinion, and I shall never be afraid to avow it, is a government resembling, as far as the nature of things will admit, the government of England; a government acknowledged by all Europe to be free and happy, and the reputation of which the subtle arguments of our upstart politicians will never be able to destroy. Let all the principles of civil and political liberty, consecrated by the French constitution, be preserved; let them receive even additional force; but, for the sake of public order, for the regular activity of administration in a great empire, for the agreement and union of all powers, for the external consideration and internal tranquillity of the kingdom, for the peaceful security of freedom itself, for all these conditions to be fulfilled, let the executive authority be invested with the dignity and authority which are absolutely necessary to it. Let a second legislative chamber be established, the suffrage of which will enhance the respect due to the laws, the political dignity of which will serve as an intervening step between the monarch and the nation, and thus become a support to the majesty of the throne. Finally, let the deputies of the legislative body be required to possess a certain degree of property, that they may be connected with the state by all kinds of ties. These are the essential points in favour of which it is to be wished that opinions would unite; otherwise the French government will degenerate into a tumultuous democracy, in the midst of which there will be no other harmony but what will be derived from the despotism of those tyrants whom the popular favor will give us.

I am aware of the difficulties attending such a conciliation, in the present disposition of the public mind; but as the constitution cannot remain in its present form, as a republic of twenty-six millions of

men is a chimerical idea, as the re-establishment of the old system is
out of the question, and as the kingdom of France cannot disappear
from the face of the globe, we would need, amidst all the challenges
we are facing today, to arm ourselves with fresh courage to encounter
all difficulties, however formidable they may be.

The principal obstacles would easily be removed, if men seriously
attached themselves to their removal, and if public interest were not
constantly sacrificed to private views. To these private interests, I will
then address myself now; and this is the last task which remains to
be completed. And in the first place, I shall not fear to address myself to those who are the most difficult to persuade, those whose attention is perpetually directed to one object, a republic, a republic at
all costs. Every day, they advance towards this end, at the same time
declaring that they have no intention to do it, or have given up all desire to attain it. These people in general have as much understanding
as it is possible to have without morality; thus, they are perfectly acquainted with the game they have to play, and the sincere and bona
fide constitutionalists are the instruments of their conspiracy. These
last maintain with blind enthusiasm and with unremitted constancy
the defects of the constitution in full vigour; these defects annihilate
the respectability of government, render its administration impotent,
and the more they are maintained, the more reason the republicans
have to promise themselves success. Thus having for the perpetual
burthen of their song, *"the constitution, the whole constitution, nothing
but the constitution,"* the democracy advances with flying colors. Those
whose task is limited to repeating these words with devotion will one
day regret the mischief they have promoted; they will see, without
being able to doubt it, the projects which their political activity has
served; and then their lamentatations may reasonably be answered,
like the grasshopper in the fable:

"What did you do in the summer and autumn?"

Let us consider, however, whether the calculation of the republicans themselves is as ingenuous and deep as they think.

People are misled regarding their interests by the very spirit they
are obliged to assume for reaching their goals. Thus, during a revolution, when their intrigues and challenges occupy their thoughts,
they are distracted and prevented by many factors from examining

whether, if the goal of their wishes were obtained, the result would indemnify them for the efforts of their pursuits. Thus, the artful democrats of the present hour meditate with transport in their secret committees, the stratagem of making use of the constitutionalists themselves, the better to arrive at a republic. They find it interesting to leave them the name of king with which to entertain themselves, until the fit moment shall arrive to take from them their last toy. They still find it delightful to inspire alarm into all the Parisians, and through them into their provincial imitators, by making them worry, sometimes by a fable artfully contrived, and sometimes by an impudent lie destitute of all shadow of probablity. Moreover they think it a great strategy to bring to march, from time to time, through the midst of the National Assembly, irregular bodies of men, armed with pikes and pitch-forks; and they amuse themselves during the ceremony with watching the stressed and worried looks with which the scrupulous friends of the constitution elaborated in 1789, 1790, and 1791 behold it. But enough of the various amusements of the same type that the republicans, Quakers, and Jacobins, to whom the Legislative Assembly is now subjected, procured to themselves. I proceed to transport them in imagination, by the shortest possible path, to the completion of all their wishes, the establishment of the most complete republic; but once they shall have reached their goal, I ask them if they would not begin to experience disgrace and setbacks of all kinds. First, many of them, surprised by their progress, will perhaps be upset for not having been told the entire truth along their voyage; but this will be a trifle. Their leaders will try to convince them that the treacherous conduct of the court, the projects of the constitutionalists, the conspiracies of the moderates, and the discoveries of the committee of surveillance have made the latest measures necessary; and the dupes will yield a ready assent to the chiefs of factions, if it were only to put on a more honorable appearance. The great difficulty will be when the legislative and executive authorities shall be united in the hands of the same class of citizens, all equal to each other, all looking the same, and determined to court the people in order to be promoted into their ephemeral functions. For the absolute destruction of all types of imposing superiorities, amidst an immense population, would weaken so much the general ideas of respect, that soon obedience would become only a chance thing, a mere accident, for which the multitude of executive and legislative chiefs would fight among themselves and finish by regarding it as good luck.

The great difficulty, above all, will be when every type of power, being united in the hands of people chosen by the nation, there will no longer be two branches of government to guarantee the public happiness. The representatives of the people, possessing all the powers, will alone be accountable to the people; and they will not be able, as now, to get rid of complaints by throwing all the blame upon the enemies that surround them and talking of the battles they have to fight against them. The victory once acknowledged, the supreme power once recognized, these excuses will no longer be admissible. For a little while, they will still try to appease this people by praising them, by pandering to them, by telling them that they rose up majestically, that they had a superb attitude, that the entire universe regards and admires them. They will still need to consult the people on what they would like to do, before ordering them to do anything; and they will probably throw out a bait to the most impatient, by giving them more houses to strip and more forests to cut, and by extending all the honors that are due to property to those who own nothing. But there are bounds to such distributions, there is a limit to fortunes to be divided by the law of the strongest; there is a limit also to promises and hopes; for the nature of things is deaf and mute, and the language of hypocrisy can do nothing against it. It will therefore sooner or later be discovered that it is impossible to bestow on twenty-six millions of sovereigns a lot proportioned to their dignity and pretensions; and when the majority of them shall remark that their condition has not improved, when they shall perceive that the rain still penetrates into their rooms, the wind still whistles through their abodes, that the price of bread and the wages of industry are not under their control, they will then discover that they have been led astray, they will incline their ear to new seductions, and their last friends, their last champions will see, like the preceding ones, their authority overthrown.

Let them then once more examine their personal interest before they sacrifice to it the interest of their country, before they take another step towards absolute democracy. It is the completion of their wishes that will prove the termination of their power; and their sole satisfaction will be the horrid spectacle of a disordered state, and a great kingdom completely overthrown. Let them at length come forth from the cloud behind which they have concealed themselves; and if they believe from their hearts, that a republic forming a single body, or a federal republic, or a republic with the vain name of king, or any other form of government composed of the three preceding ones, be suitable to France, let them submit their ideas to the nation and explain themselves openly. But it is inexcusable, it is highly criminal, to advance towards an object, which they carefully dissemble, by means which they dare not avow, means which daily and hourly weaken the pillars destined to support the social edifice. It is still more reprehensible to invite to this destructive operation a number of men who, though mistaken, are sincere in their sentiments, a numerous body of worthy citizens, in whose minds a continual alarm is kept up, and who, while they believe to participate in quelling civil tumults, are harnessed to the chariot of certain ambitious leaders and made the instruments of the basest intrigue. They will be the first to call you to a reckoning for the illusions by which they have been ruined; they will be the first to load you with reproaches when the truth, the sad truth, can no longer be concealed. You may still attempt to govern them, still attempt to keep them in a state of agitation; but there will no longer be any authority to expose to suspicion, no longer any ministers to calumniate, and your most powerful resources will thus be cut off. Then all eyes will be turned upon you, and it will be asked, are these the men whom we suffer to sway the sceptre of France? Then the sentiments of a proud nation will be awakened, and those who in the moment of faction have appeared conspicuous, will be barely noticed. I can distinguish their little boat which the furious waves lift, at intervals, almost to the skies; but it will escape my view when, the ocean being appeased, I have no other mode of discovering it, but by its form and its height.

You madmen, what are you then going to do? You see that the least enlightened class of the people, always credulous, always open to suspicion, is the most docile to your inspirations; and you govern their thoughts and direct their opinions by all the artificial means in your power. You foolishly imagine that, having once agitated the multitude, you can still lead it as you please; but dread the fatal effects that may result to yourselves from your blind confidence; and fear that you, as well as we, should be buried under the ruins of an edifice of which you have endeavored to loosen and disunite all the parts.

Be also assured, you, whom momentary triumphs lead on from project to project, from one degree of temerity to another, that, should your perfidious manoeuvres, or your continued outrages, subdue the constancy and weary the life of the august chief of the state, should his heart sink under so many hardships, so great injustice and ingratitude, you would shortly see every form of indignation spring up against his persecutors. Then, but too late, would his misfortunes, his virtues, and his benefits strike with redoubled force on the heart and feelings of a nation, too long habituated to compassion and generosity ever to be totally lost to these qualities; then you will see all their old sentiments revive, burst out with double force, and they will hate your machinations in proportion as they recover all their virtues.

It is a hazardous undertaking to wish to carry a political innovation to its farthest extreme. And it is a singular undertaking to think of executing such a plan without any profound sentiment, without any object of irritation similar to those whose memory is transmitted from age to age; we act, as it were, with the passions of the mind; and we are teaching the posterity that those passions are the most dangerous of all, because they are exaggerated beyond all limits in order to render them similar to the emotions of the heart, or the impulses of character.

All these speculative ideas would not have been able to lead the imagination astray, they would not have had at least any effect, if the first legislators of France had transmitted to us a government capable of surviving, like many others, solely through the judicious balance between its parts; if they had transmitted to us a constitution which, by its structure and combinations, could have kept all powers in harmony and made them profit from their reciprocal action. Besides, this constitution covers such a large scale that is everywhere weak, and reason cannot suffice to guard it. From afar, we can see only fanatical believers or philosophical inquisitors on its ramparts, and the prudent people, the wise ones, that militia of morality are nowhere to be seen.

You then, who love this constitution, add to it what is necessary to render it durable, or it will shortly perish in your hands. How is it that you do not perceive that, with a little dexterity, with the slightest misconstruction, it may be converted either into a government without action, or into a disorderly republic? It is then in the name of liberty, in the name of that blessing so inestimable when confined within proper limits, that all Europe solicits you to reflect upon, to adopt those principles, of which experience and political philosophy have consecrated the reasonableness and utility.

And you also ought to lend your resources and assistance to these reasonable ideas, you who appear to wish only for the pure and unqualified return of the old government. What kind of blindness is that which gives you the confidence to be able to make all the sentiments and opinions return to the point from which they began? You have, no doubt, been led to this confidence by the disorders of the kingdom, by the mischiefs to be ascribed to a systematical exaggeration of the ideas of liberty; but are you not afraid that you should support this extravagance by opposing to it your own exaggeration? How can one imagine that a government which has long been subverted by public opinion and lost all its influence and consideration from the countless errors of a succession of ministers whose arbitrary authority it supported, and from the irresistible effect of the progress of knowledge; how can one imagine that such a government could ever return to live and be able to maintain itself, when all its abuses, formerly seen only in a general light, have been discussed one by one?; when all its abuses, heretofore investigated only in books, or in the conversations of enlightened men, have been unveiled in the presence of the whole assembled nation today, and form the creed and familiar catechism of the inhabitants of France? Moreover, it would no longer be sufficient to restore the ancient government of the kingdom. A twenty-year despotism and the most frightening tyranny would scarcely be enough to achieve this goal. It would therefore be impossible to conceive it and flatter yourselves with its success, even if you had the support of all the forces in Europe. For this would be far from acquiring all the necessary means for exercising a long domination over the power of reason and the united will of a great people. One should never take counsel from resentment, even if it were entirely justified, in a political crisis without precedent, in an immense revolution that expands at every step beyond its first causes.

There are periods in the life of nations when it becomes indispensible to consider their interest in a general manner, detaching ourselves, by an effort of mind, from all the prevailing passions of the moment.

I invite those who would like to do this to reflect on the following propositions.

The ancient government of France united all the necessary means for the maintenance of the laws of property, of order and liberty, but it contained also the power of infringing them. Without exposing itself to the danger of importunate complaints, with a simple decree of the royal council, it could reduce the interest of loans or delay their imprisonment; with a bed of justice (*lit de justice*), it could augment and make taxes permanent; and with a *lettre de cachet*, it could imprison whomever it pleased.[1]

The authority of the National Assembly, that unique authority established by the new constitution, also has the power of infringing upon the laws of property, order, and liberty; but it does not possess, like the previous government, the necessary power for forcing others to obey those laws. Quite often, a decree that was voted after a motion had been introduced by a person lacking honor and property brings to our recollection both the old decrees of the Council against property, and *lettres de cachet* against individuals; and yet we are not on this account less subject to the arbitrary will of the departments, districts and municipalities, nor more secure against all the calumnies of the evil-minded and all the violent acts of the multitude.

A perfect government then would be that which should be able, by its constitution, to protect the laws of property, liberty and order, without possessing at the same time the power of violating them; and this perfection, in my opinion, is represented by the political constitution of England.

---

1. During the Old Regime, a bed of justice (*lit de justice*) was a session of the *parlement* (court of justice) attended by the king who came in person in order to have his decrees officially registered. A *lettre de cachet* was a letter bearing the seal of the sovereign, containing a royal warrant authorizing imprisonment without trial.

I believe then that every reasonable person, every real friend of the happiness of the human race, may be allowed to pay homage to this government and wish that it may serve as a model to the legislators of other nations. Had this government been bestowed on France, had we adopted a system similar to it, we would have enjoyed a better, more genuine freedom than that which we have so thoughtlessly boasted of. Peace would have also prevailed in the kingdom and public order would have been maintained; our morality, far from losing ground, would have been perfected, and we would at this moment have been an object of affection and admiration in the eyes of all people in Europe. Alas! we should have been too happy! In our distress, we are ready to scatter our reproaches upon all parties, but we do not have the courage to reproach any party except that which is crowned with success.

I well recollect that, towards the end of my administration, and for the purpose of precipitating that end, it was customary to say that I was the constant obstacle to completing the constitution; and that I was unable to raise myself to its true level. I have now shown, without thinking of me, that in this lofty atmosphere, the air is quite unhealthy, and that there are many reasons to regret that France was not content to remain in the middle regions. I have always listened with pity to these discourses; more than once, while I contemplated the proud inebriation of our first legislators, more than once when I stood in the midst of their sessions and saw the arrogant confidence to which they abandoned themselves, I pictured to my imagination the fatal hand recorded by the prophet Daniel, which once terrified the despot Balthazar by writing these words on the interior walls of his palace: "I have weighed you in the balance and found you wanting."

Doubtless, it was my wish to restrain our first legislators in the rapid progress of their excesses; I would have gladly erected the standard of reason and exhibited wisdom in the most lively colours, in order to rally round these two guides those who so frequently deserted their cause; I would have gladly done this, for the sake of the tranquillity and happiness of France and for its own glory. But let us not dwell upon the past; it is a period that is forever lost to us; it is sunk in eternal night, and our eyes which revert towards it, our regrets which so often wish to call it back, are no longer able to reach it. Reflect on this inexorable truth, you who dispose of the present moment, and who are anxious that it should contribute exclusively to your own renown. You artfully conceal from us the final object you have in view; but when, within the kingdom, the respect due to government has been destroyed, and abroad, all the sovereigns of Europe have been insulted and provoked, it is certain to bring with every type of war all kinds of confusion. It is impossible to observe without the deepest regret how a whole people can be misled by discourses; how it can be governed by a small number of men astonished themselves at their omnipotence; and it is impossible to observe without anguish so many brave men, so many virtuous citizens, abandoning over and over again, some their parents, others their wives and children, in order to defend, at the risk of their lives, not the liberty in general, not the liberty which would have brought about the happiness of France, not the liberty which would have elicited the respect of all the nations of Europe, but a speculative liberty and consecrated by certain metaphysical pontiffs, and which would terrify every man of prudence and moderation more than despotism itself.

You well know what this liberty is, you who celebrate it without having any confidence in it; you, who employ it as a stalking horse to your ardent ambition; you, who do not hesitate to offer as a sacrifice to the shrine of this idol the repose and happiness of the present generation; you, who would obliterate for its sake humanity, justice, and all the other virtues. Retire then from its altars, if you want that we love it; for all the serpents of the furies hiss around your heads; we shudder at your aspect, and your hypocritical adoration petrifies us with horror. Oh! who will save us from the abyss into which we are fallen? Will the only power that perhaps has the means deign to render us this service? Will it endeavour to arrest in their course the projects of that formidable league which threatens our country, and at the same time attempt to restore us to our senses and reason? A vulgar and shortsighted policy would no doubt dictate to that power to leave us to ourselves, and to take no interest either in our external quarrels, or our intestine divisions; but a moral and enlightened policy would give perhaps a very different counsel. Listen then to its voice, ye generous English, listen to the voice of this policy in preference to every other. Let one and the same age, adding new lustre to your destiny, aggrandize you in the eyes of posterity by three of the most brilliant public acts that can do honour to a people:

By a striking act of national gratitude, in resolving upon an immense sacrifice, for the purpose of indemnifying those numerous royalists, whose fidelity to you had caused them the loss of their whole fortune. This you have already done.

By a striking act of humanity, in prohibiting an impious commerce so long maintained by European avarice. This you have already done.

By a striking act of generosity, in giving peace to your ancient rivals, and pointing out to them the means of happiness. This also you will perhaps do.

In this conduct you would find your true interest; for it cannot be indifferent to you either, on the one hand, to have among your nearest neighbours a hotbed of anarchy and political libertinism, or, on the other, to see re-established the same old goverment, which has so long concerned you. But I would not want to present to you a personal motive, at a time when noble motives would be so badly needed to give to your intervention all the majesty required by such a great and difficult enterprise. It seems as if the character of the human race would be redeemed from the dishonour in which our atrocities have involved it, if a truly philosophical nation should undertake to lead us back to just ideas and reasonable sentiments. But alas! the eagerness of my wishes misleads me. Our regeneration ought to be our own work; and France, I well know, contains in her bosom a sufficient number of sagacious minds to expect from them our salvation, if these minds were not doubtful, dejected, and if we did not find them embarrassed with their situation, often mixing with the audacious and extravagant ones, as if to hide from themselves their own weakness.

Oh! Resume at length some degree of courage and ask whither it is that others want to lead you! Remember that the first characteristic of any free person is independence of thought, and that of all humiliations the most difficult to support is that of being governed in an absolute way by men whom we despise. Above all, do not enlist in the service of opinions which you condemn, and at least continue sincere in your actions, when prudence will prevent you from being frank and open in your language.

What a period is that in which we live! What a spectacle presents itself on every side to our regards! Never did there exist such a mixture of so many artificial ideas and extravagant opinions! Those ideas and opinions gravitate towards each other and form a league to produce our ruin. O Reason, celestial Reason, image of the supreme intelligence which created the world, I will never forsake thy altars; but, to continue faithful to thee, I will disdain alike the hatred of some, the ingratitude of others, and the injustice of all! O Reason, whose empire is so congenial and so pleasing to sensible souls and all the elevated hearts; Reason, celestial Reason, our guide and support in the labyrinth of life, alas! whither wilt thou fly in this season of discord and maddening fury? The oppressors will have nothing to say to thee, and thou art rejected by the oppressed. Come then, since the world abandons thee, to inhabit the retreat of the sage; dwell there protected by his vigilance, and be satisfied with his silent worship, so that one day thou can appear again attired in all thy ancient glory, when these times dominated by prestige and conceit shall have passed. And as at that time perhaps I shall be no more, allow my shadow to follow thy triumph from afar, and in the meantime, permit that my name, tarnished as it is with calumny, preserve its place humbly inscribed at the foot of thy statue!

The End

Appendixes

Note by Way of Appendix

The silence of the greater part of the public papers regarding the affairs of North America prevented my being informed, before the present work was printed, of a change which took place last year in the political constitution of Pennsylvania. The court of censors has been abolished, and the legislative body, instead of one, is now composed of two Houses, an innovation that tends to justify the general observations I have made, in the fourth chapter of the second volume, in speaking of the government of that state.

First Note On Page 312 of Vol. II

This deficiency has been concealed as much as possible, by constantly making up the account of the finances for a particular year, a mode by which the temporary resources are comprehended in the revenues. The following is a concise account of the present state of the revenue and expenditure.

Permanent Revenue

	Livres
Taxes on property, real and personal	300,000,000
Stamps and registers	80,000,000
Patents	20,000,000
Custom houses	15,000,000
Posts and expresses	14,000,000
Lotteries, from seven to eight millions	7,500,000
Gunpowder and saltpetre duties	1,500,000
Produce of the forests	10,000,000
Feudal rights belonging to the public, and not yet redeemed, from three to four millions	3,500,000
Total	451,500,000

The taxes do not at this time produce the above sum, but may be thus calculated in a statement of permanent revenue.

In the foregoing statement, the revenues of the national domains is not included, because these revenues will cease to exist, when all the assignats shall be converted into property of this sort, destined for their extinction. In the course of the present year, the amount of the assignats will equal the value of the national domains.

The arrears of the patriotic contributions, and the produce of the salt and tobacco which may remain in store, are also not included in the above statement. These are transitory resources which will cease with the present year.

Permanent Expenditure

	Livres
Perpetual annuities upon the Hotel de Ville, the Clergy, the Pays d'Etats, &c.	85,000,000
Life annuities,	100,000,000
interest of that part of the debt which is said to be redeemable on demand	37,000,000
Church pensions	65,000,000
Pensions, annual gratifications & charities	18,000,000
To the princes, under the titles of appenages and grants	6,500,000
For the war department, including the expense of the national gendarmerie	109,000,000
For the marine department	45,000,000
For foreign affairs	6,300,000
Expence of religious worship	1,000,000
Civil list	25,000,000
Expence of the National Assembly	6,000,000
Bridges and highways	5,000,000
General administration	5,000,000
Public buildings	4,000,000
Bounties and encouragements	4,000,000
Orphans	3,500,000
Academies, universities, king's garden	1,200,000
High national court, tribunal of appeal	500,000
Casualties	5,000,000
Total	612,000,000

The part of this expenditure which consists of life annuities, operates gradually to its own extinction.

The charge of public education, when settled, should be annexed to the above statement.

Should experience prove, as is highly probable, that in the new order of things, the sum of five millions reserved for casualties will be insufficient, the article under that head should be augmented.

None of the extraordinary expenses are carried into the above account, the object being to state only the permanent expenditure.

Comparative Statement

	Livres
The permanent expenditure amounts to	612,000,000
The permanent revenues to	451,000,000
The permanent expenditure exceeds the permanent revenue by	161,000,000

It appears to me that this statement cannot differ more than three or four millions from the precise truth.

The various expedients determined on by the National Assembly are to be applied to the lessening of this deficiency.

The above calculations were made at the close of the month of April, 1792.

Second Note On Page 312 of Vol. II

The taxes on property, real and personal, amount together to three hundred millions of livres, a sum which (when divided by twenty-seven million one hundred and ninety thousand souls, equal, according to the supposition of the committee of contributions, to the population of all the departments) gives eleven livres and eight deniers for the average contribution of each individual.

Now, by dividing in a similar way the sum each department contributes by its particular population, the result will be found to vary from six livres to eighteen, without including in this comparative statement, the extreme cases. Thus while Corsica, for instance, pays no more than twenty sous for each individual, and while the departments of Arriege and the upper Pyrenees pay a hundred sous only, Paris contributes at the ratio of thirty two-livres, and the departments which compose the ancient generality of Paris, from twenty to twenty-two livres.

The degrees of population, even with the exceptions I have just made, undoubtedly do not indicate with precision the respective competency of each part of the kingdom. It is evident, however, that to explain the great disproportion which has been introduced between the contributive quotas of several departments, it must be ascribed to the ancient branches of some of them, and to the subsidies and high duties on salt to which others have long been subjected. Without this consideration it would be impossible to account why the most unfruitful department of Champagne should be taxed at thirteen livres or thereabouts, per head, whilst the richest department in Lorraine pays ten only, and the best in Alsace and Franche-Comté only eight. How is it likewise that the departments of Normandy bordering on the sea, not comprehending the rich departments of Rouen, should be taxed at from thirteen to eighteen livres per head, while the departments of Brittany, also situated on the sea coast, should pay from an hundred sous to eight livres, and that in which Nantz is comprehended nine livres only for each individual?

I am far from finding fault with the respect which has been paid to the ancient franchises of particular provinces; but why boast so frequently, and in so pompous a style, of having abolished them?

Select Bibliography

NECKER'S MAIN WORKS

Compte rendu au roi. Paris: Impr. Royale, 1781. English translation: *State of the Finances of France Laid Before the King.* London, 1781.

Mémoire sur l'établissement des administrations provincials. Paris, 1781.

De l'Administration des finances de la France. Lausanne, 1784. English translation: *A Treatise on the Administration of the Finances of France.* London: J. Walther, 1785.

De l'importance des opinions religieuses. Paris and London: Panckoucke, 1788. English translation: *Of the Importance of Religious Opinions,* trans. Mary Wollstonecraft and W. Goodwin. London: Johnson, 1788.

Sur l'administration de M. Necker par lui-même. Paris, 1791.

Du Pouvoir exécutif dans les grands états. First edition: Paris, 1792. Republished in *Oeuvres Complètes de M. Necker,* ed. M. le Baron de Staël, vol. 8 (1 and 2). Paris: Treuttel and Würtz, 1821. English translation: *An Essay on the True Principles of the Executive Power in Great States.* London: G. G. J. and J. Robinson, 1792. 2 vols.

De la Révolution française, republished in *Oeuvres Complètes de M. Necker,* ed. M. le Baron de Staël, vols. 9 and 10. Paris: Treuttel and Würtz, 1821. English translation: *On the French Revolution.* London: T. Gadell, Jun. and W. Davies, 1797. 2 vols.

Cours de morale religieuse (Geneva: Pascoud; Paris: Maradan, 1800).

Dernières vues de politique et de finance (1802). Republished in *Oeuvres Complètes de M. Necker,* ed. M. le Baron de Staël, vol. 11 (Paris: Treuttel and Würtz, 1821).

ON NECKER AND THE COPPET GROUP

Cahiers Staëliens, published by the *Société des études staëliennes* (founded
in 1929 at Coppet; http://www.stael.org/) and Éditions Honoré
Champion, are an essential source of information about the entire
Coppet group that also included, among others, Germaine de Staël,
Benjamin Constant, and Sismonde de Sismondi. The website of the
Society contains valuable bibliographical references and offers access
to many electronic texts.

WORKS ON NECKER

Bredin, Jean-Denis. *Une singulière famille: Jacques Necker, Suzanne
Necker et Germaine de Staël.* Paris: Fayard, 1999.

Burnand, Léonard. *Necker et l'opinion publique.* Paris: Honoré Champion, 2004.

Diesbach, Ghislain de. *Necker ou la faillite de la vertu.* Paris: Perrin,
1978.

Egret, Jean. *Necker, ministre de Louis XVI.* Paris: Honoré Champion,
1975.

Grange, Henri. *Les Idées de Necker.* Paris: Klincksieck, 1974.

Harris, Robert D. *Necker: Reform Statesman of the Ancien Régime.*
Berkeley: University of California Press, 1979.

———. *Necker and the Revolutionary Decade* (Special Collections and
Archives, Moscow, Idaho: University of Idaho Library, Collection:
ma 2007-031.

———. *Necker and the Revolution of 1789.* Lanham, MD: University
Press of America, 1986.

d'Haussonville, Comte. *Madame de Staël et Necker.* Paris: Calmann-
Lévy, 1925.

Lavaquery, Eugène. *Necker: Fourrier de la révolution, 1732–1804.* Paris:
Plon, 1933.

Staël, Auguste de. "Notice sur M. Necker" in *Oeuvres diverses de M. le
Baron Auguste de Staël,* vol. 2. Paris: Treuttel and Würtz, 1829.

Staël, Germaine de. "Du caractère de M. Necker et de sa vie privée" in
Oeuvres Complètes de Madame la baronne de Staël publiées par son fils.
Paris: Treuttel and Würtz, 1821. Vol. 2, 261–90.

GENERAL BACKGROUND

"The French Revolution," Alpha History. Accessed October 31, 2019. http://alphahistory.com/frenchrevolution/.

Baker, Keith M., ed. *The Old Regime and the French Revolution*, Vol. 7. Chicago: University of Chicago Press, 1987.

Beik, Paul H., ed. *The French Revolution*. New York: Harper & Row, 1970.

Duguit, L., H. Monnier, and R. Bonnard, eds. *Les Constitutions et les principales lois politiques de la France depuis 1789*. Paris: Librairie Générale de Droit et de Jurisprudence, 1952.

Stewart, John Hall, ed. *A Documentary Survey of the French Revolution*. New York: Macmillan, 1951.

SUPPLEMENTARY WORKS (PRIMARY AND SECONDARY)

Acton, John Emerich Edward Dalberg. *Lectures on the French Revolution*. Indianapolis: Liberty Fund, 2000.

Baker, Keith. *Inventing the French Revolution*. Cambridge: Cambridge University Press, 1990.

Baker, Keith, ed. *The French Revolution and the Creation of Modern Political Culture, Vol. 1: The Political Culture of the Old Regime*. Oxford: Pergamon Press, 1987.

Burke, Edmund. *Further Reflections on the Revolution in France*, ed. Daniel E. Ritchie. Indianapolis: Liberty Fund, 1992.

———. *Selected Works of Edmund Burke, Vol. 2: Reflections on the Revolution in France*. Indianapolis: Liberty Fund, 1991.

Carré de Malberg, R., *Contribution à la théorie générale de l'État*, 2 vols. Paris: Éditions du CNRS, 1962.

Constant, Benjamin. *Political Writings*, edited and translated by Biancamaria Fontana. Cambridge: Cambridge University Press, 1988.

Craiutu, Aurelian. *A Virtue for Courageous Minds: Moderation in French Political Thought, 1748–1830*. Princeton: Princeton University Press, 2012.

Diesbach, Ghislain de. *Madame de Staël*. Paris: Perrin, 1983.

Doyle, William. *The Oxford History of the French Revolution*. Oxford: Oxford University Press, 1989.

Doyle, William. *Origins of the French Revolution*, 3rd ed. Oxford: Oxford University Press, 1999.

Duclos, Pierre. *La notion de constitution dans l'oeuvre de l'Assemblée constituante.* Paris, 1923.

Dunn, Susan. *Sister Revolutions: French Lightning, American Light.* New York: Farrar, Straus, and Giroux, 2000.

Echeverria, Durand. *Mirage in the West: A History of the French Image of American Society to 1815.* Princeton: Princeton University Press, 1957.

Egret, Jean. *The French Pre-Revolution.* Chicago: University of Chicago Press, 1977.

Fatovic, Clement. *Outside the Law: Emergency and Executive Power.* Baltimore: Johns Hopkins University Press, 2009.

Furet, François. *Interpreting the French Revolution.* Cambridge: Cambridge University Press, 1981.

———. *Revolutionary France: 1770–1880.* Oxford: Blackwell, 1995.

Furet, François, and Mona Ozouf, eds. *A Critical Dictionary of the French Revolution.* Cambridge: Harvard University Press, 1989.

Furet, François, and Mona Ozouf, eds. *Terminer la Révolution.* Grenoble: Presses Universitaires de Grenoble, 1990.

Furet, François, and Ran Halévi, eds. *La Monarchie républicaine: La Constitution de 1791.* Paris: Fayard, 1996.

Furet, François, and Ran Halévi, eds. *Orateurs de la Révolution française*, vol. 1. *Les Constituants.* Paris: Gallimard, Bibliothèque de la Pléiade, 1989.

Gauchet, Marcel. *La Révolution des droits de l'homme.* Paris: Gallimard, 1989.

———. "Necker." In *A Critical Dictionary of the French Revolution*, eds. François Furet and Mona Ozouf, 287–97.

Glénard, Guillaume. *L'Exécutif et la Constitution de 1791.* Paris: Presses Universitaires de France, 2010.

Grange, Henri. "De l'originalité des idées politiques de Necker." *Cahiers staëliens* 36 (1985): 54–55.

Grieder, Josephine. *Anglomania in France 1740–1789: Fact, Fiction and Political Discourse.* Geneva: Droz, 1985.

Griffith, Robert. *Le Centre perdu: Malouet et les "monarchiens" dans la Révolution française.* Grenoble: Presses Universitaires de Grenoble, 1988.

d'Haussonville, Othénin. "La liquidation du 'dépôt' de Necker: entre concept et idée-force." *Cahiers staëliens* 55 (2004): 153–206.

Jaume, Lucien. *Échec au libéralisme: Les Jacobins et l'État.* Paris: Kimé, 1990.

Jaume, Lucien, ed. *Coppet, creuset de l'esprit libéral: les idées politiques et constitutionnelles du group de Madame de Staël.* Aix-en-Provence and Paris: Presses Universitaires d'Aix-Marseille and Economica, 2000.

Jennings, Jeremy. "Conceptions of England and Its Constitution in Nineteenth-Century French Political Thought," *Historical Journal* 29: no. 1 (1986): 65–85.

Kleinerman, Benjamin. *Discretionary President: The Promise and Peril of Executive Power.* Lawrence, KS: University Press of Kansas, 2009.

Lahmer, Marc. *La Constitution américaine dans le débat français: 1795–1848.* Paris: l'Harmattan, 2001.

Lemay, Edna H., ed. *Dictionnaire des constituants.* Paris: Universitas, 1991.

Lemay, Edna H., Alison Patrick, and Joël Félix. *Revolutionaries at Work: The Constituent Assembly, 1789–1791.* Oxford: Voltaire Foundation, 1991.

Mansfield, Harvey C. *Taming the Prince: The Ambivalence of Modern Executive Power.* New York: The Free Press, 1989.

Chaussinand-Nogaret, Guy, ed. *Mirabeau entre le roi et la Révolution: Notes à la cour suivies de Discours.* Paris: Hachette, 1986.

Moellers, Christoph. *The Three Branches: A Comparative Model of Separation of Powers.* Oxford: Oxford University Press, 2015.

Montesquieu, *The Spirit of the Laws.* Translated by Anne Cohler, Basia Miller, and Harold Stone. Cambridge: Cambridge University Press, 1989.

Morabito, Marcel. "Necker et la question du chef de l'État." In *Coppet, creuset de l'esprit liberal,* ed. Lucien Jaume, 41–51.

Mousnier, Roland. *Les institutions de la France sous la monarchie absolue, 1598–1789.* Paris: Presses Universitaires de France, 2005.

Ozouf, Mona. "L'opinion publique." In *The Political Culture of the Old Regime,* ed. Keith Baker, 420–34.

Pasquiet-Briand, Tanguy. *La Réception de la Constitution anglaise au XIXe siècle. Une étude du droit politique français.* Paris: Institut Universitaire Varenne, 2017.

Roussellier, Nicholas. *La Force de gouverner: le pouvoir exécutif en France XIXe–XXIe siècles.* Paris: Gallimard, 2015.

Soll, Jacob. *The Reckoning: Financial Accountability and the Rise and Fall of Nations.* New York: Basic Books, 2014.

Staël, Germaine de. *Oeuvres Complètes de Madame la baronne de Staël publiées par son fils,* 3 vols. Paris: Treuttel and Würtz, 1821.

———. *Considerations on the Principal Events of the French Revolution*, ed. Aurelian Craiutu. Indianapolis: Liberty Fund, 2008.

Tackett, Timothy. *Becoming a Revolutionary: The Deputies of the French National Assembly and the Emergence of a Revolutionary Culture (1789–1790)*. University Park, PA: Pennsylvania State University Press, 1996.

Troper, Michel. *La Séparation des pouvoirs et l'histoire constitutionnelle française*. Paris: Librairie générale de droit et de jurisprudence, 1980.

Valensise, Marina. "The French Constitution in Prevolutionary Debate," *Journal of Modern History* 60 (suppl.) (1988): 22–57.

———. "La Constitution française." In *The Political Culture of the Old Regime*, ed. Keith Baker, 441–68.

Vile, M. J. C. *Constitutionalism and the Separation of Powers*, 2nd ed. Indianapolis: Liberty Fund, 1998.

Index

absolute equality. *See* equality, extreme or absolute

Acts of Union/Settlement (1701, Great Britain), 153, 154, 156

Adams, John, xxxvi

administrative structure. *See* interior administration

aides, 308, 312

Alzire ou les Américains (Voltaire, 1736), 287

ambassadors, 111–12

amendment of constitutional decrees in France, 53–63, 327–28

amercements, 109

America. *See* United States

Ami des Patriotes (journal), xviii

Anne (queen of England), 153

appointments and patronage, 100–116; ambassadors, 111–12; church dignities, 102–3, 321; collectors of direct and indirect taxes, 105–6, 321; interior administration, 109–10; invalid institutions, 108–9; judges and juries, 103–4; knighthoods, 110, 322; *maréchaussée*, 104–5, 321; military commissions, 107–8, 321; monarch's lack of control over, 21, 110–11, 321–22; national treasury, officers of, 106–7; peers of the realm, 103; police magistrates, 104, 321; royal [lack of] control over, in France, 101–2, 112–16; sinecures and pecuniary favors, 110–11; in U.S., 207–9

Areopagi, 233

Argus, 84

aristocracy: abolition of nobility and noble titles in France, 168n1, 175, 321; appointment and patronage of, 103; England, gradual transition from king to peers to commons in government of, 40; forms of respect observed towards, 120; gradations of rank, value of, 40, 170–77; House of Peers in France, Necker on appropriate establishment of, 175–76; as pejorative term, 309

Aristotle, *Politics*, xiii

arms, right to bear, 144

army. *See* military affairs

Articles of Confederation (U.S.), xvi

361

government, 232–36; in U.S., xxxiv, xxxvi, 203, 205–9, 211–12, 232, 235–36
press, liberty of, 144–45, 291, 326
Price, Richard, xxxi
The Prince (Machiavelli, 1532), xiv
Procureur-Syndics, 75, 77, 78, 89, 104
property: extreme/absolute equality, ramifications of, 178, 181; of king, 124–25; legislators required to hold, 36–40, 309; owners of versus workers on, 282–85; protection of laws regarding, without violating them, 342
Prussia, French war with (1792–93), 245n1
public morals: actions of Second National Assembly and, 325, 326, 329; civility, politeness, manners, and taste, decline of, xxix, 217–18, 272–74, 276–79; Constitution of 1791, moral effects of, xxviii, 25n4, 265–89, 306, 314, 332, 333, 336, 340, 343, 344; Constitution of 1791 and (*see also under* Constitution of 1791); *Cours de morale religieuse* (Necker, 1800), x; *Declaration of the Rights of Man* and, xxxii–xxxiii; discarding of old opinions and patterns of behavior, 273–79, 286; in English government, 151, 185; executive power and, 10, 12, 15; in federated governments, 254, 255, 256, 262; French Revolution and, 5–6, 8–9; inability

of National Assembly to form good constitution and, 290, 295, 299, 301; interior administration and, 138, 139, 140, 145; judicial power and, 71, 72, 73, 81, 83, 84, 85; legislative power and, 33, 37, 39, 41, 55, 60, 185, 276; liberty/equality and, 154, 156, 165, 172, 173, 175, 177, 180, 182, 183, 186, 337–38; mercy and right of pardon, 88, 90, 92; monarchy and, 4, 323; nature of government and, 191; Necker and, ix; peace and war, right of, 129, 132, 135; public assent to Constitution of 1791 and, 306, 314; public order and, 147; of Quakers versus French public, 218; religion, positive influence of, xxix, 112, 281–89; in republics, 230, 232, 233, 235, 243, 248, 250; in savage versus civilized state, 8; in United States, xxxii–xxxiii, 190, 191, 193, 204, 206, 212, 218
public order: liberty versus, 70, 146–48, 170, 178, 291, 344; protection of laws regarding, without violating them, 342
public science, 225

Quakers, 217–18, 337
queen, forms of respect observed towards, 120

Rabaut Saint-Étienne, Jean-Paul, xxxii
Rapport fait au Roi dans son conseil (Necker, 1788), 61n3

Reflections on the Revolution in France (Burke, 1790), xxviii
Réflexions philosophiques sur l'égalité (Necker, 1793), xiin8, 32n1
religion: appointment of church dignities, 102–3, 321; clergy, oath required of, 311; Constitution of 1791 failing to preserve salutory influence of, 281–89; *Cours de morale religieuse* (Necker, 1800), x; *De l'importance des opinions religieuses* (Necker, 1788), x; ecclesiastical committee of Constituent Assembly, 20; Necker's views on importance of, xxix; paganism and gradations of rank, 172; public morals, positive influence on, xxix, 112, 281–89
republican government: civil and foreign wars likely resulting from French formation of, 245–52; discipline of army in, 232; elected senate charged with exercise of executive power, 229–32; in France, 227–29, 236–38, 244; French monarchy, importance of continuing, 244; monarchy and, 224–29, 244, 245–52; presidential figures in, 232–36; public morals in, 230, 232, 233, 235, 243, 248, 250; separation and balance of powers in, 239–40; in Swiss cantons, 221–23; veto power/approval of legislation by executive power in, 239–44; weakening of monarchies and, 224–26. *See also* United States

revision of constitutional decrees in France, 53–63, 327–28
Revolution. *See* French Revolution
Robinson, G. G. J. and J., xxxvii
Romans, 49, 98, 150, 232, 269, 270–71, 274–75, 315
Rousseau, Jacques, xxi, xxx, 32n1; *On the Social Contract* (1762), xv, 23

St. Louis, Order of, 110
St. Patrick, Order of, 110
Sardinia, French war with (1793), 245n1
separation and balance of powers, ix, xxi–xxvii; damages by continuance of Constitution of 1791, 338; imbalance of legislative and executive power in France, 159–66; "intertwining" of powers, importance of, xxi, xxiii–xxiv, xxvi–xxvii, 41n2, 51–53, 262; liberty requiring, 161; ministry, formation of, 93–94, 98–99; moderates in early phases of Revolution and, 310n4; peace and war, right of, 127, 134; in republican government, 239–40; in United States, xxivn26, xxv–xxvi, 203–10, 239–40
sinecures and pecuniary favors, 110–11
size and population of country, effects of, 176, 192–96, 198–200, 223
small European republics. *See* republican government
Solon, 306

This book is set in Adobe Jenson, an old-style serif typeface drawn for Adobe Systems by Robert Slimbach. Its roman styles are based on a text face cut by Nicolas Jenson in Venice around 1470, and its italics are based on those created by Ludovico Vicentino degli Arrighi fifty years later.

This book is printed on paper that is acid-free and meets the requirements of the American National Standard for Permanence of Paper for Printed Library Materials, Z39.48-1992. ∞

Book design and typography by Julie Allred, BW&A Books, Oxford, North Carolina
Index by Kate Mertes, Alexandria, Virginia
Printed and bound by Sheridan Books, Inc., Chelsea, Michigan